An Introduction to
Louisiana Archaeology

An Introduction to
Louisiana
Archaeology

ROBERT W. NEUMAN

Louisiana State University Press
Baton Rouge and London

All plates, except where noted, are used courtesy of the Museum of Anthropology, Louisiana State University, Baton Rouge.

LIBRARY OF CONGRESS CATALOGING IN PUBLICATION DATA

Neuman, Robert W.
    An introduction to Louisiana archaeology.

    Bibliography: p.
    Includes index.
    1. Indians of North America—Louisiana—Antiquities. 2. Excavations (Archaeology)—Louisiana. 3. Louisiana—Antiquities. I. Title.
E78.L8N483   1984   976.3   83-19973
ISBN 0-8071-1147-3

It should come as no surprise
to those of us interested
in Louisiana archaeology
that I dedicate this book to
DR. CLARENCE H. WEBB
of Shreveport.

Contents

Illustrations

Maps

Plates

Acknowledgments

I can state, in all sincerity, that this section of the book is the most pleasing portion to write. It is a fact that I will not be able to thank each of many persons individually, but I hope that everyone concerned may feel that his or her generosity in time and interest is at least partially compensated for by the contents of this book.

As in all serious human endeavors, there are those friends and organizations that we call upon, and indeed nettle, for their specific skills and facilities, and somehow we are unfailingly rewarded. For their assistance and friendship I wish to express my gratitude particularly to the Avery Island Foundation and especially to Lanier and Ned Simmons of Avery Island. Much of my fieldwork would not have been feasible, and certainly not as enjoyable, were it not for the helping hand of Harry E. Shafer, Jr., of the Louisiana Department of Wildlife and Fisheries and his assistants, my friends Eric Lacefield and Tony Doucet. On the same tack, I wish to thank Ted Joanen of the Rockefeller Wildlife Refuge and Game Preserve and John R. Walther of the Sabine National Wildlife Refuge. I want also to acknowledge the financial assistance I received from the Morton Salt Company and the National Science Foundation.

A large part of archaeological fieldwork is directed toward locating sites, and it cannot be too much emphasized that were it not for local informants, this phase of investigation would be extraordinarily long and expensive. Individuals who have been most helpful and hospitable to me during site surveys and to whom I owe a special debt of gratitude include William and Marie Addison, Charles N. Bollich, Jack C.

Bonnin, Dominic Braud, O.S.B., Marc Dupuy, Jr., John Guy, Sr., Nelson Hardy, Paula Johnson, John S. Prescott, and Wallace J. Stroud.

After I began to compile this manuscript in 1976, I called upon a number of persons to assist me until it was completed. Those were pre-word-processor days, at least for me, so I wish to thank Edith Kleinpeter, Jinx Hunter, and Arlene J. Stephens for typing and retyping many portions of the manuscript. Their patience was remarkable. During the interim as I finished various chapters, I sent copies to people who I thought were most capable of reviewing the data, and for this I express my gratefulness to Jeffrey P. Brain, Ian W. Brown, David D. Davis, Hiram F. Gregory, Alan Toth, and Clarence H. Webb. Should they read this book, I trust that they will not feel that their time was spent in folly. As is customary, of course, I take full responsibility for what is printed here.

After completing the original draft of this manuscript, I must admit that I felt rather satisfied with what I had accomplished; perhaps what I really mean is that I was relieved that it was completed. In any event, and fortunately for the readers, that manuscript was edited, and there appeared a striking improvement in the word flow. Credit for this accomplishment must go entirely to Judith Bailey.

For the illustrations I was assisted by David R. Jeane, who provided me with a number of selected artifacts from his private collection, and by R. E. Baremore, Jr., and Jeanne H. Mason of the Louisiana State Exhibit Museum, Shreveport, who allowed me to borrow artifacts from the museum's display cases. Douglas D. Bryant worked diligently in photographing all of the artifactual specimens, and Karen A. Brandt helped me greatly in the composition of the individual plates. The figures are the work of Clifford P. Duplechin and Mary L. Eggart of the cartography section of the School of Geoscience, Louisiana State University. I express my appreciation to each of these individuals. Finally, throughout all stages of the preparation of this book, I had the good fortune to receive gainful criticism and persistent encouragement from Kathleen M. Byrd. Thank you sincerely, Kass.

An Introduction to
Louisiana Archaeology

Introduction

It has been my good fortune to have been involved daily with matters of Louisiana archaeology for the past fifteen years. I have had the invaluable opportunity of meeting and interacting with everyone who has directed archaeological investigations in Louisiana since 1967, and I have traveled extensively, visiting sites throughout every section of the state. Through these contacts and experiences, I have become aware of the wealth of archaeological data that has been gathered in Louisiana, as well as the priceless evidence that has been irretrievably lost through the settlement and development of the state. Perhaps most important, I have been conscious that more needs to be done to investigate Louisiana's prehistory before the remaining sites are destroyed to assure that this part of the state's past does not remain forever a mystery.

Unlike my predecessor, J. Ashley Sibley, Jr., whose *Louisiana's Ancients of Man* was published in 1967, I have not attempted to reconstruct the cultures of prehistoric and historic Louisiana Indians. Rather, I have written an account of the archaeology of Louisiana. I have attempted to compile and to relate in considerable detail the archaeological information relative to the aboriginal Indians of Louisiana.

Although the core of this study deals with the archaeological manifestations of Louisiana as revealed by scientific professional procedures, I have directed considerable attention toward observations reported by nineteenth-century and early-twentieth-century chroniclers. In these earlier reports there was no attempt at an organized or systematic plan to study the archaeology of the state, and only rarely were the authors engaged by scientific institutions within or outside of the state. Nevertheless, the many varied and frequently intriguing observations found in early publications are too often the only information extant on a multitude of sites that were damaged or completely destroyed as Louisiana was settled by Europeans and as commercial enterprises developed. Moreover, some of the more substantive information in early reports—site locations, site maps, excavation data, and artifactual illustrations and descriptions—have profoundly influenced the direction of present-day research. Indeed, the record of nineteenth-century and early-twentieth-century explorations is a fundamental constituent of Louisiana archaeology, the base upon which formal professional research has built.

I have organized the data from modern, professional archaeological investigations chronologically and according to culture. My study is limited to the prehistoric and early historic native populations of Louisiana, beginning with the Paleo-Indian Era (10,000 B.C.–6000 B.C.). The available data for this period are tantalizing, but not always as strongly substantive as one might desire. Paleo-Indian artifacts found in presumed association with the remains of Pleistocene big-game mammals at Avery Island and at the Trappey Mastodon Site at Lafayette, have fueled speculation over the date that man first made his way into the state. Other information about Paleo-Indians has been drawn from excavations at the John Pearce Site in Caddo Parish and from regional surface finds of diagnostic Paleo-Indian stone artifacts in Louisiana.

The Meso-Indian Era (6000 B.C.–2000 B.C.) followed the end of the Pleistocene Era and the extinction of the big-game mammals. The striking feature of this era is the emergence of social groups, perhaps extended families or bands, that had gradually localized and adapted themselves to a rich, broad spectrum of natural resources. Meso-Indian sites are markedly more numerous than those of the preceding era, and they are manifested by a multitude of diverse chipped-stone points, knives, scrapers, drills, and other tools. In addition, ground-stone artifacts appear for the first time, and the tool kits are enhanced by such artifacts as celts, grooved axes, mortars, pestles, mealing stones, and smoking pipes. It is also during the Meso-Indian Era that we see the introduction of tools and ornaments made of bone, shell, and occasionally copper. Evidence from Meso-Indian sites indicates that the atlatl, or spear thrower, had also made its appearance. Finally, from the excavations at the Banana Bayou Site on Avery Island, we may have the earliest evidence of ceremonial mound construction thus far reported in the eastern United States.

Most of the archaeological endeavors in Louisiana have been directed toward sites that were inhabited during the Neo-Indian Era (2000 B.C.–A.D. 1600), largely because the remains from this period are more extensive, more apt to be intact, and quite often more visible today than the older sites. In addition, their artifact assemblages are more abundant and varied than those from Paleo-Indian or Meso-Indian sites in the state. Because so many of these relatively undamaged sites have been carefully investigated over the past fifty years, we know infinitely more about the lifeways of the populations of the Neo-Indian Era than of either of the preceding divisions. The archaeological data that have accumulated from stratigraphic excavations and subsequent analyses have revealed distinctive cultural sequences within the period. I have used the commonly accepted names for these cultures to subdivide and order the vast amount of data pertinent to the Neo-Indian Era. The earliest of these cultures, called Poverty Point, is followed in chronological order by the Tchefuncte, Marksville, Troyville–Coles Creek, Caddo, Plaquemine, and Mississippian cultures. However, the last three cultures were not successive but rather overlapped chronologically to a considerable degree.

Our knowledge of the sequence of events within the Neo-Indian Era is enhanced considerably by the fact that we have many times more radiocarbon determinations, and even some thermoluminescent dates, from sites of this era than from both of the preceding eras. Among the archaeological manifestations introduced during the period are the large village sites, earthworks, compound pyramidal mounds, and multimound ceremonial centers. We also have evidence of a variety of house types. Shell middens and mounds of the Neo-Indian Era indicate that coastal areas were settled and exploited for the first time. From the identification and analysis of floral and faunal remains, we have the first solid evidence respecting subsistence economies of the prehistoric Indians of Louisiana. Moreover, we see the introduction of three most important technologies: maize, bean, and squash agriculture; the manufacture of ceramics; and use of the bow and arrow. And

4

too, we have considerable data on a variety of human burial forms, their funerary accompaniments, and physical anthropological analyses of the skeletal elements. These provide us with a glimpse into the socioreligious practices of the Neo-Indian Era.

Lastly, for the recent end of the Neo-Indian Era, or late prehistoric times, we are able to answer the question, What tribes of Indians lived here? with more than speculation. By carefully scrutinizing historic documents and coordinating these data with field observations, archaeologists have been able to identify certain sites occupied by particular Indian tribes in our region, namely, tribes of the Caddo, Natchez, and Tunica Indians. Furthermore, particular classes of objects, most commonly aboriginal ceramics, studied at historically documented Indian sites, can be used as keys for locating and identifying prehistoric occupations of the historic tribes. By this process, going from the known to the unknown, archaeologists are able to perceive the cultural development of a historic tribe for more than just the transient period of their historic record.

The last section of the text, Historic Indian Archaeology, addresses the archaeological data retrieved from excavations at historic Indian sites occupied during the early years of the eighteenth century. At the Bayou Goula Site, the Angola Site, the Bloodhound Hill Site, the Fish Hatchery Site, and the Trudeau Site, we can observe European traits and artifacts that have diffused into the aboriginal cultures and have made their way into Indian burial grounds. The data gathered from the excavations at the site of the Presidio de Nuestra Señora del Pillar de Los Adaes near Natchitoches are quite different in nature. From this body of information we are afforded a glimpse at the effects of the conflicts between Spain and France in North America upon a tribe of the Caddo Culture. Unfortunately, the section on historic sites is quite brief because very few historically documented Indian sites have been studied. For that matter, very few of them have been found in Louisiana. On a happier note, however, long-term programs for further excavations at the Trudeau and Los Adaes sites are being implemented by the Office of State Parks. The data gathered from these investigations will add significantly to our limited store of knowledge respecting the early period of contact between the Indians of Louisiana and the fledgling European empires in the New World.

This book is in no way an attempt to answer all of the many questions that one may ask about the archaeology of Louisiana Indians. Very much to the contrary, it is hoped that the information presented here will generate diligent inquiry into areas where our knowledge is lacking or in short supply and particularly where our judgments have been in error. Quite simply, the present study is an attempt to collate the available data, to present them objectively and clearly to the interested reader, and to provide interpretations or at least surmises only when they are appropriate.

I The Beginnings of Archaeology in Louisiana

In the area now within the boundaries of the state of Louisiana (Fig. 1), just as elsewhere in the New World, the early explorers and settlers came upon a variety of archaeological remains left here by the aboriginal Americans. Their descriptions of these cultural remnants soon began to appear in published documents. As one might expect, the accounts range from remarkably precise descriptions of archaeological remains to speculative folly conjuring up illusions of Mexican migrations. In the record of these first steps toward an understanding of Louisiana's prehistoric past we may discern the beginnings of archaeology itself as a scientific discipline. Every observer contributed toward developing the tools and the techniques that would enable an understanding of how man lived in ages past.

The Nineteenth Century

The earliest surviving description of a prehistoric Indian site in Louisiana was written shortly after the Louisiana Purchase. The United States government commissioned the naturalist William Dunbar to explore a part of the newly acquired territory. On October 23, 1804, Dunbar came upon the massive earthworks that once existed at the Troyville Site in present-day Catahoula Parish. They so impressed him that he returned in January, 1805, and recorded in his journal the first detailed description of the mounds and surrounding embankment. President Thomas Jefferson found the report of such interest that he

FIG. 1   Louisiana's Natural Areas and Parishes

commented on Dunbar's discoveries in a message to Congress and included a description of the Troyville Site.[1]

The site drew considerable attention throughout the nineteenth century. It was visited, described, illustrated, photographed, excavated, compared to other earthworks, and attributed to the Aztecs,

1. Dunbar Rowland, *Life, Letters and Papers of William Dunbar, 1749–1810* (Jackson, 1830), 317; Winslow M. Walker, *The Troyville Mounds, Catahoula Parish, Louisiana,* Bureau of American Ethnology Bulletin 113 (Washington, D.C., 1936), 4–6.

Mexicans, vanished races, and/or the Natchez Indians. At least twelve well-known and influential men wrote about Troyville before the close of the century, beginning in 1812 with writer and soldier Amos Stoddard and including jurist and author Henry Marie Brackenridge, physician and historian John Wesley Monette, Kentucky naturalist Constantine Samuel Rafinesque, Swedish immigrant and Louisiana legislator and judge Henry Bry, newspaper editor Ephraim G. Squier, Ohio physician Edward Hamilton Davis, physician Andrew R. Kilpatrick, author Samuel Langhorne Clemens, Smithsonian archaeologist Cyrus Thomas, Peabody Museum curator Lucien Carr, and Tulane University professor George Eugene Beyer.[2] In spite of the evident interest in Troyville, however, by the end of the nineteenth century most of the tremendous earthworks there had been needlessly destroyed.

Another noteworthy early archaeological document is the *Carte Generale du Territoire d'Orleans*, a detailed map dated 1806. It was compiled by Bernard La Fon, a civil engineer, real estate appraiser, and confidant of the historically popular Jean Lafitte. On the map are small circles that indicate the location of "monuments," Indian mounds. In Louisiana they are shown at the mouth of Bayou Siard, near the city of Monroe, and at the juncture of the Boeuf and Ouachita rivers in Catahoula Parish. The Troyville mounds are indicated at present-day

2. Amos Stoddard, *Sketches, Historical and Descriptive, of Louisiana* (Philadelphia, 1812), 350; Henry Marie Brackenridge, *Views of Louisiana, Together with a Journal of a Voyage Up the Missouri River, in 1811* (Baltimore, 1814), 188–89; C. S. Rafinesque, *Ancient History; or, Annals of Kentucky* (Frankfort Ky., 1824); John Wesley Monette, *History of the Discovery and Settlement of the Valley of the Mississippi* (New York, 1846), I, 267; Henry Bry, "Louisiana Ouachita Region," *DeBow's Review*, Vol. 3 (1847), No. 3, p. 228; E. G. Squier and E. H. Davis, "Ancient Monuments of the Mississippi Valley," *Smithsonian Contributions to Knowledge*, Vol. 1 (Washington, D.C., 1848), 117; Andrew R. Kilpatrick, "Historical and Statistical Collections of Louisiana," *DeBow's Review*, Vol. 12 (1852), Art. 3, 256–75; Samuel Langhorne Clemens [Mark Twain], *Life on the Mississippi* (Boston, 1883), 600–601; Cyrus Thomas, *Catalogue of Prehistoric Works East of the Rocky Mountains*, Bureau of Ethnology Bulletin 12 (Washington, D.C., 1891), 102; Cyrus Thomas, "Report on the Mound Explorations of the Bureau of Ethnology," *Twelfth Annual Report of the Bureau of Ethnology* (Washington, D.C., 1894), 250–52; Lucien Carr, "The Mounds of the Mississippi Valley, Historically Considered," *Annual Report of the Smithsonian Institution for 1891–1892* (Washington, D.C., 1892), 585; George Eugene Beyer, "The Mounds of Louisiana," *Publications of the Louisiana Historical Society*, Vol. 1 (1896), Pt. 4, pp. 15–16, 28–32.

Jonesville, and additional mounds are shown along the Tensas River near Clayton in Concordia Parish.

Also during the first decade of the nineteenth century the American Philosophical Society published two provocative communications in its transactions, describing a human skull and teeth, shell-tempered pottery, and bones of extinct mammals that had been found 30 to 35 feet below the surface of the ground, during well-digging operations near Opelousas.[3]

During the next three decades, several published pieces discussed archaeological finds. The surveyor and cartographer William Darby published his *Geographical Description of the State of Louisiana*, in which he cites several "little mounts," twelve feet taller than the surrounding terrain, along Bayou Fusillier in Saint Landry Parish. Soon thereafter, while appraising resources for suitable timber to construct naval ships, agent James Leander Cathcart compiled a most interesting journal of his reconnaissance through parts of southern Louisiana in 1819. He mentions a number of "shell banks," which today we know to be Indian middens, and he specifically describes one such midden near Morgan City, "which bounds an Indian burial ground, from whence they frequently dig human bones, and once they found a whole skeleton." Cathcart also gives a detailed description of four Indian mounds and a shell midden in the Berwick environs just west of Morgan City. In 1828 Harvey Elkins retrieved Indian pottery, animal bone, and shell from a deposit thirty feet below the surface near Lake Pontchartrain north of New Orleans. In 1838 John Wesley Monette read a paper before the Jefferson College and Washington Lyceum in Mississippi in which he talked about the remains of human cremations in a mound on the property of a Mr. John Routh, Esquire, along Lake Saint Joseph in Tensas Parish.[4]

---

3. "Abstract of a Communication from Mr. Martin Duralde, Relative to Fossil Bones, and c. of the County of Apelousas West of the Mississippi to Mr. William Dunbar of the Natchez, and by Him Transmitted to the Society. Dated April 24, 1802," *American Philosophical Society Transactions*, Vol. 6 (1809), 40, 55–58.
4. William Darby, *A Geographical Description of the State of Louisiana* (Philadelphia, 1816), 116–18; Walter Prichard, Fred B. Kniffen, and Clair A. Brown (eds.), "Southern Louisiana and Southern Alabama in 1819," *Louisiana Historical Quarterly*, Vol. 28 (1945), 789, 793–95; Daniel Drake, *A Systematic Treatise, Historical, Etiological, and Practical, on the Principal Diseases of the Interior*

Between 1837 and 1844, Montroville Wilson Dickeson, the Philadelphia physician, author of *The American Numismatic Manual,*
member of the Academy of Natural Sciences of Philadelphia, and col-
lector of fossils, geologic objects, and Indian curiosities, explored sites
in the Ohio Valley and in Mississippi and Louisiana. His notes and
collections were subsequently purchased by the Free Museum of Science and Art of the University of Pennsylvania and reported upon by
Steward Culin. In 1843 while residing in Natchez, Mississippi, Dickeson conducted excavations into four tumuli located on the William
Ferriday plantation in Concordia Parish. He drew a map of the Ferriday mounds on which he included a list of their dimensions and provided a schematic drawing of a mound cross section and another
drawing showing a skeleton, which Culin identified as that of a Choc-
taw Indian in a sitting position. Dickeson described the mound strata,
and he was, for his time, particularly attentive respecting the human
skeletal remains. He noted their state of preservation, pattern of deposition, and cranial characteristics. Culin cataloged the Louisiana artifacts that Dickeson collected from Concordia, Catahoula, Tensas, and
Morehouse parishes, as well as less definitely located sites elsewhere
in the state. Culin also provided photographs of two decorated vessels
from Morehouse Parish. In his numismatic manual Dickeson had
placed a color illustration of a decorated pottery disk from Black River
and two intriguing clay tablets, each exhibiting an impression of a human hand. He had found the latter two specimens "in a small jar finely
decorated with zigzag lines, embedded in a light-colored ash, about the
neck of a skeleton," in Ouachita Parish.[5]

The first author to provide a detailed, hachured topographic map of
an Indian mound site in Louisiana was Caleb Goldsmith Forshey (Pl.
2, *a*), educator, engineer, West Point graduate, and Confederate offi-

---

*Valley of North America, as They Appear in the Caucasian, African, Indian and
Esquimaux Varieties of Its Population* (Cincinnati, 1850), I, 76; John Wesley
Monette, "Indian Mounds; or American Monuments, in the Southwest," *South-
Western Journal,* Vol. 1 (1838), Nos. 15-16, p. 231.

5. Steward Culin, "The Dickeson Collection of American Antiquities," *Bulletin of
the Free Museum of Science and Art of the University of Pennsylvania,* Vol. 2
(1900), No. 3, pp. 132–33, plates 14, 15; Montroville Wilson Dickeson, *The
American Numismatic Manual of the Currency or Money of the Aborigines and
Colonial State, and United States Coins* (Philadelphia, 1865), plate 3, pp. 5, 7, 8.

cer. In a letter mailed from Trinity, Louisiana, dated January 19, 1845, Forshey sent the editors of the *Journal of Science and Arts* his description of the site and a map (Pl. 1) of a complex of mounds, a "causeway," and a moat on the property of Dr. Harrison, on Prairie Jefferson, Morehouse Parish. Forshey had the then uncommon forethought to document the site dimensions, for he clearly recognized that "the levelling hand of American Industry is fast obliterating these dumb, yet eloquent records of the past; and hence the necessity of early attention and accurate description." Even so, he was a product of his time and shared the contemporary view of primitives. He wrote, "The whole work, although exhibiting very little ingenuity, bears evidence of the vastness of the population, their industry, and not less certainly their ignorance and folly." Three years later Ephraim Squier and Edward Davis published Forshey's data and site maps again in their voluminous *Ancient Monuments of the Mississippi Valley*. More recently, a surface collection from the site yielded shell-tempered pottery, and three charred corncobs of eight- and ten-rowed corn were recovered from an aboriginal fire pit there.[6]

Less rigorous yet interesting notes and observations continued to appear in the literature. One report by Henry Adams Bullard, the jurist and first president of the Louisiana Historical Society, remarked upon a circular group of low mounds at Sicily Island, Catahoula Parish. As is often the case in Louisiana, one of the mounds had a house on its summit. Bullard also reported upon an earthen construction near the town of Harrisonburg that to him resembled a breastwork. He felt that these structures were built as refuges from the flood waters of the Mississippi River. It was a persistent theory, one which recurred time and again in nineteenth-century publications but which has since been discredited. Although prehistoric Indians undoubtedly retreated to the mounds in times of high water, current theory holds that mounds were built for socioreligious purposes.[7]

6. Caleb Goldsmith Forshey, "Description of Some Artificial Mounds on Prairie Jefferson, Louisiana," *American Journal of Science and Arts*, Vol. 49 (1845), Art. 4, pp. 39, 42, fig. 1; Squier and Davis, *Ancient Monuments of the Mississippi Valley*, 113–14, plate 28; Hugh Cutler, Missouri Botanical Gardens, personal communication to the author, December, 1972.
7. H. A. Bullard, "Louisiana Historical Researches," *Commercial Review*, Vol. 3 (1847), No. 1, pp. 36–37.

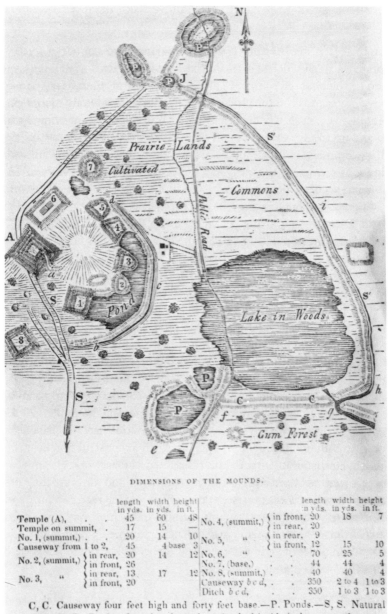

DIMENSIONS OF THE MOUNDS.

	length in yds.	width in yds.	height in ft.			length in yds.	width in yds.	height in ft.
Temple (A),	45	60	48	No. 4, (summit,) { in front,	20	18	7
Temple on summit,	17	15	—	{ in rear,	20		
No. 1, (summit,)	20	14	10	No. 5, " { in rear,	9		
Causeway from 1 to 2,	45	4 base	3	{ in front,	12	15	10
No. 2, (summit,) { in rear,	20	14	12	No. 6, "	70	25	5
{ in front,	26			No. 7, (base,)	44	44	4
No. 3, " { in rear,	13	17	12	No. 8, (summit,)	40	40	4
{ in front,	20			Causeway b c d,	350	2 to 4	1 to 3
				Ditch b c d,	350	1 to 3	1 to 3

C, C. Causeway four feet high and forty feet base.—P. Ponds.—S, S. Natural swale.—S', S'. Swale of regular channel, embanked inside in low grounds.

PLATE I

The earliest-known professionally drawn map of an archaeological site in Louisiana. This is Forshey's map of the site on Prairie Jefferson in Morehouse Parish that he drew in 1845.

In the same year in *DeBow's Review*, an anonymous writer published his description of a mound and shell midden that extended for a hundred yards along Bayou Pigeon near Grand Lake and contained human bones. The Squier and Davis volume on mounds appeared a year later, published by the Smithsonian Institution. Along with Caleb Forshey's data, the book also contained a hachured topographic map of a site "situated upon the right bank of Walnut Bayou, in Madison Parish, Louisiana, seven miles from the Mississippi. It consists of seven large and regular mounds, and a graded or elevated road-way half a mile in length. The plan exhibits the relative positions of the remains and their predominating features, and obviates the necessity of a particular description, which at best would be intricate and obscure."[8] Today these mounds, most commonly referred to as the Fitzhugh Site, remain only as bare remnants of their previous magnitude.

In 1851 two other notes regarding Indian mounds in Louisiana appeared in *DeBow's Review*. The first commented upon the fact that, along Bayous Grand, Petite Caillou, Terrebonne, and Black in Terrebonne Parish, there were fifteen to twenty mounds from which human skeletal remains had been collected. The second note discussed the two Indian mounds on the garrison grounds in Baton Rouge. One of the mounds had been destroyed, and pottery and bones had been retrieved from it. The other mound was being used as a cemetery for military officers and their wives. The author described it as nearly circular, 110 feet in diameter and 18 feet in height. He alluded to other mounds near Baton Rouge along Highland Road, and he noted two large mounds on the McHatton plantation that later became part of the present campus of Louisiana State University.[9] The two mounds are undoubtedly the oldest cultural structures that now grace the university grounds.

Another brief description of Caleb Forshey's site on Prairie Jefferson appeared in 1855, after which nothing noteworthy was published un-

8. "Indian Mounds in Louisiana," *DeBow's Review*, Vol. 3 (1847), No. 4, pp. 351–52; Squier and Davis, *Ancient Monuments of the Mississippi Valley*, 115, plate 39.
9. "Historical and Statistical Collections of Louisiana," *DeBow's Review*, New Series, Vol. 1 (1851), No. 6, pp. 601–602; "Statistical and Historical Sketches of Louisiana," *DeBow's Review*, New Series, Vol. 1 (1851), No. 6, p. 611.

til Reymond Thomassy's *Geologie Practique de la Louisiane* in 1860. The French geologist included a brief description of the extensive Morton Shell Mound at Weeks Island in Iberia Parish. That same year a newspaper agent for the New Orleans *Crescent*, J. W. Dorr, was touring Louisiana, and while stopping at Harrisonburg, Catahoula Parish, he remarked upon Indian mounds in that region and, particularly, upon one destroyed in the town itself. Dorr wrote, "Abundant remains of pottery and human bones were unearthed when the vandal shovels and hoes of modern progress ruthlessly invaded this aboriginal abode of the dead." The following year the engineers Andrew Atkinson Humphreys and Henry L. Abbot published their voluminous report *Physics and Hydraulics of the Mississippi River*. They noted two mounds "situated about 800 feet apart, near Mr. Erwins's house, on the north bank of the Bayou Grosse Tete, Iberville Parish, about 2 miles above Rosedale. Both were of the same dimensions, having the form of a square, truncated pyramid 12 feet in height, the slope of the sides being about 2.5 upon 1, and the length of each side, on the top, being about 50 feet. The western mound had a ramp on its eastern side, with a slope of about 3.5 upon 1. Both mounds were composed of the alluvial soil which surrounds them, and traces of the hollows from which the earth had been taken were plainly visible."[10]

Almost a decade later Samuel Henry Lockett, West Point graduate, Confederate officer, one-time engineering professor at Louisiana State University, and director of the first topographical survey of the state of Louisiana, wrote about the numerous mounds he had seen in Morehouse Parish, which varied "from a few yards in diameter and a few feet in length to over one hundred yards across, and from fifty to sixty feet in elevation. They are thought by the inhabitants," Lockett continued, "to be Indian mounds, and some of them have been exca-

10. "Indian Mounds in Louisiana," *DeBow's Review*, Vol. 18 [New Series, Vol. 1 (1855)], No. 4, pp. 568–71; Raymond Thomassy, *Géologie Practique de la Louisiane* (New Orleans and Paris, 1860), 82; Walter Prichard (ed.), "A Tourist's Description of Louisiana in 1860," *Louisiana Historical Quarterly*, Vol. 21 (1938), No. 4, p. 1204; Andrew Atkinson Humphreys and Henry L. Abbot, *Report upon the Physics and Hydraulics of the Mississippi River*, Professional Papers No. 4, U.S. Army Corps of Topographical Engineers, U.S. Bureau of Topographical Engineers (Philadelphia, 1861), 433.

vated, and Indian relics found. But it is hardly probable that so many tumuli, so irregularly scattered over so large a scope of country can all be the results of human labor, but rather having a natural origin, and subsequently used in some cases as burying grounds by the aborigines." Undoubtedly, some of the smaller mounds that Lockett described are examples of a geological phenomenon popularly known today as pimple mounds. These low, round to elongated mounds have often puzzled subsequent investigators.[11]

One year later Professor Americus Featherman reported on his botanical survey in Louisiana. He remarked that "shell islands," some covering quite a large area and built up high above sea level, were numerous along Bayous Barataria, Rigolettes, and Saint Denis, north of Grand Isle.[12]

The annual report of the Board of Regents of the Smithsonian Institution in 1873 contained a good deal of information about Louisiana archaeology. Lockett commented on additional data obtained during his survey of Louisiana and reported visiting another Indian site in West Carroll Parish.

> I visited, near Jackson's Ferry, four miles south of Floyd, on Bayou Macon, some very remarkable Indian mounds. Six of these are within a mile of Mrs. Jackson's. Four of them are almost perfect; the other two are partly destroyed by the caving of the banks of the Bayou Macon. They are connected with each other by a levee or narrow embankment of earth, having a nearly semi-circular figure. There are two much larger mounds nearer to Floyd, one on Mr. Mabins' and one on Mr. Motley's land. The latter must be between 20 and 30 feet in height.
>
> On the sides of all of the mounds, and in their vicinity, are found great numbers of relics, such as human bones, arrow-heads, "plumbobs" very

---

11. Samuel Henry Lockett, "Report of the Topographical Survey of Part of Louisiana," *Annual Report of the Board of Supervisors of the Louisiana State Seminary of Learning and Military Academy for the Year Ending December 31, 1869* (New Orleans, 1870), 66–67; Wilbur C. Holland, Lee W. Hough, and Grover E. Murray, *Geology of Beauregard and Allen Parishes*, Department of Conservation, Louisiana Geological Survey, Geological Bulletin 27 (Baton Rouge, 1952), 50–68; Jack Charles Bonnin, *Pimple Mound Occupation in Southwest Louisiana* (Welsh, La., 1972).
12. Americus Featherman, "Report of a Botanical Survey of Southern and Central Louisiana," *Annual Report of the Board of Supervisors of the Louisiana State University for 1870* (New Orleans, 1871), 23.

perfect in form, and immense quantities of broken pottery. Many of the pieces of pottery are highly ornamented. From the quantity of pottery, I imagine there must have been a factory of this ware in this locality.

He added prophetically, "Excavations would in all probability reveal some very valuable and interesting specimens, and I think it should be done by one accustomed to searching for archaeological remains." In the same Smithsonian publication, T. P. Hotchkiss of Shreveport reported that during well-digging operations at the edge of Post-Oak Ridge, 1½ miles east of Wallace Lake, an Indian grave was exposed at a depth of 32 feet below the surface. "In this deposit were found the bones and darts placed side by side, with a slight lap, the points directed from the body. The largest spear was 11½ inches in length. They were four in number and wrought from pure flint-rock." Hotchkiss sent with his article "ancient crockery" from a site 1½ miles above Shreveport in Bossier Parish where a cut-off was dug along the Red River in 1859. This site, exposed 18 feet below the surface, contained "numbers of remains of bodies and of articles buried with them, such as implements of cooking jugs, plates, sc., of a peculiar workmanship; also remains of something supposed to be a turtle."[13]

Also in 1873 Eugene Woldermar Hilgard, the Mississippi state geologist and professor at the University of Mississippi, wrote in his report on a geological reconnaissance of Louisiana that in the Lake Charles area near the sulphur mine, there were two large shell middens containing pottery and charcoal. Consisting "almost entirely of edible shells (Gnathodon mainly and Unio), with occasional bones of small animals, and a few land-snails (doubtless accidentally introduced), they must be considered as relics of human efforts to sustain life at the expense of the bivalve creation." That same year the Georgia antiquarian, Charles Colcock Jones, Jr., illustrated two vessels purportedly "taken from an ancient burial-ground in the Mississippi Valley, near Shreveport."[14]

13. Samuel Henry Lockett, "Mounds in Louisiana," *Annual Report of the Board of Regents for 1872, Smithsonian Institution* (Washington, D.C., 1873), 429–30; T. P. Hotchkiss, "Indian Remains Found 32 Feet Below the Surface, near Wallace Lake, in Caddo Parish, Louisiana," *Annual Report of the Board of Regents for 1872, Smithsonian Institution*, 428–29.
14. Eugene Woldemar Hilgard, *Supplementary and Final Report of a Geological*

To this period also belongs an encompassing book written by Professor John Wells Foster, a geologist and paleontologist whose observations on the archaeological record of his time include remarks on developments in Louisiana. In one chapter of his book devoted to the antiquity of man in America, Foster cites the human skeleton found in New Orleans beneath layers of vegetation at a depth of 16 feet. Since a physician named Bennet Dowler reported the find, which was exposed by excavation of foundation placements for a gas works, the skeleton was sometimes referred to as Dr. Dowler's Red Indian. Actually, these skeletal remains, exposed in 1844, were first reported in 1850 by the renowned physician and medical historian Dr. Daniel Drake, who remarked that "the cranium lay between the roots of a tree, and was in tolerable preservation, but most of the other bones crumbled on exposure. A small os ilium, which I saw, indicated the male sex. A low and narrow forehead, moderate facial angle, and prominent, widely separated cheek bones, seemed to prove it of the same race with our present Indians. No charcoal, ashes, or ornaments of any kind, were found around it." Dowler attributed an age of more than 57,600 years to the skeleton. Foster and subsequent writers, however, felt that Dowler's computations contained far too many discrepancies to be acceptable.[15]

In another section of the book Foster cites manuscript notes submitted to him by Caleb Forshey describing the Transylvania Site in East Carroll Parish, the Fitzhugh Site in Madison Parish, the site on the Harrison property in Morehouse Parish, "ten mounds in a form nearly circular, facing the temple on the Hollywood plantation, on the

---

Reconnaissance of the State of Louisiana (New Orleans, 1873), 15; Charles Colcock Jones, Jr., Antiquities of the Southern Indians (New York, 1873), 45, figs. 3, 4.

15. James Cocke Southall, The Recent Origin of Man: As Illustrated by Geology and the Modern Science of Prehistoric Archaeology (Philadelphia, 1875), 470–73; Drake, A Systematic Treatise, 77; Bennet Dowler, Tableaux of New Orleans Daily Delta (New Orleans, 1852), 17; Josiah Clark Nott and George R. Glidden, Types of Mankind (Philadelphia, 1854), 338; Aleš Hrdlička, Skeletal Remains Suggesting or Attributed to Early Man in North America, Bureau of American Ethnology Bulletin 33 (Washington, D.C., 1907); John Wells Foster, Prehistoric Races of the United States of America (2nd ed.; Chicago, 1873), 72–76; Marquis de Nadaillac, Pre-historic America, trans. N. d'Anvers (New York, 1893), 35–56.

southwest bend of Lake St. Joseph" in Tensas Parish, the Troyville Site in Catahoula Parish, and "others of like magnitude with minor ones arranged round the temple, perhaps twenty or more" along the right bank of Little River extending up to Catahoula Lake. Forshey's notes also include a most intriguing description of several large mounds on the east bank of Little River, a mile or two from its junction with Catahoula Lake. "They stand on a bluff some forty feet above the river. One is about one hundred feet square at the base, with very steep sides, and covered with the ordinary pine forest. It is the only mound with stone masonry structure which I have seen south of the Ohio. A caving face exposed blocks some twelve to eighteen inches in size, rudely carved or broken in shape, supporting its steep sides. The stone was taken from the immediate vicinity—the soft sandstone of the Tertiaries, or, perhaps, the inundated materials of the Drift as seen at Grand Gulf." There are allusions to more or less detailed descriptions of sites in the Atchafalaya Basin, "in the rear of Baton Rouge" along Bayous Grosse Tete and Fordoche. In a chapter on the geographical distribution of shell mounds, Foster, again relying on Forshey's notes, furnishes additional descriptions of shell middens and mounds in the New Orleans environs, around Lakes Pontchartrain, Borgne, and Maurepas; the Bayous Metairie, Saint John, Barataria, Perot, and Des Allemands; and south to Berwick's Bay and Point a la Hache. Forshey remarks that the shell accumulations from other sites were being used for street grading and garden walks in New Orleans. "A constant trade in small sailboats and barges is kept up, and this trade is fast exhausting these supplies. . . . There were formerly other banks, I believe, which showed artificial construction, but they have been mutilated for gain . . . many thousands of cubic yards of these shell being annually brought to the city." He laments the artifacts from shell middens in the Grand Lake area, specifically "unique specimens of axes of haematitic iron ore and glazed pottery," that were sent to the Chicago Academy of Sciences and destroyed in that city's conflagration of October 8, 1871. A Mr. Dungan of Jeanerette had donated one such stone axe, 6½ inches long, 5¼ inches broad, and 1¼ inches thick. It came from a shell midden along Grand Lake. He also donated a cup-shaped decorated vessel from a Grand Lake shell midden to the Chicago academy. Forshey describes this vessel and lauds it as the most beautiful piece of prehistoric pottery he has ever seen.[16]

As was commonly the case throughout the United States, archaeological site descriptions often appeared in very obscure survey reports written by personnel of the Department of the Army, Corps of Engineers. One such report, by Assistant H. C. Collins, who was engaged in surveying remnants of the Red River raft in northwest Louisiana, mentions several mounds and beach ridges upon which he found pottery and stone artifacts. In another report, published two years later, Assistant Engineer H. C. Ripley, who was surveying a proposed inland waterway to connect Donaldsonville, Louisiana, to the Rio Grande in Texas, remarked upon the large shell mounds and extensive middens of *rangia* shell he saw in the passes that flow into Sabine Lake. He noted other shell mounds along Bayou Connu, and at the mouth of Bayou Lacassine he came upon a shell midden 500 feet long.[17]

During the last quarter of the nineteenth century, the Smithsonian Institution undertook the classification of its extensive collection of North American Indian objects for an exhibition in celebration of the nation's centennial to be held at Philadelphia. Charles Rau, of the Smithsonian Institution, compiled a descriptive list that referred only to the typical specimens in the collection. Among those from Louisiana were stone projectile points, a knife, a celt, a cast of an atlatl weight, a cast of a perforated gorget, and another cast of a tabular implement that may have served as an abrader. Rau also described and illustrated two decorated pottery vessels from mounds in Louisiana. Four years later Thomas Wilson, curator of the Smithsonian's Department of Prehistoric Anthropology, published *A Study of Prehistoric Anthropology: Hand-Book for Beginners*, which, he admitted, contained "nothing new or original not even the illustrations."[18] Wilson had indeed republished Rau's figures.

16. Foster, *Prehistoric Races*, 118, 72–76, 114–21, 156–59, 211–12, 244–45.

17. H. C. Collins, "Geological Notes of Assistant H. C. Collins," *House Executive Documents*, 43rd Cong., 1st Sess., Vol. 2, Pt. 2, pp. 653–54, 656–57; H. C. Ripley, "Report of the Chief of Engineers," *House Executive Documents*, 44th Cong., 1st Sess., Vol. 2, Pt. 1, pp. 889–90.

18. Charles Rau, "Archaeological Collection of the United States National Museum, in Charge of the Smithsonian Institution," *Smithsonian Contributions*

In a note that appeared in the transactions of the Saint Louis Academy of Science in 1878, Joseph R. Gage, M.E., cautioned contemporary antiquarians about attributing to the Mound Builders articles that in actuality had been subsequently deposited. Referring specifically to the Transylvania Site, he explained that one of the mounds there was used by the plantation as a cemetery for the Negro workers. "I wish to draw attention," he wrote, "to the fact that too great care cannot be exercised in these investigations, as negroes are usually buried in coffins of light wood, which in that damp soil decay in a few years; and (since) they are usually interred with their necklaces of beads and other trinkets, these relics found in the mounds might add to great confusion in assigning them to their proper origin." It is, in all probability, the Transylvania Site that was fortified during the Civil War. John D. Winters, the historian, writes that Confederate forces "encountered a fort, built on an ancient Indian mound, garrisoned by Negro troops who were used to furnish protection to the leased plantations. The sides of the mound had been strongly fortified and were next to impossible to scale without great loss of life."[19]

Endeavoring to collect archaeological data for "an exhaustive treatise: on antiquities from all regions of the United States," Otis Tufton Mason, then a professor at Columbia University and subsequently curator at the Smithsonian Institution, distributed a fifteen-page request for information dated February 1, 1878, entitled *Circular in Reference to American Archaeology*, which is sometimes referred to as *Circular 316*. Thousands of copies were distributed throughout the United States, and the responses were most gratifying. There were at least four communications from Louisiana, the first and most informative of which was from Benjamin H. Broadnax. Broadnax had once written a detailed letter to Secretary Joseph Henry of the Smithsonian Institution in which he had described and illustrated a camp area along Bayou DeGlaize in Morehouse Parish. He had also sent a wide variety of

to Knowledge, Vol. 22, Art. 4 (Washington, D.C., 1876), 9–12, 15, 17–18, 23–24, 32–33, 35–36, 77–78; Thomas Wilson, "A Study of Prehistoric Anthropology," *Annual Report of the Board of Regents of the Smithsonian Institution for the Year Ending June 30, 1888* (Washington, D.C., 1890), 597–671.

19. James R. Gage, "Results of Investigation of Indian Mounds," *Transactions of the Academy of Science of Saint Louis,* Vol. 3 (1878), 232; John D. Winters, *The Civil War in Louisiana* (Baton Rouge, 1963), 203.

chipped-stone and ground-stone artifacts and biconical baked-clay objects from the Bayou DeGlaize site, as well as pottery fragments that he had collected "in almost every Southern state." In his reply to *Circular 316*, Broadnax reported on sites in the Bayou Bartholomew drainage, Morehouse Parish. His report included two detailed maps showing the location of three mounds on the G. H. Johnson plantation. Broadnax noted that the mounds had yielded human bones, stone implements, and "a small pottery jar or jug . . . of soft grayish-blue clay mixed with ground shell (I think)." He reported that campsites "where pottery was burnt and arrow-heads chipped" also abounded in the vicinity. The second site that Broadnax mentioned is the mound complex on the property of Dr. William P. Harrison, which Caleb G. Forshey had first noted thirty-three years earlier. Broadnax observed that the mounds at this site "seem to have been built in layers, covered with clay, and the canes (such as we now used for fishing-poles) were burnt on them, the impressions of the joints of the canes remaining in the burnt red clay. Bones and human remains found in them show great age. Quantities of celts, arrow-heads, chisels, wedges, sc., have been found in the fields and plantations for miles around."[20]

The other responses that Mason received from Louisiana were much less ambitious in scope. There was a communiqué from J. M. Sharp, who reported a mound located about two miles north of Lake Lafourche in Morehouse Parish. Describing the mound as 35 feet in diameter and 5 feet in height, Sharp explained, "Anywhere one digs from base to summit bones and pottery are found. The pots are generally between the legs of the skeleton, against the pelvic bones." Sharp also noted the height (30 feet) and diameter (50 feet) of one of the mounds on the previously cited Harrison property. In another Louisiana reply to *Circular 316*, A. C. Love, writing from Donaldsonville, simply stated that "there is a group of earthworks in this portion of the State—Ascension Parish—which if properly explored might yield up some relics of value to science." The fourth reply, written by George Williamson, briefly described the earthworks at what is presently the

---

20. Benjamin H. Broadnax, "Mounds in Morehouse Parish, Louisiana," *Annual Report of the Smithsonian Institution for 1879* (Washington, D.C., 1880), 386–88; Broadnax letter, copy on file at the Museum of Geoscience, Louisiana State University, Baton Rouge.

Marksville Prehistoric Indian State Park, Avoyelles Parish. Alan Toth, in an excellent history of early references to the Marksville Site, remarks that throughout the nineteenth century published reports and local tradition imaginatively attributed the earthworks to the DeSoto expedition.[21]

The responses to *Circular 316* provided information for several articles by Smithsonian researchers in which a variety of artifacts were categorized and illustrated. One such publication, by Charles Rau, entitled *Prehistoric Fishing in Europe and North America*, illustrated four polished-stone "sinkers" of various shapes from Louisiana. Thomas Wilson's "Study of Prehistoric Archaeology" drew on information Mason had accumulated by means of his circular. Cyrus Thomas used Mason's data and other material to produce the *Catalogue of Prehistoric Works East of the Rocky Mountains*. In a section devoted to Louisiana, Thomas briefly notes archaeological remains in eleven parishes, including the Ouachita Parish sites, the Pargoud mound group, "consisting of mounds and house sites," and "mounds at Monroe."[22] The latter had been reported to the Smithsonian by Dr. Edward Palmer, who also explored and reported upon earthworks in eastern Arkansas.

Four years later, incorporating all that he could learn from extensive research and fieldwork, Cyrus Thomas published his celebrated "Mound Explorations of the Bureau of Ethnology." In a section dealing with sites in Louisiana, Thomas explains that he conducted explorations only in Ouachita, Catahoula, and Tensas parishes. Beginning with the Pargoud group he provides the dimensions of the larger mound and describes the stratigraphy as well as he could judge it from a profile exposed "to obtain material for repairing the road that runs by its

21. Otis T. Mason, "Abstracts of the Smithsonian Correspondence Relative to Aboriginal Remains in the United States," *Annual Report of the Smithsonian Institution for the Year 1880* (Washington, D.C., 1881), 444; Love letter, copy on file at the Museum of Geoscience, Louisiana State University, Baton Rouge; "Abstracts from Anthropological Correspondences," *Annual Report of the Smithsonian Institution for the Year 1881* (Washington, D.C., 1883), 686; Edwin Alan Toth, *Archaeology and Ceramics of the Marksville Site*, Anthropological Papers No. 56, Museum of Anthropology; University of Michigan (Ann Arbor, 1974).

22. Charles Rau, "Prehistoric Fishing in Europe and North America," *Smithsonian Contributions to Knowledge*, Vol. 25, Art. 1 (Washington, D.C., 1885), 169–71; Wilson, "A Study of Prehistoric Anthropology"; Thomas, *Catalogue of Prehistoric Works East of the Rocky Mountains*, 102–104.

base." He was not permitted to explore further. Of the smaller Pargoud mound, he says only that it is conical and six feet high, and he
notes that in the surrounding area house sites are evidenced by beds
of burnt clay and ashes. Thomas also describes the remains of the
earthworks at the Troyville Site, illustrating his remarks with a map
and a photograph. He reports that the large mound within the enclosure, which was originally 250 feet by 160 feet at the base and 60 to 75
feet high, "with a nearly sharp summit," was "so gashed and mutilated, having been used during the war as a place for rifle pits, that its
original form can scarcely be made out." In one of the exposed gashes
there was a layer of charred cane one foot thick. He excavated Mound
6, revealing a matrix of "very hard, greasy clay." Mound 5 was, by then,
being used as a modern cemetery. Thomas remarked that "skeletons
and pottery are frequently thrown out" of newly dug graves. Mounds
2, 3, and 4 had been nearly obliterated by this time. Thomas visited
two other mounds, one 12 feet and one 7 feet in height, "4 miles
southeast of St. Joseph," in Tensas Parish, but since one mound was
being used as a cemetery and the other was occupied by a cistern, excavation was impossible.[23]

During the years 1898 and 1899, Arthur Clifford Veatch, a geologist
employed by the state experiment stations of Louisiana State University, conducted surveys in parts of Louisiana. In addition to geological
data, Veatch contributed a considerable amount of useful information
on archaeological sites he had visited. He described a number of mound
sites in "A Catalogue of Aboriginal Works on Caddo Bottoms," an ap-
pendix to his reports. He also discussed the excavation of a cellar at
Stormy Point on Ferry Lake, Caddo Parish. Colonel S. D. Pitts had discovered an iron tomahawk, two iron rifle barrels, and an iron knife
about eight inches long, as well as pottery sherds, a large vessel "full
of living ants, evidently attracted there by something the pot contained," and a smaller vessel filled with children's bones. Veatch noted
that in 1870 high waters had eroded away part of the bluff at Stormy
Point, exposing a human skeleton. "The forehead was covered with a
thin, highly ornamented piece of silver bent to fit the skull. On the

23. Thomas, "Report on the Mound Explorations of the Bureau of Ethnology," 250,
251–52.

back of the head was a circular piece of silver. These pieces are said to have been analyzed by a local jeweler and pronounced virgin silver. On the shoulders were thin crescent-shaped pieces of metal. They are described as having been coated with green, and are hence inferred to have been copper."[24]

In another section of his report, "The Five Islands," Veatch described archaeological deposits he had examined in several of the salt domes in Iberia and Saint Mary parishes. At Belle Isle in Saint Mary Parish, he noted a shell midden "150 to 200 feet long and three feet thick, from which a human skeleton was removed." Veatch mentioned that pottery fragments were rare, and he commented on "the numerous little baked clay objects" scattered about in the midden. His description of these objects, now recognized as a diagnostic trait of the Poverty Point Culture, is one of the first published. "These little objects," he wrote, "average about two inches in diameter. A common form has the shape of two cones placed base to base. This pattern is varied by making four indentations around its Equator. Others are irregular spheres with four elongated indentations about them medially." Veatch went on to speculate erroneously that "the way they fit in the hand and their shape would suggest that they were used in playing some game."[25]

Of sites in Iberia Parish, Veatch described the Morton Shell Mound at Weeks Island (Grande Cote), which Reymond Thomassy had mentioned. At the time of his visit to the site, Veatch noted, the mound was 600 feet long, 30 to 60 feet wide, and 10 feet high. "The southern end," he wrote, "has the shape of a truncated pyramid from which a narrow ridge, gradually increasing in width, extends to the northern end of the mound, which is almost as wide as the southern. The heap is composed almost entirely of common coast Gnathodon. A few animal bones, oysters and pot-shreds (sherds) are found scattered through the mass. Near the northern end numerous skeletons have been found." In his discussion of Avery Island (Petite Anse), Veatch com-

24. Arthur Clifford Veatch, "The Shreveport Area," in Gilbert D. Harris and A. C. Veatch, *A Preliminary Report on the Geology of Louisiana* (Baton Rouge, 1899), Special Report No. 2, pp. 152–208.
25. Arthur Clifford Veatch, "The Five Islands," in Harris and Veatch, *A Preliminary Report on the Geology of Louisiana*, Special Report No. 3, pp. 213–62.

mented on the fossil bone deposits and their contemporaneity with man. He also remarked upon a low domed mound on the top of Prospect Hill and another site that had yielded shells and pottery fragments.[26]

Veatch also had occasion to examine salt springs and wells in northern Louisiana and in Bienville Parish around Drake's Salt Works. He remarked upon the large quantity of Indian pottery fragments found there. He noted that the specimens were tempered with pulverized shell of a fossil oyster variety not found *in situ* at the salt works. Reasoning from ethnohistoric accounts, Veatch thought it highly probable that these salt licks had been used by the Natchitoches Indians to "make salt for themselves and for trade with the neighboring Indians." At King's Salt Works along Bayou Castor, Veatch felt that the scarcity of sherds and arrowheads and their distance from the brine indicated a temporary campsite used by Indians who came there to hunt animals attracted by the salt licks. A short distance to the north, along Lake Bistineau, another salt works yielded pottery fragments that were not shell tempered and "quantities of flint chips and partly perfected arrowheads."[27]

During the fall of 1899, a period of low water along the Ouachita River, Veatch undertook a boat trip from Monroe downstream to Harrisonburg to study geological stratigraphy exposed along the riverbanks. In his usual encompassing manner, he also examined and reported upon archaeological sites he found along the route in Ouachita, Caldwell, and Catahoula parishes. At eleven different locations he noted mound sites and middens containing shell, pottery, animal and human bone, and stone artifacts.[28] Most of these sites were soon to be more intensely investigated by an expedition from the Academy of Natural Sciences of Philadelphia.

By the year 1900 a researcher interested in Louisiana antiquities

26. Thomassy, *Géologie Practique de la Louisiane*; Veatch, "The Five Islands," 237, 253.
27. Arthur Clifford Veatch, "The Salines of North Louisiana," in Gilbert D. Harris, Arthur C. Veatch, and Jov. A. A. Pacheco, *A Report on the Geology of Louisiana* (Baton Rouge, 1902), Special Report No. 2, pp. 53–55, 77, 83.
28. Arthur Clifford Veatch, "Notes on the Geology Along the Ouachita," in Harris, Veatch, and Pacheco, *A Report on the Geology of Louisiana*, Special Report No. 4, pp. 153, 171–72.

could have read published literature bearing upon earthworks, shell mounds and middens, campsites, salt licks, human burials, and a variety of metal, stone, and ceramic artifacts. Even so, he would know next to nothing about the antiquity of the various finds or even their chronological relationships. Even if the researcher were to have perused some of the most scholarly writings on American archaeology, he would have found few dealing with the factors of cultural growth, site relationships, or the diffusion of traits. Nothing in the nineteenth-century literature pertaining to Louisiana seriously considers such matters.

Nevertheless, there were two important developments in Louisiana during the last century that presaged modern archaeological concerns and techniques. The first of these developments was a report of finding split-cane basketry in the ground *beneath* the bones of Pleistocene fauna at the Avery Island salt dome, Iberia Parish. Colonel Richard Owen made the first scientific report of the basketry find before a meeting of the Saint Louis Academy of Science on September 5, 1864. Upon resigning from the Union army at his post in New Iberia in November, 1863, Colonel Owen, a geologist and later professor at Indiana State University, visited the salt works at nearby Avery Island, where, he had heard, an unusually pure deposit of rock salt was being mined. Although the day proved very rainy, he was enabled to make a satisfactory examination of the entire locality, under the polite guidance of Mr. Henshaw. The salt deposit was overlain by 15 to 18 feet of "chiefly bluish-clay, sand and gravel, with some lumps of micaceous sandstone. . . . After an inspection of some hours, made as remarked, rather unfavorably on account of rain, but still sufficiently in detail to be certain to the facts," Owen opined that "the accumulation of 15 to 18 feet of clay, sand and gravel on the deposit had evidently been the result of comparatively recent washings of the adjoining hills; the deposit has, no doubt, been worked by the aborigines, as, at more than one place, on reaching the rock-salt, Indian relics were found. He (Owen) saw, at Mr. Henshaw's, a basket, obtained from the surface of the rock-salt, 15 feet below the surface of the soil, made of split cane; and was informed they also found pieces of charcoal, apparently the remnants of fires and torches. A rope of bark, wooden hooks, stone axes, and pottery, were likewise obtained." Colonel Owen felt that, "in all probability, the semicircular deposit of sand and gravel, thrown to the height of 160 feet and conforming generally to the contour of the sea-coast, resulted from the combined action of the winds and the waves of the ocean." Since in his opinion this could have happened over a brief period, he attributed no great antiquity to the archaeological remains. Owen made no mention whatsoever of Pleistocene mammal bones in his report.[29]

The first disclosure that such bones had been found at Avery Island appeared in a short communiqué from Dr. Joseph Leidy that was presented at the meeting of the Academy of Natural Sciences of Philadelphia on May 22, 1866. Dr. Leidy explained that he had been visited by J. F. Cleu, one of the proprietors of Avery Island. In addition to donating a sample of the rock salt from the mining operations there, Cleu reported that a number of pits had been dug to reach the salt deposit.

> In several of the pits at a depth of ten or fifteen feet they discovered in the soil bones of the Elephant, well preserved, and beneath these, within a few inches of the rock salt, abundance of matting. Portions of this matting, exhibited to Dr. Leidy, were composed of a tough, flexible, split-cane, and were plaited diagonally. The pieces were well preserved, and evidently specimens of human art. On being asked the question, Mr. Clew (sic) said he was under the impression that some stone implements had also been found in a similar position, but he was not certain. He further added, that at the sides of one of the pits, bones of the Elephant, and beneath them pieces of matting, could yet be seen, as they had been allowed to remain undisturbed.

Dr. Leidy concluded that some competent person should visit and examine the site.[30]

A year later John Wells Foster presented a paper before the Chicago Academy of Sciences in which he outlined certain discoveries that he felt were indicative of the contemporaneity of man and the Pleistocene fauna. One of the discoveries Foster cited in his report was the basketry from Avery Island. Noting that Cleu had donated a specimen of it to the Smithsonian Institution in May, 1866, Foster quotes a statement from Professor Joseph Henry, secretary of the Smithsonian:

29. Richard Owen, "On the Deposit of Rock Salt at New Iberia, La.," *Transactions of the St. Louis Academy of Science*, Vol. 2 (1868), 250–52.
30. Joseph Leidy, "Remarks," in *Proceedings of the Academy of National Sciences of Philadelphia* (Philadelphia, 1866), 109.

The fragment of matting was found near the surface of the salt, and about two feet above it were remains of tusks and bones of a fossil elephant. The peculiar interest in regard to the specimen is its occurrence, in situ, two feet below the elephant remains, and about fourteen feet below the surface of the soil; thus showing the existence of man on the island prior to the deposit in the soil of the fossil animal. The material consists of the outer bark of the common southern cane (Arundinaria macrospermum), and has been preserved for so long a period, both by its silicious character and the strongly saline condition of the water.

Foster goes on to report that he had learned from the Mississippi geologist Dr. Eugene Woldemar Hilgard that "entire baskets have been found in the same locality . . . they have been covered by the soil washed from the slight elevation surrounding the locality. This throws some little doubt upon the above interpretation of the occurrence of the elephant bones, which may have been transported from some other deposit; although, if so, they would probably have become scattered." Foster's article included an illustration of the basketry specimen presented to the Smithsonian by Cleu.[31]

Neither Leidy, Holmes, nor Foster had actually visited the site of the finds. Colonel Owen and Cleu had observed the archaeological deposits, but Owen made no mention of the fossil bone. We know that Professor Hilgard visited the locality in 1867, and his report expresses his view that

all the borings and pits which had reached the salt, had been sunk in detrital material washed down from the surrounding hills, and frequently inclosing the vestiges of both animal and human visits to the spot. Mastodon, buffalo, deer, and other bones; Indian hatchets, arrowheads, and rush baskets, but above all, an incredible quantity of pottery fragments have been extracted from the pits. The pottery fragments form at some points veritable strata, three to six inches thick; this is especially the case where Mr. Dudley M. Avery found what appeared to have been a furnace for baking the ware (a process very imperfectly performed), and near it three pots of successive sizes, inside of each other.

In a footnote Hilgard remarks, "It is very positively stated, that Mastodon bones were found considerably *above* some of the human relics.

31. John Wells Foster, "On the Antiquity of Man in North America," *Transactions of the Chicago Academy of Sciences*, Vol. 1 (1867), 227–57, plate 24.

In a detrital mass, however, this cannot be considered a crucial test."
Hilgard illustrates a geological cross section of Avery Island and a sev-
enty pound "boulder of porphyritic diorite" said to be from the detrital deposits above the salt. He notes that this is the only rock of this
type he has seen on Avery Island and assigns its origin to Missouri or
Arkansas.[32]

The Reverend Mr. Edward Fontaine, who had once been secretary
of the New Orleans Academy of Sciences and by at least one report a
geologist, accompanied Hilgard to Avery Island. In a book disputing
the antiquity of man upon the earth, Fontaine wrote, "I am inclined
to think that both men, differing in nothing essential to constitute a
'type of mankind' from the Cooshattie Indians, and these huge quadrupeds used the rock-salt of Avery's Island in an age much more recent
than the Deluge of Noah, as fixed by the *short* chronology of Usher."
Fontaine included drawings of the Vermilion Bay area and Weeks and
Avery islands, a schematic sketch of the geology of Avery Island, and
a drawing of a 70-pound diorite boulder which he said measured 15 by
14 by 9 inches.[33]

In 1889, Joseph Leidy published a description of additional fossil
bones from Avery Island. These specimens, donated to the Smithsonian Institution in 1883 and 1884, were obtained during excavations for
an air shaft in connection with the salt-mining operation. From information given to him, Leidy described the stratigraphic sequence from
the surface down to the rock salt.

1, superficial sandy soil, 6 feet; 2, sands, 4 feet; 3, black earth, like that
of the neighboring bogs, containing fragments of pottery, 4 feet; 4, sands,
2 feet; 5, dark coarse sand and gravel, in contact with the salt bed, and
varying in depth from 6 inches to 2 feet according to the dip of the latter
bed. In this deepest layer the fossil bones together with vegetal remains
were found, many of them close to if not actually in contact with the
salt. The bones and teeth are stained chocolate brown and black, are
otherwise little altered, and are not rolled or water-worn. They consist
of remains of Mastodon americanus, Mylodon, and of a Horse.[34]

32. Edward Fontaine, *How the World Was Peopled: Ethnological Lectures* (New
York, 1884), 67; Eugene Woldemar Hilgard, "On the Geology of Lower Louisiana and the Salt Deposit on Petite Anse Island," *Smithsonian Contributions
to Knowledge*, Vol. 23, Art. 248 (Washington, D.C., 1872), 14, 16–17, 20.
33. Southall, *The Recent Origin of Man*, 322; Fontaine, *How the World Was Peopled*, 82–83, 68–71.
34. Joseph Leidy, "Notice of Some Mammalian Remains from the Salt Mines of Pe-

A year later the Smithsonian curator Thomas Wilson published an article in which he reviewed all of the evidence on hand relative to the age of the basketry fragment that Cleu had presented to the museum in 1866. In summary, Wilson concurred with the findings of Hilgard and stated that the specimen "has no bearing upon the question of the antiquity of man. The same would apply with equal propriety to the buffalo, deer, and other bones, to the Indian hatchets and arrowheads, and to the incredible quantity of pottery fragments found by Professor Hilgard. These, together with the matting and fossil mastodon bones and tusks, have all been washed down from the surrounding hills and swept back and forth, in no one knows how many relative changes of position, by each recurring tide."[35]

In 1895, Professor Henry Chapman Mercer, an anthropologist and curator of the museum at the University of Pennsylvania, published a brief summary of the events pertinent to the fossil bone and artifacts found at Avery Island. He was able to include some more recent observations of the site by Dr. Joseph F. Joor. In January, 1890, when salt-mining operations exposed additional artifacts and fossil mammal bone, the president of Tulane University was notified. Since the professor of geology was absent at the time, he asked Dr. Joor, a physician who had attained prominence in the field of botany, to travel to the island and report his observations. During his eighteen-day visit to the island, Joor noted, he was hospitably received and assisted by the McIlhenny and Avery families and officials from the salt-mining company. He viewed a rectangular excavation, "about 50 × 90 feet at top, and 30 × 70 feet at bottom, with sloping sides—the greater length being north and south. The depth varied from 16 to 25 feet." Joor described four stratigraphic layers overlying the salt, noting that the third layer, of loam from 10 to 12 feet thick, contained the "pottery bed." Below this was a fourth layer, consisting of blue clay intermixed with pebbles, which contained fossil bone. A portion of this last stratum was removed in his presence.[36]

---

tite Anse, Louisiana," *Transactions of the Wagner Free Institute of Science,* Vol. 2 (1889), 33.

35. Thomas Wilson, "Ancient Indian Matting—From Petit Anse Island, Louisiana," *Annual Report of the Board of Regents of the Smithsonian Institution for the Year Ending June 30, 1888* (Washington, D.C., 1890), 673–75.

36. Henry Chapman Mercer, "The Antiquity of Man on Petit Anse (Avery's Island) Louisiana," *American Naturalist,* Vol. 29 (1895), 393–94; Joseph F. Joor, "Notes

Within the loam stratum were deposits of animal bone, shell, and pottery in addition to fire pits containing ash and pottery fragments; Joor also observed evidence of a gully that had since been filled with clay. From the south end of the excavation a fragment of cane matting about four inches square was retrieved. Joor wrote, "It seems to have come from the lower part of the loam, below the level of most of the other human vestiges." Also within the loam were found well-preserved leaves that were "still green," and twisted strips of bark that Joor conjectured were basket handles.[37]

From the blue clay, he tentatively identified bone, antler, and teeth belonging to mastodon, horse, giant sloth, and deer, as well as a "soft stercoraceous mass, found about the junction of the blue clay and loam, apparently the dung of some large herbivorous animal."[38] As to the age of these deposits, Joor, after describing the artifacts within the loam, stated:

> I see no reason for assigning any very enormous antiquity to these relics . . . the two last layers appear to be a "wash" from the neighboring hills, and may have been formed within a century, while three or four hundred years would be enough for the loam, especially if there was a slight gradual subsidence, so as to keep it subject to overflow. The deeper specimens were found near the south end, where there are signs of a gully or hollow of some kind, which would fill more rapidly than the higher ground, if the cause which produced it were removed.
>
> It is somewhat remarkable that not an arrow-head, weapon or tool was found in the excavation, although such articles are not rarely found at or near the surface, in the neighborhood.[39]

The following year William Henry Holmes, the Smithsonian archaeologist and later director of the Bureau of American Ethnology, published his work on aboriginal textile art in the eastern United States. In this illustrated report Holmes mentions the basketry fragment given to the Smithsonian by J. F. Cleu, but his description of the specimen and the find spot simply reiterates John Wells Foster's report of 29 years before.[40]

on a Collection of Archaeological and Geological Specimens Collected in a Trip to Avery's Island (Petit Anse), Feb. 1st, 1890," *American Naturalist*, Vol. 29 (1895), 394–98.

37. Joor, "Notes on a Collection of Archaeological and Geological Specimens," 396.

38. *Ibid.*, 398.

39. *Ibid.*, 396–97.

40. William Henry Holmes, "Prehistoric Textile Art of Eastern United States,"

In 1898 the president of Tulane University was notified that additional matting fragments were being exposed 16 to 18 feet beneath the surface at Avery Island. This time George Eugene Beyer, professor of biology and past curator of the Museum of Natural History at Tulane University, was sent to investigate the find. According to his report, the expanding mining operations had created numerous large openings that had subsequently collapsed. It was from the walls of one of these openings that Sidney Bradford had found and removed pieces of matting about two feet square. Beyer examined the find spot, but "with the exception of a few small pieces (of matting) there was nothing left in situ." He remarks that the stratum resting upon the salt deposit consisted of a very compact drift composed of gravel, clay, and sand about two feet thick, exhibiting two distinguishable layers. "Between these two strata of drift, nearly two feet above the salt and fifteen or sixteen feet from the surface, this basket work, as well as several well preserved pieces of wood, had been found. The wood plainly exhibited the rather jagged surfaces of cuts made with crude and in all probability, stone implements."[41]

Noting that Bradford had also found the tooth of a fossil form of horse nearby partially covered by the matting, Beyer judged that the tooth must have been washed down from higher levels. His final comment provides an interesting bit of information that had not been mentioned by any of the previous investigators. Beyer states that a variety of extinct mammal bones "have been found embedded in a strata from 8 to 10 feet above the drifts." He concluded that the basketry remains were in situ, that they were deposited prior to "the embedding in the soil of those gigantic Pachyderms," and that the earlier articles by Hilgard and Fontaine were "somewhat obscure and contradictory." Beyer's findings are themselves contradictory, however. In one place he maintains that the fossil horse molar, found partially covered by basketry fragments, was washed into its place of discovery. Later he de-

Thirteenth Annual Report of the Bureau of Ethnology, 1891–92, Smithsonian Institution (Washington, D.C., 1896), 7–46; Foster, "On the Antiquity of Man in North America," 233–34.

41. George Eugene Beyer, "Ancient Basket Work from Avery's Island," Publications of the Louisiana Historical Society, Vol. 2 (1899), Pt. 2 for 1898, pp. 23–26.

clares not only the basketry but also the fossil mammal bones, found in a stratum eight to ten feet above it, to be *in situ.*[42]

Arthur C. Veatch was the last professional to examine the site in the nineteenth century, visiting Avery Island in 1899. He "carefully searched in the bone bed for objects which could be unquestionably attributed to man but was unable to discover any. Numerous pieces of cane were found in this layer and some had a peculiar split appearance which was first thought to be artificial but turned out to be due to unequal weathering. If a piece of cane was found partially embedded in clay the exposed end almost always had the split appearance while the part enclosed in the bank was perfectly solid. Pieces of wood showed a tendency to behave in the same way." Veatch concluded that evidence for the contemporaneity of the fossil mammal bones and the basket work was unconvincing.[43]

By the turn of the century the Avery Island finds had been the subject of considerable discourse for thirty-six years. It was one of the numerous sites throughout the country where it was believed evidence existed for the presence of modern man in association with extinct fauna. If such a relationship could be proven, it would indicate that modern man had lived here thousands of years earlier than had been formerly accepted. Confronted with the evidence on hand in the year 1900, it would have been most difficult to draw any strong conclusions about the true chronological relationship of the cane basketry fragments to the fossil mammal bones. It would likewise have been impossible to confidently ascribe any great antiquity to the artifactual remains. Of those five individuals who actually examined the deposits, only Cleu, who was not a professional investigator, reported basketry *beneath* fossil bone. The geologist Owen did not so much as mention fossil bone in his communiqué and the other geologist, Professor Hilgard, felt that the remains were secondary deposits of no remote antiquity. Neither the Reverend Mr. Fontaine nor Dr. Joor really possessed the expertise to reckon with the problem. Nevertheless they did concur with Hilgard. Professor Beyer, who had directed some pre-

42. Hilgard, "On the Geology of Lower Louisiana and the Salt Deposit on Petite Anse Island," 14–19; Fontaine, *How the World Was Peopled*; Beyer, "Ancient Basket Work from Avery's Island," 25–26.
43. Veatch, "The Five Islands," 252, 253.

34

vious archaeological explorations in Louisiana, was the only visitor who believed the basketry to be *in situ*, but he was undecided as to its age. In the last analysis, convincing proof of the antiquity of man at Avery Island was not demonstrated, but as we shall see, further explorations at the site more than sixty years later provided more substantial data with which to assess the question.

The second significant nineteenth-century development pertinent to the archaeology of Louisiana occurred in 1896. In that year the Louisiana Historical Society became the first professional organization within the state to officially support and fund archaeological explorations, and George Beyer became the first archaeologist so funded. This marked the beginning of scientific, professional archaeology in Louisiana, although to be sure, it was an undramatic and tentative beginning. Fifty-two years would elapse before any state institution in Louisiana funded the salary for a full-time anthropologist, professionally trained in the subdiscipline of archaeology. Nevertheless, this was a significant milestone.

George Eugene Beyer (Pl. 2, *b*) was born in Germany in 1861. He was educated in biology at the University of Berlin, and in 1891 he came to the United States and settled in New Orleans. In 1893 he was appointed curator of the museum at Tulane University, where he remained for twenty-five years, rising to the rank of professor of biology, medial entomology, protozoology, and helminthology. Beyer's first active involvement with Louisiana archaeology began in the year 1896, when he read a preliminary report on Indian mounds in Catahoula Parish before a formal meeting of the Louisiana Historical Society. In his characteristically straightforward, if not doggedly resolute, style Beyer told the audience that the mounds should be explored in a scientific manner, that the artifacts were promised to Tulane University, and that the Louisiana Historical Society should actively support such investigations. The society membership immediately contributed the sum of fifteen dollars and discussed ways of providing additional funds. One year later the society's president, Alcée Fortier, suggested that fifty dollars be voted by the membership to aid Beyer, and the motion was passed unanimously. Beyer continued his archaeological investigations under the society's auspices until the turn of the century.

Professor Beyer conducted excavations and/or surveyed sites in

Catahoula, Franklin, Natchitoches, West Feliciana, Calcasieu, Iberia, Saint Charles, and Orleans parishes.[44] His articles must certainly stand as the first site reports concerning observations on excavated archaeological remains published in Louisiana. Beyer's digging techniques are not always described in detail, but he usually employed the trenching method, in addition to the usual procedure of the day, the sinking of a shaft down from the summit of a mound. At several sites he simply cleaned off profiles that had been exposed by riverbank erosion or railroad construction, and at least once, he seems to have peeled an extensive area of horizontal strata from the top of a mound in order to expose an underlying layer that contained human interments. His labor force was apparently provided by the proprietors of the land at each site, supplemented by local volunteers. Beyer illustrated his site reports with site maps, excavation profiles, plan views, and drawings of artifacts and human crania. It is evident from comparison with the actual artifacts that his rather plain line drawings are not very carefully executed facsimiles.

The existence of Indian sites in Louisiana had long been known, but Beyer was one of the first investigators whose object was other than collecting artifacts. He was interested in the methods of mound construction and clearly demonstrated their multistage structure. He theorized that the Indians had built the earthen tumuli, at least in part, as refuges from floodwaters. Since, as others before him, Beyer was intrigued by the pimple mounds located near an Indian site, he mapped their locations and dug into a number of these small, low eminences. Finding no archaeological deposits, he concluded that they were built up by the aborigines for the placement of dwellings in areas of poor drainage. While examining shell middens in Calcasieu Parish, Beyer observed their various lenses, which contained pottery, fire pits, animal bones, and human burials, and correctly reasoned that they represented deposits from intermittent occupations. He also described a variety of burial patterns that he had observed in his excavations. Be-

44. Beyer, "The Mounds of Louisiana" (1896); George Eugene Beyer, "The Mounds of Louisiana," *Publications of the Louisiana Historical Society*, Vol. 2 (1898), Pt. 1, pp. 7–27; Beyer, "Ancient Basket Work from Avery's Island"; George Eugene Beyer, "Investigations of Some Shell-Mounds in Calcasieu Parish," *Publications of the Louisiana Historical Society*, Vol. 2, (1899), Pt. 2 for 1898, pp. 16–23.

yer remarked on several occasions that archaeological sites should be excavated with utmost care and scientific attention. He decried the plundering of sites and the removal of artifacts from the state, as well as the destruction of still other sites by road and railway construction projects.

Beyer, however, was a product of the times. He believed that the brain of the Indian was inferior to that of the Caucasian, and he shared the prevalent view that the Mound Builders were not of the same race as the present-day Indians. His attempts at physical anthropology, based upon measurements of a very limited number of excavated crania, were incredibly naïve and fallacious, even for the times. No less incredible are his remarks regarding designs on a vessel retrieved from a mound in Natchitoches Parish. Beyer felt that the incised designs, which he likened to swastikas and Maltese crosses, were too intricate to have originated in the mind of a North American Indian.

In spite of these impossible theories and interpretations, Beyer's efforts were undoubtedly of value to Louisiana archaeology. His site reports, obviously, cannot be measured against present-day standards, but they were quite innovative compared to others of their time and place. Beyer's work foreshadowed the methods that are now considered standard professional practice.

The Twentieth Century

Shortly after the turn of the century, the geologist A. C. Veatch again contributed descriptions of sites and artifacts he found situated near salines in north Louisiana. In his *Report on the Geology of Louisiana*, in a section relative to the Ouachita River, he provided data on eleven mounds and/or campsites that he had visited along the river route between Monroe and Harrisonburg, Louisiana.[45]

Near the beginning of the new century, physical anthropologists began to study skeletal remains retrieved from sites in Louisiana. This represented an extremely important advance in archaeological tech-

45. Veatch, "The Salines of North Louisiana," 53–54, 77, 83, 91; Veatch, "Notes on the Geology Along the Ouachita," 171–75.

nique. Assuredly, diseased human skeletons had been studied (Jones 1877–1878) and their burial patterns illustrated by previous reporters. Indeed, craniological or, more accurately, phrenological studies that included Louisiana specimens had been published by prominent physicians many years earlier. Not until 1907, however, did a professional, physical anthropologist comment upon human skeletal remains from Louisiana. In that year Aleš Hrdlička of the Smithsonian Institution published a volume refuting evidence for the presence of people in North America during the terminal stages of the Pleistocene period. In regard to the matter of Doctor Dowler's Red Indian, or the "New Orleans Skeleton," Hrdlička concluded correctly that the argument for attributing tremendous age to this skeleton "shows so many weak points that it can not be accepted for anything more than an individual opinion."[46]

Subsequently, Hrdlička analyzed human skeletal material excavated by Clarence Bloomfield Moore during the latter's exploration of the Ouachita River drainages in Louisiana and Arkansas. Hrdlička mistakenly included the bones of two adult males from a site in Union County, Arkansas, in his tabulations of material from six sites in Morehouse, Ouachita, Caldwell, and Franklin parishes in Louisiana. Nevertheless, Hrdlička provides comprehensive data on bones representing twenty-eight adult females and a like number of adult males. For the first time we have detailed cranial and postcranial dimensions and descriptions of artificial cranial deformation and pathologies such as syphilis, arthritis, exostoses, and lesions.[47]

46. Joseph Jones, "Explorations and Researches Concerning the Destruction of the Aboriginal Inhabitants of America by Various Diseases, as Syphilis, Matlazarica, Pestilence, Malarial Fever and Small Pox," *New Orleans Medical and Surgical Journal*, New Series, Vol. 5 (1877–78), 926–41; George Samuel Morton, *Crania Americana* (Philadelphia, 1839); J. Aitken Meigs, "Observations upon the Cranial Forms of the American Aborigines Based upon Specimens Contained in the Collection of the Academy of Natural Sciences of Philadelphia," *Proceedings of the Academy of Natural Sciences of Philadelphia* (Philadelphia, 1866), 197–235; Hrdlička, *Skeletal Remains Suggesting or Attributed to Early Man in North America*, 15.

47. Clarence Bloomfield Moore, "Antiquities of the Ouachita," *Journal of the Academy of Natural Sciences of Philadelphia*, Vol. 14 (1909), 7–170; Aleš Hrdlička, "Report on an Additional Collection of Skeletal Remains, from Arkansas and Louisiana," *Journal of the Academy of Natural Sciences of Philadelphia*, Vol. 14 (1909), 171–249.

Several years later Hrdlička published his detailed analysis of material that Moore had excavated at Bayou Sorrel, Iberville Parish. From sixteen skulls and a few bones Hrdlička identified eight adult females and eight adult males between the ages of thirty-five and sixty. All of the crania were artificially deformed and none showed evidence of pathologies, although diseases were apparent on some of the postcranial bones. It is also interesting that, of the 401 teeth he examined, Hrdlička found only 6 teeth from 5 skulls that exhibited caries.[48]

Hrdlička later used the information gathered from all of these Louisiana skeletal remains as comparative data in a volume on the physical anthropology of the Lenape Indians. The data appeared again twenty-four years later in his inventory of Indian crania from the Gulf Coast states. The inventory listed the cranial dimensions, the sex, and the approximate age at the time of death of each individual. The Louisiana sample consisted of thirty-four males and twenty-nine females from Morehouse, Ouachita, Caldwell, Franklin, Richland, Madison, Avoyelles, Iberville, and Vermilion parishes. He found that forty of the skulls—twenty-three males and seventeen females—were artificially deformed.[49] By and large, Hrdlička's work stands alone. Aside from his reports, there continued to be a dearth of comprehensive information on the physical anthropology of prehistoric Indians from Louisiana.

Of all the archaeological investigations discussed thus far, none was as important as the work of Clarence Bloomfield Moore (1852–1936; see Pl. 2, c). He was born in Philadelphia and received an A.B. degree from Harvard University in 1873. He then spent seven years traveling extensively: to Asia Minor, Greece, Turkey, Egypt, Syria, Europe, and even over the Andes and down the Amazon River to its mouth. During the early 1890s, while associated with the Academy of Natural Sciences in Philadelphia, Moore began archaeological explorations in

48. Aleš Hrdlička, "A Report on a Collection of Crania and Bones from Sorrel Bayou, Iberville Parish, Louisiana," in C. B. Moore, "Some Aboriginal Sites in Louisiana and Arkansas," *Journal of the Academy of Natural Sciences of Philadelphia*, Vol. 16 (1913), 95.
49. Aleš Hrdlička, *Physical Anthropology of the Lenape or Delawares and of the Eastern Indians in General*, Bureau of American Ethnology Bulletin 62 (Washington, D.C., 1916); Aleš Hrdlička, "Catalog of Human Crania in the United States National Museum Collections: Indians of the Gulf States," *Proceedings of the United States National Museum*, Vol. 87 (1940), 315–464.

Florida and later expanded his work into Georgia, South Carolina, Alabama, Arkansas, Mississippi, Louisiana, Tennessee, and Kentucky. When he was searching for sites, Moore characteristically transversed stream drainages, using a one-hundred-foot stern-wheeler appropriately named *Gopher* for transportation (Pl. 4). His crew complement would comprise a captain, a pilot, an engineer, a physician, and five crewmen. In addition he employed eight other men to conduct excavations, assisted by members of the regular boat crew.

By the time Moore began his explorations in Louisiana in 1908, he had worked for sixteen years in six other southeastern states, and he had developed field techniques that would compare favorably with those of any of his peers in the region. Although Moore generally omitted site maps and excavation dimensions, he did describe soil strata from his trial or bore holes. He also employed the trenching technique, troweling, and occasionally screening the material from his excavations. Between 1908 and 1917, Moore visited 104 archaeological sites located in twenty-seven parishes. He and his entourage steamed to sites in the Ouachita, Little River, Boeuf, and Bayou Bartholomew drainages, and along the Mississippi River, the Red River, the Atchafalaya River, the Tensas River, and Macon and D'Arbonne bayous.[50] He did not excavate at every site he visited, even though a number of those sites had been reported earlier by Beyer and Veatch, but Moore's accomplishments are nonetheless impressive, and his publication record is even more gratifying. Moore customarily compiled and published the achievements of each field season within a year of completing his fieldwork. In elegantly illustrated volumes, Moore provided the type of high-caliber archaeological information found only in the more comprehensive reports of that period. Moreover, he was the first investigator in Louisiana to incorporate data derived from specialists in other fields of science. He consulted experts like Aleš

50. Moore, "Antiquities of the Ouachita"; Clarence Bloomfield Moore, "Some Aboriginal Sites on the Mississippi River," *Journal of the Academy of Natural Sciences of Philadelphia*, Vol. 14 (1911), 365–480; Clarence Bloomfield Moore, "The Northwestern Florida Coast Revisited," *Journal of the Academy of Natural Sciences of Philadelphia*, 2nd Series, Vol. 16 (1918), Pt. 4, pp. 514–77; Clarence Bloomfield Moore, "Some Aboriginal Sites on Red River," *Journal of the Academy of Natural Sciences of Philadelphia*, Vol. 14 (1912), 481–644; Moore, "Some Aboriginal Sites in Louisiana and Arkansas."

Hrdlička for physical anthropological analysis of human skeletal remains and for animal bone, shell, and pigment identifications. The
nature and extent of Moore's work and his contributions to the common store of knowledge were indeed superlative.

Aside from the explorations of Clarence Moore, the first three decades of this century held no particularly outstanding developments
for Louisiana archaeology. At least one writer has attributed the dearth
of archaeological publications in the United States between 1920 and
1933, to the passage of the Volstead Act.[51] Even so, Louisiana antiquities continued to be mentioned in the literature, and a limited amount
of fieldwork was reported. In his excellent study, "Aboriginal Pottery
from Eastern United States," William Henry Holmes illustrated several vessels from Louisiana. In 1918 Joe Mitchell Pilcher described
several mound sites in the vicinity of Marksville and briefly reviewed
C. B. Moore's findings from along the Red River. The following year
David I. Bushnell, Jr., of the Smithsonian Institution, reported artifacts and human bones intermixed with shell and sand along the "shore
of Lake Pontchartrain, about 12 miles northeast of New Orleans."[52]

The paleontologist Oliver P. Hay published an article in 1924 in
which he reviewed the data relative to finds of fossil mammals in central North America. He included a summary of the discoveries at Avery Island. In regard to the artifacts found in the salt-mine excavations
he offered a cautious and objective opinion.

An opinion must be expressed more guardedly respecting the age of the
objects of human origin found there. It will not do to dismiss too lightly
the statements of those who have affirmed that the human objects and
bones were intermingled before disinterment. There is no occasion to
question the honesty of Mr. Clew (sic), who affirmed that the basket-
work had been found two feet below elephant bones and that there was
more of the basket-work and bones for the examination of experts.

51. William B. Butler, "Archaeology and Prohibition," Plains Anthropologist, Vol.
21 (1976), No. 71, pp. 67–71.
52. William Henry Holmes, "Aboriginal Pottery from Eastern United States,"
Twentieth Annual Report of the Bureau of American Ethnology (Washington,
D.C., 1903), fig. 52, plate 51 (c and d), plate 52 (a), pp. 31, 48, 57, 102–103; Joe
Mitchell Pilcher, "The Story of Marksville," Publications of the Louisiana
Historical Society, Vol. 10 (1918), 68–82; David I. Bushnell, Jr., Native Villages
and Village Sites East of the Mississippi, Bureau of American Ethnology Bulletin 69 (Washington, D.C., 1919), 65.

However, it is possible that he was in some way mistaken as to the relative position of the materials and that others were mistaken as to the commingling of bones and pottery; or it may be that the artifacts in some unknown way got into their places in rather late times. The case offered here at Petit Anse (Avery Island) is not greatly different from that which presents itself at Natchez and at a considerable number of other localities in the United States.[53]

In 1926 Gerard Smith (1855–1933), who adopted the name Fowke (Pl. 2, d), came to Louisiana as a special archaeologist for the Smithsonian Institution to explore sites in the Red River Valley. He had spent the previous twenty-two years investigating archaeological sites in Siberia, the Hawaiian Islands, British Columbia, Oregon, Kansas, Missouri, Illinois, Indiana, Ohio, Kentucky, Tennessee, and Alabama, and had been variously employed by the American Museum of Natural History, the Missouri Historical Society, and the Smithsonian Institution. Between the Arkansas-Louisiana state line and the Marksville environs, in Avoyelles Parish, he reported no less than forty-eight tumuli and several villages or campsites. Fowké, like several of his predecessors, misinterpreted the pimple mounds of the region as prehistoric habitation sites, although he also felt that at least some of them might be burial mounds. At a salt lick west of Natchitoches, near Shamrock Mills, he reported a site strewn with pottery and chipped-stone and ground-stone artifacts. A plowman had unearthed a human scapula that exhibited a hole. Fowke, surmising that it was a bullet hole, attributed the scapula to the Civil War. Near the right bank of Bayou Boeuf, south of Alexandria, he visited a site where there were two tumuli from which a number of prehistoric and historic objects were removed. Fowke then proceeded to the Marksville vicinity. He spent three months there, conducting excavations into six tumuli located in and near the present Marksville State Commemorative Area. Fowke published a complete description of his Marksville investigations, including the first detailed map of the tumuli and encircling earthworks. Unfortunately, none of the excavated artifacts from this site was illustrated, although in the earlier, more condensed report of

53. Oliver P. Hay, *The Pleistocene of the Middle Region of North America and Its Vertebrated Animals*, Carnegie Institution of Washington Publication No. 322a (Washington, D.C., 1924), 219–20.

his Red River explorations, Fowke had furnished photographs of his excavations and two illustrations exhibiting a stone plummet, a clay pipe, and three vessels.[54]

Fowke also visited archaeological sites along Bayou Maçon in the vicinity of Delhi and Epps in Richland and West Carroll parishes, respectively. He described the tumuli and earthworks and some of the artifacts he collected from plowed fields, but he did not conduct any excavations in the region. A map of the site on the Neil farm, seventeen miles north of Delhi, which Fowke included in his report, shows eight tumuli and an angular earthwork, where Fowke found fragments of a steatite vessel. He remarked that, "In every direction from these mounds, and in the adjoining fields, many flints and fragments of pottery have been found."[55] In neither of his articles does Fowke provide more than a shadow of a remark respecting chronological placement of the reported sites. It is evident that most archaeological investigations in Louisiana were still purely descriptive.

In 1926 the Smithsonian Institution also sent Henry Bascom Collins, Jr. (Pl. 2, e), its assistant curator of ethnology, to conduct fieldwork in Mississippi and Louisiana. A native of Geneva, Alabama, Collins had received an A.B. degree from Millsaps College. He had participated in the National Geographic Society expedition at Pueblo Bonita, New Mexico, had worked for the Mississippi Department of Archives and History, and had directed Smithsonian explorations in Florida. He would, in later years, become one of the most renowned specialists in Arctic archaeology, a field that he pioneered.

Collins' explorations in Louisiana began along Bayou Grande Cheniere in Plaquemines Parish, where he found nine mounds. He next spent ten days in Terrebonne Parish, gathering data from earth middens with the help of Randolph A. Bazet of Houma. Collins continued west from there. He examined sites in the Gibson, Lake Palourde, Bayou L'Ours, Berwick, Charenton, and Avery Island environs. Later

---

54. Gerard Fowke, "Archaeological Work in Louisiana," *Smithsonian Miscellaneous Collections,* Vol. 78 (1927), No. 7, pp. 254–59, figs. 246, 247; Gerard Fowke, "Archaeological Investigations—II," *Forty-fourth Annual Report of the Bureau of American Ethnology* (Washington, D.C., 1928), 409.
55. Fowke, "Archaeological Investigations—II," 434–36, fig. 6.

he spent three weeks excavating human burials found along the chen-
ier ridge at Pecan Island, Vermilion Parish.[56]

The data he had gathered from his survey and excavations led Collins to conclude that the mounds and shell middens in Louisiana were
the farthest extension south and west of the better-known mound cultures of the lower Mississippi Valley. He also noted that certain distinctive pottery styles appearing along the Gulf Coast from Florida to
western Louisiana were indicative of prehistoric cultural relationships. Fourteen years later Collins would be able to draw more detailed conclusions about cultural origins and their affinities between
the Pecan Island sites and excavated remains elsewhere in the eastern
United States and Mexico. These will be discussed in the chapter on
the Tchefuncte Culture.[57]

In 1928 the Smithsonian anthropologist John Reed Swanton offered
a hypothesis linking the prehistoric construction of mounds with certain ethnohistorically documented ceremonial customs of the Creek
Indians. His article makes use of data from the Morehouse Parish site
first described in 1845 by Caleb G. Forshey. In *The Mound Builders,*
the Ohio archaeologist Henry Clyde Shetrone mentions certain Louisiana site plans and artifacts, illustrating some of them. His discussion of Louisiana is essentially a résumé of Clarence Moore's work. In
1934 Caroline Dormon, the Louisiana artist and conservationist, wrote
an article for the journal *Art and Archaeology* in which she called attention to the fine quality of surface finish, color, and decorative techniques and forms characteristic of pottery found in northwest
Louisiana and the adjacent areas of Texas and Arkansas and attributed
it to the historic Caddo Indians and their predecessors. She provided
fourteen illustrations of vessels and decorative motifs to accompany
the articles. It was also in 1934 that a very interesting and comprehensive report of explorations at a shell mound along Bedico Creek,

56. Henry B. Collins, Jr., "Archaeological Work in Louisiana and Mississippi: Explorations and Field-Work of the Smithsonian Institution in 1926," *Smithsonian Miscellaneous Collections,* Vol. 78 (1927), No. 7, pp. 200–207.
57. Henry B. Collins, Jr., "Relationships of an Early Indian Cranial Center from
Louisiana," *Journal of the Washington Academy of Sciences,* Vol. 31 (1941), No.
4, pp. 145–55.

Tangipahoa Parish, appeared in the *Abbey Chronicle*, published at the Saint Benedict Abbey near Covington. The Reverend Odilo Alt, O.S.B., gave detailed descriptions of the human burials, hearths, and pottery that he and his assistants had excavated. He mentions finding two rough pieces of obsidian, an exotic stone not heretofore reported from Louisiana sites.[58]

It has long been recognized that the era of professionalism in American archaeology began in the 1930s. Before that time there were very few professionals, and those were widely scattered and poorly funded. During the late 1920s and early 1930s, a notable increase in public interest brought marked expansion of state archaeological societies. Many more institutions of higher learning also began offering professional training in the subject. From these societies, colleges, and universities came the individuals who organized the national Society for American Archaeology in 1934 and began publishing the society's first journal, *American Antiquity*, in 1935.

Ironically, it was the economic depression of the 1930s that revolutionized archaeology in the United States. The federal government soon realized that archaeological investigations were ideally suited to reducing the massive unemployment of the period. Professors and even many graduate students were soon directing hitherto unheard of numbers of workers in large-scale excavations in almost every state. As elsewhere in the nation, federal relief projects under the aegis of the Federal Emergency Relief Administration first and, subsequently, the Civil Works, and the Works Projects, and the Works Progress administrations were created in Louisiana. By August, 1933, Frank M. Setzler (Pl. 2, *f*) of the Smithsonian, directing a FERA project employing more than one hundred workmen, began excavation and restoration at the Marksville Site, Avoyelles Parish.[59] He continued his investi-

58. John R. Swanton, "The Interpretation of Aboriginal Indian Mounds by Means of Creek Indian Customs," *Annual Report of the Board of Regents of the Smithsonian Institution for 1927* (Washington, D.C., 1928), 495–506, fig. 4b; Henry Clyde Shetrone, *The Mound Builders* (New York, 1930); Caroline Dormon, "Caddo Pottery," *Art and Archaeology*, Vol. 35 (1934), No. 2, pp. 59–68; Odilo Alt, "A Prehistoric Find at Bedico, La.," *Abbey Chronicle* (St. Benedict, La.), Vol. 8 (1934), No. 4.

59. Carl E. Guthe, "Twenty-five Years of Archaeology in the Eastern United States," in James B. Griffin (ed.), *Archaeology of Eastern United States* (Chicago, 1952), 1–12; William G. Haag, "The Archaic in the Lower Mississippi Valley," *Amer-*

gations until December, 1933, after which there was a hiatus in federally sponsored archaeological projects in Louisiana. Whereas large-scale CWA and WPA projects were launched early on in other states, for reasons totally unrelated to archaeology the federal government funded no new Louisiana projects until September, 1938, when a coordinated Louisiana State University–Works Progress Administration program was established.

James Alfred Ford (Pl. 2, *i*) (1911–1968) of Water Valley, Mississippi, then a graduate student at the University of Michigan with a B.A. degree from Louisiana State University, planned and directed the program. Ford, already an experienced archaeologist, having conducted fieldwork in the Arctic, New Mexico, Georgia, Mississippi, and Louisiana, was later to be recognized as one of the most eminent American archaeologists of our time. Edwin Lyon, historian of WPA archaeology in Louisiana, noted that Ford selected experienced professional archaeologists for his staff, including Edwin B. Doran, Jr., Preston Holder, Arden R. King, William T. Mulloy, Robert S. Neitzel, George I. Quimby, Jr., Carlyle S. Smith, and Gordon R. Willey (Pl. 3). A headquarters and processing laboratory originally set up in New Orleans was transferred to the Geology Building on the university campus at Baton Rouge a year later. The field units, with crew complements of thirty to forty-five workmen, conducted extensive excavations at sites in LaSalle, Avoyelles, Saint Martin, West Baton Rouge, Iberville, Saint Tammany, and Orleans parishes. Neitzel, who was in charge of the Avoyelles Parish unit, reported typical statistics from his fieldwork: "The work on the present projects was begun on the 19th of September, 1938, and, at present (19th of December, 1938), is still being continued. To date the project has been in operation fifty days, an average of thirty-seven and three tenths men being present each day, and one thousand-eight hundred and sixty-six man days of work having been expended. One thousand five hundred and fourteen cubic

ican Antiquity, Vol. 26 (1961), No. 3, Pt. 1, pp. 317–23; Frederick Johnson, "A Quarter Century of Growth in American Archaeology," *American Antiquity*, Vol. 27 (1961), No. 1, pp. 1–6; James E. Fitting (ed.), *The Development of American Archaeology* (Garden City, N.Y., 1973); Edwin Lyon, "The Louisiana WPA Archaeological Project," *Southeastern Archaeological Conference Bulletin*, No. 19 (1976), 50–52.

yards of earth have been moved." In addition to these excavations, Doran conducted a brief field reconnaissance for sites in Lafayette, Vermilion, Acadia, Jefferson Davis, and Calcasieu parishes, and Andrew C. Albrecht, the staff ethnohistorian, compiled a bibliographic manuscript of ethnographic sources relative to southeastern Indians.[60]

Certainly one of the most transcendent benefits archaeologists derived from these federally funded projects was the opportunity to see and study the enormous quantity and variety of archaeological remains unearthed in different areas. In Louisiana and elsewhere in the Southeast, formal conferences and, more commonly, impromptu meetings led to a greatly expanded theoretical framework of cultural chronologies, artifact varieties and associations, earthwork construction, village pattern, and burial practices. Prehistoric cultural dynamics at last began to be understood. As theorists became aware of primary cultural manifestations and their geographical distributions through time, they began to recognize the development and basic cohesiveness of a southeastern cultural region. Evidence of this new understanding appeared in descriptions of pottery types, site reports, and the first broad regional synthesis.[61]

Two other important developments during the 1930s that had a lasting effect on the archaeology of Louisiana were the establishment of the School of Geology at Louisiana State University and the creation of the Louisiana Geological Survey. The School of Geology, which was composed of the Department of Geography and Anthropology, the Department of Geology and the Department of Petroleum Engineering, was under the direction of the noted geologist Henry V.

60. Lyon, "The Louisiana WPA Archaeological Project"; Robert S. Neitzel, Quarterly Progress Report, WPA Project, Avoyelles Unit, manuscript on file at the Museum of Geoscience, Louisiana State University, Baton Rouge.
61. William G. Haag, untitled article, *Southeastern Archaeological Conference Newsletter*, Vol. 1 (1939), No. 2; James A. Ford and Gordon Willey, *Crooks Site: A Marksville Period Burial Mound in LaSalle Parish, Louisiana*, Department of Conservation, Louisiana Geological Survey, Anthropological Study No. 3 (New Orleans, 1940); James A. Ford and George I. Quimby, Jr., *The Tchefuncte Culture: An Early Occupation of the Lower Mississippi Valley*, Society for American Archaeology Memoirs No. 2 (Menasha, Wis., 1945); James A. Ford and Gordon Willey, "An Interpretation of the Prehistory of the Eastern United States," *American Anthropologist*, New Series, Vol. 43 (1941), No. 3, Pt. 1, pp. 325–63.

Howe. It was through his efforts that the university chose such scholars as Richard J. Russell, a geologist, and Fred B. Kniffen (Pl. 2, *h*), a geographer, to head up the school's fledgling departments. The Louisiana Geological Survey began publishing its Geological Bulletin series, which dealt with the geology and mineral resources of the state, in the early 1930s. From the very beginning, many of the articles that appeared in these bulletins resulted from research conducted by Howe, Russell, and Kniffen. In order to interpret the state's stream-drainage patterns and its coastal physiography, they and their colleagues gathered and utilized geomorphological, archaeological, and botanical data, thus initiating an interdisciplinary approach that made possible a relative chronological dating technique that proved most fruitful to all fields. Many of the bulletins contain historical and archaeological information; the Geological Survey also published a separate series of studies devoted to archaeological investigations. The *Louisiana Conservation Review*, responding to the expanding public interest in archaeology, published reports and illustrations of excavations and artifact classification.[62]

62. Henry V. Howe, Richard J. Russell, and James H. McGuirt, "Submergence of Indian Mounds," in *Reports on the Geology of Cameron and Vermilion Parishes*, Department of Conservation, Louisiana Geological Survey, Geological Bulletin No. 6 (New Orleans, 1935), 64–68; Richard J. Russell and H. V. Howe, "Cheniers of Southwestern Louisiana," *Geographical Review*, Vol. 25 (1935), No. 3, pp. 449–61; Richard Joel Russell, "Physiography of the Lower Mississippi River," in *Reports on the Geology of Plaquemines and St. Bernard Parishes*, Department of Conservation, Louisiana Geological Survey, Geological Bulletin No. 8 (New Orleans, 1936), 3–199; Fred B. Kniffen, "Preliminary Report on the Indian Mounds and Middens of Plaquemines and St. Bernard Parishes," in *Reports on the Geology of Plaquemines and St. Bernard Parishes*, 407–22; Fred B. Kniffen, "Indian Mounds of Iberville Parish," in *Reports on the Geology of Iberville and Ascension Parishes*, Department of Conservation, Louisiana Geological Survey, Geological Bulletin No. 13 (New Orleans, 1938), 189–207; W. D. Chawner, *Geology of Catahoula and Concordia Parishes*, Department of Conservation, Louisiana Geological Survey, Geological Bulletin No. 9 (New Orleans, 1936), Clair A. Brown, "The Vegetation of Indian Mounds and Middens and Marshes in Plaquemines and St. Bernard Parishes," in *Reports on the Geology of Plaquemines and St. Bernard Parishes*, 423–40; James A. Ford, "An Introduction to Louisiana Archaeology," *Louisiana Conservation Review*, Vol. 4 (1935), No. 5, pp. 8–11; James A. Ford, *Analysis of Indian Village Site Collections from Louisiana and Mississippi*, Department of Conservation, Louisiana Geological Survey, Anthropological Study No. 2 (New Orleans, 1936); Ford and Willey, *Crooks Site*; J. Richard Czajkowski, "Preliminary Report of Archaeological Excavations in Orleans Parish," *Louisiana Conservation Review*, Vol. 4 (1934), No. 3, pp. 12–18; James A. Ford, "Outline of Louisiana and

To this decade of the 1930s belong the endeavors of Winslow M. Walker (Pl. 2, g), an associate anthropologist of the Smithsonian Institution with prior archaeological experience in the Hawaiian Islands and Arkansas. During a four-week period in 1931, Walker, assisted by Mrs. Cammie G. Henry of Melrose plantation and Caroline Dormon, attempted to locate the vestiges of certain historic Caddo Indian sites in the northern Red River area. Alerted to the fact that Indian burials associated with aboriginal and European artifacts were being destroyed by the construction of a federal fish hatchery one mile south of Natchitoches, he went immediately to the site and was able to salvage one burial, that of an adult female associated with two pottery vessels. Walker subsequently analyzed his excavated material and other specimens collected at the fish hatchery site. After researching pertinent ethnohistoric documents and comparable artifactual pieces from other sites in Louisiana and Arkansas, he correctly concluded that the site was once a cemetery of the historic Natchitoches Indians. His fifteen-page illustrated article may well stand as the first really scientific archaeological report relative to Louisiana antiquities.[63]

From the fish hatchery site Walker traveled to the Marksville area, stopping briefly on the way to visit a site of four mounds along Bayou Boeuf, in Rapides Parish. At Marksville he examined the mounds that Fowke had previously reported and excavated. Of the mounds, in bottomland on the property of Alfred Greenhouse northeast of the present Marksville park, Walker remarked, "It is interesting to note that this group was completely submerged to a depth of 4 feet over the top of the highest mound during the floods of 1927, thus removing any

---

Mississippi Pottery Horizons," *Louisiana Conservation Review*, Vol. 4 (1935), No. 6, pp. 33–38; James A. Ford, *A Ceramic Decoration Sequence at an Old Indian Village Site near Sicily Island, Louisiana*, Department of Conservation, Louisiana Geological Survey, Anthropological Study No. 1 (New Orleans, 1935); James A. Ford, "Archaeological Exploration in Louisiana During 1938," *Louisiana Conservation Review*, Vol. 7 (1939), No. 4, pp. 15–17; Fred B. Kniffen, "Historic Indian Tribes of Louisiana," *Louisiana Conservation Review*, Vol. 4 (1935), No. 7, pp. 5–12.

63. Winslow M. Walker, "A Reconnaissance of Northern Louisiana Mounds," *Explorations and Field-Work of the Smithsonian Institution in 1931* (Washington, D.C., 1932), 169–74; Winslow M. Walker, "A Variety of Caddo Pottery from Louisiana," *Journal of the Washington Academy of Sciences*, Vol. 24 (1934), No. 2, pp. 99–104; Winslow M. Walker, "A Caddo Burial Site at Natchitoches, Louisiana," *Smithsonian Miscellaneous Collections*, Vol. 94 (1935), No. 14.

possibility of their having been erected to serve as places of refuge during high water periods."[64]

Once again Walker was alerted to the destruction of archaeological remains, this time at the famous Troyville Site, in Catahoula Parish. In August, 1931, Walker hastened to Troyville, where he learned that the largest mound had been leveled to the ground three days earlier "by a construction company which used the dirt as a fill for the approach to a new highway bridge being built at that point. . . . This was the first time such an enormous mound had ever been so thoroughly razed." In examining the ground surface exposed by the destruction of the mound, Walker found cane fragments outlining what he then surmised were the remains of a temple or chief's house. He also observed clays of various colors not native to the area, "brought from some unknown locality." In November of the same year and again in the fall of 1932, Walker returned to the Troyville Site, where he directed extensive excavations. Subsequently, he compiled a preliminary article and then a most comprehensive final report about the history of the site and the details of his own excavations there.[65]

In December, 1932, Walker, along with thirty-nine other experts, attended the Conference on Southern Pre-History that convened in Birmingham, Alabama, under the auspices of the National Research Council. The purpose of this most important conference was to review and evaluate all that was presently known about southeastern prehistory, to discuss general problems, and to develop new approaches and methods that would lead to a better understanding of prehistory throughout the entire United States. Walker contributed an excellent synopsis of archaeological conditions in Louisiana to the conference. He theorized that there were three somewhat overlapping prehistoric culture areas in Louisiana—the Gulf Coast, the lower Mississippi Valley and the Red River Valley—each of which possessed distinctive traits. In order to best understand the cultural developments within these areas, Walker proposed that archaeologists,

64. Fowke, "Archaeological Investigations—II"; Walker, "A Reconnaissance of Northern Louisiana Mounds."
65. Walker, "A Reconnaissance of Northern Louisiana Mounds"; Winslow M. Walker, "Trailing the Moundbuilders of the Mississippi Valley," *Explorations and Field-Work of the Smithsonian Institution in 1932* (Washington, D.C., 1933), 77–80; Walker, *The Troyville Mounds*.

working closely with ethnohistorians, locate and investigate sites of the historic tribes before attempting any classification of the prehistoric remains. There was already much solid evidence from sites attributed to the Natchez and Caddo tribes, but the Gulf Coast manifestations were still a matter of pure speculation.

This is not to say, however, that Walker was unaware of prehistoric or "nonhistoric" site relationships, for he cites artifactual similarities and other traits that extend along the Gulf Coast from Louisiana to Florida and northward into Ohio. Walker felt that little could be learned about regional archaeological chronologies from the dendrochronological (tree-ring) technique because of the climate of Louisiana. On the other hand, he was optimistic about the interdisciplinary approach of Howe, Russell, and Kniffen. "If we only knew the history of such large mound groups as now appear to be some distance away from the larger rivers," he wrote, "we would find that at the time the mounds were built the rivers ran much nearer than they do today. . . . If it were possible to determine the length of time required for this shift in the channel, we could perhaps establish the period of the building and occupation of the mounds."[66]

Not surprisingly, Walker was quite concerned about the wanton destruction of archaeological sites in the state. He expressed the hope that citizens would promptly report such instances to the proper authorities and would themselves take the steps necessary to protect these sites for future generations. In order to document the state's antiquities, Walker recommended a statewide archaeological survey, "parish by parish, listing all aboriginal sites known, whether still in existence or not," and suggested that the survey "enlist the aid of interested amateurs by asking all collectors to furnish the survey with photographs and descriptions of specimens in their collections together with all available data as to the places and circumstances of discovery."[67] It is unfortunate that many years would pass before the recommendations in this first comprehensive summary of the state of archaeology in Louisiana would be implemented.

66. Winslow M. Walker, "Pre-Historic Cultures of Louisiana," in *Conference on Southern Prehistory, Held Under the Auspices of the Division of Anthropology and Psychology, Committee on State Archaeological Surveys, National Research Council, Birmingham, Alabama, Dec. 18, 19 and 20, 1932* (Washington, D.C., 1932), 47.
67. *Ibid.*, 48.

Although Walker obviously recognized and differentiated the pre-historic from the historic, neither his publications nor any others of the period have been much help toward understanding the prehistoric cultural sequences. Toward this end, in the summer of 1933 James A. Ford, who more than anyone else was instrumental in developing ceramic chronologies for the prehistoric cultures of the area, began excavating midden deposits at the Peck Site, Catahoula Parish. Since 1927, Ford, Henry B. Collins, Jr., and Moreau B. Chambers of the Mississippi Department of Archives and History had excavated and/or surface-collected artifacts from more than a hundred sites in Mississippi and Louisiana. After careful study of the potsherds from these sites, Ford organized the collections into seven ceramic complexes based upon pottery design or ornamentation and reasoned that these had spatial-temporal significance. When pottery belonging to three ceramic complexes that he had previously ascribed to the prehistoric period was found eroding from a midden 20 inches thick, Ford saw an excellent opportunity to test for a stratigraphic sequence and, by implication, a chronological scale. The excavation data he obtained from the site bore out his hopes and provided further corroboration of his ceramic chronology. Using the stratigraphic, seriational, and classificatory techniques described in his two 1935 articles and one published a year later, Ford was able to devise the first valid scheme for determining the prehistoric cultural sequence in the lower Mississippi Valley.[68]

This description of chronological sequence represented an extraordinarily important advance over the contemporary practice whereby archaeological remains were simply classified as historic or prehistoric. Ford's methodology offered a means by which prehistoric cultural changes could be recognized and studied. There was as yet no method that would permit the archaeologist to assign absolute dates to the regional complexes, but now at least their relative ages could convincingly be shown. Not until the 1950s and the development of the radiocarbon, or carbon-14, dating techniques, would archaeologists be able to date Louisiana sites.[69]

68. Ford, A Ceramic Decoration Sequence; Ford, "An Introduction to Louisiana Archaeology"; Ford, Analysis of Indian Village Site Collections from Louisiana and Mississippi.
69. Willard F. Libby, Radiocarbon Dating (Chicago, 1955).

In 1935 Emmet Chisum, a student at what is now Northeastern Louisiana State University, conducted additional excavations at the Peck Site in an undisturbed area of midden deposit. In addition to finding potsherds marking the same prehistoric sequence Ford had reported, Chisum unearthed sherds attributed to the historic Natchez complex in association with a human skeleton. Off to one side from this skeleton, and at a greater depth, he exposed the remains "of five (human) skulls found with fragments of other bones." An exceedingly interesting finding of his excavations was postmolds, "which appeared to contain decayed wood" and which formed the outline of the rectangular floor plan of a prehistoric structure. The pattern measured 8 by 14 feet, and within it Chisum found mussel-shell fragments, animal bones, cord-marked sherds, a small stone bowl, a stone plummet, and the remains of a hearth.[70] These structural remains are unique in the publication record of Louisiana archaeology.

No discussion of archaeology in the 1930s would be complete without acknowledging the contributions of the Shreveport physician Clarence Hungerford Webb (Pl. 3, *h*), whose association with archaeology began early in that decade. His meticulous excavations, conference presentations, and publications are hallmarks in American archaeology. His enormously important work, as it pertained to individual cultures in prehistoric Louisiana, will be discussed in detail in the following chapters.

During most of the period from 1800 through the 1920s, the archaeological record may be characterized as loosely descriptive and generally devoid of methodological and theoretical considerations. By the beginning of the 1930s, though, dedicated and competent professionals had begun rigorously to apply the scientific method to unravel the chronological and distributional attributes of the region's archaeology. By the end of the 1930s much of the basic framework of Louisiana archaeology was formulated. We shall now turn our attention to the documentation for at least 12,000 years of culture change that scientific archaeology has made available.

70. Emmett Chisum, "The Excavation of an Indian Village near Sicily Island, Louisiana," *Proceedings of the Louisiana Academy of Sciences*, Vol. 4 (1938), No. 1, pp. 54–57; Ford, *A Ceramic Decoration Sequence*.

Contributors to Louisiana archaeology: *a*, Caleb G. Forshey; *b*, George E. Beyer; *c*, Clarence B. Moore (photo courtesy of Harvard University); *d*, Gerard Fowke; *e*, Henry B. Collins, Jr.; *f*, Frank M. Setzler; *g*, Winslow M. Walker; *h*, Fred B. Kniffen; *i*, James A. Ford.

a   b   c

d   e   f

PLATE 3   g   h   i

Contributors to Louisiana archaeology: *a*, Gordon R. Willey; *b*, George I. Quimby, Jr.; *c*, Robert S. Neitzel; *d*, Carlyle S. Smith; *e*, Edwin B. Doran, Jr.; *f*, William T. Mulloy; *g*, Arden R. King; *h*, Clarence H. Webb; *i*, William G. Haag.

PLATE 4

The paddle-wheeled quarterboat *Gopher of Philadelphia* used by C. B. Moore, purportedly docked along the Tombigbee River at Columbus, Mississippi, during the winter of 1900–1901.

II Paleo-Indian Era:

10,000 B.C.—6000 B.C.

Before reviewing the current evidence on hand for Paleo-Indians in Louisiana, it would be well to set the stage for their presence here by beginning with a few statements relative to man in the New World. One may rightly ask, Just how did the Paleo-Indians enter the New World, when did they arrive and what are the data that document their presence? While the detailed evidence, or lack thereof, respecting this most ancient epoch is still a subject of no little speculation, the general picture is still a point of agreement among most professional archaeologists. Furthermore, lest the reader become perplexed by unanswered questions, let him bear in mind that the archaeologist, unassisted by chariots from outer space, specters of lost tribes, or mythical sunken continents, is left to deal with only the accidently preserved objects of man's activities, namely his tools, constructions, middens, and his human skeletal remains.

From all that is presently known through physical anthropological research on a very limited inventory of human skeletal remains attributed to Paleo-Indians in the New World, and from additional data gathered from American Indian populations of lesser antiquity, it is evident that the first Americans were Mongoloids that had evolved from racial stocks in Asia. By the time the Paleo-Indians entered the New World, they were equipped with all of the physical characteristics of modern man. Culturally they were prodigious, unrivaled hunters and predators. Additionally, all collaborative research by archaeologists, physical anthropologists, and paleontologists testifies that

Paleo-Indians represent the first human population to inhabit the New World.[1] Although there is considerable controversy among archaeologists respecting the exact time of Paleo-Indian's arrival in the New World, it is unanimously agreed that his route from Asia was across the Bering Land Bridge into Alaska.[2] This was the only land connection between Asia and the Western Hemisphere, and there is no physical evidence that the Paleo-Indians had yet developed a water-craft technology capable of transoceanic voyages in the area under consideration.

Regarding the problem of when the Paleo-Indians arrived in the New World, geological investigations and radiocarbon dates have shown that the Bering Land Bridge was only available during particular climatic intervals of the Pleistocene, or Ice Age. The last major glacial advance, called the Wisconsin, reached its maximum sometime between 60,000 and 50,000 years ago, and the enormous body of water impounded by the expanding glaciers lowered the sea level as much as 460 feet, exposing a land bridge 1,300 miles wide north to south between Asia and Alaska.[3] The fossil record from the Pleistocene period testifies to the fact that numerous and varied fauna migrated across the land bridge from Asia to the New World. After about 40,000 years ago, a climatic warming trend resulted in glacial melting and a sea-level rise that submerged that land bridge until around 23,000 years ago. Final emergence of the land bridge occurred between 23,000 years ago and 12,000 years ago, after which a warming climate caused sea levels to rise, and it is estimated that by 8,000 years ago the land bridge had disappeared.[4] Thus, in the broadest of terms, the Paleo-Indians had the op-

1. T. S. Genovés, "Some Problems in the Physical Anthropological Study of the Peopling of America," *Current Anthropology*, Vol. 8 (1967), No. 4, pp. 297–312; T. Dale Stewart, *The People of America* (New York, 1973).
2. Alan Lyle Bryan, "Early Man in America and the Late Pleistocene Chronology of Western Canada and Alaska," *Current Anthropology*, Vol. 10 (1969), No. 4, pp. 339–65; Irving Rouse, "Peopling of the Americas," *Quaternary Research*, Vol. 6 (1976), No. 4, pp. 597–612.
3. William G. Haag, "The Bering Strait Land Bridge," *Scientific American*, Vol. 206 (1962), No. 1, pp. 112–23.
4. C. Wylie Poag, "Late Quaternary Sea Levels in the Gulf of Mexico," *Transactions of the Gulf Coast Association of Geological Societies*, Vol. 23 (1973), 394–

portunity to migrate across the Bering Land Bridge and enter the Western Hemisphere sometime before 40,000 years ago and again between 23,000 and 8,000 years ago.

From a number of locations in the Americas radiocarbon-dated archaeological deposits, in conjunction with geological and paleontological data not altogether uncontroversial, have led some investigators to maintain that the Paleo-Indians entered the New World *at least* as early as 40,000 years ago.[5] On the other hand there is a great deal less trepidation over a large store of indisputable, radiocarbon-dated archaeological remains documenting the presence of the Paleo-Indians over broad environmentally diverse regions of the Americas between 23,000 and 8,000 years ago. The cultural spread of the Paleo-Indians was such that by at least 10,000 years ago they were occupying caves and killing now-extinct animals near the Strait of Magellan at the southern tip of South America.[6] As we have seen, indications of Paleo-Indians in America came to the fore during the mid-nineteenth century. We shall now examine the more current endeavors to document their remains in Louisiana.

The time period for the Paleo-Indian era in Louisiana, 10,000 B.C.– 6000 B.C., is not altogether arbitrarily selected. This is not to say that people were not here earlier; it is only that archaeological evidence along that vein is most inconclusive. The era is characterized by glacial melt and retreat and rising sea levels during the waning years of the Pleistocene period. One can only speculate as to how many of our earliest archaeological sites now lie mantled below the present sea level along the continental shelf and previous coastlines now located many miles seaward.

Regional pollen studies and finds of extinct megafauna, such as

400; Reid A. Bryson and Wayne M. Wendlund, "Tentative Climatic Patterns for Some Late Glacial and Post-Glacial Episodes in Central North America," in William Mayer-Oakes (ed.), *Life, Land and Water* (Winnipeg, 1967), 9–15.
5. Richard S. MacNeish, "Early Man in the New World," *American Scientist*, Vol. 63 (1976), No. 3, pp. 316–27.
6. *Ibid.*; Bryan, "Early Man in America"; C. Vance Haynes, Jr., "The Earliest Americans," *Science*, Vol. 166 (1969), No. 3906, pp. 709–15; Gordon R. Willey, *An Introduction to American Archaeology: Volume I, North and Middle America* (Englewood Cliffs, N.J., 1966); Alex D. Krieger, "Early Man in the New World," in Jesse D. Jennings and Edward Norbeck (eds.), *Prehistoric Man in the New World* (Chicago, 1964), 23–81.

mammoth, mastodon, dire wolf, giant ground sloth, giant bison, horse, tapir, and saber-toothed tiger, in the southeastern United States indicate that the climate of this period was cooler and drier than today, supporting xeric, mixed pine and oak forests, and open prairies. By 6000 B.C. the regional climate had warmed, bringing about changes in vegetation and the gradual extinction of most of the Pleistocene faunal species. It is important to realize, however, that this climatic change was most gradual. In the extreme, the annual temperature would not average more than five degrees centigrade cooler than today, and the slow change would be almost imperceptible to man.[7]

There is evidence that Paleo-Indian hunters and gatherers lived in Louisiana at least as early as 10,000 B.C., contemporaneously with Pleistocene megafauna (Fig. 2). This is not to say that people were not here earlier, but evidence of human occupation of the state before 10,000 B.C. is sketchy. As previous workers who dealt with eastern North America, the southeastern region, and more specifically, the lower Mississippi Valley, have testified, most of the evidence for man's coexistence with Pleistocene megafauna is secondhand. Investigators have found diagnostic stone artifacts, whose association with Pleistocene species has been authenticated at sites in the plains and southwest regions, and they have reasoned by analogy that the tool-users who lived in this area were contemporaries of those in other regions. Very close to Louisiana there is one notable exception to this pattern of indirect evidence, however, that involved human bones.[8]

Natchez Man

In 1846 Dr. Montroville Wilson Dickeson reported finding a fragmented human pelvis in a blue matrix "about two feet below the skel-

7. Carl O. Sauer, "Seashore—Primitive House of Man?" *Proceedings of the American Philosophical Society*, Vol. 106 (1962), No. 1, pp. 41–47; Jim J. Hester, "Late Pleistocene Extinction and Radio Carbon Dating," *American Antiquity*, Vol. 26 (1960), No. 1, pp. 58–77; S. David Webb (ed.), *Pleistocene Mammals of Florida* (Gainesville, 1974); William G. Haag, "Southeastern United States: Post-Pleistocene Adaptations, 9000–4000 B.C.," manuscript on file at the Department of Geography and Anthropology, Louisiana State University, Baton Rouge.
8. Willey, *An Introduction to American Archaeology*, Vol. I; Don W. Dragoo, "Some

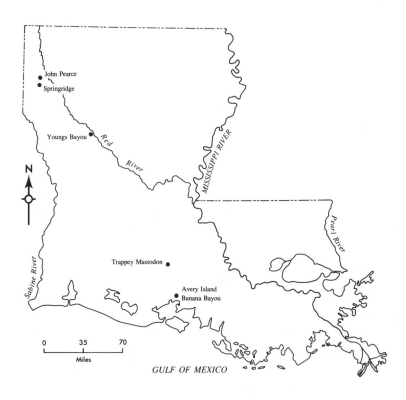

FIG. 2   Locations of Paleo-Indian and Meso-Indian Sites Discussed in the Text

etons of the Megalonyx and other extinct genera of quadrupeds,"
beneath the loess bluffs just west of Natchez, Mississippi. This find

Aspects of Eastern North American Prehistory: A Review," *American Antiquity*, Vol. 41 (1976), No. 1, pp. 3–27; Walter S. Newman and Bert Salwen (eds.),
Amerinds and Their Paleoenvironments in Northeastern North America, Annals of the New York Academy of Sciences, Vol. 288 (New York, 1977); Stephen
Williams and James B. Stoltman, "An Outline of Southeastern United States Prehistory, with Particular Emphasis on the Paleo-Indian Era," in H. E. Wright, Jr.,
and David G. Frey (eds.), *The Quaternary of the United States* (Princeton, N.J.,
1965); Jeffrey P. Brain, "The Lower Mississippi Valley in North American Prehistory," manuscript, Arkansas Archaeological Survey, Fayetteville.

reached notoriety under the name "Natchez Man" even though Dickeson himself identified the pelvis as belonging to a sixteen-year-old boy. Several prominent scientists of the day examined the mammal bones. Two scientists who visited the site were of the opinion that the human bone had fallen from the bluffs thirty feet above and therefore was not found *in situ*. The question of the contemporaneity of the human and mammal bones was all but put to rest until 1895. In that year fragments of the human pelvis and associated *Mylodon* (ground sloth) bone were analyzed for their fluorine content by R. L. Packard of the Smithsonian Institution. If the fluorine proportions in the bones were found to be equal and there were no other extenuating circumstances to the contrary, the bones would be judged to have the same antiquity. After the fluorine tests were completed, Dr. Thomas Wilson, the Smithsonian curator who requested the analysis, concluded that "the bones under present consideration, the man and the mylodon, are substantially of the same antiquity."[9] In our area, this was the first and last instance that human and extinct Pleistocene animal remains were reported in association, tested for their fluorine content, and adjudged to be of the same age.

Avery Island

The site yielding both Pleistocene fauna and artifacts that has been most intensively explored is Avery Island. The basketry fragment found there in conjunction with the bones of extinct animals provoked discussion throughout the nineteenth century.[10] However, no conclusion was possible from the data and techniques then available.

During the summers of 1960 and 1961, in the hope of clarifying the archaeological situation in the deposits overlying the salt cap, the McIlhenny Company and the International Salt Company sponsored

9. Montroville Wilson Dickeson, "Report at Meeting of October 6, 1846," *Proceedings of the Academy of Natural Sciences of Philadelphia*, Vol. 3 (1846), No. 5, pp. 106–107; Thomas Wilson, "On the Presence of Fluorine as a Test for the Fossilization of Animal Bones," *American Naturalist*, Vol. 29 (1895), 301–17, 439–56, 719–25; George I. Quimby, Jr., "The Locus of the Natchez Pelvis Find," *American Antiquity*, Vol. 22 (1956), No. 1, pp. 77–79.
10. See Chapter 1 for a history of the find.

investigations. Sherwood M. Gagliano, then a graduate student at Louisiana State University, made auger and core borings in an effort to find undisturbed Pleistocene deposits in the pond fill overlying the salt cap in Salt Mine Valley. It was in this area that the much-publicized nineteenth-century finds had been retrieved. The tests indicated that the southeastern portion of the valley had been relatively undisturbed by salt-mining operations, and so it was here that Gagliano chose to conduct excavations. Using a backhoe and later a dragline, Gagliano excavated a pit measuring 10 feet by 40 feet at the surface, which contracted to an apical point 25 feet below the surface. The pit was excavated in twenty-one irregular levels. Inasmuch as a large share of the excavation extended below the water table, slumping walls were a constant problem. Excavating in such a situation is no mean task, but Gagliano made every effort to minimize the chance of mixing the strata or misinterpreting the proveniences of the material brought up in the buckets.

The material from each of the twenty-one levels was examined for its sedimentary characteristics and then water-screened for artifactual retrieval. The stratigraphy revealed a white and olive gray sand and gravel unit overlying the salt cap in Levels 20 and 21. On top of that unit were interbedded silty clays, sands, and gravel 10 to 20.5 feet below the surface in Levels 12 through 19. From this latter unit "approximately 600 bipolar cores, flakes and irregular fragments were collected."[11] Gagliano believes these bipolar cores were made by removing flakes from opposite ends of a piece of parent gravel. The resulting sharp-edged flakes may themselves have served as cutting and/ or scraping tools.

From this excavation, designated Pit V, and two boreholes, Gagliano was able to obtain organic clays for radiocarbon dating. Leaf mold and twigs from Level 7 in Pit V yielded a date of A.D. 1512 ± 105 years, which is confirmed by the Plaquemine period ceramics also found at that level. Peat deposits in Borehole B, located about 60 feet northwest of Pit V, were dated 1613 ± 120 years B.C., and peat in Borehold D,

11. Sherwood M. Gagliano, *An Archaeological Survey of Avery Island* (Baton Rouge, 1964); Sherwood M. Gagliano, *Occupation Sequence at Avery Island* (Baton Rouge, 1967), 25.

about 70 feet north northwest of Pit V, provided a date of 1363 ± 120
years B.C. The much-discussed split-cane matting that J. F. Cleu had
presented to the Smithsonian Institution in 1866 was also subjected
to radiocarbon analysis along with two fossil mammal bones. The
reader will recall that this matting fragment was purportedly found
near the salt cap and about two feet *beneath* fossil mammal bones. Radiocarbon dating revealed that the matting fragment was made in 2310
± 590 years B.C., whereas a fossil mammal bone, unidentified as to
species, that Joseph Joor had collected somewhere in Salt Mine Valley
in 1890 was dated 6440 ± 140 years B.C. A second fossil mammal bone,
also unidentified as to species, that was found in the early 1960s with
other fossil bones "in situ in the walls of a small gully at the base of
the railway embankment," was radiocarbon-dated 7750 ± 550 years
B.C.[12]

In 1968 the McIlhenny family and the International Salt Company
again provided facilities for Gagliano to conduct archaeological explorations in Salt Mine Valley. Gagliano made core drillings in selected
areas that were to be disturbed by the construction of a new mine shaft
and a loading structure. At Borehole I, located about 130 feet east of
Pit V, an organic horizon was found 16 to 18 feet below the surface,
immediately above the rock salt.[13] Samples taken from this organic
horizon yielded radiocarbon dates of 10,050 ± 400 years B.C., and 8950
± 300 years B.C.

In 1969 at the site selected for the construction of a new mine shaft
in Salt Mine Valley, a unit of interlocking sheet metal pilings, 40 feet
in diameter, was driven into the ground down to the surface of the salt
cap. Using a mechanical clam bucket, the earth overlying the rock salt
was removed from inside the steel unit in thirty-four arbitrary levels
extending to a depth of 31.5 feet. Gagliano was present during part of
this operation, and he "examined the overburden material *in situ* and
after removal from the shaft" the material from each location was
loaded into a dump truck and transported to an open field where it was
deposited in orderly, segregated piles. During the shaft excavations

12. Gagliano, *Occupation Sequence at Avery Island*, 36.
13. Sherwood M. Gagliano, *Archaeological and Geological Studies at Avery Island, 1968–1970* (Baton Rouge, 1970), 4.

Gagliano noted fossil mammal bone and artifactual materials being exposed in Levels 29 through 34. Subsequently, the piles for these levels were troweled and water-screened, and a number of interesting artifacts were recovered. Gagliano identified fossil teeth of mastodon and horse at Level 32, and in Levels 33 and 34 he found "shells of *Rangia cuneata* . . . in a matrix of clean sand and ash (?), suggesting a hearth." Also in Levels 33 and 34 were a number of bipolar tools, notched-shaft scrapers, and concentrations of chert spalls. "Cordage," he reported, "occurs both as short, individual strands (5 to 15cm in length and 2 to 8mm in diameter and in interwoven bundles)." The cordage, two-stranded and made from plant fiber, sometimes appeared to be fragments of bags or mats. Split-cane matting and a mammal-bone point wrapped in a bundle of grass were found in Level 34. Gagliano summarized his progress as follows: "The new data seem to confirm the interpretation advanced in the 1967 report, that is, the earliest occupation was by peoples with a 'pre-Clovis' culture."[14]

To be sure, Gagliano provided excellent data relative to the geological history of Salt Mine Valley, and proved that archaeological materials, some of which are extraordinarily well preserved, occur at various depths at several locations in the strata overlying the salt cap. Unfortunately he has not convincingly demonstrated the presence of Paleo-Indians or a "pre-Clovis" culture. He has not found a single diagnostic Paleo-Indian artifact *in situ*, either isolated or in primary association with fossil mammal bone. The bipolar specimens are comparable to specimens reported from the more recent Archaic, or Meso-Indian inventories.[15] Certainly they are more common in Archaic collections. Moreover, Gagliano has not documented their direct associations in unmixed Paleo-Indian assemblages. In terms of the fossil mammal bone, there are no reports of possible butchering patterns, cut scars, or burning on the bones that would indicate use by man. Nor is there any inventory of the number, kind of bone, and species for the skeletal elements recovered in any of the tests during the 1960s. Although the radiocarbon dates are interesting, it is not possible to conclude from them that Paleo-Indians occupied the site. Nei-

14. *Ibid.*, 6, 10, 11, 20.
15. Jefferson Chapman, *The Rose Island Site*, University of Tennessee, Department of Anthropology, Report of Investigations No. 14 (Knoxville, 1975).

ther of the two fossil mammal bones dated was reported in direct
association with any diagnostic Paleo-Indian artifacts. Since the species of the fossil bones are not given, we cannot judge the validity of
the date by the accepted time range of the species. The radiocarbon date
obtained from the split-cane matting found below the fossil bones deposit is certainly incongruous if the deposits were *in situ*, and the two
radiocarbon dates obtained from the organic horizon at Borehole I have
no unequivocal artifactual association. The question of the contemporaneity of man and Pleistocene fauna at Avery Island has, therefore,
not been resolved, but the data thus far reported indicate that further
exploration would be warranted.

Trappey Mastodon Site

Another interesting find of Pleistocene remains was made at the Trappey Mastodon Site in Lafayette. There, while constructing a waste
water facility for the B. F. Trappey canning plant in 1970, workmen
exposed the remains of a mastodon 4 meters below the surface. Notified of the find, Jon L. Gibson, an archaeologist, and Layton J. Miller,
a geographer, both from the University of Southwestern Louisiana,
conducted explorations in hopes of exposing additional materials. Unfortunately, after stripping 150 square meters of the site, no additional
remains were found.

The original mastodon find included four teeth as well as pieces of
mandible and scapula and a fragment tentatively identified as the ar-
ticular surface of a tibia. The two scientists felt that "the general appearance of the bones and the absence of the posterior portion of the
skeleton suggest that the mastodon may have died elsewhere and then
been transported by man to its final resting place."[16] During the excavations two corner-notched stone projectile points were found. Neither was *in situ* or, in any discernible way, associated with the mastodon bones. Gibson and Miller attribute the points to a much more
recent period, between 3000 B.C. and 1000 B.C.

Two radiocarbon assays were run on the mastodon remains—an

16. Jon L. Gibson and Layton J. Miller, *The Trappey Mastodon*, Research Series No.
27, Anthropology, University of Southwestern Louisiana (Lafayette, 1973), 4.

enamel specimen dated at 10,010 ± 450 years B.C. and a bone specimen dated at 4330 ± 180 years B.C. By evaluating comparable paleontological evidence and radiocarbon dates from other sites, Gibson and Miller believe that the earlier date is more concordant with the situation at the Trappey site. Obviously, aside from the two scientists' impression that the bones had been deposited at the site by man, there is no evidence of the contemporaneity of Paleo-Indians and Pleistocene fauna at the Trappey site.

Diagnostic Points

In the state of Louisiana the most solid evidence for the presence of Paleo-Indians is more than 500 diagnostic stone points. The earliest of these points, dating between 10,000 B.C. and 8000 B.C., are lanceolate in outline, fluted or unfluted. The points are categorized according to their variations as Clovis, Folsom, Scottsbluff, Plainview, and Meserve (Pl. 5). These "honest to God" Paleo-Indian points were manufactured by the pressure flaking technique, and their basal-edge portions, which are either straight or concave, are characteristically smoothed by grinding. It cannot be overemphasized that, with one exception, all Louisiana finds are surface collections without unequivocal archaeological associations. The exception, "two lanceolate points, one certainly and one possibly of Clovis type . . . found lying flat on the smooth bottom of the pit," were recovered from an excavation, five feet in diameter, at the John Pearce Site, Caddo Parish. No other artifactual materials were found in direct association with these points. Therefore, their chronological placement can only be inferred by comparison with comparable specimens recovered from excavated and radiocarbon-dated sites in other regions.[17]

David I. Bushnell, Jr., of the Smithsonian Institution made possibly the first report of Paleo-Indian points in Louisiana. In 1935 remarking

17. H. M. Wormington, *Ancient Man in North America*, Denver Museum of Natural History, Popular Series, No. 4 (Denver 1957); Clarence H. Webb, Joel L. Shiner, and E. Wayne Roberts, "The John Pearce Site (16CD56): A San Patrice Site in Caddo Parish," *Bulletin of the Texas Archaeological Society*, Vol. 42 (1971), 7; George F. MacDonald, "A Review of Research on Paleo-Indians in Eastern North America," *Arctic Anthropology*, Vol. 8 (1971), No. 2, pp. 32–41.

PLATE 5

Artifacts of the early Paleo-Indian Era: *a*, Clovis point; *b–c*, Folsom points; *d–f*, Scottsbluff points; *g–j*, Plainview points; *k–l*, Meserve points; *m–n*, end scrapers.

upon a pentagonal point from Virginia, he noted that comparable "examples have been discovered in the northwestern part of Louisiana in a region where Folsom points have likewise been found, but the relation to the two types, if any actually exists, has not been determined." It was not until 1948, however, that any evidence of this culture came to the fore in Louisiana. Dr. Clarence H. Webb was the first to report and illustrate Clovis and Scottsbluff points from the hill country of central and northern Louisiana. Subsequently, almost two decades passed before any other pertinent articles appeared; but then during the 1960s, a number of papers were published that dealt with Paleo-Indians in Louisiana. The upshot of these reports was that the known distribution of the Paleo-Indian points was restricted to upland areas of the Tertiary and Quaternary ages. It also became apparent that the vast majority of these lanceolate points were manufactured from shiny gray or brown flints and novaculites from areas in Texas and Arkansas respectively. The overall picture has not changed substantially to date. The number of known Paleo-Indian points, the majority made of flints foreign to the state, has increased, and the distributional base, although still restricted to older land surfaces, has been broadened. Data from Louisiana are still far too scanty, however, to tell anything at all about the physical stature of Louisiana's earliest Paleo-Indians, their settlement patterns, stone-tool and bone-tool inventory, ornaments, art, clothing, or hunting and butchering techniques.[18]

18. David I. Bushnell, Jr., "The Manahoac Tribes in Virginia, 1608," *Smithsonian Miscellaneous Collections*, Vol. 94 (1935), No. 8, p. 36; Clarence H. Webb, "Evidence of Pre-Pottery Cultures in Louisiana," *American Antiquity*, Vol. 13 (1948), No. 3, p. 230; "Some Paleo-Indian Points in the Williamson Museum," *Louisiana Studies*, Vol. 1 (1962), No. 3, pp. 60–61; Hiram F. Gregory, Jr., "Scottsbluff Points: Trademarks of Texas Tourists," *Louisiana Studies*, Vol. 2 (1963), 176–77; Sherwood M. Gagliano, "A Survey of Preceramic Occupations in Portions of South Louisiana and South Mississippi," *Florida Anthropologist*, Vol. 16 (1963), No. 4, pp. 105–32; Sherwood M. Gagliano and Hiram F. Gregory, Jr., "A Preliminary Survey of Paleo-Indian Points from Louisiana," *Louisiana Studies*, Vol. 4 (1965), No. 1, pp. 62–77; Clarence H. Webb, "The Paleo-Indian Era: Distribution of Finds, Louisiana," *Proceedings of the 20th Southeastern Archaeological Conference*, Bulletin No. 2 (1965), 4–6; Jon L. Gibson, "Burins from Louisiana," *American Antiquity*, Vol. 31 (1966), No. 5, pp. 746–47; Jon L. Gibson, "A Preliminary Survey of Indian Occupations in LaSalle Parish, Loui-

The Later Paleo-Indians

Sometime around 7500 B.C. new regional projectile point forms, which, most archaeologists agree, evolved from the Clovis tradition, developed and spread throughout much of North America. Of course in some places the early Paleo-Indian styles continued to be made. Some of the new types in the eastern United States, such as the Cumberland and Quad points, are lanceolate in outline and fluted with ground concave bases. By now, however, the bifacial fluting is generally produced by the removal of multiple flakes rather than a single flake as was the characteristic of the earlier Paleo-Indian points. Dalton and San Patrice points, two other styles derived from the Clovis prototypes, have a wide distribution in portions of the southeastern United States. These points have a pentagonal outline and a concave base that has been ground smooth and, characteristically, thinned and fluted. Also during this interval, concave-based points exhibiting side or corner notches first appear, although they became more popular toward the end of the era. These, too, continue to display the traditional traits of fluting and basal grinding.

As the shapes of these stone projectile points were changing, the human population in the area was growing. A good indication of this population expansion is the profound increase in the number of sites attributable to the more recent stages of the Paleo-Indian Era. The archaeological remains do not demonstrate a major change in life-style, but almost all of the stone artifacts were made from locally available materials, in sharp contrast to early Paleo-Indian points. This fact, the point-type distributions, and hunting patterns, suggest that a measure of regionalization was developing. Hunters of the period became quite successful at killing deer, as is evident from the number of deer bones found at sites within the period. Deer do not migrate long distances seasonally; they restrict their movements to a relatively small area. Therefore, the exploitation of these animals and other smaller game

siana," *Louisiana Studies*, Vol. 5 (1966), No. 3, pp. 193–237; Joe Ben Wheat, "Lifeways of Early Man in North America," *Arctic Anthropology*, Vol. 8 (1971), No. 2, pp. 22–31.

may have enabled groups to remain within a smaller territory, thus encouraging regionalism. The question of whether the Paleo-Indians were the prime factor in the extinction of Pleistocene megafauna is still being debated, but none of the era's more recent point types has ever been reported in primary association with megafaunal remains in the state.[19]

The archaeological deposits of the more recent period of this era in the southeast region afford a much-expanded inventory of stone tools. From the earlier period, only projectile points were found, but archaeological sites attributed to the later Paleo-Indian period have yielded a variety of implements formed by percussion-flaking and pressure-flaking techniques (Pl. 6). The more recent tool kit includes knives, scrapers, drills, chisels, gravers, and adzes for butchering, working wood and bone, and hide preparation.[20] Some sandstone abraders have been found, but they are rare. In fact, grinding implements, mealing stones, or ground-stone ornaments of any kind are not at all characteristic of this era.

The John Pearce Site

One of the most interesting, well-explored, and comprehensively reported sites of the late Paleo-Indian period is the John Pearce Site, at which San Patrice points were found in association with a variety of other chipped-stone implements. The site was excavated and reported by Clarence H. Webb, who had been the first to recognize the distinctiveness and relative chronological placement of San Patrice points and to note that they were found in northwest Louisiana and the contiguous parts of Texas. Almost twenty years later he reported "over 300

19. P. S. Martin and H. E. Wright, Jr. (eds.), *Pleistocene Extinctions: The Search for a Cause* (New Haven, 1967); Donald K. Grayson, "Pleistocene Avifaunas and Overkill Hypothesis," *Science*, Vol. 195 (1977), No. 4279, pp. 691–92; Haag, "Southeastern United States: Post-Pleistocene Adaptations, 9000–4000 B.C."
20. Dan F. Morse, "The Hawkins Cache: A Significant Dalton Find in Northeast Arkansas," *Arkansas Archaeologist*, Vol. 12 (1971), No. 1, pp. 9–20; Albert C. Goodyear, *The Brand Site: A Techno-Functional Study of a Dalton Site in Northeast Arkansas*, Arkansas Archaeological Survey Publications in Archaeology, Research Series, No. 7 (Fayetteville, 1974).

found on at least 75 to 100 sites in from ⅓ to ½ of the total parishes in Louisiana." By 1971 San Patrice points had been reported from excavations and surface collections at sites from as far west as the Brazos River in Texas east to the Mississippi River, and from Lake Pontchartrain north to Missouri.[21] Webb's longtime interest in the San Patrice points culminated in his careful excavation of the John Pearce Site, which is located on a gently sloping spur of land about 25 feet above the floodplain of Cypress Bayou in Caddo Parish.

By superimposing a grid of 5-foot squares over the site and carefully recording the vertical and horizontal proveniences of the artifacts within the grid system, the investigators were able to discern two discrete areas of occupation, or encampments. Area A, measuring about 35 feet in diameter, contained 355 stone artifacts, including 19 San Patrice points. Area B, a short distance to the north, measured about 65 feet by 75 feet and contained 566 stone artifacts among which were 20 San Patrice points. By meticulously analyzing all of the artifacts from each area separately, Webb and his associates were able to observe and tabulate major tool categories, utilization of raw material, processes of manufacture, technological traits, and use-wear patterns.[22] They noted that although the frequencies of the major tool categories from Areas A and B differed, their proportions were quite similar and the total tool assemblages were almost identical. Tool types included points, end scrapers, side scrapers, notched scrapers, denticulates, notched flakes, gravers, drills, and burins. Most of the artifacts were manufactured preferentially from local cherts and fine-grained petrified wood, but some exotic materials—flints, fossiliferous cherts, novaculite, and quartzites—were also used.

Macro- and microscopic examination of the John Pearce Site specimens revealed the techniques of manufacture. First the toolmaker struck off flakes from the parent cobble; then he thinned them and shaped them into preforms. The longitudinal, bifacial fluting was then accomplished by pressure flaking. Next, the toolmaker refined the lat-

---

21. Clarence H. Webb, "Two Unusual Types of Chipped Stone Artifacts from Northeast Louisiana," *Bulletin of the Texas Archaeological and Paleontological Society*, Vol. 17 (1946), 9–17; Webb, "The Paleo-Indian Era: Distribution of Finds, Louisiana," 5; Webb, Shiner, and Roberts, "The John Pearce Site."
22. Webb, Shiner, and Roberts, "The John Pearce Site."

eral edges by bifacial pressure retouching, and then he ground the basal edges smooth. Lastly, he applied the final touches, bifacial thinning and refining to the distal portion of the point. Some points had evidently been resharpened. Non-projectile-point artifacts displayed marked homogeneity in length, width, and edge angle. All of these tools in both Areas A and B were small and thin, only rarely exceeding 40mm in length. The San Patrice assemblage at the John Pearce Site was indeed a small-tool complex.

Drawing on the data from the John Pearce excavations, the authors made several inferences about the prehistoric activities at the site. First, they declared, the artifactual and stratigraphic similarities between Area A and Area B suggest contemporaneous or closely contemporaneous occupations by culturally similar bands. The artifactual density, the sparsity of hearths, and the lack of habitational evidence, such as postmolds, indicate temporary encampments. The tool categories suggest hunting and butchering activities as well as cutting, scraping, and boring on bone, antler, hide, and possibly wood. Furthermore, Webb and his associates, judging by the complete lack of grinding implements and large knives and choppers, believed that there was little or no grinding of seeds or cutting of trees for log constructions. In fact, the investigators expressed their disappointment that none of the archaeological data from John Pearce provide "any real clue to the amount of food gathering in the economy, which must have been considerable in this environment."[23]

As is so often the case in archaeological explorations at sites of this era, no material was found that could be used for radiocarbon dating. The authors therefore drew upon data from extra-areal sites with comparable assemblages and found that "radiocarbon dates from several of these sites place these (San Patrice) assemblages between 8000 and 6000 B.C."[24] This is the only comprehensive site report on the San Patrice complex and, in fact, the only such report relative to a site of this age in the state of Louisiana. This situation is not altogether due to the neglect of archaeological exploration, for as we have already seen San Patrice points have been documented from innumerable sites in

23. *Ibid.*, 42.
24. Webb, Shiner, and Roberts, "The John Pearce Site."

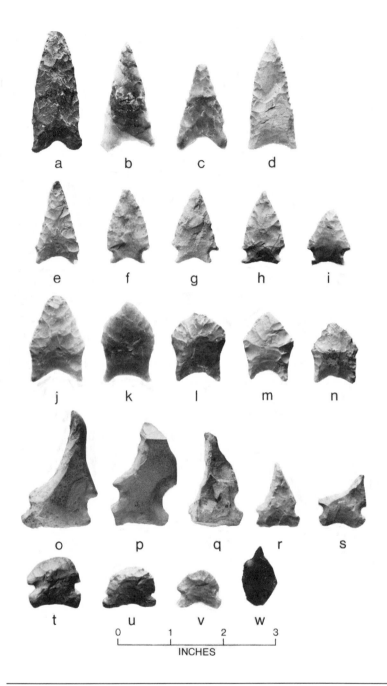

a   b   c   d

e   f   g   h   i

j   k   l   m   n

o   p   q   r   s

t   u   v   w

0   1   2   3
INCHES

PLATE 6

Artifacts of the late Paleo-Indian Era: *a–n*, varieties of San Patrice points; *o–s*, Albany scrapers; *t–v*, notched scrapers; *w*, graver.

the state. Part of the problem is the nature of the sites themselves. Because most of the sites are located in hilly terrain, erosion has lowered and mixed artifacts from various levels and times of occupation to a common surface, thus eliminating any opportunity to discern distinct tool assemblages or sequential stratification. Conversely, low-lying sites in the same regions have been covered by deposition that has concealed the archaeological remains.

Summary

Despite the absence of recorded *in situ* archaeological remains, numerous surface finds of diagnostic stone artifacts comparable to specimens from excavated and radiocarbon-dated sites outside this area demonstrate that humans were occupying Louisiana at least as early as 10,000 B.C. These small bands of hunters and gatherers were ecologically adaptable, and they exploited a wide variety of habitats while pursuing the big game herbivores and smaller species of the Pleistocene period. With the waning of the Pleistocene period, gradual climatic warming was accompanied by corresponding changes in the flora and fauna. Large herbivores, such as the mammoth, mastodon, giant bison, tapir, and ground sloth, disappeared. Toward the latter half of the Paleo-Indian Era, the population expanded, producing a noticeable increase in the number of recorded archaeological sites. Although many of the earlier stone-tool attributes lingered, new projectile point styles evolved, and by the end of this era their distributions reflect the development of social regionalism.

III Meso-Indian Era:

6000 B.C.—2000 B.C.

Many of the early archaeological elements of the Meso-Indian Era derived directly from those of Paleo-Indian times. The innovations of the earlier period gradually evolved into characteristic traits of the Meso-Indian archaeological record. Accompanying and certainly influencing these cultural adaptations were new climatic and eustatic changes. The altithermal period, sometimes called the Thermal Maximum, which occurred between 5000 B.C. and 2000 B.C., brought warmer and drier conditions to our continent than have existed since that time. The altithermal's effects on human populations in the Southeast are largely conjectural. Certainly the resultant modification in the flora also affected the fauna and contributed to the extinction of the last, lingering big game animals. How greatly this extinction affected the human subsistence activities is not clearly understood. There is considerable evidence from the southeastern United States, however, that during this era and even earlier, humans were mainly exploiting the smaller species of animals for their subsistence.[1]

It was during the altithermal period, around 3000 B.C., that the oceans rose to their present level. The rise in sea level lessened the stream gradients, and meandering stream courses, with their accompanying natural levees, backswamps, oxbows, and deltas developed,

---

1. E. Antevs, "Geological-Climatic Dating in the West," *American Antiquity*, Vol. 20 (1955), No. 4, Pt. 1, pp. 317–35; National Research Council, *Understanding Climatic Change: A Problem for Action* (Washington, D.C., 1975), 35–40; Herbert L. Alexander, Jr., "The Levi Site: A Paleo-Indian Campsite in Central Texas," *American Antiquity*, Vol. 28 (1963), No. 4, pp. 510–28.

providing new riverine environments. As Haag and Brain have noted, this eustatic change had paramount effects upon human subsistence activities, particularly in the lower Mississippi Valley.[2] Nor can we ignore Louisiana's intimate relationship with the sea. The eustatic change was a major factor in the formation of our coastal marshes, lakes, and estuarine environments. The Meso-Indians accommodated themselves to these natural forces and new ecological niches.

By 6000 B.C., and for at least four millenia after that, hunting and gathering bands with distinctive arrays of stone tools occupied a number of preferentially selected areas in the eastern United States. In the Southeast along the Atlantic coast, the multiplicity of extensive shell middens and/or shell rings attests to human adaptation to the coastal ecosystems. Other regional sites provide substantive evidence for man's successful adaptation to the eastern forest environments and to a wide variety of riverine environments.[3] Cultural deposits at some of the sites, particularly those in more protective settings like caves and rock shelters, are more than 20 feet thick. These middens may be

2. Haag, "The Archaic in the Lower Mississippi Valley"; Brain, "The Lower Mississippi Valley in North American Prehistory."
3. Willey, An Introduction to American Archaeology, Vol. I; Dragoo, "Some Aspects of Eastern North American Prehistory"; Antonio J. Waring, Jr., "The Archaic Hunting and Gathering Cultures: The Archaic and Some Shell Rings," in Stephen Williams (ed.), The Waring Papers, Papers of the Peabody Museum of Archaeology and Ethnology, Harvard University, Vol. 57 (Cambridge, Mass., 1968), 243–46; Stephen L. Cumbaa, "A Reconsideration of Freshwater Shellfish Exploitation in the Florida Archaic," Florida Anthropologist, Vol. 29 (1976), No. 2, Pt. 1, pp. 49–59; Rochelle A. Marrinan, "Assessment of Subsistence Strategy Evidenced by Shell Ring Sites," Southeastern Archaeology Conference Bulletin No. 19 (1976), 61–63; Joseph R. Caldwell, Trend and Tradition in the Prehistory of Eastern United States, American Anthropological Association Memoir No. 88 (Menasha, Wis., 1958); Melvin L. Fowler, "Summary Report of Modoc Rock Shelter, 1952, 1953, 1955, 1956," Report of Investigations No. 8 (Springfield, Ill., 1959); D. L. DeJarnett, E. B. Kurjack, and J. W. Cambron, "Stanfield–Worley Bluff Shelter Excavations," Journal of Alabama Archaeology, Vol. 8 (1962), Nos. 1–2, pp. 1–124; John W. Griffin, Investigations in Russell Cave, National Park Service Publications in Archaeology No. 13 (Washington, D.C., 1974); William S. Webb and David L. DeJarnett, An Archaeological Survey of the Pickwick Basin in the Adjacent Portions of the States of Alabama, Mississippi, and Tennessee, Bureau of American Ethnology Bulletin 129 (Washington, D.C., 1942); William S. Webb and Charles G. Wilder, An Archaeological Survey of Guntersville Basin on the Tennessee River in Northern Alabama (Lexington, Ky., 1951); Thomas M. N. Lewis and Madeline Kneberg Lewis, Eva: An Archaic Site (Knoxville, 1961); William S. Webb, Indian Knoll (Knoxville, 1974); Chapman, The Rose Island Site.

viewed as indicating residential stability, a social prerequisite for plant manipulation, or horticulture. They record repeated, probably seasonal, occupations throughout the era. These stratified deposits, if carefully excavated, provide the archaeologist with a chronological framework within which he can record changes in tool types and artifactual associations.

The Meso-Indian stone tools are generally larger than those of the previous era, and the number of new projectile point types seems almost limitless.[4] The points, characteristically fabricated from locally available stone, are crude in appearance with straight to convex, jagged side edges. Their bases have straight, contracting, or expanding stems sometimes accompanied by side, corner, or basal notches, and basal grinding is no longer a characteristic element. The crude appearance of these points should not, however, be taken as an indication that they were awkward or less serviceable than the more finely chipped and finished Paleo-Indian points. Quite to the contrary, the point types of the Meso-Indian were made and used for thousands of years, by which we can assume that they adequately handled the tasks at hand.

In contrast to projectile points, most of the other early tool types, such as knives, scrapers, drills, and gravers, continued to be made in the same way. In addition, many new tools made their first appearance. The chipped-tool inventories now include adzes and choppers. Moreover, during this period new techniques of working stone by grinding, pecking, and polishing permitted the manufacture of an astonishing assortment of tools and ornaments. These artifacts are fabricated from lithic materials, including granitic rocks, sandstone, slate, steatite, and scoria, that were unsuitable for chipping. It is evident from the sort of objects the Indians made that they were becoming more proficient at exploiting their respective regions (Pl. 7). The stone pipes, mortars, pestles, and mealing stones made by means of the new tech-

4. Robert E. Bell, *Guide to the Identification of Certain American Indian Projectile Points*, Oklahoma Anthropological Society Special Bulletins Nos. 1 and 2 (Oklahoma City, 1958, 1960); James W. Cambron and David C. Hulse, *Handbook of Alabama Archaeology: Part I, Point Types* (University, Ala., 1964); Gregory Perino, *Guide to the Identification of Certain American Indian Projectile Points*, Oklahoma Anthropological Society Special Bulletins Nos. 3 and 4 (Oklahoma City, 1968, 1971).

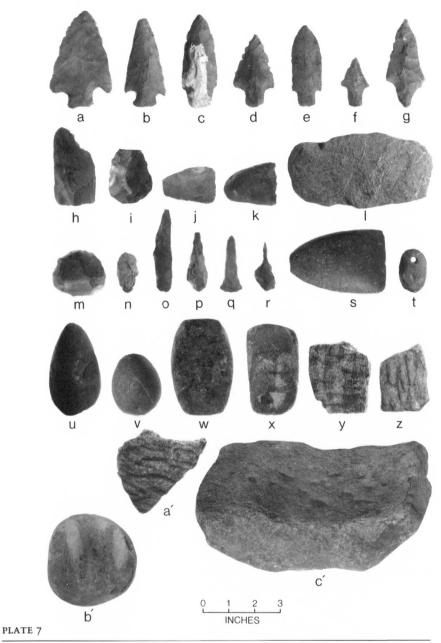

```
0   1   2   3
└───┴───┴───┘
    INCHES
```

PLATE 7

Chipped- and ground-stone artifacts of the Meso-Indian Era: *a–g*, projectile points; *h–i*, knives; *j–l*, choppers; *m–n*, scrapers; *o–r*, drills; *s*, celt; *t*, ornament; *u*, plummet; *v*, pecking stone; *w*, atlatl weight; *x*, sandstone abrader; *y–a′*, steatite vessel fragments; *b′–c′*, mealing stones.

niques provide the first physical evidence from which we can infer that the people were knowledgeable of plants, nuts, and seeds and were using them for food. We may also suppose that man was cognizant of the habitats in which important plant species grew and the seasons in which they matured and ripened. Since the Meso-Indians made ground-stone celts, hammerstones, grooved axes, and large chipped-stone choppers to be used, it is thought, for working wood, it is likely that they were making use of the timber resources of the eastern woodlands.

Another important innovation of the period is the atlatl, or spear thrower.[5] The atlatl resembles a wooden lath, usually about two feet long, on which there is a grip carved—sometimes elaborately so—at one end and a carved notch or hook at the opposite end. The hook was sometimes made of bone or antler and was attached to the wood with sinew or resin. The atlatl was held in the hand at the grip, and the hook was engaged into the butt of a spear shaft that rested upon the atlatl. When the spear was thrown, the atlatl became an extension of the thrower's arm, providing greater leverage that allowed the spear or dart to be thrown much farther than had ever been possible before. Apparently use of the atlatl waned after the introduction of the bow—sometime after 900 A.D. in Louisiana—but there is at least one sixteenth-century account of an Indian wounding a Spanish soldier, near the mouth of the Mississippi River, with a dart hurled from an atlatl.[6]

Clay, stone, or shell objects, variously called boatstones, bannerstones, or atlatl weights, were attached to the distal portion of the atlatl.[7] Some archaeologists believe that the weights were a means of increasing the force with which the dart was released, but the information supporting this theory is inconclusive. Some researchers speculate that the atlatl weights functioned only as fetishes or ornaments comparable to the decorative gunsmithing found on firearms.

5. James H. Kellar, *The Atlatl in North America*, Indiana Historical Society Prehistory Research Series, Vol. 3, No. 3 (Indianapolis, 1955); Calvin D. Howard, "The Atlatl: Function and Performance," *American Antiquity*, Vol. 39 (1974), No. 1, pp. 102–104.
6. John R. Swanton, "Historic Use of the Spear-thrower in Southeastern North America," *American Antiquity*, Vol. 3 (1938), 356–58.
7. Robert W. Neuman, "Atlatl Weights from Certain Sites on the Northern and Central Great Plains," *American Antiquity*, Vol. 32 (1967), No. 1, pp. 36–53; John L. Palter, "A New Approach to the Significance of the 'Weighted' Spear Thrower," *American Antiquity*, Vol. 41 (1976), No. 4, pp. 500–10.

The conceptualization of this most complex composite tool was, without doubt, a major technological advance. Not only did the use of this device increase man's success in hunting wild game, but it also must have effected a marked change in his hunting patterns. Equipped with the atlatl, a spear or a javelin, an axe, and a knife, adept at fishing, hunting, and at gathering mollusks and plant foods, the Meso-Indians were indeed becoming formidable predators in their local environments.

Not only did the hunted animals provide sustenance, they yielded the raw material for the manufacture of a large assortment of tools and ornaments. Meso-Indian occupation sites provide the earliest examples of bone technology found in the Southeast. The faunal collections from such sites include raccoon, opossum, dog, groundhog, squirrel, fox, beaver, bear, wildcat, rabbit, skunk, chipmunk, mink, muskrat, otter, porcupine, wild turkey, turkey vulture, passenger pigeon, goose, sandhill crane, turtle, snake, and fish. Unquestionably, though, deer bones and antlers dominate the lists. At the Indian Knoll Site along the Green River in west central Kentucky, for example, "of the 25,756 fragments identified 23,177 are bones of the Virginia Deer."[8] Further zooarchaeological analyses demonstrated that those bones represented no less than 1,551 deer. The Meso-Indians cut, sawed, ground, and bored long bones, vertebrae, bacula, mandibles, turtle shells, antlers, and teeth to form awls, fishhooks, whistles, flagellates, spatulates, scoops, beads, pendants, needles, points, hairpins, handles, atlatl hooks, and rattles. All of these articles are replicated in a wide array of sizes with various degrees of finish and/or embellishment.

Shell and copper were other raw materials that began to be widely used during this era. Their distribution patterns document prehistoric trade relationships, for shell and copper occur as raw materials or finished products at sites far from their native sources. The Meso-Indians used their new manufacturing techniques to make tubular, globular, and discoidal beads, columella pendants, atlatl weights, pins, gorgets, and cups from marine and freshwater mollusk shells and pearls. From copper they made pendants, bars, and coils.

8. Lewis and Lewis, *Eva: An Archaic Site*; DeJarnett, Kurjack, and Cambron, "Stanfield–Worley Bluff Shelter Excavations"; Webb, *Indian Knoll*, 340.

Another most important manifestation of some of the southeastern Meso-Indian sites are the human burials, for the human skeletal material from these interments provides cardinal cultural and biological data on human populations of the era.[9] In the characteristic Meso-Indian burial pattern the skeleton is found lying on one side in a flexed position at the bottom of a circular, basin-shaped pit. The skeleton, usually that of an adult male or female, is quite often accompanied by stone, bone, shell, and/or copper artifacts, and it is not uncommon to find red ochre sprinkled over and around the remains. On occasion a dog skeleton is also found in the pit. There are other, less common burials in which more than one individual of either sex and of all age groups lie in flexed or extended positions in a common pit. These, too, may have funerary accompaniments. Secondary interments, sometimes called bundle burials, were also practiced. In this type of burial, the corpse, perhaps wrapped and tied to a tree limb or a rafter, is allowed to decay until the flesh is gone. The bones of one or more individuals are then gathered up and deposited in a pit. They are not in anatomical order, and more often than not, some of the bones are missing from the burial. Both sexes and all age groups are represented, and they may be associated with artifacts and red ochre. Occasionally, burials are found in which an individual is placed in a fully extended supine position on the ground surface and then covered with dirt and/or shell. These, too, may have artifactual accompaniments.

In summarizing the very detailed measurements and indices obtained from the skeletons of more than 1,200 Meso-Indian individuals at the Indian Knoll Site, Kentucky, Charles E. Snow characterized the occupants as follows:

> The unusually well preserved skeletal remains indicate a people who were rather short, small, and gracile, and beset with diseases. The average age of the adults at death was about 27 years. These people, who probably lived as an inbred, comparatively isolated group, were characterized by mesocephaly with a definite tendency toward dolichocephaly, by their large, protruding faces of medium proportions and typically wide, flaring lower jaws. The group as a whole were remarkably free of dental decay, but due to their apparently staple diet of the gritty,

9. W. M. Krogman, *The Human Skeleton in Forensic Medicine* (Springfield, 1962); William M. Bass, *Human Osteology: A Laboratory and Field Manual of the Human Skeleton*, Special Publications, Missouri Archaeological Society (Columbia, Mo., 1971).

freshwater mussel, their teeth show pronounced degrees of mechanical wear with subsequent dental abscesses. It is remarkable to find that over half of the adult population was afflicted with arthritis.

Subsequent analyses of another Meso-Indian population from the Eva Site in Benton County, west Tennessee, generally corroborated the data from Indian Knoll.[10] It would seem acceptable, therefore, to assume that a large majority of the Meso-Indians in the southeastern United States fell within the ranges of the physical types described from the Indian Knoll and Eva sites.

Much is known about cultural developments during the Meso-Indian Era in some parts of the southeastern region, but in Louisiana the specifics of such phenomena for the most part remain to be determined. Not a single Louisiana site with a discrete archaeological deposit unequivocally attributable to this era has been systematically excavated, analyzed, and comprehensively reported. Furthermore, most of the data we do have applies to the very end of the Meso-Indian Era. Nevertheless, there have been some limited excavations and surface collections from which we can discern certain broad developments (Fig. 2).

Our primary data bank consists of reports documenting finds of diagnostic stone projectile point types whose attributed chronologies have been established outside the state. One such extra-areal site that has an important bearing on this matter is the multicomponent Resch Site. Located near Marshall, Texas, less than forty miles west of Shreveport, the site rests on a terrace about 8 feet above the Potters Creek floodplain. The site was excavated by Clarence Webb in arbitrary 6-inch layers, and midden was found to a depth of 5 feet. "Altogether 288 five-foot squares were dug, covering 7,200 square feet of surface and incorporating approximately 25,000 cubic feet of midden."[11] Although human factors, such as land clearing and cultivation, and natural disturbances, such as erosion and animal burrowing, resulted in a measure of horizontal and vertical midden displacement,

10. Charles E. Snow, "Indian Knoll, Skeletons of Site Oh 2, Ohio County, Kentucky," *Reports in Anthropology*, Department of Anthropology, University of Kentucky, Vol. 4 (1948), No. 3, Pt. 2; Lewis and Lewis, *Eva: An Archaic Site*.
11. Clarence H. Webb *et al.*, "The Resch Site (41HS16), Harrison County, Texas," *Bulletin of the Texas Archaeological Society*, Vol. 40 (1969), 12.

Webb and his colleagues were adroit enough to retrieve important artifactual data that relate closely to comparable artifact types in Louisiana. For example, the excavation levels at this multicomponent site demonstrated that the use of dart points, presumably propelled by the atlatl, declined from early to late times. The investigators also reported that the forms of the point bases, or stems, change from early to late, with side-notched and expanded-base styles giving way to straight-sided stems, and the latter to contracting stems. The upper levels of the Resch Site contained ceramics, and the excavation data indicated that most of the chipped-stone artifact types prevalent during the Meso-Indian Era continued to be made and utilized for many hundreds of years after the introduction of pottery.

In Louisiana the literature reports that stone projectile points, diagnostic of this era, were surface-collected on Avery Island, along the Amite River, and in the Lake Pontchartrain environs.[12] The point types include Kirk, Morrow Mountain, Tortugus, Williams, Marshall, Frio, Carrollton, Trinity, Morhiss, Marcos, Gary, Macon, Ensor, and Wells. In addition to these surface finds, there is a genuinely interesting manifestation, once again, on the Avery Island salt dome. Gagliano investigated a low domed earthen mound, 5 feet high and 80 feet in diameter, located near Banana Bayou in the southern area of the salt dome. He excavated several 5-foot squares and a small lateral extension into the center of this mound and found stratigraphic zones that suggested to him that the mound had been constructed in two stages. The tests also exposed the remains of an oval pit that extended from the secondary stage down into the primary one. The silt, or fill, from this pit contained only several unworked stones. Charcoal fragments were found scattered in the mound profiles, and two chert chips were retrieved from the fill of the primary mound. "A number of amor-

12. Gagliano, "A Survey of Preceramic Occupations in Portions of South Louisiana and Mississippi"; Gagliano, An Archaeological Survey of Avery Island; Sherwood M. Gagliano, "Post-Pleistocene Occupations of Southeastern Louisiana Terrace Lands," Proceedings of the 19th Southeastern Archaeological Conference, Bulletin No. 1 (1964), 18–26; Sherwood M. Gagliano, "Kirk Serrated: An Early Archaic Index Point in Louisiana," Florida Anthropologist, Vol. 20 (1967), No. 1, pp. 3–9; Sherwood M. Gagliano, "Late Archaic–Early Formative Relationships in South Louisiana," Proceedings of the 23rd Southeastern Archaeological Conference, Bulletin No. 6 (1967), 9–22; Gagliano, Occupation Sequence at Avery Island.

phous fired clay objects were found just below the top of the primary mound. These were apparently confined to one level but showed no special pattern or orientation."[13] Charcoal from the top of the primary mound was radiocarbon-dated at 2490 ± 260 years B.C., which places it within the accepted dates of the Meso-Indian Era. It is important to realize, however, that this date precedes any other dated, earthen constructions in the southeastern region by almost one thousand years. The date, if it were accepted, and there seems to be no apparent reason to discount it, would establish the mound as the earliest constructed in the eastern United States.

Subsequently, during his 1978 investigations at Avery Island, Ian W. Brown conducted limited excavations into the Banana Bayou Mound. These tests generally confirmed the stratigraphic sequence Sherwood Gagliano had reported. Furthermore, the 1978 investigations expanded the artifact inventory from the primary mound. From that stratum Brown found 132 amorphous clay objects; worked and unworked stone chips; a piece of pumice; fire-cracked rocks; deer, fish, and turtle bones; mollusk fragments; and nut shells. Particularly interesting were the finds of two stone projectile points of the Pontchartrain and Williams varieties.[14] These point types date from sometime between 2000 B.C. and 1500 B.C.

Elsewhere in the state we have only brief reports of Meso-Indian projectile points found on the surface or excavated from archaeological deposits containing later materials. For example, there are Williams, Marshall, Macon, and Gary points, and a lanceolate specimen from the Lake Rodemacher area, Rapides Parish; Williams, Gary, and Carrollton points from the Springridge Site near the Caddo-DeSoto parish line; and Williams, Marshall, Carrollton, Marcos, and Ensor points from Young's Bayou sites, Natchitoches Parish.[15] In addition,

---

13. Gagliano, *An Archaeological Survey of Avery Island*, 13.
14. Ian W. Brown and Nancy Lambert-Brown, "Lower Mississippi Survey, Petite-Anse Project," *Research Notes*, No. 5.
15. John H. House, *Archaeological Salvage in the Basin of Lake Rodemacher, Rapides Parish, Louisiana, 1972* (Baton Rouge, 1973); James H. Long, "The Springridge Site," *Louisiana Archaeological Society Newsletter*, Vol. 2, (1975), No. 1, pp. 9–10; Brent W. Smith, "Prehistoric Settlement Patterns of the Young's Bayou Drainage, Natchitoches Parish, Louisiana," *Louisiana Archaeology*, Bulletin No. 2 (1975), 163–200.

another mass of material in private surface collections has been examined by every archaeologist in the state. Many of the sites have been visited by archaeologists and the collections recorded and photographed for official site files. We can, therefore, state unequivocally that Meso-Indian points of many styles have been found in Louisiana. Unfortunately, we have no specific physical data regarding structures of subsistence and burial patterns. These aspects of the culture are presently totally conjectural.

Clearly, the relative abundance of diagnostic point types and other stonework characteristically fabricated from local lithic sources is strong evidence for inferring successful local adaptation. If we may draw analogies from data from other southeastern sites of this era, even though they are admittedly far afield, it would appear that the Meso-Indians had evolved a measure of sedentism not achieved heretofore in Louisiana.

IV Neo-Indian Era:

2000 B.C.—A.D. 1600

Several important new traits were introduced into Louisiana during the Neo-Indian Era. The Indians of this time period adopted these innovations and successively exploited them, developing cultures that evolved into the tribal societies first chronicled by European explorers. The narrative of this era has been plausibly presented in a number of developmental frameworks.[1] I have chosen a scheme denoting seven generally distinct cultures that developed during this time: Poverty Point, Tchefuncte, Marksville, Troyville–Coles Creek, Caddo, Plaquemine, and Mississippian (Fig. 3).

In actuality the beginning of the Neo-Indian Era precedes the Poverty Point time period, and as Webb observes, during the second millennium B.C., a number of the general cultural phenomena that underlie much of the southeastern United States prehistory occurred.[2] At the beginning of this era hunting and gathering techniques were systematic enough to provide stable, and more likely, surplus food resources in a wide variety of geographical environments. The fact that sites were larger than during the Meso-Indian Era is at least indicative of sedentism. Perhaps in some locales small-band social units became community or village settlements with their concomitant communal endeavors. Certainly, it is difficult to account for the innumerable or-

1. William T. Sears, "The Southeastern United States," in Jennings and Norbeck (eds.), *Prehistoric Man in the New World*, 259–87; Willey, *An Introduction to American Archaeology*, Vol. I; William G. Haag, *Louisiana in North American Prehistory*, Mélanges No. 1 (Baton Rouge, 1971).
2. Clarence H. Webb, *The Poverty Point Culture*, Geoscience and Man, Vol. 17 (Baton Rouge, 1977).

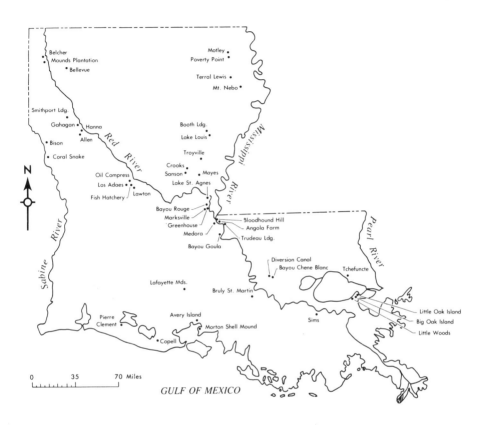

FIG. 3   Locations of Neo-Indian Sites Discussed in the Text

naments and esoteric stone, bone, and shell objects, many of which
were deposited with the dead, without envisioning a social organization capable of accommodating nonessential crafts.

Although artifactual inventories show regional distinctiveness, certain technologies were introduced and diffused throughout the Southeast. One such technology was the use of steatite and sometimes
sandstone to shape containers for food preparation and storage. These
bowls range from shallow to deep and are generally conical with flat
to convex bases. Louisiana specimens complete enough to be mea-

sured are from 3 to 11 inches tall, from 5 to 16 inches in diameter at the orifice, and from 2 to 6 inches in diameter at the base. The vessel exteriors are usually plain, but they may exhibit appendages, incised designs, and stylized zoomorphic motifs carved in relief. Steatite vessels or fragments thereof have been recovered from a number of sites in Louisiana, although at most of the sites they are not numerous (Pl. 16). At the Poverty Point Site in West Carroll Parish, however, Clarence H. Webb collected 2,724 fragments of steatite vessels from an area having a radius of about 45 feet. Traditionally, archaeological reports have maintained that the source for the steatite was the southern Appalachians, and recent trace-element studies on steatite fragments from the Poverty Point, Terral Lewis, and Young's Bayou sites in Louisiana trace the specimens to more specific locales in northwestern Georgia, eastern Alabama, southeastern Virginia, and North Carolina.[3]

Some time after stone vessels were introduced, fiber-tempered pottery, the earliest ceramic ware discovered in North America, began to be manufactured. It was made from materials that were readily available throughout the southeast region, and eventually replaced steatite vessels. Bullen and Stoltman argue persuasively that fiber-tempered-pottery technology originated at shell-midden sites on the Caribbean coast of Colombia and was subsequently diffused to comparable coastal sites in South Carolina and Georgia. In any event, by 2000 B.C. it was being made in Florida, and by several hundred years later the trait had been diffused into coastal Louisiana. In at least one instance laboratory tests indicated that fiber from the palmetto (*Sabal palmetto*) was the tempering agent for sherds from three widely separated areas in the southeastern United States. Not surprisingly, the vessels are shallow to deep bowls, similar to their stone-vessel prototypes. The bases are circular, flattened, or rounded, and occasionally they exhibit tetrapodal supports.[4] Some vessels are plain, while others are decorated on

3. *Ibid.*; Clarence H. Webb, "Stone Vessels from a Louisiana Site," *American Antiquity,* Vol. 9 (1944), No. 4, pp. 386–94; Brent W. Smith, "The Late Archaic–Poverty Point Steatite Trade Network in the Lower Mississippi Valley: A Preliminary Report," *Newsletter of the Louisiana Archaeological Society,* Vol. 3 (1976), No. 4, pp. 6–10.

4. Ripley P. Bullen and James B. Stoltman, "Fiber-Tempered Pottery in Southeastern United States and Northern Columbia: Its Origins, Context and Significance," *Florida Anthropologist,* Vol. 25 (1972), No. 2, Pt. 2; Jeffrey P. Brain and Drexel Peterson, "Palmetto Tempered Pottery," *Proceedings of the 27th Southeastern Archaeological Conference,* Bulletin No. 13 (1971), 70–76; Sherwood M.

the lip and wall exterior with punctations, nodes, incised straight or curved lines, simple stamping, or dentate stamping. As early as 1500 B.C. fiber-tempered pottery was being utilized at the Claiborne Site along the Pearl River in southwest Mississippi and at the Linsley and Tchefuncte sites in Orleans Parish and the Bayou Jasmine, Beau Mire, Ruth Canal, Meche, and Poverty Point sites in Saint John the Baptist, Ascension, Saint Martin, Saint Landry, and West Carroll parishes, respectively.

Another easily recognizable innovation early in the Neo-Indian Era was the manufacture of "baked-clay objects," as they are most commonly known. These are characteristically hand-sized, sometimes decorated, untempered clay objects of various shapes, which were fired and used just as people today use briquettes for baking and roasting food. These baked-clay objects substitute for stone in regions where that commodity is inadequate or absent; there is an ethnohistoric account of Australian aborigines manufacturing and using comparable objects. "Ovenstones" have been reported at sites in Australia said to be more than 6,500 years old. Specimens of such objects have also been found in California and in coastal Lincolnshire, England, and the Channel Islands.[5]

Stone containers, fiber-tempered pottery, and baked-clay objects, along with ground-stone zoomorphic effigies have been found in dozens of coastal shell middens and inland sites in the southeastern United States. Many of the sites, which have been radiocarbon-dated at between 2000 B.C. and 1500 B.C., may be considered antecedents or developmental indicators of the Poverty Point Culture.[6]

Gagliano and Clarence H. Webb, "Archaic–Poverty Point Transition at the Pearl River Mouth," *Southeastern Archaeological Conference Bulletin* No. 12 (1970), 47–72.

5. Donald G. Hunter, "Functional Analyses of Poverty Point Clay Objects," *Florida Anthropologist*, Vol. 28 (1975), No. 2, pp. 57–71; James A. Ford, Philip Phillips, and W. G. Haag, *The Jaketown Site in West-Central Mississippi*, Anthropological Papers of the American Museum of Natural History, Vol. 45 (1955), Pt. 1; Edmund D. Gill, untitled article in *Current Anthropology*, Vol. 10 (1969), No. 5, p. 473; Robert F. Heizer, "Baked Clay Objects of the Lower Sacramento Valley, California," *American Antiquity*, Vol. 3 (1937), No. 1, pp. 34–50; Edward Thomas Stevens, *Flint Chips: A Guide to Pre-historic Archaeology, as Illustrated by the Collections in the Blackmore Museum, Salisbury* (London, 1870).

6. Webb, "The Extent and Content of Poverty Point Culture"; Webb, *The Poverty Point Culture*; Gagliano and Webb, "Archaic–Poverty Point Transition at the Pearl River Mouth."

V Poverty Point Culture

There are more than one hundred known Poverty Point occupation sites in Louisiana, Arkansas, and Mississippi, as well as other closely related cultural manifestations in Missouri, Tennessee, Alabama, and Florida. At six of the Poverty Point occupations in Louisiana, no less than twenty-eight radiocarbon dates have been established, ranging from 2040 B.C. to 865 B.C. The thermoluminescent process has yielded dates of 1090 B.C. to 750 B.C. from six other assays of Poverty Point occupations in Louisiana and Mississippi.[1] These dates suggest that diagnostic Poverty Point developments began along the Gulf Coast and spread inland through the Mississippi River Basin, where they reached their zenith.

Sites are located along stream levees, on terrace edges, at stream-lake junctions, and in coastal environments. In each of these milieus the inhabitants could exploit a wide variety of natural resources. Poverty Point occupations characteristically occurred as clusters of small sites around a large regional center. The sites vary in size from the Poverty Point Site itself, which covers more than one square mile and at the time of its construction was the largest earthwork in both Americas, to sites that are only about 100 feet in diameter. Clarence Webb notes that some of the larger sites, supposed regional centers, are horseshoe-shaped or oval. This is certainly true at the Poverty Point, Claiborne,

1. Webb, *The Poverty Point Culture*; Cynthia J. Weber, "Thermoluminescent Dating of Poverty Point Objects," In Bettye J. Broyles and Clarence H. Webb (eds.), *The Poverty Point Culture, Southeastern Archaeological Conference Bulletin,* No. 12 (1970), 99–107.

Cole Crossroads, and Teoc Creek sites. However, his attribution of groups of six to eight small, domed mounds, arranged in arcs or in an arcuate pattern, to the Poverty Point Culture, is to a degree sagacious speculation. To the best of my knowledge, Mound G at the Jaketown Site in west-central Mississippi is the only such mound ever tested and reported in the literature.[2] Since no primary diagnostic artifacts of the Poverty Point Culture were retrieved from Mound G, the most that can be said of it is that it was probably constructed during Poverty Point times. Almost without exception these small mound sites were constructed or occupied by several successive cultures, and until the mounds themselves have been examined individually, their cultural attribution will remain speculative.

Poverty Point, the type site for this culture, is located near the present community of Epps, in West Carroll Parish. By about 1500 B.C. the inhabitants of this rich riverine environment had developed a way of life that produced a stable supply of and presumably a surplus of food items. Efficient hunting and gathering techniques, perhaps augmented by the cultivation of native plants and even the tropical cultigen squash, increased the quantity of food, while decreasing the number of people required to produce it. Socially elite classes capable of mandating the construction of massive geometrical and, possibly astronomically oriented earthworks may also have developed. Jon Gibson postulated that the Poverty Point society was a stratified organization ruled as a chiefdom and that the "culture arose independently as a consequence of local cultural adaptations to the specific environmental conditions of the Lower Mississippi Valley." Other archaeologists have reasoned from comparisons of particular artifacts and of massive ceremonial centers that the Poverty Point Culture was Meso-American in origin. The exact nature of the spark that ignited the patterns of thought and behavior that grew to typify the Poverty Point Culture will probably never be firmly documented, nor is this requisite. It seems likely, in the absence of more pragmatic evidence, that both local adaptation and Meso-American influence provided the impetus for the earliest developmental stages of the Poverty Point Culture. Undoubtedly the location of the site was also a profoundly

2. Webb, *The Poverty Point Culture;* Ford, Phillips, and Haag, *The Jaketown Site.*

important factor in the settlement and florescence of the Poverty Point Site. It was situated near to and between two immense streams, the Mississippi River just to the east, and the Arkansas River, which at that time was flowing southward just to the west of the site.[3] These tremendous rivers and their subsidiary drainages near the site were cardinal factors in the vast trade network that characterized the Poverty Point Culture.

Today the major portion of the Poverty Point Site is a recently established state park situated on an escarpment about 15 feet high along the right bank of Bayou Maçon (Pl. 8). Mound A, which reaches a height of 70 feet, is the largest earthen construction at this site. In the plan view it is triangular with the apex pointing east. In profile the west face of Mound A is quite steep, while the east face is gently sloped and is thought to have functioned as a platform and ramp. The maximum dimensions at the mound base are 640 feet north-south and 710 feet east-west. Immediately to the east of Mound A are six concentrically placed earthen ridges, which form six semicircles that terminate at Bayou Maçon. They are transected in four places by aisles that radiate from a vacant area, called the central plaza, within the inmost ridge. These ridges are about 5 to 9 feet high and 164 feet broad, and they are approximately 150 feet apart from crest to crest. The maximum diameter of the outer ridge is 3,964 feet, and that of the inner ridge measures 1,950 feet. About 2,220 feet north of Mound A is Mound B, a conical tumulus, 21 feet in height with a base diameter of 195 feet. The Motley Mound, located one and one half miles due north of the center of the semicircles, is also assigned to the site complex. Similar in shape, but smaller than Mound A, the Motley Mound is oriented north-south with the ramp slope facing south. Conclusions about the true relationship of the Motley Mound to the Poverty Point Site are presumptive, however. Although the mound resembles Mound A and seems to

3. Jon L. Gibson, "Poverty Point, the First North American Chiefdom," *Archaeology*, Vol. 27 (1974), No. 2, pp. 104–105; James A. Ford, A Comparison of Formative Cultures in the Americas, Smithsonian Contributions to Anthropology, Vol. 11 (Washington, D.C., 1969); Webb, *The Poverty Point Culture*; Roger T. Saucier, *Quaternary Geology of the Lower Mississippi Valley*, Arkansas Archaeological Survey Publications in Archaeology, Research Series, No. 6 (Fayetteville, 1974).

PLATE 8

Aerial view of the Poverty Point Site in West Carroll Parish. The ridges are accentuated by plantings of crimson clover. Mound A is to the left center. (Courtesy of Wylie Harvey, Office of State Parks.)

be astronomically affiliated with it, the only exploration of the Motley Mound consisted of clearing an 8-foot profile halfway down the mound, which "exhibited artificial fill with soil containing fragments of Poverty Point clay objects."[4]

For that matter, the oft-quoted relationship of Mound B to the Poverty Point Culture is not much more empirical. Excavations into Mound B revealed several interesting manifestations, but no artifacts diagnostic of the Poverty Point Culture were reported in the mound itself. James A. Ford directed excavations of Mound B and in the ridge areas of the site in 1942, 1943, and 1955. On the ground surface over

4. James A. Ford and Clarence H. Webb, *Poverty Point: A Late Archaic Site in Louisiana*, Anthropological Papers of the American Museum of Natural History, Vol. 46, Pt. 1 (New York, 1956); Gibson, "Poverty Point, the First American Chiefdom"; William G. Haag and Clarence H. Webb, "Microblades at Poverty Point," *American Antiquity*, Vol. 18 (1953), No. 3, p. 247.

which Mound B was built, he exposed a large burned area of ash, charcoal, and small fragments of charred bone, one of which was said to be the proximal end of a human femur. Near the burned area, "in the ground surface beneath the ash bed in the North 10–20 trench," he found a fire pit containing thirty-two baked-clay balls.[5] The only conclusion that can be safely drawn is that, since Mound B overlies the baked-clay objects, it must date from Poverty Point times or later.

Ford found as he dug into the mound proper that it was constructed in several stages. The demarcations of the basket loads of dirt used to build Mound B were plainly visible in his excavations, for the baskets left impressions on the clay. Woven in a simple plaited style, the baskets were 11 to 22 inches in diameter. There were soil stains, as well, that were judged to be animal-hide containers which averaged 17.1 inches in diameter. It has been estimated that 30 million, 50-pound basket-loads, or .75 million cubic yards, of earth went into the construction of Mounds A and B and the ridges at Poverty Point.[6]

Carl Kuttruff's excavations in the ridge area were the only other excavations of the site published in detail. He concluded, as had Ford and Webb in the original site report, that the ridges functioned as low elevations upon which people lived, built structures, dug fire pits, and left behind their trash. Clearly, the archaeological data indicate that many ridge areas were lived upon during different periods of their construction. Nevertheless, since Ford and Webb found no certain evidence of postmolds and Kuttruff reported only one, the inference that the ridges at the Poverty Point Site served as substructures for houses lacks substantiation.[7]

Ford and Webb were able to isolate the basic traits of Poverty Point Culture from analysis of their excavation data and almost 20,000 artifacts from the type site. By 1968 they had examined about 70,000 artifacts from the Poverty Point Site, many of which were systematically collected by Carl Alexander of nearby Epps. The efforts of a number of such dedicated nonprofessionals have made Poverty Point, almost

5. Ford and Webb, *Poverty Point.*
6. Webb, *The Poverty Point Culture.*
7. Carl Kuttruff, "The Poverty Point Site: North Sector Test Excavations," *Bulletin of the Louisiana Archaeological Society,* No. 2, pp. 129–51; Ford and Webb, *Poverty Point.*

indisputably, the largest systematically surface-collected site in North America. It is indeed a tribute to their efforts that these controlled surface collections have been the very basis for distribution studies relative to the occupational history of the site.[8] By 1977 Webb was able to report that he and his colleagues had examined 120,000 artifacts from this and other sites of the Poverty Point Culture.

The Poverty Point baked-clay object is one of the most numerous artifacts: there are over 18,000 from this type site alone (Pls. 9 and 10). These objects have been recovered from many sites of the Poverty Point and other cultures, but nowhere are they as numerous, as variable in form, and as ornate as at the Poverty Point type site. They have been sorted into five general types and labeled, in order of their frequencies: melon-shaped, cylindrical, cross-grooved, biconical, and spheroidal. Each type comprises a number of variants, such as melon-shaped twisted; cylindrical with lateral incising; cross-grooved, multiple crosses; biconical extruded; and spheroidal dimpled. There are also atypical specimens, such as amorphous, biscuit-shaped, cuboidal, rectangular, finger-squeezed (some showing fingerprints of adults and children), mushroom-shaped tetrahedral, barrel-shaped, and pyramidal. One of the baked-clay objects from Poverty Point exhibits a human face. Many of these artifacts have been found in fire pits intermixed with ash and charcoal. Anywhere from one dozen to two hundred have been recovered from a single pit, and most of the specimens "in a given pit are of a single type, indicating the individual housewife's or family's preference for a certain shape or decoration."[9]

At the Poverty Point Site most of the baked-clay objects, as well as stone vessel fragments and potsherds, were found in the north and south sectors close to Bayou Maçon. Since all of these specimen categories are considered culinary items, it is not at all surprising that they would have been used and discarded close to a water source. Most of the potsherds are fiber-tempered specimens or Tchefuncte wares,

8. Ford and Webb, *Poverty Point*; Webb, "The Extent and Content of Poverty Point Culture"; Jon L. Gibson, "Intersite Variability at Poverty Point: Some Preliminary Considerations on Lapidary," *Southeastern Archaeological Conference Bulletin*, No. 12 (1970), 13–20; Clarence H. Webb, "Settlement Patterns in the Poverty Point Culture Complex," in Broyles and Webb (eds.), *The Poverty Point Culture*, 3–12.

9. Webb, "The Extent and Content of Poverty Point Culture," 308.

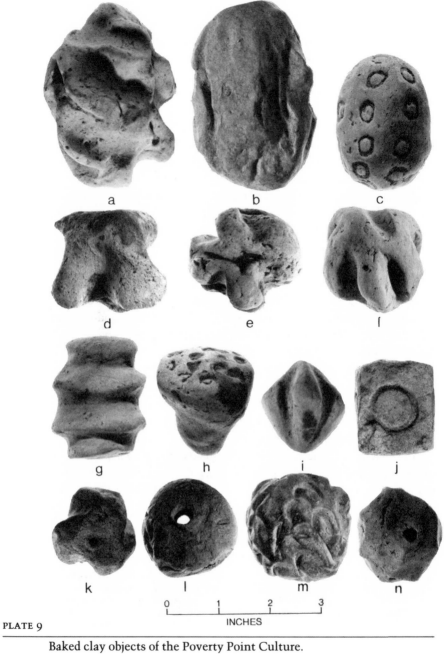

PLATE 9

a

b

c

d

e

f

g

h

i

j

k

l

m

n

0   1   2   3
INCHES

Baked clay objects of the Poverty Point Culture.

which will be discussed in the following chapter that describes the Tchefuncte Culture. A minority of sherds, made from a kaolinitic clay, represent trade vessels from sites in the Saint John's River area of northeastern Florida.

Other clay artifacts include plummetlike objects, casts of wild cane, tubular pipes, pendants, beads, and fragments of wattle and daub. In addition, many small human figurines about 1 to 2.5 inches tall and 1 to 2 inches wide were found. Typically, these represent seated females with lifelike torsos, breasts, and buttocks, but lacking arms (Pl. 10). The faces are characterized by molded noses and punctated and/or incised eyes and mouths. Often they display a smile. Ears are lacking, but hair is indicated by punctations and incised lines. It has been remarked that the faces closely resemble that of the comic character Casper the Friendly Ghost. They also bear a remarkable resemblance to specimens from Olmec Culture manifestations in Mexico, which were contemporary with the Poverty Point Culture. Only 16 of the 107 figurines found at Poverty Point retain their heads, leading Webb to surmise that breaking off the heads may have been a cultural trait.[10] The majority of these ceremonial figurines was concentrated in the north sector of the Poverty Point Site.

Inasmuch as large lithic deposits are not a characteristic of this alluvial region, it is quite intriguing to find that the stone artifact inventory at Poverty Point is extraordinarily extensive. The only lithic resources of the region, small chert cobbles and pebbles, are to be found 25 to 30 miles from the site. The Indians, using these gravels as cores, ingeniously chipped tools for scraping, cutting, sawing, incising, engraving, drilling, and polishing. Indeed, one of the cardinal diagnostics of the Poverty Point Culture is the microflint technology whereby lamellar blades, struck from cores measuring about 3 inches in their greatest dimension, were made into a variety of tool categories. Almost 30,000 of these microflints were retrieved from the Poverty Point Site itself (Pl. 15). They predominated in the southwest sector, indicating to Webb that this must have been a special activity area.[11] Undoubtedly, the quite similar microflint technology practiced in Meso-

10. Webb, *The Poverty Point Culture.*
11. *Ibid.*

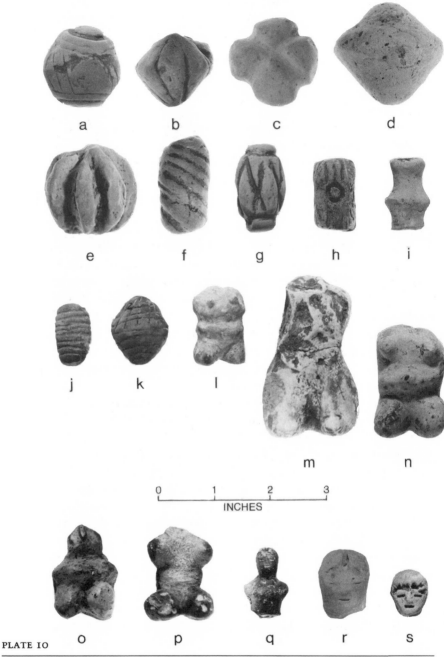

a   b   c   d

e   f   g   h   i

j   k   l   m   n

0   1   2   3
INCHES

o   p   q   r   s

PLATE 10

Artifacts of the Poverty Point Culture: *a–k*, baked clay objects; *l–s*, human figurines.

America before and during Poverty Point times, was the source for the technology at Poverty Point.

Projectile points, many of which are types continuing from late in the Meso-Indian Era, are also numerous at Poverty Point (Pl. 11). They include over 12,000 specimens, most of which were made from the local cherts. Many others, however, were manufactured from exotic flints, novaculites, and fossiliferous cherts transported from Indiana, Illinois, Ohio, Missouri, Tennessee, Arkansas, and Oklahoma. A particularly outstanding example is the type called the Motley point (Pl. 11, a–d). It is a carefully finished, distinctive triangular point with large, deep corner notches, an expanding stem, and a straight to convex base. Motley points are one of the most popular point types from the site, and 80 percent of them are made of flints from the Ohio River area, Tennessee, and Oklahoma. Furthermore, it is notable that although projectile points occur in all sectors of the Poverty Point Site, Motley points show a differential treatment and predominate in the northern sector.

Celts, hoes, and adzes make up the remainder of the chipped-stone assemblages. Since adzes are particularly numerous, woodworking must have been a significant task. Besides these large tools, there are thousands of smaller chipped-stone blades and flakes that exhibit use wear from cutting and scraping (Pl. 12). As we might expect, chipped-stone tools are found in all areas of Poverty Point, but they are proportionally more numerous in the north and south sectors nearest Bayou Maçon.

Among the ground-stone implements found are mealing stones, one of which is a metate with a trough "formed by to-and-fro movement, another Mesoamerican trait."[12] There are also whetstones, pitted stones, hammerstones, saws, reamers, polishers, atlatl weights, gorgets, pipes, tubes, cones, spheres, cylinders, cubes, and a variety of other multifaceted objects made from limonite, hematite, chert, sandstone, slates, shales, siltstone, talc, galena, cannel coal, and jasper (Pls. 13 and 14). Ground-stone plummets are found regularly at most sites of the Poverty Point Culture, but they are particularly numerous (numbering 2,790) at the type site. Made of hematite and magnetite imported

12. *Ibid.*, 42.

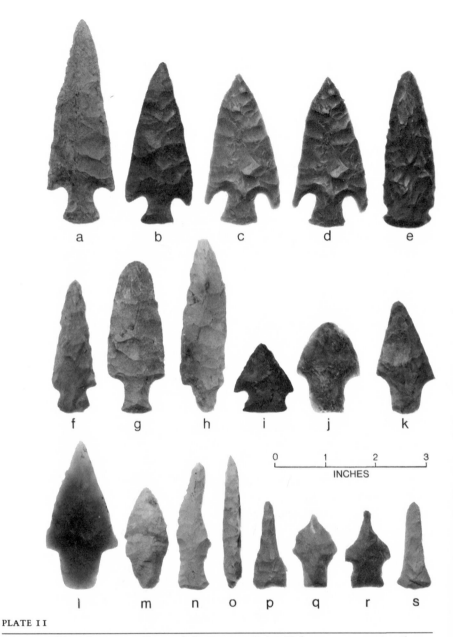

a b c d e

f g h i j k

0 1 2 3
INCHES

l m n o p q r s

PLATE II

Chipped-stone artifacts of the Poverty Point Culture: *a–m,* projectile points; *n–s,* drills.

a

b

c

d

e

f

g

0   1   2   3
INCHES

h

i

0   1   2   3
INCHES

j

PLATE 12

Artifacts of the Poverty Point Culture: *a–c*, ground-stone celts; *d–g*, chipped-stone choppers; *h–i*, knives; *j*, antler atlatl hook.

from northern Arkansas and Missouri, plummets are ovoid forms, perforated or grooved at the top for suspension. Additionally, 35 of the plummets are finely decorated with incisions, punctations, engravings, and intaglio depicting stylized human and zoomorphic motifs and geometric designs. Some archaeologists feel that these objects functioned as weights on bolas used to capture mammals and waterfowl. It is just as likely that they served as net weights to entrap waterfowl and/or fish.

Certainly one of the most exquisite vestiges of the Poverty Point Culture is the lapidary technology that characteristically utilized exotic raw materials, such as red jasper, talc, slates, quartzites, crystal clear quartz, magnetite, hematite, limonite, galena, feldspar, amethyst, fluorite, and other unidentified translucent stones, imported from many parts of the central United States. A most exceptional manifestation at the Poverty Point Site was a bead-maker's cache excavated by King Harris, of Dallas, Texas. The cache contained 56 items of red and green talc in various stages of manufacture, a drill, and a blade apparently used for sawing. Most of the 1,536 finished lapidary items from Poverty Point are beads and pendants. Many of the beads are tubular, and there are lesser numbers of globular, barrel-shaped, discoid, and hourglass-shaped beads as well. Some beads are made from crinoid stems. Others are splendidly engraved and embossed, and there are two zoomorphic forms. The pendants include bird effigies, a turtle form, geniculate, spade, anchor, butterfly, triangular, rectangular, ovoid, and cylindrical forms (Pl. 15). In addition there are Y-shaped, pear-shaped, rattle-shaped, and claw-shaped pendants, as well as axe, celt, and plummet miniatures and a polished red jasper tablet, on one surface of which is a human face "carved in a style that strikingly resembles an Olmec jade figure from La Venta."[13] For that matter, the entire lapidary technology of the Poverty Point Culture parallels that of the contemporary Olmec Culture.

Another category of raw material attributed to the Poverty Point occupation at the type site is native copper, thought to have been traded from the Lake Superior region. Webb reports 155 copper items, in-

13. *Ibid.*, 50; Clarence H. Webb, "Archaic and Poverty Point Zoomorphic Locust Beads," *American Antiquity*, Vol. 36 (1971), No. 1, pp. 105–14.

a   b   c   d   e

f   g

h

0   1   2   3
INCHES

i

j   k

PLATE 13

Ground-stone artifacts of the Poverty Point Culture: *a–g*, plummets; *h*, pipe fragment; *i–k*, celts.

PLATE 14

Stone artifacts of the Poverty Point Culture: *a–f*, gorgets; *g*, atlatl weight; *h*, tablet; *i–k*, quartz ornaments.

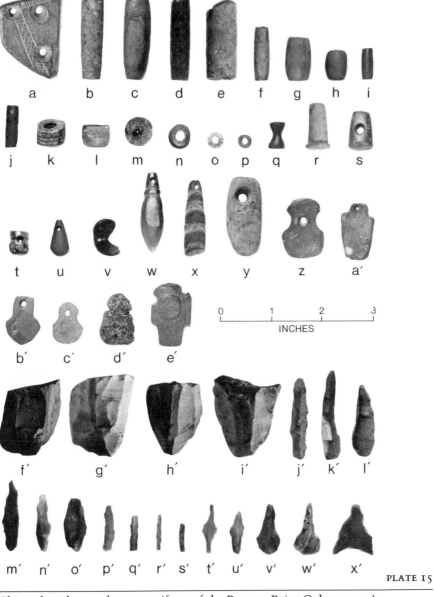

a b c d e f g h i

j k l m n o p q r s

t u v w x y z a′

b′ c′ d′ e′

0   1   2   3
INCHES

f′ g′ h′ i′ j′ k′ l′

m′ n′ o′ p′ q′ r′ s′ t′ u′ v′ w′ x′

PLATE 15

Chipped- and ground-stone artifacts of the Poverty Point Culture: *a–e′*, objects of the lapidary technology; *f′–x′*, artifacts of the microflint technology.

a

b

c

d

e

f

g

h

0   1   2   3
INCHES

PLATE 16

Steatite vessel fragments of the Poverty Point Culture.

cluding a plummet; an awl; sheet fragments; globular, tubular, and discoid beads; wire fragments; and amorphous lumps. Of these specimens, the majority of which are surface finds, only the plummet and a laminated fragment have been described in detail. "In December, 1961, Carl Alexander found several copper beads washing out of the midden; subsequently, other beads, including 19 beads in a double row suggesting a burial placement, and small copper objects were found in the same place." Although the laminated fragment was excavated at Poverty Point, neither its provenance nor its archaeological associations necessarily align it with the Poverty Point Culture, and the archaeological association of the beads is equally obscure. Nevertheless, in light of the vast Poverty Point trade network and the numerous similar artifacts excavated from Poverty Point middens at the Claiborne Site, the attribution of these native copper artifacts to the Poverty Point Culture seems valid.[14]

Bone objects do not preserve well at Poverty Point because of the high soil acidity. Webb records only 81 worked objects, which include deer antler points, flakers, a wedge, and an atlatl hook (Pl. 12, j).[15] There are also a bone awl, decorated pins and pin fragments, tubes, pendants, a spatula, a worked human jaw, several perforated human teeth, and five perforated animal teeth. Since most of these items were dredged from Bayou Maçon, their exact archaeological association with the Poverty Point Culture is unclear.

There are many other Poverty Point Culture sites in or near Louisiana. The Claiborne Site, located in Hancock County, Mississippi, along the left bank of the Pearl River very near its mouth, is a Poverty Point regional center.[16] The site was dominated by a large, horseshoe-shaped, *rangia* shell midden with an outside diameter of 660 feet and an inside diameter of 460 feet, whose ends abutted the riverbank. The exact height of the midden was not reported because, just prior to an archaeological investigation, most of the site was disturbed in prepa-

14. Webb, *The Poverty Point Culture*; Robert E. Bell, "A Copper Plummet from Poverty Point, Louisiana," *American Antiquity*, Vol. 22 (1956), No. 1, p. 80; Ford and Webb, *Poverty Point*; Webb, "The Extent and Content of Poverty Point Culture," 317; Clarence H. Webb, personal communication to the author, 1978.
15. Webb, *The Poverty Point Culture*.
16. Gagliano and Webb, "Archaic–Poverty Point Transition at the Pearl River Mouth."

ration for the construction of a port facility. The midden was at least 4 feet high in the eastern sector, as I was able to judge from undisturbed remnants. A small, conical, earthen mound about 1,000 feet from the center of the horseshoe was destroyed before being tested, so its relationship to the midden is undetermined. Systematic excavations at Claiborne were minimal, consisting only of several test pits, and most of the artifacts were discovered from uncontrolled digging. Nevertheless, although fewer artifacts were found, the inventory from Claiborne virtually duplicates that from the Poverty Point type site. Furthermore, "The quantity and variety of artifacts eclipse all other site collections of the Poverty Point Culture in the coastal area." A truly unusual manifestation at the Claiborne site was a concentration of ten steatite vessels exposed by a bulldozer near the apex of the horseshoe. The vessels, all inverted and found within an area of about 10 square feet, were lying below the Poverty Point deposits in sterile sand. Gagliano and Webb surmise that this peculiar concentration of vessels may denote a ritualistic deposit.[17]

The radiocarbon date from Claiborne indicates that its occupation commenced earlier than that of the Poverty Point Site. The evidence suggests that Claiborne eventually evolved into a principal regional center in the trade network between Poverty Point and the southeastern coastal region. Other such regional centers in Mississippi are the Jaketown Site, a multimound complex about 150 acres in extent, and the Teoc Creek Site, characterized by a semicircular midden deposit extending for about 1,000 feet along the crest of a natural levee. Its configuration is certainly reminiscent of the Claiborne Site. Among the examples of small support settlements of the Poverty Point Culture is the Terral Lewis Site along Joe's Bayou, in Madison Parish. The midden remains from this occupation, though 3 feet thick, cover an area only 300 feet in circumference. Gregory *et al.* feel that the site most likely represents a short-term occupation by an extended family group. Within the occupation area were a number of hearths containing broken and whole Poverty Point baked-clay objects. More of these objects were also concentrated adjacent to the hearths and earth ovens from which they obviously had been removed. Unlike the hearths at

17. *Ibid.*, 57.

Poverty Point, which typically contained a single type of baked-clay object, most Terral Lewis hearths contained a variety of shapes. There were no bone or shell items found at the site, but 551 stone artifacts were recovered. In an unusual distribution pattern, many of the specimens were found in areas away from the hearths. Gregory *et al.* speculate that activity away from the source of warmth indicates that the site was occupied seasonally in late spring and/or summer. They also maintain that the distribution pattern indicates a division of labor.[18]

The stone inventory includes points, bifaces, several atlatl weights, steatite vessel fragments, magnetite plummets, quartz crystals, and a greenstone celt. Unlike Poverty Point and other regional centers, Terral Lewis yielded almost no microflints and none of their cores, nor did the site yield a single lapidary item. Most of the stone objects were large bifaces or flakes struck from sharpening them. A high surface sheen indicates that these artifacts were used as digging implements. Although these bifaces were made from northern flints and some of the other artifacts were of exotic stone, the entire artifact inventory and its depositional distribution bespeak a secular, subsistence-oriented settlement.

Postmolds, the archaeological manifestations of habitational structures, have been reported from a number of Poverty Point Culture occupations. Only at the Jaketown Site, however, did they form a pattern. This pattern, an oval, about 13 feet on its longest axis and partially interrupted by overlying pits, showed no evidence of an entryway, nor were there any of the fire pits that might be expected within the oval outline. Although the exact artifactual associations are not reported, it is generally assumed that the structure relates to the Poverty Point Culture.[19]

By about 800 B.C. the culture that had fostered the massive earthen constructions at Poverty Point and lesser, though prominent, earthworks at regional centers, had declined. In this region there was no other culture characterized by a far-reaching trade network and extensive earthworks until almost the time of Christ, and no succeeding ab-

18. Hiram F. Gregory, Jr., Lester C. Davis, Jr., and Donald G. Hunter, "The Terral Lewis Site: A Poverty Point Activity Facies in Madison Parish, Louisiana," *Southeastern Archaeological Conference Bulletin* No. 12 (1970), 35–46.
19. Ford, Phillips, and Haag, *The Jaketown Site*; Webb, *The Poverty Point Culture*.

original culture in Louisiana was ever able to match the achievements of the Poverty Point Culture in earthwork construction, trade relationships, and lapidary technology. It is entirely justifiable to ask how this fascinating and embellished culture sustained itself for at least one thousand years. What means of support left the people sufficiently free to expend a considerable amount of time and labor on earthen constructions and craft industries? In respect to the type site, nothing can be said with certainty on the basis of so little excavation data. Several hypotheses have been offered, however; Clarence Webb, who has studied the Poverty Point manifestations more closely than any other scholar, is of the opinion that the economic base was agriculture supplemented by hunting and gathering. "Agriculture or horticulture is not proved," he writes, "but it is implied by the riverine settlement patterns; by the usual association of agriculture with large year-round villages and ceremonial centers; by the known presence of maize, beans, squash and other cultigens in contemporary Mesoamerican centers; and by the occurrence, at the Poverty Point site, of artifacts like trough metates, loaf-shaped manos, and clay figurines, which are associated with agriculture in Mesoamerica."[20] More recently, he opined that "the transport of multiplied tons of desired raw materials, the advent of pottery making, and possibly, the knowledge of squash or maize horticulture are evidences of far-reaching cultural interaction."[21] These hypotheses are worth consideration, but it is important to note that while squash remains dating from 2000 B.C. have been found in Missouri and Kentucky, the earliest convincing evidence on hand of maize is in Illinois during the first century before Christ, and beans make their first appearance almost one thousand years later! Of course, the Poverty Point peoples may have cultivated such native plants as the sunflower, marsh elder, lamb's quarters, pigweed, and knotweed.[22]

Jon Gibson offers an alternative hypothesis in his dissertation on the Poverty Point Culture. He suggests that "forest-edge efficiency" in

20. Webb, "The Extent and Content of Poverty Point Culture," 319.
21. Webb, The Poverty Point Culture, 60.
22. Kathleen M. Byrd and Robert W. Neuman, Archaeological Data Relative to Prehistoric Subsistence in the Lower Mississippi Alluvial Valley, Geoscience and Man, Vol. 19 (Baton Rouge, 1978).

hunting and gathering would supply sufficient sustenance to maintain such a culture in the area, one of the most nutritionally bountiful in the eastern United States. In respect to the lower Mississippi Valley, Gibson remarks, "I am convinced that a harvesting program geared to the seasons and coupled with regional distribution could have produced the communal surplus, and spare time associated with spiraling cultural advances."[23] I concur with Gibson on this point.

It is a generally accepted dictum among North American archaeologists that the most likely means of freeing a large work force from constant pursuit of subsistence is an agricultural surplus. Moreover, it is generally assumed that in prehistoric North America maize agriculture was the only really successful system to produce a surplus. These theories have generally stood the test of time, but there is at least one example of a site situation somewhat comparable to Poverty Point where the archaeological evidence shows that the cultivation of food plants was not at all important. The El Paraiso Site, encompassing an area of about 120 acres, was the largest preceramic maritime settlement along the Peruvian coast between 2500 B.C. and 1700 B.C. It is true that this littoral zone, the lushest area of the New World in terms of the availability of nutritional foods, was easier to exploit than the Poverty Point area.[24] However, the masonry constructions at El Paraiso also required more labor to build than the Poverty Point earthworks. About 100,000 tons of igneous bedrock had to be hauled to the site, cut into blocks, set into mortar to form walls, and then plastered with pigmented mud!

It is difficult to explain what caused the decline of the Poverty Point Culture, and not everyone is in agreement on this matter. From the scanty archaeological evidence, we know that after 800 B.C. most of the aggrandized traits—the massive earth constructions, the extensive trade network, lapidary crafts, and microflint technology—dissolved away. Steatite vessels and fiber-tempered pottery, which, it seems, were never particularly plentiful except at the larger sites, also disappeared from the scene. They were replaced by the sand-tempered

23. Gibson, "Poverty Point, the First American Chiefdom," 104.
24. Mary Hrones Parsons, "Preceramic Subsistence on the Peruvian Coast," *American Antiquity*, Vol. 35 (1970), No. 3, pp. 292–304; Michael Edward Mosely, *The Maritime Foundations of Andean Civilization* (Menlo Park, Calif., 1975).

and clay-tempered wares of the succeeding Tchefuncte Culture. Many of the techniques for making the Poverty Point chipped-stone tool assemblage survived, as did the custom of making baked-clay objects, although fewer were made and their variety was limited. We have no evidence of climatic fluctuation nor of any other natural phenomena that would have disrupted the culture. Likewise, there are no archaeological remains indicative of warfare or of conquering legions. The only thing we can say with certainty is that whatever socioreligious aggregates held the Poverty Point Culture together in a viable, integrated unit gradually disintegrated. By the very nature of archaeology, where the only clues are accidentally preserved remains, some important questions must remain unanswered.

VI Tchefuncte Culture

Before 1939 the Marksville Culture, which existed from about 200 B.C. to A.D. 400, was considered the oldest ceramic-manufacturing mound-building culture in Louisiana. Archaeologists first became aware of the distinctive traits of an even older pottery-making culture as a result of the first federally sponsored archaeological salvage project in Louisiana. We now have acceptable radiocarbon dates and diagnostic artifacts from the marsh just east of New Orleans from as early as the fifth century B.C.[1] It is the earliest culture for which we have sufficient human bone to derive physical anthropological data. It is also the earliest culture for which we have excellent physical remains from the middens to furnish us with information about subsistence patterns. And lastly, it is the earliest culture to be characterized by pottery.

In 1934 a number of shell (*Rangia cuneata*) middens in the Little Woods community, near the south shore of Lake Pontchartrain, were being gutted for their shell content and for the construction of a radio station. News of numerous human skeletons and artifacts in these middens reached state and federal officials, who, in turn, provided facilities for archaeological salvage excavations. J. Richard Czajkowski and Maurice K. Weil of the Louisiana Department of Conservation directed a fifty-man crew in excavations that lasted for at least six

---

1. J. Richard Shenkel and Jon Gibson, "Big Oak Island: An Historical Perspective of Changing Site Function," *Louisiana Studies*, Vol. 13 (1974), No. 2, pp. 173–86; J. Richard Shenkel and George Holley, "A Tchefuncte House," *Proceedings of the 31st Southeastern Archaeological Conference*, Bulletin No. 18 (1975), 226–42.

months. Fred B. Kniffen acted as adviser to the project, and Czaj-kowski summarized the findings.[2]

An enormous amount of material was excavated. Unfortunately, much of it, along with the field notes, was displaced, and eventually the material from a number of middens was consolidated into one collection. Czajkowski recognized two separate horizons in the middens. The deepest, which subsequently became known as the Tchefuncte component, was from 2 to 7 feet in depth. In addition to bone, stone, shell, and ceramic artifacts, this deposit contained six primary adult human burials, each lying in a semiflexed position. They were parallel to each other and about 4 feet apart. Associated with one individual were two quartz crystals. Another human burial was found lying face down in an extended position, and one isolated skull was found lying on top of a decorated potsherd. The topmost deposit, containing the remains of a culture subsequently known as Coles Creek, extended from the surface to a depth of about 18 inches. It, too, contained artifacts and human burials. The latter were poorly preserved, however, and the burial positions are not reported. One skull was restored, and Czajkowski provided craniometric measurements. Although it is not specifically stated, the skull's state of preservation and its provenience seem to indicate that it came from the Tchefuncte horizon.[3]

Between 1934 and 1939 regional archaeologists became aware that the Little Woods middens contained a culture complex quite different from anything previously studied. In July, 1939, a Louisiana State University–Works Progress Administration project to reexamine what remained of the middens got under way. Until October of that year Preston Holder and his assistant, Edwin B. Doran, Jr., directed a 35-man crew that worked at middens designated 16OR1 through 16OR5. Although the quantity of material excavated fell short of expectations, it did demonstrate the validity of Czajkowski's observations. Thirty years later, in 1969, the human skeletal material from 16OR3 and 16OR4 was loaned to Dr. Elizabeth S. Watts, a physical anthropologist at Tulane University. Students under her supervision iden-

2. Czajkowski, "Preliminary Report of Archaeological Excavations in Orleans Parish."

3. Ford and Quimby, *The Tchefuncte Culture*; Czajkowski, "Preliminary Report of Archaeological Excavations in Orleans Parish."

tified and sorted the bones and estimated that the collection represented a minimum of thirty individuals.[4]

For two weeks in September, 1939, Doran and a 10-man crew augered and dug test pits in midden 16OR6 at the Big Oak Island Site located in the marsh area presently called New Orleans East. This large crescent-shaped shell midden, measuring 725 feet by 75 feet with a maximum height of 9 feet above the marsh, contains a Tchefuncte component among its deeper deposits. Although in their first report Ford and Quimby asserted that the Tchefuncte component at Big Oak Island included primary flexed human burials, they neglected to mention them in their summary of Tchefuncte period burials. Nor were they included with Charles Snow's analysis of Tchefuncte skeletal remains.[5]

The Tchefuncte type site was first excavated as an archaeological salvage project during the winter of 1939. Two shell middens within the confines of the Tchefuncte State Park (now known as Fontainebleau State Park) in Saint Tammany Parish were being destroyed for their shell content. The Civilian Conservation Corps, assigned to the park improvement project, provided facilities and personnel to investigate the middens. The easternmost midden, designated Midden A, measured 250 feet by 100 feet; Midden B was 150 feet by 100 feet. Their long axes paralleled the Lake Pontchartrain shoreline. Clarence L. Johnson, a historian, conducted an investigation limited to a portion of Midden B. He imposed a grid of 5-foot squares over the midden and excavated 53 of them to sea level (about 2½ feet), even though the midden actually extends to more than 5 feet below sea level. Johnson's excavation was deep enough to amply demonstrate that the site contained a major Tchefuncte component.

In January and February, 1941, a 35-man LSU–WPA project, directed by Edwin B. Doran, Jr., excavated both middens. This time the middens were excavated to their basal deposits, which varied in depth according to the tide and the winds. In addition to almost fifty thou-

4. Records on file at the Department of Geography and Anthropology, Louisiana State University, Baton Rouge.
5. Shenkel and Holley, "A Tchefuncte House"; Ford and Quimby, The Tchefuncte Culture. In the latter work, see especially Charles E. Snow, "Tchefuncte Skeletal Remains."

sand sherds, to say nothing of the numbers of stone, bone, shell, and ceramic objects, forty-three human burials were exposed in Midden A. Of this number, twenty-one were primary flexed interments, and the remainder, manifested as bundles of bones, were presumably secondary burials. In the usual pattern of Tchefuncte interments, none had funerary associations.[6]

Another Tchefuncte culture occupation site having human burials is the Copell Site, Vermilion Parish. From his 1926 excavation at this site, Henry B. Collins reported human interments, some of which were lying on red and yellow pigments. Although he does not mention the burial positions, Collins does remark that the skulls were wide-formed and that none of the bones showed evidence of pathologies. Artifactual associations, which are unique at this site, included a number of stone, bone, and shell objects. Aleš Hrdlička conducted craniometric examinations of the Copell skulls and published his results in his catalog series, "Indians of the Gulf States." He lists twenty-one males, whose age at death ranged from forty-five to seventy-five years. There were also fifteen females, whose age at death ranged from twenty to sixty-five years. Collins lists only thirteen females, two less than Hrdlička, and he notes that one of the males listed by Hrdlička really came from another site. Generally, Collins found the females to be much broader in their facial dimensions than the males. In fact, in five of the Copell females, the face was broader than any that Collins had seen previously. Both sexes exhibited particularly low orbits, males slightly more so than females.[7]

In a subsequent study of Tchefuncte skeletons, Charles E. Snow incorporated eleven more males and nine more females in the Copell series. His craniometric data generally corroborated Collins' finding. Both sexes exhibited extremely high, vaulted crania; low, broad orbits; long faces; broad, long palates; and lower jaws of moderate dimensions. Males were mesocranic, and females were brachycranic

6. George I. Quimby, Jr., "The Tchefuncte Culture," Newsletter of the Southeastern Archaeological Conference, Vol. 2 (1941), No. 4, pp. 29–30; Ford and Quimby, The Tchefuncte Culture.
7. Collins, "Archaeological Work in Louisiana and Mississippi"; Collins, "Relationships of an Early Indian Cranial Series from Louisiana"; Hrdlička, "Catalog of Human Crania in the U.S. National Museum Collections: Indians of the Gulf States."

(broad-headed). Females also had broader noses than males. Because the postcranial bones were poorly preserved, only limited information was available from examining humeri, femorae, tibiae, and pelves. Nevertheless, Snow estimated that the men ranged from 62.5 inches to 64.8 inches in height. The long bones and skulls exhibited pathologies that Snow identified as osteoporosis symmetrica and periostitis. In fact almost all of the specimens showed some evidence of disease. On the other hand, no dental caries were noted, although abscesses were common. Tooth wear was extreme, but considering the death-age and dietary patterns, this is to be expected.[8]

Collins, Ford, and Quimby, Jr., assigned the Copell Site to the Tchefuncte Culture, but in a subsequent report Sherwood Gagliano has reassigned it to an earlier, preceramic or late Archaic horizon. This reassignment was based largely upon the fact that no pottery was found at the Copell Site, indicating that the site occupation predated the Tchefuncte Culture. Gagliano then added that, "recent data verifies this interpretation."[9] However, since the Copell Site has a complex of traits correlative to the Tchefuncte Culture and since the physical anthropological analyses indicate that human crania from Copell are morphologically comparable to those from Tchefuncte sites, until substantive data to the contrary are presented, I shall concur with the assignment by Ford, Quimby, Jr., and Collins.

Collins noted that the Copell Site inhabitants were bigger than comparable populations reported in Kentucky, and he surmised that this disparity might be explained by diet. It is not a question easy to resolve, but we do have some primary information on Tchefuncte subsistence patterns. Our earliest information is quite general. In 1934 Czajkowski noted that the animal bones from the Little Woods middens indicated that the animals were killed away from the site and only selected parts were brought into the camp area to be eaten. "The jaws," he wrote, "are mostly deer, peccary, and small rodents." Since Louisiana is far east of their known range, peccary bones have never been excavated at any other prehistoric archaeological site. Therefore, the identification of peccary bones is somewhat doubtful. There is no

8. Snow, "Tchefuncte Skeletal Remains."
9. Gagliano, "Late Archaic–Early Formative Relationships in South Louisiana," 12.

doubt, however, that the inhabitants ate the meat from the brackish-water clam, *Rangia cuneata*. The shells of this mollusk make up the major constituent by volume of the Louisiana coastal shell middens. However, the tens of thousands of tons of these shells that compose Louisiana coastal middens may mislead the observer into overestimating the *rangia*'s importance as a food source. In a recent zooarchaeological study, Kathleen M. Byrd analyzed the *rangia* for the amount of meat it provides, its nutritional value, and how it is affected by gathering strategies. She found that 81 clams would leave 162 valves whose total volume would average 64.88 cubic inches, but these clams would provide only 2.4 ounces of wet meat—not very much meat for the volume of shell. In order to obtain the equivalent of 50 pounds of deer meat, it would be necessary to gather 25,300 clams, leaving behind 50,600 valves and a midden volume of 11.8 cubic feet. Nutritionally, the *rangia* is low in protein, fats, carbohydrates, and calories when compared to other wild food resources. Nevertheless, they were persistently exploited because they were numerous, easily procured, and provided a reliable continuous supply of food.[10]

In the Tchefuncte Site middens, entire and broken animal bones were plentiful, with deer (*Odocoileus virginianus*) being the most common species. Other species represented include raccoon (*Procyon lotor*), opossum (*Didelphis virginiana*), muskrat (*Ondrata zibethicus*), otter (*Lutra canadensis*), bear (*Euarctos americanus*), grey fox (*Urocyon cinereoargenteus*), dog (*Canis familiaris*), ocelot (*Felis pardalis*), alligator (*Alligator mississippiensis*), catfish (Ameriuridae), alligator gar (*Lepisosteus spatula*), and black drum (*Pogonias cromis*). In addition to *rangia* shell, the middens also contained some marine mollusks, such as oyster and *Busycon* sp. Ford and Quimby remark that bird bones were common, but they do not identify them by species. It should be noted that the ocelot remains are considerably east of the known range for that animal.[11]

---

10. Collins, "Archaeological Work in Louisiana and Mississippi"; Czajkowski, "Preliminary Report of Archaeological Excavations in Orleans Parish"; George H. Lowery, Jr., *The Mammals of Louisiana and Its Adjacent Waters* (Baton Rouge, 1974); Kathleen Mary Byrd, "The Brackish Water Clam (*Rangia cuneata*): A Prehistoric 'Staff of Life' or a Minor Food Resource," *Louisiana Archaeology*, Bulletin No. 3 (1977), 23–31.
11. Ford and Quimby, *The Tchefuncte Culture*; Lowery, *The Mammals of Louisiana and Its Adjacent Waters*.

A Tchefuncte component at the Morton Shell Mound, Iberia Parish, was situated in a peat deposit 6 to 7 feet below sea level. Unusually well-preserved faunal and floral remains from the mound provided excellent material for a study of Tchefuncte subsistence patterns. After identifying the animal bone from the Tchefuncte component, Byrd was able to estimate the minimum number of individuals represented for each species. She then computed the amounts of edible meat provided by the sample, their dietary ratios, and their nutritional value. She also determined what percentage of the total each class of animals (*i.e.*, mammals, birds, fishes, and reptiles) contributed in terms of numbers and amount of edible meat. Deer, muskrat, raccoon, goose, crane, turtle, bowfin, catfish, and sunfish predominated, numerically, but the greatest amounts of edible meat were provided by deer, alligator, raccoon, goose, and catfish, in that order. These were the most important sources of animal protein.[12]

The floral remains were also identified and their nutritional values computed. Hickory nuts, acorns, plums, grapes, and persimmons were among the important edible wild species.[13] The presence of squash (*Cucurbita pepo* var. *ovifera*) and bottle gourd (*Lagenaria siceraria*) seeds and rinds is evidence of horticultural activity, although the bottle gourd does occur in the wild. The five acceptable radiocarbon dates, from 325 B.C. to A.D. 295, for the Tchefuncte component at the Morton Shell Mound, represent the earliest presence of squash reported anywhere along the northern coast of the Gulf of Mexico.

It is difficult to understand the absence of crustacean remains in these Tchefuncte midden deposits. Crustaceans are plentiful in this region and easy to gather. They are also nutritious and, at least by modern viewpoint, delectable. Nevertheless, not a single professionally identified example of crab or crawfish remains has been recovered from *in situ* deposits at Tchefuncte middens. In fact, no crustacean re-

---

12. Robert W. Neuman, *Archaeological Investigations at the Morton Shell Mound, Weeks Island, Iberia Parish, Louisiana* (Washington, D.C., 1972); Kathleen Mary Byrd, "Tchefuncte Subsistence Patterns, Morton Shell Mound, Iberia Parish, Louisiana" (M.A. thesis, Louisiana State University, Baton Rouge, 1974); Kathleen Mary Byrd, "Tchefuncte Subsistence: Information Obtained from the Excavation of the Morton Shell Mound, Iberia Parish, Louisiana," *Southeastern Archaeological Conference Bulletin*, No. 19 (1976), figs. 1–3, table 1.
13. Hugh C. Cutler and Leonard W. Blake of the Missouri Botanical Gardens made most of the identifications. Byrd, "Tchefuncte Subsistence Patterns, Morton Shell Mound"; Byrd, "Tchefuncte Subsistence," tables 2 and 3.

mains have been reported from any prehistoric sites in Louisiana. It is not likely that the lack of remains can be explained by poor preservation. At the Morton Shell Mound and in almost 735 cubic feet of Tchefuncte deposits excavated at the Bayou Jasmine Site in Saint John the Baptist Parish, preservation is excellent.[14] Crustaceans simply were not used for food. Even the ethnohistoric literature makes no reference to the use of crustaceans as food among Louisiana Indians. No doubt the Tchefuncte people would find it remarkable that Louisiana's present-day inhabitants do not eat *Rangia cuneata*.

Knowledge of the animal foods that the Tchefuncte culture employed can be used to derive information about their hunting and fishing techniques. Previous studies have shown that hunting and gathering groups can productively exploit the area within about 6 miles of the base camp. Applying that range to the Tchefuncte component at the Morton Shell Mound, Byrd computed the faunal populations supportable in each microenvironment. She observed that deer, blue goose, box turtle, and fish were overexploited; mink and rabbit were present in about their expected numbers; and muskrat and raccoon were underexploited. Duck, one of the most abundant seasonal food resources, seems to have been almost ignored.[15]

We have tangible evidence of Tchefuncte hunting and fishing methods in the form of stone and bone artifacts, including stone points, antler points, splintered-bone points, bone harpoon heads, antler atlatl hooks, stone atlatl weights, bola stones, and bone fishhooks. From cord impressions on Tchefuncte sherds at the Norman Site in Mississippi and on sherds from the Tchefuncte Site itself, we can conclude that cord was present and may have been used to weave nets for trapping game. Taking into consideration the artifacts found, the behavioral traits of the animals represented, and pertinent ethnohistoric accounts, Byrd suggested that the Tchefuncte people at the Morton

14. Jack Fiser, "The Treasure of Bayou Jasmine," *LSU Alumni News*, Vol. 51 (1975), No. 5, pp. 2–6.
15. E. S. Higgs and C. Vita-Finzi, "Prehistoric Economies: A Territorial Approach," in E. S. Higgs (ed.), *Papers in Economic Prehistory* (Cambridge, Mass., 1972), 27–36; Byrd, "Tchefuncte Subsistence Patterns, Morton Shell Mound"; Byrd, "Tchefuncte Subsistence."

Shell Mound used the atlatl to kill deer. Since muskrat are so poorly represented, it is likely that these animals were killed while the hunters were pursuing other game. The nocturnal raccoon and opossum would be most easily caught by trapping or night hunting. The migratory birds, which would be in residence from October to April, could be killed with bolas or projectiles or trapped in nets. The bowfin could be caught with hook and line or speared. Small gar could be hooked or netted, but the scales of a large gar would protect it from a spear, and the hook-and-line or netting techniques would be incapable of holding it. The freshwater drum is a bottom feeder in muddy water, so spearing would be impractical. This fish could, however, be hooked or netted. Most of the other fish could also be taken by line fishing or less productively, by spearing and netting.[16]

The hunting-and-gathering economy must adjust to the changing seasons. As flora and fauna react to climatic change, humans exploit these seasonal adjustments. For many years archaeologists have debated the question of whether the coastal shell middens were occupied throughout the year or only during particular seasons. One approach to deciding this question is analysis of the animal and botanical specimens recovered from the shell middens. Byrd performed such an analysis on remains from the Tchefuncte midden at the Morton Shell Mound. She reasoned that the goose remains indicated occupation of the site in late fall to early spring. Turtles are most active from early spring to winter. The common box turtle, however, will devour great quantities of poisonous mushrooms, which are most profuse in the spring. Humans who eat turtles that have consumed poisonous mushrooms might be poisoned themselves. If they were aware of this danger, the Indians at the Morton Shell Mound would only have eaten turtles during the summer and late fall. The hackberry ripens during the fall and winter, and the remaining fruit pits, seeds, and nutshells indicate occupancy from early summer into late fall. From these data, which are not entirely conclusive, it appears that

16. Edwin Alan Toth, "Early Marksville Phases in the Lower Mississippi Valley: A Study of Culture Contact Dynamics" (Ph.D. dissertation, Harvard University, 1977); Byrd, "Tchefuncte Subsistence Patterns, Morton Shell Mound"; Byrd, "Tchefuncte Subsistence."

Indians of the Tchefuncte Culture occupied this site during the summer, autumn, and possibly the spring as well.[17] However, the data from this single component at one site will have to be augmented by comparable studies of remains from many sites before we can begin to speak authoritatively of seasonal occupation patterns in the Louisiana marshland. Barring hurricanes or other storms that would upset the ecological balance over a wide region for an extended period of time, people with a hunting-and-gathering technology would certainly be able to remain in the semitropical marsh environment during any season of the year.

The Indians of the Tchefuncte Culture were the first in Louisiana to make widespread use of pottery. The fiber-tempered sherds recovered from earlier Poverty Point sites are extremely rare. So few samples are available for study that very little can be concluded about the pottery of those times. The innumerable sherds of Tchefuncte ceramics that have been found, however, provide us with direct evidence that these people were adept at the new technology. The sherds are also evidence of new culinary techniques. One need only read of experiments utilizing animal skin receptacles for cooking to appreciate the advantages of clay pots.[18] The introduction of pottery undoubtedly brought innovations in food preparation and changes in eating habits. Pottery also provided a new method for storing and transporting goods. Pottery is an artifact of unique importance to the archaeologist. The sherds from broken vessels are almost indestructible, and they are generally the most abundant class of artifacts at the sites where they occur. The methods employed in tempering and molding the clay and the decorative devices and colors applied to the pot make the ceramic artifact a precisely selected cultural expression. The method of tempering the clay, and the vessel shape and decoration change through time, from one geographical area to another. These changes are excellent indicators of such cultural phenomena as migration, trade, and territorial boundaries.

Thousands of potsherds have been recovered from Tchefuncte sites, described, and categorized (Pls. 17, 18, 19), but only one complete ves-

17. Byrd, "Tchefuncte Subsistence Patterns, Morton Shell Mound"; Byrd, "Tchefuncte Subsistence"; Archie Carr, *Handbook of Turtles* (Ithaca, N.Y., 1952).
18. John Coles, *Archaeology by Experiment* (New York, 1973).

a

b

c

d

e

f

g

h

0   1   2   3

INCHES

PLATE 17

Vessel rim sherds of the Tchefuncte Culture.

a

b

c

d

e

f

g

h

0   1   2   3
INCHES

PLATE 18

Vessel rim sherds of the Tchefuncte Culture.

0 1 2 3
INCHES

0 1 2 3
INCHES

PLATE 19

Ceramic artifacts of the Tchefuncte Culture: *a*, restored vessel from the
Resch Site; *b–f*, Tchefuncte vessel bases; *g–m*, pipe fragments; *n–o*,
baked-clay objects.

sel has ever been found (Pl. 19, a).[19] It was excavated from the Resch Site in Harrison County, northeast Texas. Tchefuncte pottery was tempered with either sand or clay particles, but on many of the more chalky-textured sherds the tempering agent, if there really was one, is not visible. The potters built the base and walls of coils, which were then malleated and molded to form a vessel of the desired size and shape. They made globular pots with shoulders, constricted necks, and flaring rims, and they made bowls, either globular with an incurving rim, or with straight to slightly expanding walls and rims. The lips are generally rounded, and some are quite irregular. Bases are flat to slightly concave in cross section with teat-shaped or wedge-shaped podal supports. One partially restored vessel from the Tchefuncte Site is a round-bottomed, shallow bowl, and another partially restored vessel is trough-shaped with a rounded bottom. Characteristically, the vessels range from 10 to 40 centimeters in diameter; their walls are from 5 to 10 millimeters thick. Vessel heights are not generally calculable, but the vessel from the Resch site is 17 centimeters tall. The pots are buff to light gray to black, and quite often they are discolored by smoke or encrusted with charcoal. Exterior surfaces and the lips may be plain and smooth, or embellished with a number of specific decorative patterns

19. Ford and Quimby, *The Tchefuncte Culture*; Philip Phillips, James A. Ford, and James B. Griffin, *Archaeological Survey in the Lower Mississippi Alluvial Valley, 1940–1947*, Papers of the Peabody Museum of American Archaeology and Ethnology, Vol. 25 (Cambridge, Mass., 1951); Joe Ben Wheat, *An Archaeological Survey of the Addicks Dam Basin, Southeast Texas*, Bureau of American Ethnology Bulletin 154 (Washington, D.C., 1953), 143–252; Jon L. Gibson, "Russell Landing: A North Louisiana Phase of the Tchefuncte Period" (M.A. thesis, Louisiana State University, Baton Rouge, 1968); Lawrence E. Aten and Charles N. Bollich, "A Preliminary Report on the Development of a Ceramic Chronology for the Sabine Lake Area of Texas and Louisiana," *Bulletin of the Texas Archaeological Society*, Vol. 40 (1969), 241–58; Philip Phillips, *An Archaeological Survey in the Lower Yazoo Basin, Mississippi, 1949–1955*, Papers of the Peabody Museum of Archaeology and Ethnology, Vol. 60, Pts. 1 and 2 (Cambridge, Mass., 1970); Philip George Rivet, "Tchefuncte Ceramic Typology: A Reappraisal" (M.A. thesis, Louisiana State University, Baton Rouge, 1973); J. Richard Shenkel, "Big Oak and Little Oak Islands: Excavations and Interpretations," *Bulletin of the Louisiana Archaeological Society*, No. 1 (1974), 37–65; Webb et al., "The Resch Site"; Richard A. Weinstein and Philip G. Rivet, *Beau Mire: A Late Tchula Period Site of the Tchefuncte Culture, Ascension Parish, Louisiana*, Anthropological Report No. 1, Department of Culture, Recreation and Tourism, Louisiana Archaeological Survey and Antiquities Commission (Baton Rouge, 1978).

applied by a combination of techniques, including punctating, incising, stamping, pinching, notching, brushing, and cord impressing. In some cases the vessel exterior was coated with red ochre.[20]

Pipes and Poverty Point baked-clay objects were also among the Tchefuncte ceramic inventory (Pl. 19). The pipes, made of sand-tempered clay, are tubular, about 15 centimeters long, and up to 2 centimeters in diameter. The bore hole tapers from the smoke-blackened chamber to the mouthpiece, which is sometimes flattened. The pipe exterior ranges from buff to gray to red in color and on several specimens is decorated with a combination of incised and punctated patterns. The baked-clay objects are types of the biconical, cylindrical, and spherical forms reported from the Poverty Point Culture. These baked-clay objects and the tubular pipes illustrate a cultural continuity from the Poverty Point Era. Indeed, the stone and bone artifacts found in Tchefuncte deposits are indistinguishable from those recovered at late Meso-Indian or Poverty Point sites.

In addition to the stone and bone objects used in hunting and fishing that have already been discussed, many other stone and bone tools are listed in Tchefuncte inventories (Pls. 20, 21, 22). There are stone knives, drills, scrapers, choppers, sandstone abraders, mealing stones, hammerstones, sandstone saws, celts, and quartz crystals. Bone specimens include awls, flakers, chisels, cut and ground animal jaws, perforated animal canine teeth, perforated penis bones, antler flakers and socketed handles (Pl. 23), and ground sections of turtle shell. At the Tchefuncte Site an interesting, though problematical group of three hundred cut distal ends of deer metapodials was found.[21] Among the shell artifacts found are gouges, a chisel, fragments of *Busycon* shell containers, perforated circular gorgets, and columella punches and pendants (Pl. 22, *a–f*).

Tchefuncte sites are identified mainly by the presence of Tchefuncte pottery types. In the original synthesis, which has not been superseded, Ford and Quimby felt that certain Tchefuncte pottery types were comparable to reported wares in northern Alabama and northern Florida. Since that time Tchefuncte or Tchefuncte-like ceramics have

20. Webb *et al.*, "The Resch Site,"; Ford and Quimby, *The Tchefuncte Culture*.
21. Ford and Quimby, *The Tchefuncte Culture*.

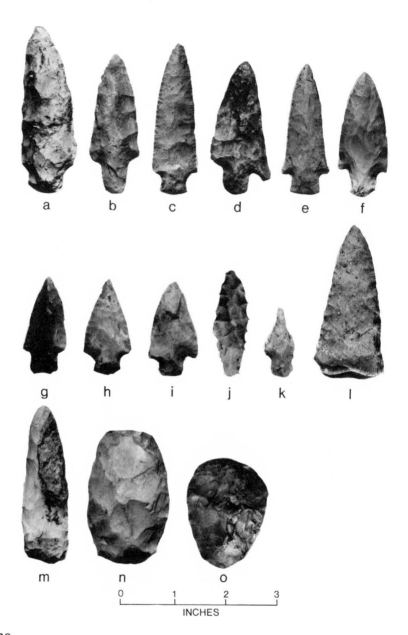

PLATE 20

Chipped-stone artifacts of the Tchefuncte Culture: *a–j*, projectile points; *k*, drill; *l–m*, knives; *n–o*, choppers.

a

b

c

d

e

f

g

0   1   2   3
INCHES

PLATE 21

Ground-stone objects of the Tchefuncte Culture: *a*, mealing stone; *b–e*,
pecking stones; *f–g*, sandstone abraders.

a   b   c

d   e   f   g

0   1   2   3
INCHES

h   i   j   k

PLATE 22

Shell and ground-stone objects of the Tchefuncte Culture: *a–f*, marine shell ornaments and tools; *g*, ground-stone ornament; *h–k*, plummets.

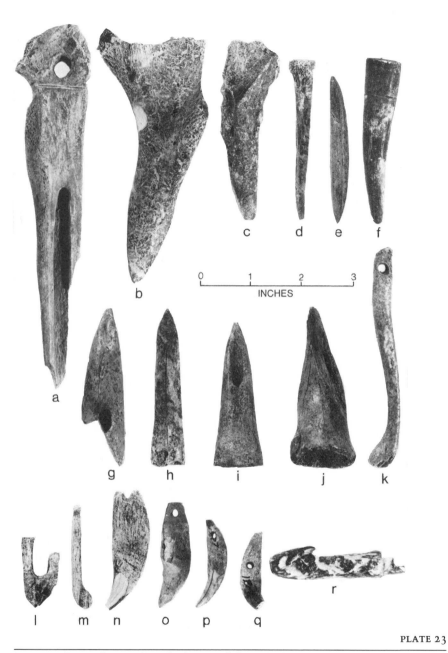

PLATE 23

Bone, antler, and animal teeth objects of the Tchefuncte Culture: *a–j*,
perforators; *k*, ornament; *l–m*, fishhooks; *n–q*, canine-teeth pendants;
r, antler atlatl hook.

been reported at sites in southeast Missouri, northwest Mississippi, the Yazoo River Basin in Mississippi, coastal Alabama, northeast Texas, and coastal southeast Texas.[22]

Edwin Alan Toth notes that Tchefuncte settlements are generally absent along major stream courses. The Indians of this culture tended to locate in slack water environments, "coincident with the slow-moving secondary streams which drain the bottomlands (e.g., Cassidy Bayou, Tensas River, Bayou Macon, Bayou Teche), the floodplain lakes (e.g., Panther Lake, Catahoula Lake), and a littoral zone including the Prairie Terrace adjacent to Lake Pontchartrain." Toth hypothesized that these sites would be inundated annually by Mississippi River floodwaters, and the inhabitants would be forced to relocate on nearby uplands. If such refuge sites containing Tchefuncte ceramics and animal bone refuse are found, his hypothesis may be tested by zooarchaeological analyses. However, historical data does not corroborate the theory of annual flooding over the tops of natural levees in slack water environments. It was precisely and particularly along these natural levees that European settlements began and thrived. Flooding over these eminences was an exception rather than the rule. Furthermore, Jon L. Gibson, in his study of Tchefuncte sites in the Bayou Vermilion drainage, south-central Louisiana, noted that seasonal flooding imposed a constraint on the selection of places for settlement. Five of his eleven sites are located on the crests of natural levees, two others are on an escarpment 13 feet high, two are along bankline ridges of a crevasse, one is on an elevated apron of alluvium or colluvium, and another occupies the edge of a characteristically wet meadow. Of this settlement pattern, he writes, "An overriding founding consideration appears to have been hydrologic fluctuations; site locations were chosen to place village residents above all but the most severe annual floods and inundations."[23]

22. *Ibid.*; Phillips, Ford, and Griffin, *Archaeological Survey of the Lower Mississippi Alluvial Valley*; Phillips, *An Archaeological Survey in the Lower Yazoo Basin*; Brain, "The Lower Mississippi Valley in North American Pre-history"; Steve B. Wimberly, "Bayou La Batre Tchefuncte Pottery Series," in James B. Griffin (ed.), *Prehistoric Pottery of the Eastern United States* (Ann Arbor, 1953); Webb *et al.*, "The Resch Site"; Wheat, *An Archaeological Survey of the Addicks Dam Basin*; Lawrence E. Aten, "Coastal Southeast Texas Archaeology," manuscript, University of Texas, 1970.
23. Toth, "Early Marksville Phases in the Lower Mississippi Valley," 50; Jon L. Gibson, "The Tchefuncte Culture in the Bayou Vermilion Basin, South Central

The littoral zone amply demonstrates Tchefuncte occupation patterns. Here sites are located on cheniers, terrace remnants, and salt domes, and along lake shores and natural levees. Most of the reported Tchefuncte sites have been found in the littoral zone. Since most of the Tchefuncte data were obtained in this zone, it would be an excellent place to begin a careful study of Tchefuncte settlement patterns.

Settlement studies attempt to deduce a broad spectrum of activities. From their excavations into the Tchefuncte midden at the Big Oak Island Site, Orleans Parish, Shenkel and Gibson hypothesized a chronology of specialized activities. The sherds were found in their greatest density in the basal deposit, a black clay matrix lacking shell. From this evidence, the scientists speculated: "The large number of potsherds and high evidence of decorated sherds suggests that a relatively large number of women were on the site at this period. It is not unreasonable to assume that the presence of women means that men and children were there also. The presence of both sexes and various age groups can be interpreted as representing a much fuller range of activities than would be encountered at sex-or-activity-specific camps." Because artifacts were sparse in the middle deposit, which was characterized by lenses of shell and humic silt, Shenkel and Gibson felt that the site had been seasonally occupied at that time by men who were gathering and processing the shellfish at Big Oak Island, but who were living somewhere else. The topmost deposits, located on two elevated areas at opposite ends of the site, were distinguished by a thick humic matrix and concentrations of human skeletal parts. Shenkel and Gibson hypothesized that during this period the Tchefuncte people only utilized the site for mortuary purposes. "There is no general occupational refuse attributable to this late component, nor is there evidence for specialized mortuary preparation areas anywhere on the island. The people who were laid to rest on Big Oak Island probably did not live there."[24]

Another most important aspect of settlement studies has to do with structures such as habitations, outbuildings, scaffolds, and fences. For the Tchefuncte Culture, archaeological evidence for such structures is both slight and speculative, but it should not be ignored. In the pre-

Louisiana: A Developmental Case Study," *Bulletin of the Texas Archaeological Society*, Vol. 45 (1974), 85.
24. Shenkel and Gibson, "Big Oak Island," 183, 184.

mound surface at the Lafayette Site, excavations revealed small vertical postmolds, some of which were arranged to form an arc. If these were part of the outline of a circular structure, it would have measured about 30 feet in diameter. Excavations at Little Oak Island, Orleans Parish, revealed a compact humic lens overlying "a solid cemented calcareous mass of shell." After the humus was removed, numerous postmolds about 3 to 4 inches in diameter became apparent as dark, humus-filled holes in the shell matrix. The postmolds, which numbered about 160, extended along the crest of the site for a distance of about 60 feet. Unfortunately, they were not distributed in any recognizable pattern, and the report theorizes that some of the postmolds may represent replacement poles. In the postmold area, along the crest were 8,647 potsherds and bone and stone artifacts indicative of a high-activity area. The report suggests, from ethnographic analogy, that the postmolds at Little Oak Island could represent wall posts and roof supports for long, shedlike habitations comparable to those built by the Yanomamo Indians in northern South America.[25]

With the data presently on hand, we can say little about the arrangement of buildings or their manner of construction at Tchefuncte Culture sites. This is not to say that we will never know what sort of structures these people built. Because of its unique deltaic history, Louisiana has more extensive peat deposits than any other state along the Gulf of Mexico. The excellent preservative properties of these peat deposits have been documented at two sites containing Tchefuncte Culture materials, and other comparable sites in the region await scientific investigation.[26]

It has generally been assumed that Tchefuncte sites sometimes comprised low domed earthen mounds along with the middens.[27] This assumption, however, has been based upon very imprecise interpre-

25. Ford and Quimby, The Tchefuncte Culture; Shenkel and Holley, "A Tchefuncte House," 232.
26. James M. Coleman and William G. Smith, "Late Recent Rise of Sea Level," Geological Society of American Bulletin, Vol. 75 (1964), 833–40; Neuman, Archaeological Investigations at the Morton Shell Mound; Fiser, "The Treasure of Bayou Jasmine."
27. Ford and Quimby, The Tchefuncte Culture; Gibson, "Russell Landing"; Haag, Louisiana in North American Prehistory; Robert W. Neuman, An Archaeological Assessment of Coastal Louisiana, Mélanges No. 11 (Baton Rouge, 1977).

tations of artifactual associations. Tchefuncte sherds at the Lake Louis Site, Catahoula Parish, were not in direct association with the human interments. Rather, they came from the mound fill. The Tchefunte sherds from the Lafayette Site, Saint Martin Parish, were retrieved from the mound fill and the premound floor. At the Booth Landing Site, Catahoula Parish, the Tchefuncte sherds were obtained from the midden, not the mound nearby. At the multicomponent Bayou Rouge mound site, Saint Landry Parish, the Tchefuncte sherds were collected from the surface, in no way warranting their assignment to the mounds there. The associated proveniences reported for Tchefuncte ceramics at multicomponent mound sites in east-central Louisiana provide no data to validate assigning those mounds to the Tchefuncte Culture. And finally, for Tchefuncte-related Tchula period sites in the Yazoo Basin, Mississippi, some of which have small domed mounds, Philip Phillips states that "in no case has the association been established even by surface correlations, let alone excavation." In sum then, the evidence to support the theory that the Tchefuncte Culture Indians were mound builders is most vague.[28]

In summation then, we find that the Tchefuncte Culture existed in Louisiana from 500 B.C. until A.D. 300. Most of the sites—sixty of which are recorded in Louisiana State University files—are located in the coastal zone, but others extend into south-central Louisiana and the alluvial valley. This is the earliest culture for which we have physical data on human morphology, mortuary practices, subsistence patterns, and the manufacture of pottery. The published record indicates widely scattered camps of seminomadic hunters and gatherers, while the seeds of the squash and bottle gourd found at one site suggest horticultural beginnings.

It might be pointed out, however, that the focus of attention on Tchefuncte Culture has blurred much of the regional picture. Sixty or even a hundred Tchefuncte sites probably do not represent the total human population living in Louisiana during the period. Yet not a single word has been published regarding contemporary cultures. It is impossible not to wonder what happened to the large population that

28. Ford and Quimby, The Tchefuncte Culture, 22; Moore, "Antiquities of the Ouachita"; Gibson, "Russell Landing"; Phillips, An Archaeological Survey of the Lower Yazoo Basin, 965.

survived the decline of the Poverty Point Culture. Are there no archaeological manifestations of these people? Undoubtedly, there are more Tchefuncte sites to be recorded, but just as assuredly there are as many or more sites of Tchefuncte contemporaries that remain to be studied and defined. When this has been accomplished we will have a more factual picture of Louisiana's inhabitants between 500 B.C. and about A.D. 200.

VII Marksville Culture

During the nineteenth and early twentieth centuries, the popular fantasies about the Mound Builders, who had built magnificent earthworks in the eastern United States, were gradually unraveled. Robert Silverberg has so superbly related the tale of discovery that it would not be improved upon here and need not be recounted.[1] The Marksville Culture, however, is very much a part of that story, for most of what we know about Marksville concerns earthen tumuli and their funerary contents.

A good deal of the evidence concerning this culture originates from archaeological explorations at a site in the city of Marksville, Avoyelles Parish (Pl. 24). The site and a museum interpretative center have been a Louisiana state park since the 1930s. Recently, Edwin A. Toth has carefully compiled the history of the Marksville Site and skillfully analyzed its archaeological data. He found that the first known description of the site was a newspaper account published in 1851 that attributed the earthworks to the DeSoto expedition. This myth proliferated and prevailed right up into the present century. The first scientific exploration of the site was under the auspices of the Smithsonian Institution during the 1926 Red River Valley survey conducted by Gerard Fowke. As mentioned previously, Fowke spent three months in the area, during which time he tested five mounds and composed a detailed map of the Marksville Site and other nearby earthworks.[2] He described the site in detail.

1. Robert Silverberg, *Mound Builders of Ancient America* (Greenwich, Conn., 1968).
2. Toth, *Archaeology and Ceramics of the Marksville Site*; Fowke, "Archaeological Work in Louisiana"; Fowke, "Archaeological Investigations—II."

PLATE 24

Aerial view of the Marksville Site and the surrounding environs. (Photo by Dache Reeves, USAF, ca. 1935.)

The largest and most complicated group of ancient remains in the State is located from a mile to 2 miles eastwardly from Marksville. . . . They reach for more than a mile along Old River. . . . The enclosures or embankments, the lodge sites, and some of the mounds are on a bluff, other mounds are on ground subject of floods. . . . The most conspicuous feature of the group is the large enclosure . . . on the farms of Greenhouse, Schaub and DuPre. It forms an irregular curve, the ends resting on the bayou bluff. . . . Its total length is almost 3,000 feet; the height ranges from less than 3 to nearly 7 feet for most of its length, but there is a space of more than 400 feet at the northern end where it is almost obliterated by cultivation. The breadth increases and extends proportionately. These variations raise a question as to whether the work was ever fully completed to the extent that it was planned. There are two openings or passageways toward the south and one toward the west; no doubt there was also one toward the north. South of the west opening is an extension of the inner side of the embankment, continuous with it, which forms a platform 30 feet across; it appears as if intended for the foundation of a building. . . . An outside moat . . . now filled by wash and decayed vegetation until it is swampy for most of its length, borders the outside of the wall for its entire extent.[3]

Two of the mounds Fowke tested yielded artifactual material diagnostic of the Marksville Culture. The first one, Mound 4, located within the space encircled by the earthen enclosure, measured 20 feet high and had a basal diameter of 100 feet. Into this domed mound Fowke excavated a trench 25 feet wide and 60 feet long. From these excavations he found that the mound was constructed in two stages, both of which contained human interments and artifacts. Characteristically, the bone was very poorly preserved, but teeth and surviving bone parts aided in identifying the remains of children and adults buried in the mound. Most of the interments were multiple secondary burials in pits lined and covered with wood or bark matting. In one instance an adult was found lying between two small logs. Some of the burial pits were basin-shaped, 3 feet deep and about 5 feet in diameter. Two pits were saucer-shaped, 6 inches deep and about 4 feet in diameter. In another instance the remains of six or more skeletons were found lying on the surface of the first construction stage and associated with postmolds, which led Fowke to surmise that some sort of protective shelter had been erected over the bodies. In all, seventeen human burials were excavated.

The artifacts Fowke retrieved from Mound 4 included twenty clay vessels of various shapes, two clay pipes, and one sandstone pipe. Of cardinal interest, "among the remains was one decorated pot 2 inches high containing minute dessicated fragments of corn, squash, and perhaps other forms of food. A leaf, apparently a corn blade, had been placed over the top. Earth settling into the vase and hardening had preserved the form of these substances." This statement is the only extant evidence for crop cultivation by the Marksville Culture; unfortunately a search for these botanical specimens, or casts of them in the Smithsonian Institution, failed to reveal their whereabouts. The

3. Fowke, "Archaeological Investigations—II," 411–12.

small vessel said to have contained the specimens is illustrated by Toth. In 1930 the Smithsonian anthropologist John R. Swanton visited the Marksville Site while conducting his study of Louisiana Indian languages. From Fowke's open trenches at Mound 4 he "extracted portions of two decorated vessels and a number of potsherds."[4]

The second tumulus, designated Mound 8, was originally about 16 feet high and had a basal diameter of 80 feet (Pl. 25). Fowke began a trench 15 feet wide at the mound edge and expanded it to 20 feet as he reached the mound center. The mound fill, which resembled the subsoil, exhibited "irregular stratification as if each load has been thrown or scattered instead of being dumped in a pile." Within the fill were occasional sherds, stone artifacts, and particularly noteworthy, fragments of basketry. "They were made of very thin strips of cane or of white oak one-fourth of an inch wide, laid close together side by side with interwoven cross strips an inch apart. Usually the cross strips lay at a right angle to the others, though some were placed bias. They were thoroughly carbonized and fell apart with the dirt."[5] At various places in the central region of the mound Fowke exposed seven subsurface pits, some of which contained extended or secondary burials and pottery. Two pits were about six feet long. In one of these were the remains of a child and a concentration of several hundred periwinkle or snail shell fragments. There was no trace of bone in the second pit, but it contained two pottery vessels. Of the five circular pits, two contained one pottery vessel each, one other contained fragments of burned bone, perhaps human, and the remaining two contained no trace of bone in their fill. Fowke gave the dimensions of only one of the circular pits: 2 feet in diameter. He noted that all of the pits were lined with matting made of bark or wood and, furthermore, that a comparable matting covered the ground surface around the mound center. It should be noted that, although all of the subsurface pits were assumed to contain human burials, only one pit contained identifiable bones and one

4. *Ibid.*, 420–21; George Metcalf, personal communication to the author, October 23, 1969; Toth, *Archaeology and Ceramics of the Marksville Site,* 21, fig. 27d; John R. Swanton, "Indian Language Studies in Louisiana," *Explorations and Field-Work of the Smithsonian Institution in 1930* (Washington, D.C., 1931), 195–200.
5. Fowke, "Archaeological Investigations—II," 423.

PLATE 25

Remnant of Mound 8 excavated by Gerard Fowke at Marksville in
Avoyelles Parish, 1933.

other pit contained unidentified burned bone fragments. The remaining five pits were void of any bone remains. As we shall see, except for
their ceramic contents, Mound 4 and 8 have very little in common.

It is quite probable that Fowke, whose previous explorations were
in Ohio, recognized the similarity between the vessels from Mounds
4 and 8 and specimens from Hopewell Culture sites in Ohio. Nevertheless, Frank Maryl Setzler, also of the Smithsonian Institution, was
the first archaeologist to remark upon this relationship in a publication. Of the specimens from Mounds 4 and 8 he wrote, "It is significant that pottery vessels similar to a type recognized in the upper or
northern Mississippi Valley as belonging to the Hopewell Indian culture have been found in the east-central part of Louisiana, near Marksville." He detailed the ceramic similarities again in another publication

that same year.[6] It was, at least in part, because of this striking resemblance between the Marksville and Hopewell vessels that important subsequent developments took place in Marksville and at the Crooks Site in LaSalle Parish. Therefore, it is well to understand, at least generally, what Hopewell Culture was.

The culture was named for a site in the Scioto River Valley, near Chillicothe, Ohio. On the farm of Captain M. C. Hopewell there was a rectangular earthen enclosure encompassing 111 acres, within which there were about 30 earthworks. It has been estimated that no less than 3,000,000 cubic feet of dirt was required for these constructions. Excavations conducted there during the nineteenth century yielded an unparalleled array of exquisite artifacts from the burial mounds. These artifacts, along with others from sites in the region, became the diagnostic specimens of what came to be called the Hopewell Culture. By itself the Hopewell Site provided an artifact inventory that illustrates the culture's lavishness. The list includes cloth or woven fabric, cordage, netting, leather, basketry, pottery, fossils, marine shell, pearls; tortoise shell pendants, beads, disks, gorgets, and containers; copper axes, celts, adzes, tubes, and beads, and terra-cotta human and animal effigies; awls, needles, earspools, bracelets, anklets, breastplates, head plates, copper-covered teeth, bone, antler, wood, and clay objects, and silver and silver-coated objects; worked animal and human jaws, teeth, and long bones; various colored earth pigments, bark matting, and stone points; blades, axes, adzes, cores, abraders, rings, tablets, atlatl weights, pendants, disks, effigies, and pipes made from granite, argillite, meteoric iron, quartz crystals, obsidian, sandstone, hematite, slate, mica, galena, and chlorite. Professor James B. Griffin of the University of Michigan, who studied the Hopewell Culture more closely than any other archaeologist, places its existence between 200 B.C. and A.D. 400. Its two major centers of development were in Ohio and Illinois, and from these the culture expanded north to Ontario, Canada, south to the Gulf of Mexico, east to the Atlantic, and west into the Dakotas. This diffusion was not accomplished by the migration of large

6. Frank M. Setzler, "Pottery of the Hopewell Type from Louisiana," *Proceedings of the United States National Museum*, Vol. 82 (Washington, D.C., 1933), 1; Frank M. Setzler, "Hopewell Type Pottery from Louisiana," *Journal of the Washington Academy of Sciences*, Vol. 23 (1933), No. 3, pp. 149–53.

populations, but by traveling traders, missionaries of a sort, who inspired local peoples to embrace the "High Church," so to speak. "The art, the procurement of exotic raw materials, the earthwork complex, and the elaborate burial procedures were all a part of a religious ceremonialism centered on a propitiation of the spirit world which affected the hunting, trading, warfare, games, health, death, and, in fact, every phase of the existence of these people."[7]

It was, to a certain extent, because of its recognized affinity with the Hopewell Culture that the city council of Marksville acquired Enclosure A in June, 1933, for development into a park. The council and officials of the Emergency Relief Administration then requested that personnel from the Smithsonian Institution be sent to Marksville to supervise the park development. Frank Setzler was the obvious choice, and he arrived in August, 1933. He was assisted by James A. Ford, then an undergraduate at Louisiana State University. Between August 22 and December 1, 1933, with a crew of a hundred men, Setzler and Ford conducted excavations into Mounds 4, 5, and 6 and two nonmound village areas within Enclosure A. Unfortunately, no final detailed report of these investigations was ever published. Nevertheless, much can be gleaned from several general accounts by Setzler and Ford. Happily, there are also ninety-five annotated negatives of the 1933 excavations as well as Toth's comprehensive research.[8]

7. Warren K. Moorehead, "The Hopewell Mound Group of Ohio," *Field Museum of Natural History, Anthropological Series*, Vol. 6, No. 5 (Chicago, 1922), 73–184; Henry Clyde Shetrone, *Explorations of the Hopewell Group of Prehistoric Earthworks*, Ohio Archaeological and Historical Publications, Vol. 35 (Columbus, 1927); Joseph R. Caldwell and Robert L. Hall (eds.), *Hopewellian Studies*, Illinois State Museum Scientific Papers, Vol. 12 (Springfield, 1964); Robert W. Neuman, *The Sonota Complex and Associated Sites on the Northern Great Plains*, Nebraska State Historical Society Publications in Anthropology, No. 6 (Lincoln, 1975); James B. Griffin, "Eastern North American Archaeology: A Summary," *Science*, Vol. 156 (1967), No. 3772, p. 184.
8. Setzler, "Hopewell Type Pottery from Louisiana"; Setzler, "Pottery of the Hopewell Type from Louisiana"; Frank M. Setzler, "A Phase of Hopewell Mound Builders in Louisiana," *Explorations and Field-Work of the Smithsonian Institution in 1933* (Washington, D.C., 1934), 38–40; Frank M. Setzler, "Archaeological Perspectives in the Northern Mississippi Valley," in *Essays in Historical Anthropology of North America: Publications in Honor of J. R. Swanton, Smithsonian Miscellaneous Collections*, Vol. 100 (Washington, D.C., 1940), 253–90; Frank M. Setzler, "Archaeological Explorations in the United States, 1930–1942," *Acta Americana*, Vol. 1 (1943), No. 2, pp. 206–20; James A. Ford, "Mound Builders Were Pit Dwellers," *El Palacio*, Vol. 36 (1934), 74–75; James A. Ford, "Out-

The 1933 excavations at Marksville made it clear that Fowke had barely touched upon a large burial pit that had been dug into the first construction stage or clay platform of Mound 4. An undetermined number of human burials were placed in the pit (although traces of twelve are reported). Evidence of log uprights along the pit walls and roof rafters covered with cane and clay indicates that the pit was sheltered, but the roof subsequently collapsed under the weight of the second construction stage. Several other human burials were said to be located in the clay mantle topping the primary construction stage. The excavations into Mound 4 in 1933 also yielded thirteen Marksville-type vessels, numerous sherds, "two platform pipes, fifteen projectile points, three stone knives, a quartz crystal, a copper fragment and a piece of worked shell."[9] After the excavations, the mound was restored to its original dimensions (Pl. 26 and 27).

Little can be said about the excavations into Mound 5; even photographs are lacking. Ford and Willey described it as about 3 feet high and 40 feet in diameter. Setzler and Ford found no burials in this mound. Toth examined a small collection of sherds cataloged as coming from Mound 5, and he felt that "the pottery is classic Marksville, thus demonstrating, at the minimum, that the mound was constructed of Marksville midden."[10]

The excavation data on hand from Mound 6, a large truncated structure 13 feet in height, consists almost entirely of eleven photographs with brief notations. They show wooden stakes placed at 5-foot intervals, marking the location of a 20-foot-wide trench extending up the sides and across the top of the mound. Several other photographs illustrate excavations on the east and west sides extending to a depth of about 5 feet and across the summit to a depth of "a few feet below the surface." One photograph is of Ford kneeling in a trench about 3 feet deep on the mound summit, excavating the fill from a postmold.

line of Louisiana and Mississippi Pottery Horizons," *Louisiana Conservation Review*, Vol. 4 (1935), No. 6, pp. 33–38; Ford, "An Introduction to Louisiana Archaeology"; Ford, *Analysis of Indian Village Site Collections from Louisiana and Mississippi*; Toth, *Archaeology and Ceramics of the Marksville Site*.

9. Ford and Willey, *Crooks Site*, 23; Toth, *Archaeology and Ceramics of the Marksville Site*, 25.

10. Ford and Willey, *Crooks Site*; Toth, *Archaeology and Ceramics of the Marksville Site*, 28.

PLATE 26

Bark and cane matting imprints of the covering over burials in Mound 4 at the Marksville Site, Avoyelles Parish, 1933.

Although it is quite evident that the excavations were extensive, the artifactual yield was sparse. Toth, who examined the collection from Mound 6, lists only thirteen decorated sherds—all of Marksville varieties—as well as a stone point, a scraper, and one hammerstone.[11] Since all were from the mound fill, they contribute little toward a culture assignment for Mound 6. Obviously, the data only indicate that the mound was built during Marksville times or later (Pl. 28).

The excavations in the village area consisted of trenches, none of which exceeded fifteen inches in depth. The single photograph of these excavations shows two groups of men digging at opposite ends of a grid marked by wooden stakes. Artifact, catalog, and provenience data indicate that there were 5 trenches and that the 317 sherds excavated

11. Toth, *Archaeology and Ceramics of the Marksville Site.*

PLATE 27

Workers restoring Mound 4 after excavation at the Marksville Site, Avoyelles Parish, 1933.

were Marksville and a minority of later types. Although Toth analyzed the sherd collection from the village excavations, the only published record of the nonceramic inventory from surface collections in the village area is a general statement that "the surface of the village site was strewn with incised decorated potsherds, fragments of platform pipes, flint knife blades, crudely chipped projectile points and a crystal quartz bannerstone fragment." A photograph accompanying the article illustrates a small number of these ceramic and stone artifacts.[12]

One of the most intriguing features exposed during the 1933 explorations was the remains of a rectangular, semisubterranean structure designated House A. Although the function of this building is a matter of conjecture, it seems highly improbable that it was used as a

12. *Ibid.*; Setzler, "A Phase of Hopewell Mound Builders in Louisiana," 38, fig. 45.

PLATE 28

Progress photograph of 20-foot trench into Mound 6 at the Marksville
Site, Avoyelles Parish, 1933.

house. It measured 20 feet by 25 feet and had postmolds extending
down each side of the long axis. Occupying its center was a rectangular pit, 8 feet by 15 feet, which extended to a depth of 6 feet below
the floor surface. There was a postmold in each corner of this pit. Photographs show cane impressions and burnt log fragments on the pit
floor. On the house floor itself were the remains of a hearth and a cache
pit. Potsherd varieties from House A excavations indicate that the
structure "was possibly used at or until a time that postdates the construction of the burial mounds at the site."[13] To this day nothing comparable to this structure has been reported from any archaeological site

13. Ford, "Mound Builders Were Pit Dwellers"; Ford, *Analysis of Indian Village
 Site Collections from Louisiana and Mississippi*; Setzler, "A Phase of Hope-
 well Mound Builders in Louisiana"; Toth, *Archaeology and Ceramics of the
 Marksville Site*, 72.

affiliated with the Marksville Culture in the southeast region or with Hopewell manifestations anywhere in the eastern United States.

The final excavation of the 1933 project was a cross trench, of unstated dimensions located on a slight rise near Mound 6. Forty-eight potsherds are the only artifacts reported, and they are indicative of a Marksville occupation.[14]

In 1938 the LSU–WPA archaeological program was conducting investigations in Avoyelles Parish. In order to confirm the suspected succession of prehistoric cultures, the Greenhouse Site was selected for excavation. This site was located on the bottomland below the bluff on which the Marksville Site lay. It was, therefore, determined that if the Greenhouse Site were flooded, the crews would be sent to work at Marksville. Just as Fowke and Walker had predicted, the Greenhouse Site was inundated in the spring of 1939. Excavations had to be abandoned temporarily, and the work crews were detailed to go up onto the bluff to the Marksville Site. Robert S. Neitzel and Edwin B. Doran, Jr., were in charge of these investigations, and their goal was to obtain stratigraphic information relative to the occupation sequence at Marksville. Accordingly, 1,350 feet of trenching, 5 feet wide, was excavated to a depth of 15 inches, and an additional 320 feet of trenching, 10 feet wide, was dug to a depth of about 8 inches. These excavations, which were next to Mound 2 and touched upon three of its sides, yielded 6,640 sherds, 29 stone projectile points, 10 scrapers, 6 drills, 3 hammerstones, 1 plummet, and 74 worked stone fragments. In general, the ceramic sequence, as it was known from elsewhere at the Marksville Site, and its stratigraphic data accord well with what has been found subsequently at other regional sites. The trenching also revealed the rather nebulous remains of what is called House B. This structure was manifested by a rectangular pit, 10 feet by 8 feet (depth unstated) with an uneven floor and a central fire pit. Only two postmolds were observed, and a portion of an undecorated Marksville vessel was exposed just above the house floor."[15]

14. Toth, *Archaeology and Ceramics of the Marksville Site.*
15. Fowke, "Archaeological Investigations—II"; Walker, "A Reconnaissance of Northern Louisiana Mounds"; G. S. Vescelius, "Mound 2 at Marksville," *American Antiquity*, Vol. 22 (1957), No. 4, pp. 416–20; Toth, *Archaeology and Ceramics of the Marksville Site.*

About 350 feet southeast of Mound 2 was a saucer-shaped depression 65 feet in diameter. Fowke labeled this feature and similar ones in the vicinity "Lodge Sites," but when Neitzel and Doran trenched this one, they found no sign of structure or habitation. There were no fire pits, postmolds, or wall trenches, and even the delineation of the hypothesized house floor and its walls were extremely vague. Of the sherds found in the fill, only one was diagnostic, and its affinity was with a post-Marksville period. The identification and cultural assignation of this so-called lodge site remains doubtful.

Another saucer-shaped depression, designated Lodge Site 6 by Fowke, was excavated in 1970 by Thomas A. Ryan, then a graduate student at Louisiana State University. Located about 800 feet north-northwest of Mound 6, it measured about 55 feet in diameter. At the center of this depression was a semisubterranean pit whose floor was about 8 inches below the surrounding ground surface. The pit outlines, although very indefinite, appeared rectangular, enclosing an area of about 325 square feet. Extending north from the pit floor was a semisubterranean depression that Ryan interpreted as an entryway. Centrally located in Lodge Site 6 was a circular pit about 11 feet in diameter and 7 feet deep. The bottom of this pit was covered with 2 inches of charcoal, which was mantled with subsequent deposits of silt that eventually eroded into and filled the pit. Intermittent trenches formed an arc along the eastern rim of the saucer. They may have functioned as a method of wall construction, but they were not in association with postmolds. Ryan speculates that Houses A and B and Lodge Site 6 represent the remains of nonsecular structures, perhaps sweat houses.[16] However, since no diagnostic artifacts were retrieved from Lodge Site 6, its chronological association with Houses A and B or even with the Marksville Culture has yet to be demonstrated.

Although many of the details are not recoverable, the published record of archaeological excavation at the Marksville Site clearly illustrates a Hopewellian introduction into the area. The same can be said for Mound 8 outside of Enclosure A. The development, content, and

16. Fowke, "Archaeological Investigations—II"; Vescelius, "Mound 2 at Marksville"; Thomas M. Ryan, "Semisubterranean Structures and Their Spatial Distribution at the Marksville Site (16AV-1)," *Proceedings of the 31st Southeastern Archaeological Conference*, Bulletin No. 18 (1975), 215–25.

structure of Mounds 2, 5, and 6 still await examination. As for Mound 3, or the remnant thereof, and the enclosure itself, their cultural history has not even been touched upon.

The record confirms that it was part of the LSU–WPA strategy to commence field activities at the Greenhouse Site in order to investigate the Troyville–Coles Creek Culture. When the Greenhouse excavations were flooded, it was logical to detour the investigations to the Marksville Site on the bluff nearby. Originally, however, it was the Crooks Site that had been selected for excavations to elucidate aspects of the Marksville Culture. The two domed earthen tumuli of the Crooks Site were located on the Mississippi River floodplain about four miles from Archie in LaSalle Parish. The large mound was being used as a cattle refuge during the usual spring inundations of the area. Therefore, in order to obtain permission to excavate, the archaeologists had to agree to restore the mound when their investigations were completed. These excavations, directed by William T. Mulloy and Arden R. King with a 45-man crew, began in October, 1938, and continued into April, 1939.

Mound A, the larger tumulus, measured 85 feet in diameter and 17 feet in height (Pl. 29). Its first construction stage, which covered a human burial bundle, consisted of a flat-topped, steep-sided rectangular earthen platform, measuring 20 feet by 40 feet, with a height of about 2 feet. Several basin-shaped and straight-sided pits, containing ash and exhibiting burnt walls, had been dug into the top of the platform. After a period of time, at least long enough for the platform to erode and begin to fill its encircling borrow pits, 168 primary flexed and secondary human burials were placed on top of the platform and then covered with a thin lens of dirt. Over these burials but concentrated toward the platform center in an area 30 feet in diameter, 214 primary flexed and secondary human burials were added. These burials were, in turn, mantled with dirt that formed the primary mound. Additional human burials were found in this stratum. Ford and Willey reported finding 220 burials there in shallow pits. They were primary, extended or flexed, and secondary interments. Upon completion, the primary mound measured about 10 feet high and had a basal diameter of 46 feet. Also exposed in the primary mantle were the remains of two postmolds, one near the mound apex and another down into the northwest

PLATE 29

Progress photograph of excavation into Mound A at the Crooks Site,
LaSalle Parish, January 31, 1939.

slope. On top of the primary mantle were the remains of fifteen logs
lying parallel to each other and extending up the east slope of the
mound. Ford and Willey speculated that these were part of a stepped
construction or ramp.[17]

After another interval of time, during which the surface of the primary mound was exposed to the elements and partially eroded, a secondary mantle of dirt was added, and it also showed two strata. The
inner stratum contained single human interments placed in small pits.
To the south, near the apex, however, the Indians dug a pit measuring
about 14 feet by 7 feet by 2 feet, the bottom of which was lined with
what appear to be four mats about 6 feet in diameter.[18] Three human

17. Ford and Willey, *Crooks Site.*
18. *Ibid.*

interments were placed in the pit, after which they were sealed over and the pit filled with dirt. Altogether 503 extended and flexed primary and secondary human burials were recorded in this stratum. The mound was then capped with a final stratum in which could be seen fragments of baskets used to haul the earth fill for the mound construction. Subsequently, erosion took its course and mound fill washed down the slopes. Into this washed fill were deposited one primary flexed and two secondary human burials.

All of the human skeletal remains in Mound A were in a very poor state of preservation. No physical anthropological measurements were possible, and quite often even the burial position was not discernible. Nevertheless, certain trends were apparent. Primary flexed burials were the most common; they were followed in order of frequency by "isolated skull, indeterminate, bundle, semiflexed, partially disarticulated and extended."[19] The tightly flexed primary burials appeared to have been wrapped in some type of shroud before interment, and most of them were lying on their sides. The semiflexed burials were lying on their sides or on their backs with legs to the side. All extended burials were supine. About 60 percent of the primary burials were positioned with their heads toward the mound center. The remainder were arranged with their heads toward the cardinal directions.

In secondary bundle burials the long bones and crania appeared to have been tightly wrapped in a hide or vegetal fiber container. Since the isolated skulls were always accompanied by a mandible in the proper anatomical position, it is likely that these were in flesh at their time of interment. These skulls were characteristically placed near the head or pelvis of a primary burial.

Obviously, poor bone preservation hindered age determination, but it was ascertained that the majority of the individuals were adults. Others identified as to age included four infants, seventeen children and twenty-four juveniles. In terms of sex, skull fragments indicated only that adults of both sexes were represented. Accompanying a few human interments in the secondary mantle of Mound A were three dog burials. The dogs—small animals—were lying on their sides at the feet of the human burials.[20]

19. *Ibid.*, 36.
20. *Ibid.*

Mound B at the Crooks Site was a small earthen structure located 110 feet south of Mound A. It was ovoid in plan and measured about 50 feet down the long axis and was 2 feet high. Treasure hunters had dug a large hole down into its center. The archaeological excavations revealed that Mound B was a single-stage structure, originally rectangular in outline with dirt ramps extending out from the northern, western, and possibly eastern corners. Thirteen adult human interments in primary flexed and secondary burial patterns were found in the mound fill. Most of the burials were primary flexed, but one was a secondary bundle burial, another was an isolated skull, and a third was too poorly preserved to determine its pattern. Inasmuch as Mound B partially covers a borrow pit that supplied the dirt fill for Mound A, it is reasonable to assume that Mound B was a later construction. The report speculated further that "during the later part of Mound A construction, Mound B was utilized as a site for a mortuary building."[21]

A fundamental trait of the Marksville Culture is the deposition of artifacts with the human remains. At the Crooks Site it was not always determinable which burial or burials the artifacts were originally meant to accompany. Nevertheless, 169 of the burials (16.1 percent) were found in association with funerary offerings of more than 200 artifacts. Among the various types of burials, the flexed were most commonly associated with offerings. Indeterminate and bundle burials were the next most likely to be found with artifacts, followed, in order, by isolated skulls, semiflexed, and partially articulated burials. No artifacts were attributable to the primary extended interments. There did not appear to be any trend to deposit specific types of artifacts with a particular burial pattern.

The Crooks Site yielded more artifacts than any other Marksville Culture burial mound thus far excavated in the Lower Alluvial Valley. Mounds A and B contained over 12,700 Marksville Culture pottery sherds, including 84 restorable vessels. There is nothing comparable in the published record of Louisiana archaeology. Ford and Willey, Phillips, and Toth have provided detailed descriptions of the pottery types, which need not be repeated here.[22] Broadly speaking, the pottery was manufactured by the coiling method, and the clay was

21. Ibid., 131.
22. Ibid.; Phillips, An Archaeological Survey of the Lower Yazoo Basin; Toth, "Early Marksville Phases in the Lower Mississippi Valley."

tempered with clay particles and smaller amounts of sand and grit. There were hemispherical pots with a constricted neck and an everted rim, pots with straight to constricted to slightly convex sides, and cambered rims. Straight-sided beakers, and bowls that were shallow to deep with convex, flat, or podal bases were also found. The vessels were of various sizes and at least one of them was reported to have a one- to two-gallon capacity.[23] Some vessels were plain; others were decorated on their exterior surfaces with combinations of dentate, rocker-stamped, incised, or trailed lines, notches, punctations or cord impressions. The decorative motifs are curvilinear and/or rectilinear patterns or zoomorphic motifs. The exterior of a minority of the vessels is colored with a red pigment, presumably hematite, but most of the vessels are buff to brown or gray and black (Pls. 30, 31, 32, 33).

In addition to ceramics, more than 307 chipped-stone artifacts were found either scattered in the mounds or associated with the human interments. Of this number, 130 were stemmed projectile points with corner and/or side notches. A quarter of these were associated with burials. There were also 25 scrapers, 19 celts, 6 drills, 5 hammerstones, 2 chipped and polished objects (probably celts), and 3 flake tools that had evidently been used (Pl. 34). Of 61 ground-stone artifacts found, 21 accompanied burials in Mound A, and the remainder were scattered throughout Mounds A and B. Among these specimens were 10 boatstones or atlatl weights, "manufactured of argillaceous sandstone, limonite, pumice, yellow ochre, leopardite and chalk."[24] Two of these objects were near skulls of flexed skeletons; one was near the thorax of another flexed skeleton; and one was found near the feet of still another flexed skeleton. Two other boatstones were located near the pelvic region of a partially articulated burial and to the side of a semiflexed burial. The remaining specimens of this group were found in the fill of Mounds A and B. Other ground-stone objects included a small hollowed cone (Pl. 33, g), a limonite plummet, 3 ring-shaped beads, 7 celts, 20 hammerstones, 3 slabs of unknown purpose, and 4 pendants of siltstone, quartz, and bituminous shale. The quartz specimens were associated with a bundle burial in Mound A, and the shale

23. Toth, "Early Marksville Phases in the Lower Mississippi Valley."
24. Ford and Willey, *Crooks Site*, 106.

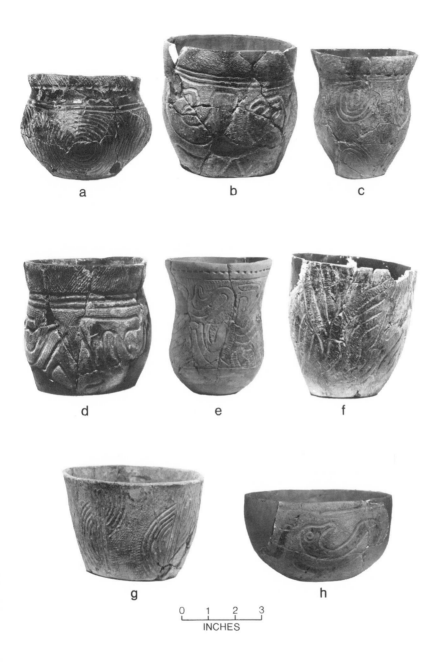

a   b   c

d   e   f

g   h

0   1   2   3
INCHES

PLATE 30

Ceramic vessels of the Marksville Culture.

a

b

c

d

e

f

PLATE 31

Ceramic vessels of the Marksville Culture.

0   1   2   3
INCHES

a

b

c

d

e

f

PLATE 32

Ceramic artifacts of the Marksville Culture: *a–d,* vessels; *e–f,* platform
pipes.

PLATE 33

Artifacts of the Marksville Culture: *a–f*, ceramic vessels; *g–h*, problematical stone objects; *i*, ceramic figurine.

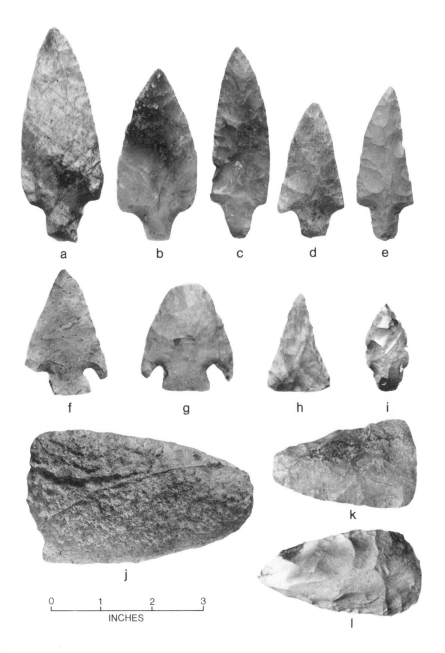

a   b   c   d   e

f   g   h   i

j   k   l

0   1   2   3

INCHES

PLATE 34

Stone artifacts of the Marksville Culture: *a–g*, projectile points; *h–i*, knives; *j–l*, choppers.

specimen was associated with a flexed burial in the same mound. The latter burial was also accompanied by a small sandstone slab with a human face fine-line engraved on one surface. Three other effigies, all of bituminous shale, resembled grasshoppers. The most complete and ornate specimen "was found with the skull of a burial on top of the burial platform [Mound] A."[25] The other two are from the fill in the same mound (Pl. 35). A rectangular, water-smoothed pebble associated with a flexed burial in Mound B was described as having a rectangle scored into one face at one end. Five lines radiate across the top of the pebble and extend down onto the face and sides at the same end. Three amorphous limonite objects, which seem to have been smoothed, were also found with flexed burials in Mound A.

Among Hopewellian mortuary artifacts, platform pipes are second only to pottery in importance.[26] We have already noted the ones from the Marksville Site. Five clay platform pipes and the bowl section of a siltstone one were recovered from Mounds A and B at the Crooks Site. Resting on the platform of one of the clay pipes from Mound A was an effigy of a four-legged animal with a short tail and small ears positioned to face the smoker (Pl. 32, *f*).

Another clay effigy not part of a pipe was found in Mound A (Pl. 33, *i*). It was a small, hollow, stylized human head. "The top, back and sides of the head are incised with fine, closely spaced lines simulating hair. A long prominent nose, which forms an unbroken line with the forehead, eyes made by incised ovals, and a part of the mouth are all that remain of the face. The lower facial portion and the body of the figure had been broken away and were not recovered."[27]

The only other ceramic specimens retrieved from excavations at Crooks were forty-one baked-clay objects of the sort that first appeared in Louisiana with the Poverty Point Culture. Along with certain point types, drills, scrapers, and hammerstones, these objects persist, but there are fewer of them and they display less variety. Two of the specimens, one from each mound, are biconical, and two others, from Mound A and a borrow pit nearby, are of the finger-squeezed type.

25. *Ibid.*, 114.
26. Toth, "Early Marksville Phases in the Lower Mississippi Valley."
27. Ford and Willey, *Crooks Site*, 119.

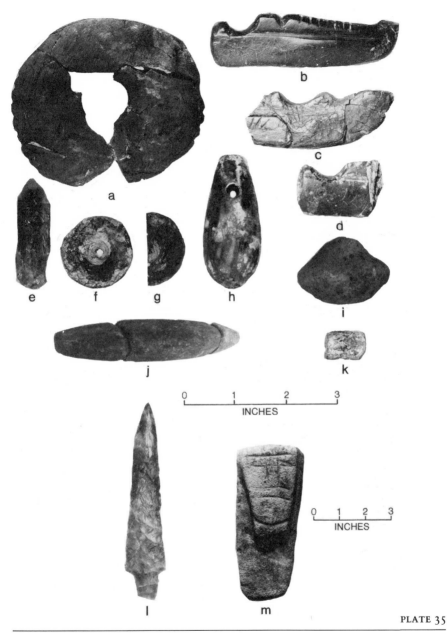

PLATE 35

Artifacts of the Marksville Culture: *a–d*, bituminous shale ornaments; *e*, quartz crystal ornament; *f–g*, copper ear spool; *h*, stone plummet; *i*, baked-clay object; *j*, stone atlatl weight; *k*, galena bead; *l*, stone point; *m*, sandstone figurine.

The remaining specimens are amorphous. None of the baked-clay objects was in direct association with the human interments.

As was to be expected, bone artifacts were rare. However, two awls made from deer ulnae and five fishhooks were found in Mound A. One of the awls was associated with the skull of a disarticulated human burial, and four of the hooks were funerary accompaniments with other human burials. The remaining awl and fishhook were retrieved from the mound fill.

Pearl and shell objects were also found in Mound A. Five perforated pearls were in association with a copper ear spool and a human skull. The fifty-seven shell beads, about 2 millimeters in diameter, were from the thorax region of a human burial. Other shell objects included a columella pendant, pointed at one end and rounded and perforated for suspension at the opposite end. Twenty-three caches of opened freshwater mussel shells were found on top of or beside human interments, and five similar deposits were exposed in the mound fill.

Five ear spools were among the copper artifacts found in Mound A (Pl. 35). The spools were in position on each side of two skulls, while a third skull had only one spool. Rolled copper tubes 1 to 4 centimeters long and 2 to 5 millimeters in diameter were found. Inside the tubes were the remains of vegetal fiber, and in one instance, two-strand twisted cord. Fifteen other beads, small copper nodules that were perforated for suspension, were found singly and in groups near the mandible, in the thorax region, and with the wrist of human burials. A bracelet in the form of flat, copper strands was found at the wrist of another human burial, and three small copper fragments were with other human skeletons.

Two tubular beads, slightly flattened on four sides and at each end, made from galena, were exposed with two human skulls in Mound A. Other objects of adornment found in Mound A included twenty-one quartz crystals, which were found in association with human crania and mandibles. One specimen was grooved toward one end, presumably for suspension.

Forty-six matting and basketry impressions remained in the fill or were associated with the burials in Mound A. Ford and Willey remarked that round-cane matting was used to line shallow graves, and occasionally, plain plaiting of cane splint covered the burials.[28] The interesting impression of a conical plaited basket, 1 foot in diameter at the top and 1.2 feet deep, with a rounded bottom, was found in an inverted position in the ground fill. Ford and Willey surmised that the impression was made by a basket used to carry dirt for the mound construction.

The final notable finds were two small clusters of pebbles in Mounds A and B. The sixty-two pebbles in Mound A were deposited alongside the skull of a flexed skeleton. The cluster of twenty-nine pebbles found in Mound B was in association with six stone projectile points, several stone chips, and sherds. The pebbles in each mound had been worn smooth, leading Ford and Willey to suspect that the pebbles were all that remained of rattles that had otherwise decomposed.[29]

Quite obviously, the excavation of the Crooks Site not only enhanced the artifactual inventory of Louisiana prehistory but also, even more so than the Marksville Site data, provided elemental information for the formulation of the Marksville Culture. The Crooks Site investigations also expanded the list of diagnostic Hopewell traits in Louisiana and, therefore, were paramount in substantiating Hopewellian influence in the Lower Alluvial Valley.

Still another Marksville Culture funerary mound, the westernmost such tumulus reported in Louisiana, is the Coral Snake Mound in Sabine Parish. It was one of many archaeological sites that were soon destined to be flooded by the creation of the Toledo Bend Reservoir, along the Sabine River. Burney B. McClurken and Harold P. Jensen, Jr., of the Texas Archaeological Salvage Project, conducted investigations there during two intervals between 1965 and 1967. Their excavations revealed that the mound, a domed earthen tumulus 80 feet in diameter and rising to a height of about 8 feet above the Sabine River floodplain, was constructed in three stages and used by three cultures. First, a basin-shaped pit about 20 feet in diameter and 4 feet deep was dug into the original ground surface. Into it were deposited the remains of human cremations, and within its fill there was evidence of

28. *Ibid.*
29. *Ibid.*

several fires. The basin was filled with dirt, and excess dirt was used to form a small mound over and around the pit. This mound measured about 50 feet in diameter and 3 feet in height. The mound fill was called Stage 2.[30] Finally, covering Stage 2 was a sand stratum, designated Stage 3, which contained additional human interments, hearths, and artifacts.

The interments were single and multiple secondary types. The bones, except for burned fragments and teeth, some of which were copper stained, were generally not preserved. Neither the number of individuals, nor their sex or age, was reported. Twenty-seven of twenty-nine cremations were in Stage 2. Only one human cremation was exposed in Stage 3 fill. In most cases, the bodies had been cremated elsewhere, and the ashes brought to the mound and interred. However, the cremations exposed in the large basin were *in situ*.

Artifacts were found in clusters or in cache pits or isolated in the mound fill. Unfortunately, since several different culture groups used Coral Snake Mound, the cultural assignment of each and every artifact that was excavated would be impossible. Nevertheless, two unmistakable Marksville vessels (one plain, the other stamped), the copper beads and ear spools, the ground-stone atlatl weights and human effigy, and certain of the chipped-stone points, clearly bespeak a Marksville occupation. A radiocarbon date of 20 B.C. ± 100 years, obtained from charcoal found in association with the stamped vessel, lends further credence to this identification.[31]

The most recently reported explorations into a mound containing a Marksville Culture component was at the Lake Saint Agnes Site, in Avoyelles Parish. At the request of the landowners, Marc, Richard, Robert, and Charles Dupuy, and with their full assistance, a portion of the mound and the surrounding village areas were tested in the spring of 1972. Edwin Toth, then a graduate student at Louisiana State University, directed the fieldwork.

The most obvious feature at the Lake Saint Agnes Site is a flat-

---

30. Burney B. McClurkan, William T. Field, and J. Ned Woodall, *Excavations in the Toledo Bend Reservoir, 1964–65*, Papers of the Texas Archaeological Salvage Project, No. 8 (Austin, 1966); Harold P. Jensen, Jr., "Coral Snake Mound (X165A48)," *Bulletin of the Texas Archaeological Society*, Vol. 39 (1968), 9–44.
31. Jensen, "Coral Snake Mound."

topped, pyramidal earthen mound, 5 feet high and about 55 feet by 45 feet at the base. Borrow pits bordering three sides of the mound accentuate its height to about 10 feet above the surrounding ground surface. Since the initial Marksville Culture occupation here, about A.D. 200, at least 6 feet of alluvium have accumulated over the site.[32] Future researchers may be advised to keep this in mind when conducting surveys for Marksville village sites in the Lower Alluvial Valley.

Excavations into the Lake Saint Agnes mound consisted of the removal of its southwest quadrant. Toth found that the first construction stage, the Marksville component, was a clay platform several feet in height. The lateral dimensions were undetermined. A pit one foot deep had been dug into the top of the platform, and secondary human interments and midden containing sherds diagnostic of the late Marksville period had been deposited in it. There were seven bone concentrations of adult and subadult crania, mandibula, long bones, and ribs. In one instance, an adult cranium and infant rib bones had been "covered by a loose frame of small poles about one inch in diameter which, in turn, were covered with split cane matting. The covering had been allowed to burn partially, and as a result all bones except the skull were badly charred."[33] The burials, their associated midden fill, and the clay platform were later covered with a thin stratum of silt, which formed the base of the second stage of mound construction that is assigned to the subsequent Troyville-Coles Creek Culture.

Although the clay platform, or at least the portion of it exposed, seems comparable to previously reported Marksville manifestations, Toth acknowledges that the burials themselves lacked purposeful funerary accompaniments. The characteristic clay mantle on top of the burials was not present, nor was there any evidence of a conical mound. Inasmuch as the ceramic types associated with Stage 1 are indicative of the late period of the Marksville Culture, their differences and/or modifications are exactly what we might expect.

The resumé I have given here lists all of the Marksville tumuli that have been at all extensively excavated and reported on. It must be emphasized, however, that this list by no means indicates the number and

32. Edwin Alan Toth, *The Lake St. Agnes Site*, Mélanges No. 13 (Baton Rouge, 1979).
33. *Ibid.*, 22.

distribution of known Marksville components in Louisiana. Phillips and Toth record numerous other mounds in the Lower Alluvial Valley from which they have examined Marksville vessels, sherds, and copper objects. McIntire, in his extensive study of the deltaic plain, reported many other Marksville components reaching from the Sabine River eastward to the Chandeleur Islands.[34] Most of the coastal sites are shell middens located on cheniers and remnant natural levees. All of these coastal Marksville ceramic collections are deserving of further study in order to determine their chronological position within the Marksville Culture. Such fundamental data could then be utilized to establish priorities for future research into diffusion, settlement patterns, and subsistence economies.

The picture we have of the Marksville Culture from unpublished manuscripts, site files, literature, and illustrations is far from complete. Because almost all of the reported excavations involve mortuary tumuli, most of these data pertain to socioreligious aspects of the culture. We know that earthen mounds were constructed in various stages, and during corresponding intervals humans were interred in them. There were primary interments in the form of extended and flexed skeletons and secondary interments represented by bundle burials, partially articulated skeletons, isolated skulls, and cremations. Because of the poor state of bone preservation, at least at those sites reported in the literature, there are almost no physical anthropological data respecting sex, age, or skeletal morphology. It is possible to say only that all age groups seem to be represented. The burials, single or multiple, were in deep or shallow rectangular or basin-shaped pits, or the remains were laid on top of a construction stage and mantled with a thin layer of dirt. Sometimes the pits were lined and covered with bark or cane matting, or as evidenced by postmolds, the pits may have been temporarily sheltered by a roof. On several occasions, dogs were buried in association with the human interments, and it would not be absurd to imagine that they were slain and offered up to accompany their owners into the hereafter. In fact, funerary accom-

---

34. Phillips, *An Archaeological Survey of the Lower Yazoo Basin*; Toth, "Early Marksville Phases in the Lower Mississippi Valley"; William G. McIntire, *Prehistoric Indian Settlements of the Changing Mississippi River Delta*, Louisiana State University Studies, Coastal Studies Series, No. 1 (Baton Rouge, 1958).

paniments were a distinctive feature of this mortuary complex. Artifacts of pottery, bone, stone, shell, copper, galena, pigment concentrations, asphaltum, vegetal cordage, basketry, and matting were associated with the human interments.

The Marksville Culture was a regional manifestation of the vast Hopewell complex. It was part of a trade and exchange network unsurpassed by any subsequent prehistoric culture. We see evidence of this in the stylized motifs on the ceramics, human effigies, platform pipes, copper and galena ornaments, quartz crystals, asphaltum, and marine shell artifacts. Indeed, the very ideas of mound burial and funerary accompaniments were exotic principles transmitted geographically and modified regionally. The Tchefuncte burial mounds discussed in the previous chapter may, in fact, be the initial expression of Hopewell influence in Louisiana. One researcher has presented some very convincing evidence "to the effect that earthen burial mound construction is not an element of the Tchefuncte cultural system per se, but rather an example of stimulus diffusion in which isolated late Tchefuncte groups adopted the Marksville practice of mound burial."[35]

The artifactual remains suggest a Marksville subsistence base much like that of the Tchefuncte Culture that preceded it. Chipped-stone points, knives, scrapers, and drills; ground-stone atlatl weights and plummets; bone awls and fishhooks; mussel shells; and the baked-clay objects from the Marksville and Crooks sites are the same tools used by the Tchefuncte people. The animal bones from the burial platform in Mound A at Crooks included one bone each of an opossum and a turkey, but since the animal bones from the secondary mantle were a mixture of native and European species, they were uninformative respecting the prehistoric diet. The purported find of domesticated plant remains at the Marksville Site is presently unauthenticated and therefore of limited usefulness.

About the Marksville habitations, we simply do not have any information. The semisubterranean structures excavated at the Marksville Site are the only candidates, but they seem inordinately inappropriate habitations for the ecological setting they occupy. There

35. Toth, "Early Marksville Phases in the Lower Mississippi Valley," 63.

is slim evidence of a Marksville house at the Peck Site near Sicily Island in Catahoula Parish. In the lower section of Pit 4, postmolds outlining a rectangular floor pattern 8 feet by 14 feet were exposed. If this was, in fact, the basal deposit, it would have been the Marksville component, and the structure, a Marksville structure. This suggestion could be confirmed by reexamining the potsherds from a large cord-marked pot, which were presumably associated with the floor pattern.[36]

As Edwin Toth has remarked, there have been more conical burial mounds investigated, with varying degrees of proficiency, in the lower Red River region than anywhere else in the Lower Alluvial Valley.[37] Therefore, we have far more information about the Marksville mortuary complex than about the culture's villages and middens. Until such sites are located and systematically excavated, we can only speculate about how these people earned their livelihood.

36. Chisum, "The Excavation of an Indian Village near Sicily Island, Louisiana," 56.
37. Toth, "Early Marksville Phases in the Lower Mississippi Valley."

VIII Troyville–Coles Creek Culture

The Troyville–Coles Creek Culture derives its name from two archaeological sites whose combined manifestations span the entire period of this culture's existence. Twenty-three radiocarbon dates have
been established from fourteen Troyville–Coles Creek sites in Louisiana, and they extend from A.D. 395 to A.D. 1250, with a median date
of A.D. 875. The first site is the Troyville Site in Catahoula Parish, and
the second is the Coles Creek Site, named for the stream along which
it is located just north of Natchez, Mississippi. As with the preceding
period, most of the published information about inland sites of this
culture pertain to earthen tumuli. Whereas the external shape of the
Marksville Culture mounds is characteristically conical, most Troyville–Coles Creek mounds are pyramidal and flat-topped, used as substructures for civic and/or religious buildings. These mounds are generally larger than Marksville Culture tumuli, and they exhibit more
construction stages. They are also considerably more numerous. In fact,
if one were to ask a Louisiana archaeologist which sites are most conspicuous throughout the inland regions of the state, almost without
exception the reply would be "The Troyville–Coles Creek tumuli."
There are also many sites attributed to this culture in the coastal region, where in addition to mounds we have an impressive list of shell
middens (Pls. 36, 37, 38).[1]

1. Walker, *The Troyville Mounds*; Ford, *Analysis of Indian Village Site Collections
from Louisiana and Mississippi*; Neuman, *An Archaeological Assessment of
Coastal Louisiana*.

PLATE 36

View toward a shell midden delimited by trees and shrub vegetation in the marsh region of St. Bernard Parish, July 18, 1972.

The earliest descriptions of the Troyville Site date from 1804, and the tale of its destruction is a matter of public record. Located at the confluence of the Black, Little, and Ouachita rivers, it was a point of land four hundred acres in extent, enclosed on the north and west sides by an L-shaped earthen embankment 10 feet high (Pl. 39). It is not known whether the embankment served as a defensive structure, but tests at various locations along it failed to reveal any evidence of stockade posts. The other two sides of the site were bordered by steep banks along Little River to the east and Black River to the south. Within the enclosed area there are said to have been as many as thirteen mounds. The largest of these mounds, sometimes called the "Great Mound," was estimated to contain 626,700 cubic feet of dirt.[2] Before

2. Walker, *The Troyville Mounds*.

it was destroyed, it was seen and described by a number of prominent visitors to the site. There is credible evidence that it was constructed in the form of two stepped terraces surmounted by a cone and that it reached a height of 80 feet. The first terrace was about 30 feet high, the second about 15 feet high, and the cone about 35 feet in height. The mound base occupied most of the block now encompassed by Willow, Second, Pond, and Third streets in Jonesville (formerly Troyville). The original plat of the town of Troyville was within the enclosed area, and the town's settlement and growth were instrumental in the demise of the earthworks. Most of the earthworks at Troyville had been cut down, plowed, surmounted by houses, or used as a modern cemetery by 1931, and their contents had been scattered over the surface of the site (Pl. 40). During the summer of that year, the remnants of the Great

PLATE 37

Aerial view of mounds delimited by trees in the marsh region of St. Bernard Parish, August 28, 1973.

PLATE 38

View toward a large temple mound remnant in Lafourche Parish, June 18, 1981.

Mound were being removed to provide "dirt as a fill for the approach to a new highway bridge."[3] Such was the fate of one of the largest, most magnificent group of tumuli in the eastern United States.

During the summer of 1931, Winslow M. Walker of the Smithsonian Institution visited the site and concluded from his observations that portions of the mound base or terrace were still intact and that they merited immediate archaeological investigation. His excavations soon revealed that not all of the remaining *in situ* construction could be attributed definitely to the Troyville–Coles Creek Culture because some of the ceramic pieces signaled a Marksville horizon and others pointed to a later occupation. Nevertheless, most of the constructional remains exposed by Walker's excavations had their closest

3. Walker, "A Reconnaissance of Northern Louisiana Mounds," 174.

affinity to the Troyville–Coles Creek Culture. The structural complexity and elaborations found in the lower terrace of the Great Mound are unrivaled in the published record of Louisiana archaeology or elsewhere in the eastern United States.

Even before he began his own excavations, Walker noted some interesting phenomena. In the profiles of the terrace base exposed by the steam shovel cuts were "a variety of colored clays—red, brown, gray, blue, and olive—and extensive layers of the cane, some of which were quite thick, separated from other layers by masses of clay. This cane was still a greenish yellow when first exposed, but almost immediately turned black on coming in contact with air and sunlight."[4] Walker

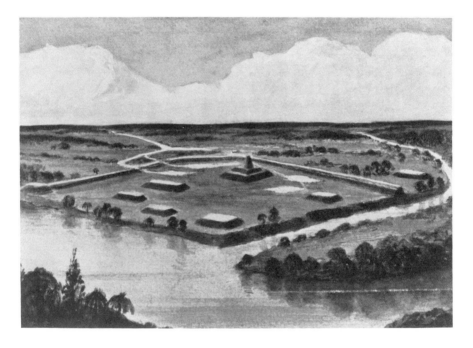

PLATE 39

Idealized drawing of the Troyville Site, Catahoula Parish. (From Winslow M. Walker, *The Troyville Mounds, Catahoula Parish, Louisiana,* Bureau of American Ethnology Bulletin 113 [Washington, D.C., 1936].)

4. Walker, *The Troyville Mounds,* 14.

PLATE 40

View toward the remnant of the Great Mound used as a refuge during the flood of 1922. Note tent peaks on the mound. (Courtesy of State Representative Bill B. Atkins of Jonesville.)

also noted that the geologist H. V. Howe had observed four conical domes incorporated in the dirt matrix of the mound base. The domes, built of concentric layers of clay and crisscrossed cane stalks, were about 24 feet in diameter and 20 feet in height. They were exposed as the base was being dismantled by the steam shovel. Walker felt that these domes and others he found later had once served as mounds themselves before becoming part of the fill for the construction of the Great Mound.

In November, 1931, Walker attempted preliminary excavations, but inclement weather forced him to cease these efforts and not until September, 1932, did he resume digging. With a crew of about eight men, Walker worked at the site until mid-November. By the time he began excavating, the surface remains of the Great Mound had been com-

pletely removed, and the locations of the mound boundaries, therefore, had to be ascertained from the highway engineer's maps, profiles,
and elevations. Walker found that the mound base, or aboriginal occupation level, was located from 6 to 8 feet below the present ground
surface. This fortunate circumstance enabled him to expose *in situ*
many of the surprisingly well-preserved constructional features.

Excavations revealed two stages of mound construction, but since
the steam shovel had removed the tops of each stage, only portions of
the mound's side slopes remained. It is not clear exactly how much of
the remains could be definitely assigned to the first construction stage.
Apparently, the portion of its western slope that was exposed was
mantled with thick layers of cane. "But unless the shallow cane patch
first uncovered, on the opposite (EAST) slope, represents a continua-
tion of this same sheet or layer, no other corresponding descending
layer was found."[5] Much of the upper portion of the eastern slope that,
without too much exactitude, I attribute to the second construction
stage for the base of the Great Mound, was also thickly mantled with
crisscrossed layers of cane. At several spots on the mound, wooden
stakes had been driven through these cane layers as if to hold them in
place. In other areas the mound slope was covered with units of wooden
planking. The individual planks measured as much as 20 feet long, 1½
inches thick, and 4 inches wide. They were found lying side by side in
units of up to seventeen planks, parallel and perpendicular to the long
axis of the mound slope. Occasionally they partially overlapped with
each other. The eastern end of the south slope was rather steep. The
western end was of a gradual incline and was covered with layers of
grass and palmetto fronds, interrupted at intervals up the slope by logs.
The logs seem to have functioned as risers and the fibers as treads to
form a stepped ramp leading toward the mound summit. Almost below the lowest log, or riser, at the foot of the slope, isolated remains
of a crushed human skull were found.

The eastern portion of the mound slope steepened as it extended
downward from the planking, and in this area Walker uncovered a clay
shelf capped with a distinctive reddish yellow sand. The shelf was 2
feet wide and extended along the south slope base for a distance of about

5. *Ibid.*, 20.

12 feet. Just to the outside of the shelf there were fifteen posts placed at intervals up to 3 feet and sunk into the earth as deep as 6 feet. The posts were in an east-west alignment, parallel to the slope base, and they extended for a distance of 40 feet. The posts had diameters ranging from several inches to more than one foot and "the ends had been crudely hacked off by some blunt edged tool, presumably a stone ax." Interestingly enough, there were no basket-load impressions. Instead, definite cleavage lines appeared as the clay fill was exposed to the elements. "By taking advantage of this situation it was possible to remove large irregular sized chunks of clay, which presumably represented the original loads dumped into place." Walker surmised that animal-hide containers had been used instead of baskets to transport the clay to the mound site.[6]

Other trenches were cut north-south and east-west so that profiles exposed numerous cane and bark layers separated by clay strata in the mound base. By the time he had completed his excavations, Walker had located three sides of the mound and was able to show almost conclusively that, upon its completion, the base of the Great Mound measured about 180 feet on a side and had ramps at the four corners leading to the summit.

In analyzing the data from his excavations at Troyville, Walker had experts identify the wood, bark, and cane from the Great Mound. He even tried, albeit unsuccessfully, to utilize dendrochronological techniques. It was found that the posts were of cypress, willow, ash, gum, and locust, and several log poles consisted of locust, pine, cypress, and chinquapin. While most of the planks were of hickory, some were of gum, pecan, or persimmon. It is quite evident that the Indians were exploiting a variety of upland and wetland environments in the site vicinity. The cane was of the type commonly seen growing today, *Arundinaria tecta*. The cane used in the massive layers covering the Great Mound had been trimmed and split into halves and quarters, but elsewhere in the mound the cane was found still round and intact. There were also several locations where it appeared that cane had been bundled and tied with "withes of grass." Walker also identified faunal and floral remains that he had retrieved from the occupational level at

6. *Ibid.*, 23, 24.

the mound base. None of these were quantified, but the animal bone, particularly deer, was abundant. Identified species consisted of bear (*Euarctos americanus*), deer (*Odocoileus virginianus*), gray squirrel (*Sciurus carolinensis*), snapping turtle (*Chelydra serpentina*), soft-shell turtle (*Trionyx* sp.), catfish (*Ictaluridae*), drumfish (*Aplodinotus grunnius*), alligator gar (*Lepisosteus spatula*), and one shark tooth. Wild turkey (*Meleagris gallopavo*) and duck (*Anatidae*) bones were also recorded. Freshwater mollusks were present but not abundantly so, and one broken gastropod shell was reported. The botanical material included seeds, stems, and leaves of thirty-eight plant species, of which only "the grapes, berries, gourd, and possibly the Nightshade and Passionflower are considered edible."[7]

The artifactual remains from Walker's excavations into the site of the Great Mound present a sort of dilemma. Walker does not quantify the ceramic collection, but there is no doubt from his report that most of the sherds "in the bottom of the Great Mound"[8] were Marksville Culture varieties. Present knowledge of the regional ceramic chronology allows us to place them as examples of late Marksville ceramics. The only nonceramic artifacts found were two modified-bone specimens. The reader might rightfully ask how the Great Mound can be assigned to the Troyville–Coles Creek Culture on the basis of such limited artifactual data. Admittedly, the evidence is indirect, but the fact that the Marksville ceramics are from the bottom of the mound could mean that the mound dates from late Marksville times and/or a later period. In addition, there can be no doubt about a Troyville– Coles Creek occupation at the site since diagnostic ceramics of this culture were found on the surface. Finally, the shape of the mound, disregarding the cone, reflects most of what we know about the pyramidal tumuli of the Troyville–Coles Creek Culture. The cone, however, and the complex mantling along the mound base slopes are unique in the published record. It seems reasonable in light of all of the present evidence to attribute the Great Mound at the Troyville Site to the Troyville–Coles Creek Culture, at least until evidence is presented to the contrary.

7. *Ibid.*, 50, 39.
8. *Ibid.*, 40.

The Greenhouse Site in Avoyelles Parish is the only Troyville–Coles Creek Site that has been really extensively excavated and comprehensively reported. It was one of the LSU–WPA projects under the direction of James A. Ford. The field excavations were supervised by Robert S. Neitzel and Edwin B. Doran, Jr., who, with a crew of thirty to forty men, began work there in October, 1938, and finished about a year later. The site consists of seven earthen tumuli originally mapped by Fowke and numbered 14 through 20, then more accurately mapped in 1938 and designated as Mounds A through G.[9] Mounds A and B are connected by a low ridge, as are Mounds E and F, and the entire group is arranged around an open space or plaza, measuring about 350 feet by 200 feet. From borings conducted during the 1938 investigations it was learned that at the time of its aboriginal occupance the site was situated on the crest of a natural levee next to a lake formed by an old Mississippi River meander scar. Subsequently, because of channel changes in the Mississippi and Red rivers north of Greenhouse, the lake was silted in and all of the site, except parts of the highest mounds, was mantled with the distinctive silt of the Red River.

Excavations were conducted into the mounds, and extensive trenches were dug across the entire site (Pl. 41). In addition, shorter exploratory trenches were dug in other locales of the site to trace out particular features and/or pertinent strata. The trenches exposed midden deposits of various thicknesses and sometimes in several lenses. They were composed of a black, greasy soil matrix containing varying quantities of potsherds, bone and stone artifacts, and charcoal and ash. By typing no less than 125,000 decorated sherds, calculating their percentages, and then relating the types back to their proveniences, Ford was able, with considerable reliability, to work out a relative chronology for the different areas tested at the site.[10] Greenhouse was excavated and then reported before the radiocarbon-dating technique was perfected.

The earliest earthwork excavated at Greenhouse was Mound C, a

9. Ford, "Archaeological Exploration During 1938"; James A. Ford, *Greenhouse: A Troyville–Coles Creek Period Site in Avoyelles Parish, Louisiana*, Anthropological Papers of the American Museum of Natural History, Vol. 44, Pt. 1 (New York, 1951); Fowke, "Archaeological Investigations—II."
10. Ford, *Greenhouse*.

low, barely perceptible rise connected to Mound D, a similar structure. Both mounds were mantled with Red River silt. Although the mounds of this culture are not funerary structures *per se*, human interments are quite often found in those that have been extensively excavated, and this was the case at Mound C. In an area 25 feet by 30 feet, eighty-four human and nine dog skeletons were found in the top of the mound. "Apparently the skeletons were dumped on the surface more or less carelessly, raked into any shallow surface depressions and then covered with the upper midden soil and the thin stratum which capped the low mound."[11] Most of the skeletons were in extended positions, some partially overlying others, but four were in a flexed position, and thirteen were semiflexed. Twenty-three other individuals were represented by articulated segments of the skeleton, such as an arm, legs, or feet, and others by isolated skulls. The collection included twenty-two male and twenty-seven female adults, as well as fourteen subadults. The sex and age of twenty-one other individuals was not determined. Of the dog skeletons, six were complete, and the other three were only represented by skulls. In the northeast area of this skeletal concentration, there was a pit containing the fragmented and charred human bones of five individuals. The pit was oval, measuring 5.5 feet by 3.5 feet with a depth of 2.0 feet. In the usual fashion of Troyville—Coles Creek burials, these were not associated with purposeful funerary offerings.

It is difficult to think of a reason for this disorderly array of skeletons. Only the four flexed individuals seem to have been purposefully positioned, and even the charred human bone fragments in the pit may have been an unintentional deposit. Evidently, most of the individuals were still in flesh when they were brought to the mound, and it does not seem likely that there was much of a time differential between the times of their deaths. It is quite probable that a physical anthropological study of these skeletal remains would elucidate this mystery for us, but until that task is accomplished the present data and our imaginations must suffice.

Coexistent with Mound C was Mound A (Pl. 42), the highest tumulus at Greenhouse. It measured 12 feet high with a base dimension

11. *Ibid.*, 43–44.

of 120 feet on a side. The flat summit was 80 feet square. Its shape gave some suggestion that its last construction stage may have included an earthen ramp or stairway on the side facing the plaza.[12] The first two of six earlier constructions were traceable, but the third stage was more fully intact. The mound at Stage 3 was 8 feet high and had reached its maximum basal dimensions. Activity on the summit was indicated only by several large burned areas and a scattering of postmolds. The surfaces of Stages 4 and 5, which increased the mound's height by 2 more feet, showed the same sort of burned areas and postmolds as at Stage 3. In Stage 6, which consisted of 3 feet of gray clay, one dog skeleton and eight human skeletons were found. There were no burial pits or grave goods. The skeletons were simply incorporated into the clay in about the same fashion as those in Mound C. Among the four infant skeletons, two were supine with flexed arms and legs, the third lay on its left side with its legs slightly flexed and its arms at its side, and the fourth was represented by skull fragments only. There were two juvenile skeletons; one supine with legs flexed and arms at its side, and the other lying prone and extended with the dog skeleton between the legs. An adult female was found in a supine position, legs extended and arms flexed. The skeleton of an adult male was lying on its right side, the arms and legs disarticulated, and the skull, hands, and feet were not present. On the surface of Stage 6 was a postmold pattern indicative of a structure 35 feet in diameter. The postmolds were paired and each set was about 2 feet apart. Inside the pattern were several burned areas but no evidence of a fire pit. Sometime later 2 feet of brown clay were added to the summit and slopes in preparation for Stage 7. Exposed on this platform was another pattern of postmolds, which also measured 35 feet in diameter, but these postmolds were not paired, and within the floor pattern was a fire pit 2 feet in diameter and 4 feet deep. At least one additional construction stage was evident on Mound A, but recent farming practices and erosion had largely destroyed its archaeological value.

Mound G at the northwest side of the plaza is one of the three largest tumuli at Greenhouse, measuring 6 feet high and 160 feet on a side at its base. This mound was not extensively excavated, but a trench

12. Ford, *Greenhouse.*

that cut through 70 feet of its southern flank revealed that the original mound base was 4 feet below the present ground surface. The trench profiles also exposed three construction stages. Ceramics from these trenches indicate the mound was one of the earliest at the site.

Mound D, the barely perceptible rise comparable to and located only about 20 feet west of Mound C, was excavated in expectation of finding burials like those in Mound C, but no burials were discovered. Instead, the excavations revealed that construction at this mound began considerably later than at Mound C. At least two construction stages and postmolds arranged in circular patterns outlining several buildings were exposed. Some of the postmolds were situated in wall trenches, which were about 4 inches wide and 1 foot deep and which extended almost half of the distance around the floor patterns. Two or possibly three buildings about 25 feet in diameter are represented. One of the buildings was constructed over an earlier bathtub-shaped pit with round corners and vertical walls that measured 3 feet wide, 3 feet deep, and about 8 feet long. The clay walls were baked and 6 inches of ash, overlain by midden soil, half filled the pit.

Another pit quite similar to this one was found in a higher stratum of Mound D, and in addition, Ford reported eight other such pits exposed by exploratory trenches. All of these were located near the mounds and the plaza border along the lakeshore side of the site. They range from 12 to 6 feet long, from 2 to 6 feet wide, and from 1 to 4 feet deep. Characteristically, the walls have been fire baked, and there is a layer of ash in the pit bottom, which is usually overlain by midden fill. Aside from the pits' location along only one side of the site, there does not appear to be any particular pattern in their orientation. At least four comparable pits were excavated at the Mount Nebo Site, a Troyville—Coles Creek Culture mound in Madison Parish. Like the Greenhouse pits, those at Mount Nebo date from the later half of this culture period. Their function is not known, although it has been suggested that they could have been used as cooking pits, crematories, or pottery kilns.[13]

Unfortunately Mound E at Greenhouse was not excavated, but Mound F, to which it was connected by a low earthen ridge, was in-

13. *Ibid.*

vestigated (Pl. 43). The construction of Mound F began late in the life of the site, and the ceramic refuse found in this mound indicated that it was used later than any of the other excavated tumuli at Greenhouse. About 6 feet in height, the mound is a rectangular structure, the long axis of which faces the plaza. When first constructed the mound was about 2.5 feet tall with a basal width of 50 feet and a summit measuring 35 feet on a side. On the summit of this stage was a rectangular area, 25 feet by 28 feet, characterized by burned clay, refuse, and a scattering of postmolds. "With the assistance of some imagination a rectangular building about 30 feet square can be traced."[14] Near its center were two superimposed fire pits, the most recent of which was basin-shaped, 4.5 feet in diameter and 10 inches deep.

The second construction stage added 2 feet of clay to the mound. A floor area 26 feet by 17 feet, with scattered postmolds and burned clay, suggested another rectangular structure. In its northeastern quarter the floor exhibited a fire pit 3 feet in diameter and 4 inches deep.

Only 1 foot of clay was added for the third construction stage at Mound F. Here the mottled and burned-clay floor of another rectangular structure, 24 feet by 26 feet, was outlined. The postmold pattern in this instance was clearly defined, but curiously enough, the corner posts were not evident. The rather obscure remains of a shallow fire pit were exposed about 6 feet south of the center of the postmold pattern.

The fourth construction stage, an addition of about 8 inches of clay, was only 1 foot below the present plow zone. Therefore, except for two postmolds and the remains of a circular fire pit, little information was gleaned from the disrupted strata. The primary investigators felt, however, that at least one additional construction stage followed Stage 4.[15]

The extensive exploratory trenches dug in addition to those through the mounds proper clarified the environmental picture of the Greenhouse Site during the period of its aboriginal occupation, showing its relationship to past stream courses and the lakeshore. These trenches also revealed that, unlike the areas bordering the plaza and around and

14. *Ibid.*, 41.
15. Ford, *Greenhouse.*

PLATE 41

View of coordinate trenches from the top of Mound A at the Greenhouse Site in Avoyelles Parish, December 12, 1938.

under the mounds, the central zone, or plaza, was quite free of refuse.
This refuse distribution suggests that a site plan had been followed
since the time of the earliest utilization of the area by the Troyville–
Coles Creek people. Furthermore, since tests outside of the side periphery yielded no refuse indicative of houses or of village occupations, it was concluded that Greenhouse functioned primarily as a
ceremonial center.[16]

   Several of the exploratory trenches bisected the low ridges, or
causeways, between Mounds A and B and E and F. The ridge between
Mounds A and B was constructed in three stages. On the second of the
stages were postmolds outlining the floor pattern of a structure 22 feet
in diameter. Several concentric arcs of wall posts, some in wall

16. *Ibid.*

PLATE 42

Stripping the southwest side of Mound A at the Greenhouse Site in Avoyelles Parish, October 3, 1939.

trenches, and two fire pits within the floor pattern suggest that the structure was built and then altered several times. The trench across the ridge between Mounds E and F revealed no comparable data, but "the cultural accumulation here averages about 60 inches: black, refuse-bearing soil interrupted by two zones of loaded earth which later investigation proved to connect with building stages in Mound F."[17]

The pottery collection from Greenhouse is the largest excavated, analyzed, and reported sample from any site of the Troyville–Coles Creek Culture. Ford and Phillips have reported in detail on the pottery types, their varieties, and their chronological and geographical distributions.[18] Troyville–Coles Creek vessels that were fashioned from lo-

17. *Ibid.*, 27.
18. Ford, *Greenhouse*; Phillips, "Archaeological Survey in the Lower Yazoo Basin."

cal clays, were usually tempered with clay particles, some quite large, and particles of white stone, but occasionally the sherds were shell tempered. Using the coiling method and by paddling and stamping the clay, the walls were shaped and sometimes highly polished. Most often the wall exteriors were smoothed somewhat—although they were still bumpy—and not polished. The bases are square or round and usually flat, although in some instances they are convex. Vessel forms are of two general classes, jars and bowls. The walls range from 2 mm to 12 mm thick, while the bases are usually slightly thicker. Vessel diameters reach up to 90 mm. The jars may be barrel-shaped or globular with faint shoulders, and cambered, direct, or incurved rims. Beakers are also common. Bowls may be shallow or deep with flaring sides or rounded, incurving walls. There are some bowls with four triangular ears ex-

PLATE 43

Mound E center, Mound F to the right, at the Greenhouse Site in Avoyelles Parish, December 15, 1938.

tending horizontally out from the rim so that in plan the bowl top appears quadrate, but these are uncommon. Since no whole vessels were found at Greenhouse, their heights were not determinable. Most of the Troyville–Coles Creek vessel fragments are buff to dark brown and gray to black, and, two of the types are embellished with a brownish pink wash applied as a decorative element to the vessel surfaces. The pottery is decorated with complicated stamping, rocker-stamping, check-stamping, net impressions, and cord marking. There are also various designs executed with straight and curvilinear incised lines, stippling, hachuring, and herringbone arrangements and punctations (Pls. 44, 45, 46, 47).

Just as one would expect, a number of the decorative patterns and elements on Troyville–Coles Creek pottery were clearly derived from the earlier Marksville Culture wares, but the zoomorphic motifs so characteristic of Marksville have no counterparts in the Troyville–Coles Creek Culture. Another notable difference is that the walls of Marksville vessels were often covered by decoration, whereas on Troyville–Coles Creek ceramics the decoration is characteristically confined to the upper half of the vessel. Troyville–Coles Creek vessels are also, on the average, decidedly larger than those reported from Marksville sites.

Other fired-clay objects retrieved from the Greenhouse Site included ear spools, elbow-shaped pipes, one platform pipe, a disk with a central perforation, a miniature, cone-shaped vessel or cup, two mushroom-shaped implements, crude head and/or torso fragments of human figurines, and other figurines depicting stylized bird heads that are thought to have been broken off from vessels (Pl. 47). The presence of seven biconical baked-clay objects suggests that this Poverty Point trait lingered at least into Troyville–Coles Creek times.

Stone and bone artifacts from Greenhouse were quite sparse. The forty-four stone projectile points are about evenly divided between earlier larger forms and the new small triangular, corner-notched points, which appear to be arrow points. If they are arrow points, they represent the introduction of the bow to Louisiana. Other chipped-stone artifacts include two drills and seventeen scrapers. Ground-stone artifacts consist of hammerstones and mealing stones, a celt fragment, two atlatl weights, and two plummets (Pl. 48). Bone and antler tools include two pins, eleven split-bone awls, ten trimmed and pointed deer ulnas, two points, and seven worked sections of deer antler (Pl. 49). The paucity of stone and bone artifacts may be another indicator that the site was primarily a ceremonial center.

The Troyville–Coles Creek Culture has also been investigated at a number of nonmound village and camp middens. For example, during the early 1970s Richard A. Weinstein, then a Louisiana State University graduate student, examined sites in the lower Amite River drainage of Livingston and Ascension parishes. His tests at seven middens showed that they were composed of *rangia* shell in the downstream areas and *rangia* intermixed with freshwater mollusks in sites farther upstream. The midden deposits were evident on the ground surface and/or along the stream banks for as much as 200 feet. They ranged from several inches to 3 feet in thickness, and one midden was reported to be 20 feet wide. Some of the sites were situated on remnants of the Pleistocene terrace, which are generally relatively high, dry land parcels that could be occupied all during the year. Indeed, they were inhabited year-round during the historic era. Other sites, located on natural levees, would have been subject to sporadic flooding. At several sites the middens were associated with a single, low domed earthen mound, usually less than 3 feet in height. However, "whether they are Marksville burial mounds or eroded Troyville–Coles Creek temple mounds cannot be answered at present."[19] Aside from sherds, the artifactual inventories at these sites are not particularly plentiful, but they do usually include stone points, drills, knives, chips, mealing stones, and hammerstones. A few bone awls, fishhooks, and points are also listed. The faunal remains, although not abundant, represented an expectable range of species. Deer, bear, dog, beaver, skunk, muskrat, opossum, raccoon, rabbit, alligator, turtle, bowfin, catfish, drum, and gar remains were found. In addition, there were bird bones, isolated human skeletal remains, coprolites, and of course, the mollusks.

Human burials were excavated at two of the sites. The Bayou Chene Blanc midden contained a flexed adult skeleton placed in the shell matrix with no evidence of a burial pit. Another human burial at Chene

19. Richard Alan Weinstein, "An Archaeological Survey of the Lower Amite River, Louisiana" (M.A. thesis, Louisiana State University, Baton Rouge 1974), 295.

a   b

c   d

e

f   g

0   1   2   3
INCHES

PLATE 44

Ceramic vessels of the Troyville–Coles Creek Culture.

PLATE 45

Ceramic rim sherds of Troyville–Coles Creek vessels.

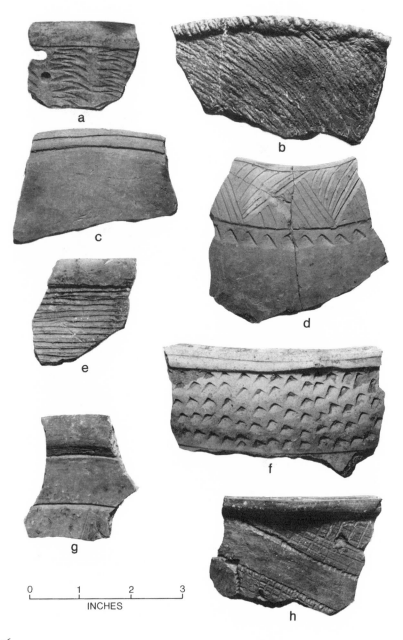

a

b

c

d

e

f

g

h

0   1   2   3
INCHES

PLATE 46

Ceramic rim sherds of Troyville–Coles Creek vessels.

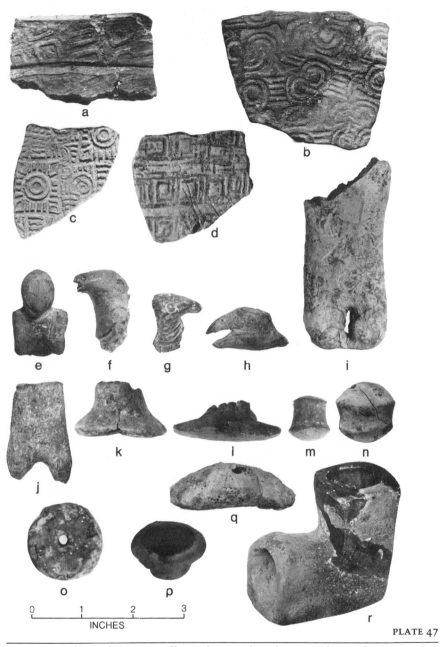

a   b   c   d   e   f   g   h   i   j   k   l   m   n   o   p   q   r

0   1   2   3

INCHES

PLATE 47

Ceramic artifacts of the Troyville–Coles Creek Culture: *a–d*, vessel sherds; *e–j*, figurines; *k–l*, ear spools; *m–n*, labrets; *o–p*, ornaments; *q*, atlatl weight; *r*, elbow pipe.

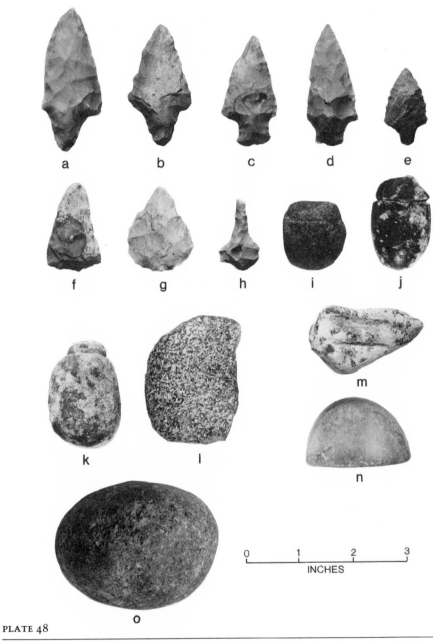

a   b   c   d   e

f   g   h   i   j

k   l   m

n

o

0   1   2   3

INCHES

PLATE 48

Chipped- and ground-stone artifacts of the Troyville–Coles Creek Culture: *a–e*, projectile points; *f–g*, knives; *h*, drill; *i–k*, plummets; *l*, celt fragment; *m*, sandstone abrader; *n*, atlatl weight; *o*, mealing stone.

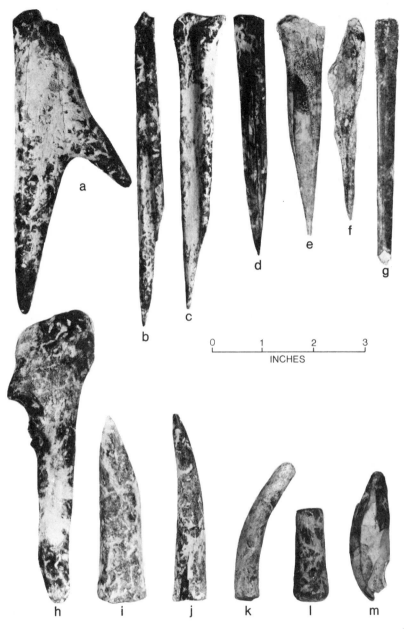

PLATE 49

Bone, antler, and animal teeth artifacts of the Troyville–Coles Creek
Culture: *a–j*, perforators; *k*, antler flaker; *l*, antler tine handle; *m*, canine tooth ornament.

Blanc was a secondary interment. The articulated torso was overlain with the disarticulated bone elements of the hands and feet. Cut marks, or incisions, on one tibia and a fibula may be indications of postmortem removal of the flesh. On the left side of this individual's skull there was a bulge surrounded by "perforations that pierced completely through the skull."[20] This curious anomaly was probably a pathology. At the Diversion Canal Site an adult, labeled Burial 1, was found in a flexed position within a prepared basin-shaped pit. Burial 2 at the same site was represented only by the lower torso and the limbs because the upper portion of the skeleton had been removed by canal dredging. Weinstein surmised from the bent knees that this skeleton was a flexed interment. There was no evidence of a pit for Burial 2, and neither individual at this site was directly associated with burial offerings.

During the early 1970s, James W. Springer, then a doctoral candidate at Yale University, employed an innovative approach to the study of the Troyville–Coles Creek Culture.[21] He wanted to compare sites of the same culture occupying different ecological environments to see what would change in response to the surroundings. He selected the Bruly Saint Martin Site along Grand Bayou in Iberville Parish as an example of an inland occupation along a natural levee adjacent to a heavily forested swamp area. After he had investigated this site, he examined the Pierre Clement Site in Cameron Parish, which is located on Little Cheniere, an ancient beach ridge, at its junction with the Mermentau River about nine miles north of the present coastline.

At Bruly Saint Martin the village area—at least that part made apparent by debris exposed in a plowed field—encompasses 127,500 square feet. In the northern section of the site there is a flat-topped, pyramidal earthen mound with a base measuring 150 feet on a side and a height of 12 feet above the surrounding ground surface. Springer excavated an area 10 feet by 30 feet down to 5 feet beneath the surface in the village sector south of the mound. In the plow zone he encountered prehistoric artifacts intermixed with historic objects, but below this disturbed zone, historic objects were rare and intrusive, and prehistoric sherds, stone and bone artifacts, ash lenses, *rangia* and fresh-

20. *Ibid.*, 204.
21. James W. Springer, "The Prehistory and Cultural Geography of Coastal Louisiana" (Ph.D. dissertation, Yale University, 1973).

water mollusks predominated. The refuse became quite sparse at the 4-foot level, and below that the soil contained no artifacts. Objects of technology, other than pottery, were not plentiful at any level. As was to be expected in southern Louisiana, stone artifacts were scarce. Five projectile points and a gorget were found, but most of the stone artifacts were utilized pebbles and chips.

Botanical specimens were rare, although ten persimmon and one grape seed were identified, but animal bone was abundant. Animals not only provided sustenance for the people, they also furnished bone for the manufacture of tools, and we can infer that their hides or feathers were used for clothing, implements, rope, and adornment.[22] Fish seem to have made up the major part of the diet, at least in terms of the total live weight that they represent. Among the identified species, which include shark, gar, bowfin, pike, sucker, catfish, bass, and freshwater drum, catfish predominate. Springer reported that "17 examples were over 39½ inches long."[23] Some of the fish species could have been caught with a hook and line, but no hooks were found at the site. Nets and weirs may have been used in the nearby bayou, and bone harpoons and points like those retrieved from the excavations could also have been used to catch fish.[24] The shark, which is represented by a single tooth and is unidentified as to species, may seem exotic to this environment. Indeed, Springer guesses that the tooth was a trade object imported to the site. But sharks are not unknown in these inland waters. In fact, George Beyer saw a shark more than eight feet long being caught much farther north, in the Lake Larto environs, Catahoula Parish.[25] The mammal remains from Bruly Saint Martin are next in dietary importance, of which slightly more than half was provided by deer. Other species include bear, bobcat, raccoon, opossum, muskrat, mink, rabbit, and squirrel. Avian species include goose, grebe, cormorant, heron, egret, eagle, duck, and coot. None of these species are

22. Joan Gardner and Mary Elizabeth King, *Textiles from Spiro Mound, Oklahoma* (New Orleans, 1977); Springer, "The Prehistory and Cultural Geography of Coastal Louisiana."
23. Springer, "The Prehistory and Cultural Geography of Coastal Louisiana," 115.
24. Erhard Rostlund, *Freshwater Fish and Fishing in Native North America,* University of California Publications in Geography, Vol. 9 (Berkeley, 1952).
25. Beyer, "The Mounds of Louisiana"; Springer, "The Prehistory and Cultural Geography of Coastal Louisiana."

uncharacteristic of a swamp environment, but the geese and ducks are seasonal inhabitants. Oddly enough, reptilian remains were sparse at Bruly Saint Martin, and only the snake and the turtle are represented.

From his stratigraphic data, Springer noted no particular change in the diet of the site occupants from early to late times. There was simply more of the same evidence. He speculated that, initially, while the stream levee was being built up, the site was occupied seasonally. Once the levee reached its maximum height and flooding became sporadic, the village became a more permanent settlement and began to grow. At that time the mound was constructed. Springer's is certainly a credible hypothesis, but inasmuch as the mound was not excavated, its assignment to the Troyville–Coles Creek occupation at Bruly Saint Martin is premature.

At the Pierre Clement Site, there is a Troyville–Coles Creek de-

PLATE 50

Excavations at the Pierre Clement shell midden, Cameron Parish, April 27, 1971.

posit in the form of 11,250 square feet of midden on the beach ridge, which rises 5 feet above sea level. Springer excavated eight adjoining 10-foot squares and exposed four different levels of shell and dirt (Pl. 50). Level 1, the uppermost, consisted mainly of *rangia* shells, black dirt, and a few oyster shells. It contained a mixture of modern and prehistoric detritus. Level 2, mostly black dirt and a small number of *rangia* shells, contained prehistoric remains and one historic piece of metal. Level 3 was characterized by a dense oyster deposit mixed with brown dirt and void of cultural material. Level 4 was a matrix of fragmented marine shells, which characterizes the body of the cheniere, or beach ridge. It, too, was sterile of cultural remains.

A basin-shaped pit that measured about 2.5 feet down its longest axis and 2.1 feet deep was found in the scattered midden of Level 1. The pit fill contained prehistoric sherds, powdered shell, burned *rangia* shells noticeably smaller than those found elsewhere at the site, and large amounts of charcoal. The pit seems to have been used to burn shell, thus making it easier to crush to provide shell particles for pottery temper. Also in Level 1 were three human burials. The first was less than a foot below the surface, and not all of the skeletal elements were present. There was no evidence of a pit, nor were there any funerary accompaniments. The age and sex of this individual were not reported, but from the illustration, it appears to have been a primary extended burial.[26] About 10 feet farther south were two other human skeletons. These were primary extended burials, lying adjacent to each other but oriented in opposite directions. Both were adults who had been placed in a shallow pit without any funerary accompaniments. Their sex was not reported.

In speaking of the artifacts from Pierre Clement, Springer noted that enough of the ceramics were of the types identifiable with the Troyville—Coles Creek Culture, but the excavated collection also contained sherds with recognizable affinities or correlations with assemblages from the Louisiana-Texas border region.[27] Pierre Clement is very far from the Mississippi Valley, the cultural center of the

26. Springer, "The Prehistory and Cultural Geography of Coastal Louisiana," fig. 23.
27. Springer, "The Prehistory and Cultural Geography of Coastal Louisiana"; Aten and Bollich, "A Preliminary Report on the Development of a Ceramic Chronology for the Sabine Lake Area."

Troyville–Coles Creek people. It is not at all surprising, therefore, to find that the diagnostic ceramic traits were altered in various degrees as they diffused into this marginal zone. Some of the ceramics at Pierre Clement differed from those found at sites closer to the cultural center in decorative motifs and in materials used to temper the clay. In addition to 912 sherds, the site also yielded a small quantity of stone and bone artifacts. They included both large, stemmed stone points and smaller varieties, scrapers, worked flakes, cores, and cobblestones. Bone implements include 5 mammal or fishbone awls, 2 points, and a fragmented fishhook.

In respect to subsistence, it has already been noted that the midden was composed largely of *rangia* shell. Nevertheless, as Byrd has demonstrated, the actual amount of edible food obtained from the *rangia* is quite small in proportion to the volume of shell remaining.[28] Faunal bones found at Pierre Clement include remains of deer, raccoon, otter, weasel, muskrat, gar, freshwater drum, sucker, bowfin, turtle, and bird. All of the identified species, except possibly the birds, inhabit the site environs throughout the year.

Clearly, the excavations and report of the Bruly Saint Martin and Pierre Clement sites demonstrate, albeit in a very narrow vein, just some of the differences and variability to be found at Troyville–Coles Creek settlements that thrived in two contrasting ecological zones. Of course, neither of these is a type site for its zone. It may well be that there is as much or more variability to be found between Troyville–Coles Creek sites existing in the same ecological zone. However, the necessary data for this conclusion are just not yet available.

The excavations of mounds, villages, and middens of the Troyville–Coles Creek people has given us a good deal of information about the socioreligious and economic aspects of this culture. In addition, thanks to the meticulous analyses provided by Professor Louise M. Robbins, University of North Carolina-Greensboro, there is more biocultural information available on the Troyville–Coles Creek people than on any other prehistoric culture in Louisiana. Robbins worked with human skeletal material that was excavated under my direction between 1969 and 1971 at the Morton Shell Mound.

The site is one of the largest *rangia* middens along the northern coast

28. Byrd, "The Brackish Water Clam."

of the Gulf of Mexico. It is 700 feet long, has a maximum width of 110 feet, extends 12 feet above sea level, and reaches a depth of 8 feet below sea level (Pls. 51 and 52). During the Troyville–Coles Creek habitation of the site, which had previously been occupied by the Tchefuncte and Marksville cultures, the northern end of the midden was selected as a cemetery. For whatever reason, the people covered the flat shell surface with a distinctive mantle of fine gray silt. Human remains were placed on this gray stratum or sometimes in very shallow pits dug into it and then covered with shell midden. The burials were often disrupted by subsequent interments, which were, in turn, covered with additional shell midden. In time the cemetery area above the gray mantle took on the appearance of a dome about 40 feet in diameter with a maximum apical height of about 4 feet.

Although several primary flexed burials and articulated sections of the torso and/or limbs were present, the most characteristic burial pattern was the secondary interment of one or more individuals. At times the bones were found loosely scattered, but in other instances they were in a compact concentration as the remains of a bundle burial. Never were all of the skeletal remains present. Apparently, at death the body was exposed to the elements for a selected period of time on a scaffold or in a special shelter until the flesh had decomposed. In some instances the body may have been purposefully defleshed, as described in regional historic accounts.[29] The bones would be gathered up later and ordinarily they would be deposited at a final burial site. At the Morton Shell Mound, however, a peculiar intermediate step was taken. The burial ritual included the breaking of the bones before their final interment—not only the long bones, but also smaller ones in the hands and feet, as well as infant bones. Robbins noted that, unlike the breaks in animal bones, which showed splintering because the bones were fresh when they were broken, the breaks in the human bones were clean and unsplintered. This indicated that they were broken after they had become dry. Such purposeful bone breakage was also a feature of a human bundle burial beneath Mound F, at the Greenhouse Site.[30]

29. John R. Swanton, *The Indians of the Southeastern United States*, Bureau of American Ethnology Bulletin 137 (Washington, D.C., 1946).
30. Louise M. Robbins, "Analysis of Human Skeletal Material from Morton Shell Mound (16IB3), Iberia Parish, Louisiana," manuscript on file at Department of Geography and Anthropology, Louisiana State University, Baton Rouge; Ford, *Greenhouse*.

PLATE 51

Aerial view of the Morton Shell Mound at Weeks Island, Iberia Parish, March 21, 1975.

Although there were no unequivocal occurrences of funerary accompaniments with the Morton Shell Mound burials, the shell midden matrix did contain sherds attributable to late Marksville and Troyville–Coles Creek times. This midden matrix was undoubtedly obtained from elsewhere than at the site, and the sherd associations would lead one to conclude that the human interments are no older than the Troyville–Coles Creek pottery types with which they were found. By isolating certain diagnostic bones, such as the proximal end of right or left humeri or femora, or particular portions of specific bones, such as the anterior section of the mandible, Robbins was able to estimate the number of individuals represented by the human skeletal collection that included about 25,000 bone fragments.[31] Using the most

31. Robbins, "Analysis of Human Skeletal Material from Morton Shell Mound."

conservative figures, she estimated that the Morton Shell Mound series contained the partial remains of 7 fetuses (of 5 to 8 months ges-
tation), 14 infants (newborn to 2 years), 25 children (2 to 11 years), 28
adolescents (11 to 17 years), 83 female and 105 male adults, and 13
adults of indeterminate sex. The population, therefore, is at least 275
individuals. Because of the extremely fragmented condition of the
skeletal collection, osteometric determinations were limited.

Robbins determined ages and sexes of adults by examining cranial
and mandibular bones and long bone epiphyses. She found conspicuous sexual dimorphism between adults. Male bones, although only
moderately robust, are massive in size. For example, the diameter of
the femoral condyle averages 3.4 inches and the femoral head ranges
from 1.8 inches to 2.0 inches in diameter. Male facial morphology also

PLATE 52

Excavation profile of the shell midden at the Morton Shell Mound, Iberia Parish, February 17, 1971.

exhibits pronounced characteristics. Males have massive brow-ridges, large and thick zygomatic bones, large broad maxillae with shallow palates and upper and lower teeth significantly larger than those of female adults. All adults have large mastoid processes and su-prameatal crests, but they are noticeably larger for males. Both sexes have large mandibles and well-defined chin forms. Adult males range from 66.3 inches to 70.3 inches in height, while adult females, who are slighter and shorter, range from 62.4 inches to 64.3 inches in height. These distinctive sexual dimorphisms are also apparent to a lesser de-gree in the mandibular, frontal, temporal mastoid, iliac and long bone morphology of adolescents and children.[32]

All of the adult females were right-handed, except two who were ambidextrous. Robbins found several common anomalies of the skel-etal elements. There were perforated olecranon fossae on the distal humeri of adult females. This anomaly was also present on some of the children's humeri, suggesting that the trait may have been trans-mitted genetically. Taurodont dentition, an expansion of the pulp cavity that can sometimes lead to the fusion of teeth roots, was a rather common anomaly. The trait appeared as early as adolescence and was prevalent among the older adults. It was not limited to any particular group of teeth; rather it could occur in any of an individual's teeth. Ear exostoses, or bony outgrowths, characterized about 20 percent of the adult population. Single ear exostoses were more frequent among male adults and multiple ear exostoses were found only on adult males. Bony nodules occurred frequently and were found on a variety of skeletal elements, such as the occiput, the mastoid process, the long bones, and even the phalanges.[33]

Two bones were distinctive for having been culturally modified. In the first, a fragmented femur, a hole had been drilled through the med-ullary cavity. In the second, a fragment of frontal bone from an adult, "a number of 6 mm holes had been drilled in a roughly oblong pattern through the frontal vault at various times during the life of the indi-vidual. Most of the holes were healed or in the final healing stage.

32. *Ibid.*
33. *Ibid.*

However, 3 holes had barely closed, and 2 were in a very early healing stage at the time of death.[34]

During her analysis of the Morton Shell Mound series, Robbins found that a small percentage of the skeletal elements were notably dissimilar from the phenotype range of the majority of the population. The skeletal fragments of both sexes of these "strangers" indicate smaller, more gracile individuals. Their cranial morphology was particularly different, and they lacked the distinctive sexual dimorphism of the majority of the population. Nevertheless, "whoever the strangers may have been, they were still accorded the Morton burial ritual."[35] It is tempting to speculate on the origins of these individuals.

The population suffered pervasive treponemal infection that was particularly prevalent among the adults. Robbins diagnosed the disease as yaws and described its process.

Initially this disease seems to appear in the bloodstream of children, adolescents, or very young adults, affecting the hemopoietic regions of the skeleton. Destruction of bone is more intensive and extensive than that resulting from periostitis, osteoporosis, or osteomalacia; shafts of long bones are affected by the disease but the cancellous bone in distal and proximal ends of long bone is also modified, as are medial and proximal sections of clavicles. A few fragments of broken and rehealed bones (femurs and ribs) reveal an abnormal profuseness of reparative bone. In contrast to periostitis, which tends to be more severe in tibial and fibular regions, the Morton pathology seems to work upon the humerus, radius and ulna to the same degree that it affects the bones of the legs; even the phalanges of the hands and feet are not omitted. Nearly all parts of the skull exhibit some evidence of the pathology, i.e., lesions of the cranial vault extending from the outer table into the enlarged diploe, increased vascularization of the inner vault table, obliteration of frontal, sphenoidal, and maxillary sinuses and in the interference with the regularity of periodontal destruction. Whether or not the pathology contributed to the formation of the sporadic bony nodules on various bones cannot be established. However, the opposition of irregularly-shaped bony spicules along lines of tendonous and ligamentous attachments (like linea aspera, deltoid tuberosity, nucha lines, and such) seem to be definitely linked to the severity of the pa-

34. *Ibid.*, 17.
35. *Ibid.*, 72.

thology, as does the lateral torsion of the humerus at the deltoid tuberosity and the anterior bowing of the tibial shaft.[36]

The immunological defenses of individuals afflicted with advanced stages of this disease would have been weakened. Therefore, treponema may have been an indirect cause of death. Certainly a disease manifested by open, running, stenchful sores in its advanced stages might have restricted an individual's social activities.

Clarence H. Webb, who read these data while they were in manuscript form, is of the opinion that the described pathologies are probably symptomatic of syphilis. Robbins disagrees. "If the diseased fragments from Morton Shell Mound are examined individually, some of them may resemble bones with syphilitic ostitis;" she wrote, "but when the fragments are examined in their proper context, i.e., representative of the Morton *series* and not as a single fragment with no cultural associations, a diagnosis of syphilis can not be substantiated." There are now three schools of thought respecting the origins of syphilis. The first theory holds that it originated in the Old World and was introduced into the New World on Columbus' voyages. Some scientists believe, on the contrary, that the American Indians infected Columbus' sailors. More recently, some scholars have postulated "that venereal syphilis is but one syndrome of a multi-faceted world-wide disease, treponematosis."[37]

Marco Joseph Giardino, in his master's thesis for Tulane University, provides another valuable source of physical anthropological data pertaining to the Troyville–Coles Creek Culture at Mount Nebo Mound.[38] This Troyville–Coles Creek tumulus situated on a natural levee along the Tensas River, Madison Parish, is a flat-topped, pyramidal mound measuring 190 feet by 180 feet at the base and reaching a height of 11 feet above the present ground surface (Pl. 53). In 1968 and 1969 I directed the mound excavation, a cooperative project of Loui-

36. *Ibid.*, 70–71.
37. Clarence H. Webb, personal communication to the author, January 21, 1978; Robbins, "Analysis of Human Skeletal Material from Morton Shell Mound," 70–71; Alfred W. Crosby, Jr., *The Columbian Exchange* (Westport, Conn., 1972), 123.
38. Marco Joseph Giardino, "An Osteological Analysis of the Human Population from the Mount Nebo Site, Madison Parish, Louisiana" (M.A. thesis, Tulane University, 1977).

siana State University and the Louisiana Department of Highways. The mound was constructed in eight stages, but all of the human bones were retrieved from Stage F near the mound base and from Stage A, the most recent phase of construction at the site. A minimum of 86 individuals was examined.

During Stage F times, circular pits containing more than one primary extended skeleton were the characteristic burial pattern. Skeletons would be lying side by side in a prone position with the heads to the south. It was sometimes obvious that the individuals had been placed in the pits at different times. Later burials intruded into and disrupted some of the earlier remains. Flexed skeletons, single and multiple bundle burials, and isolated skeletal elements, usually fragmented skulls, were also found in the pits. Several sherds, a deer man-

PLATE 53

View of the cross section of the Mt. Nebo Mound showing the multi-stage construction. Madison Parish, January 30, 1969.

dible, calcaneum, and antler, a worked bone fragment, and a pebble were associated with five adults in Stage F. These may have been purposeful burial offerings. The molars of one adult female were encrusted with red ochre. Perforated olecranon fossae on female humeri, such as were found at the Morton Shell Mound, occurred here on four specimens from Stage F. A stone projectile point was deeply imbedded in the right tibia of an adult female skeleton found in an extended, prone position in a multiple burial pit. The wound was not fatal, but it resulted in the synostosis of her tibia and fibula.[39] The small projectile point, of the type known as Alba Barbed, has been aptly described as fir-tree shaped. It is thought to indicate use of the bow and arrow.

By Stage A times at Mount Nebo, a different burial pattern had been adopted. Flexed skeletons, single and multiple bundle burials, isolated bones, and fragmented skulls were still represented, but now, in the preferred pattern, the pits were found to contain one or more primary burials, lying extended in a supine position with the head to the north. In one instance the cranium of an adult male was found in a vessel lying inverted on the Stage A floor. This find is similar to those Clarence B. Moore reports at mounds in Alabama and northwest Florida. In terms of funerary offerings, one Stage A burial pit contained five stone projectile points and a galena fragment. In another pit the rib cage and molars of an adult male and an adult female had been sprinkled with red ochre. The Troyville–Coles Creek people at Mount Nebo did not practice postmortem bone breaking.

Among the population examined, the "marked sexual dimorphism of the skeletal remains from Mount Nebo is duplicated by the population recovered from the Morton Shell Mound."[40] This population was not beset with the destructive effects of yaws or syphilis, however, although the symptoms were evident on the skeletal remains of two young females. Other pathologies included osteosarcoma and osteoarthritis in one adult male, synostosis and arthritic lipping that afflicted an adult female, and arthritic lipping on the vertebrae of six other adults—two males and four females. Only two males and one female exhibited healed fractures. Both males had fractured one of their tibiae, and the female had broken her ulna.

39. *Ibid.*, 49.
40. *Ibid.*, 6–7.

Because of the absence or fragmentation of many of the mandibular and maxillary elements, periodontal analysis was hampered. Nevertheless, Giardino examined 2,400 teeth, from which he derived age and sex data. He also found evidence of periodontal disease in about 8 percent of the Mount Nebo population and caries in 29 percent of the teeth he examined. Dental anomalies included Carabelli's Cusp, a tubercle situated on the lingual surfaces of maxillary molars on a young female and mesial rotation of the incisors on another individual.[41]

Demographic data from the analysis indicate that the skeletal material represents twenty-four males, twenty-four females, and thirty-eight other individuals of undetermined sex. A high percentage of females at Mount Nebo died between the ages of seventeen and twenty-five. In Stage F, 29 percent and in Stage A, 43 percent of the females were in this age range. Most of these women probably died during childbirth. Subadults, individuals between birth and seventeen years of age, represented 31 percent of the Mount Nebo population. Just as at the Morton Shell Mound and, apparently, at the Greenhouse Site, infant remains are notably rare at Mount Nebo. It is likely that their absence indicates that this age group was treated differently from the rest of the population at death. The human skeletons at Mount Nebo exhibit the same pronounced sexual dimorphism as was found in those from the Morton Shell Mound, but their stature ranges are quite surprisingly different. The Mount Nebo population is far shorter; males ranged in height from 61.2 to 66.3 inches and women were from 49.6 to 57.4 inches tall. The tallest men at Mount Nebo were only as tall as the shortest men at the Morton Shell Mound and the tallest women at Mount Nebo were, almost unbelievably 5 inches shorter than the smallest women at the Morton Shell Mound. It is possible that statistical error or skewed data are responsible for this difference in stature.

The nine earthen tumuli at the Mounds Plantation Site in Caddo Parish are another interesting expression of the Troyville—Coles Creek Culture. The mounds are located along a low-lying terrace of the Red River. Some are quadrilateral and flat-topped; others are dome shaped. The tallest is 15 feet in height, and the maximum lateral dimension of any of the mounds is about 220 feet. Adjacent to several sets of these

---

41. Giardino, "An Osteological Analysis of the Human Population from the Mount Nebo Site."

mounds are three borrow pits from which, presumably, came the dirt for mound construction. Midden debris, comprised principally of sherds strewn on the ground surface, suggest a settlement area extending for about 656 yards north to south and 1,300 yards east to west. The mounds are arranged in an ellipse oriented east-southeast to west-northwest. They enclose an open area, or plaza.[42] From the surface collection and excavations at the Mounds Plantation Site it is evident that the Troyville–Coles Creek Culture was the first in a sequence of occupations. Most of the mounds were not excavated, and their exact cultural assignments remain to be determined. But in 1959 Mound 3, located in the northern periphery of the site, was being bulldozed by the landowner. Fortunately, before its removal, Ralph R. McKinney was allowed time to excavate several trenches in it. The flat-topped circular mound, 9 feet high and 118 feet in diameter, had been erected over a black, premound midden, which, in turn, rested upon red clay devoid of archaeological remains. The 6- to 8-inch-thick midden stratum contained an abundance of sherds and animal bones. The sherds were predominantly Troyville–Coles Creek types, and McKinney and Clarence Webb felt that the midden, because of "its propinquity to the plaza but detachment from the major plaza axis," could have been an activity area devoted to ceremonial feasting.[43] As time passed the function of this area changed, and people of the Caddo Culture erected Mound 3 over the midden.

Mound 5 was also destined for destruction, and so it too was explored by McKinney. This tumulus at the southeastern end of the ellipse was described as quadrangular with a base measuring 160 feet by 220 feet. The summit, which was 15 feet high, measured 90 feet by 145 feet. Strata exposed in Mound 5 revealed a dome-shaped primary mound about 4 feet in height covering a stratum of premound midden. "Just above the premound level and cut down to a pit floor between 24 and 30 inches below the midden" was Burial Pit 6, which McKinney and Webb assign to the Troyville–Coles Creek Culture. The pit, below the crest of the primary mound, was ovoid in plan, oriented

42. Moore, "Some Aboriginal Sites on Red River"; Clarence H. Webb and Ralph R. McKinney, "Mounds Plantation (16CD12), Caddo Parish, Louisiana," *Louisiana Archaeology*, Bulletin No. 2 (1975), 39–127.
43. Webb and McKinney, "Mounds Plantation," 47.

northwest to southeast, and measured 16 feet by 14 feet. Lying side by side on the pit floor in extended supine positions were seven human skeletons. They had been placed along one side of the pit perpendicular to its long axis. Included was a young female adult, 65 inches in height. Her skeleton was "flexed to the left and the left arm flexed with the hand on the shoulder. Between her leg and the pit wall were ten smooth stones and two bone pins." Next to her was a male adult 66 inches tall. Near his left thigh were twenty-five small stone arrow points of the Homan type. There were copper stains near the left side of his skull, and concentrations of small pebbles were exposed near each of his ankles that may represent the remains of rattles. The next skeleton was that of an adult female 63 inches tall. Copper stains near her right wrist suggested the presence of a bracelet. Next in line were an adolescent 51 inches tall, a female adult 64 inches tall, another female adult 65 inches tall, and a male adult 67 inches tall. On the opposite side of Burial Pit 6, oriented perpendicularly to these seven skeletons, were three more skeletons. They, too, were lying side by side in an extended supine position. All were adult females with statures of 65 inches, 60 inches, and 64 inches. None of the three was associated with funerary offerings, but between one of the individuals and the burial pit wall was found the skeleton of a crane or egret.[44] (Parenthetically, it should be noted that Webb's skeletal measurements were conducted on the *in situ* interments, therefore they must not be interpreted as exact determinations of stature.)

Explorations elsewhere in Mound 5 revealed other human burials whose similarities in "compass orientation, levels of origin, skeleton orientation, pit size and paucity of offerings" suggest cultural and temporal affiliation with Burial Pit 6. The bone preservation in these five pits was not particularly rewarding however. Pit 10, measuring 9.2 feet by 3.9 feet, contained two adults and one adolescent whose statures were 66 inches, 62 inches, and 55 inches, respectively, lying side by side in extended supine positions. In Pit 11, which was 7.5 feet by 3.2 feet, the excavations revealed only one adult skull. Pit 12, parallel to the adjoining Pit 11, measured 8.4 feet by 3.9 feet. It contained an

---

44. Moore, "Some Aboriginal Sites on Red River"; Webb and McKinney, "Mounds Plantation," 64.

adult skull and vestiges of the torso and limb bones. Along each side and parallel to the skeletal remains "were depressed longitudinal stains, possibly from litter poles; dark stains on the floor suggested rotted fabrics." Near the right side of the skull, with tips aligned upward, were ten stone arrow points. Nine were identified as Colbert points, and one was of the Homan type. Pit 13, measuring 6.6 feet by 3.6 feet, contained only traces of one skull lying in the northeast corner. In Pit 14, which was 6.3 feet by 3.4 feet, were the poorly preserved remains of an adult 64 inches tall. Of this individual it was noted that "there was congenital absence of the lateral incisors and the upper third molars; the lower third molars were horizontal (impacted) and other teeth were badly worn."[45]

The investigations and report of the Troyville–Coles Creek component of Mounds Plantation are important contributions to our store of knowledge regarding that culture because they and the other excavations conducted there demonstrate quite clearly culture change at a site that lies on the periphery of the Troyville–Coles Creek settlement region. The evidence is somewhat comparable to but even clearer than that encountered at the Pierre Clement Site in western Louisiana.[46] Through time, in northwest Louisiana, Troyville–Coles Creek artifactual and ceremonial traits blended with and ultimately became dominated by what archaeologists regard as Caddo Culture manifestations.

The preceding pages have reviewed the more substantive investigations at Troyville–Coles Creek occupations in Louisiana. Ford, McIntire, Phillips, Brain, and I have reported site locations distributed throughout the major stream drainages of the alluvial valley from about the latitude of Greenville, Mississippi, to the Gulf of Mexico.[47] As one proceeds up the Red River from its mouth, Troyville–Coles Creek sites become less frequent, particularly upstream from Campti in Natchitoches Parish. West of there and in the southwest quadrant of Loui-

---

45. Webb and McKinney, "Mounds Plantation," 68, 69, 70.
46. Springer, "The Prehistory and Cultural Geography of Coastal Louisiana."
47. Ford, *Analysis of Indian Village Site Collections from Louisiana and Mississippi;* McIntire, *Prehistoric Indian Settlements of the Changing Mississippi River Delta;* Phillips, *An Archaeological Survey in the Lower Yazoo Basin;* Brain, "The Lower Mississippi Valley in North American Prehistory"; Neuman, *An Archaeological Assessment of Coastal Louisiana.*

siana, north of the marshes and west of the Opelousas-Lafayette environs, Troyville–Coles Creek mounds seem to be lacking, or at least they have not been documented. However, a relatively small number of Troyville–Coles Creek campsites, manifested by diagnostic sherds, have been reported in the riverine environments of those western areas. The same situation seems to prevail in the Florida parishes as one leaves the alluvial valley and lakeshore areas.

It is as yet difficult and perhaps even premature to define the attributes that may delimit sites of the Troyville–Coles Creek Culture. The variations evident in the sites just reviewed are to be expected, for after all, we are dealing with a cultural continuum of no less than 700 years. Some of the sites are multiple mound occupations with three or more tumuli oriented around an open area or plaza. There are also numerous sites with only a single mound, or at least that is how they appear today. It is agreed that the mounds are characteristically flat topped, but there is some question as to whether they are typically square sided or rectangular since, in many cases, the sites were reoccupied by subsequent cultures who added their own construction stages. Causeways connect two or more mounds at the Lake Larto mounds, Troyville, Greenhouse, and perhaps, the Neil Farm Site, but this construction feature has never been evaluated as a Troyville–Coles Creek settlement trait.[48]

The published data are insufficient for determining the cultural origin of the earthen ridge that enclosed the mound area at Troyville. Likewise, there are as yet no substantive data relative to the settlement systems of nonmound Troyville–Coles Creek occupations. We still do not know anything about domiciles or any other structures at such sites. Only by large-scale excavations at selected sites can concrete data be obtained on residential patterning and demography at nonmound sites.

It appears that the Troyville–Coles Creek people were the first of Louisiana's inhabitants to use the bow and arrow. The bow is generally acknowledged to be a European innovation of the Mesolithic period, about 7000 B.C. From there the weapon diffused into Asia and

48. Phillips, *An Archaeological Survey in the Lower Yazoo Basin*; Beyer, "The Mounds of Louisiana"; Walker, *The Troyville Mounds*; Ford, *Greenhouse*; Fowke, "Archaeological Investigations—II."

thence to North America. Harold Driver and William Massey suggest that it was probably introduced into the southwest region by southward-moving Athapaskan peoples and from there into Mexico and the southeastern United States. Small stone points, like the one found imbedded in the tibia of an adult female at Mount Nebo, initially appeared in Louisiana at Troyville–Coles Creek occupations. It is generally assumed that these small points were the tips of arrows shot from a bow.[49] Exactly how the bow-and-arrow complex altered hunting and fishing strategies is largely speculative, but without doubt it increased the speed, distance, and accuracy—in present-day parlance, the fire power—with which missiles could be propelled.

Another important Troyville–Coles Creek innovation was the development of large socioreligious centers with large and numerous temple mounds oriented around a plaza. This is almost certainly a trait that had diffused from Meso-America into the eastern United States, although exactly how and by which route or routes remains to be determined.[50] It would appear that by A.D. 400 the tropical cultigen corn (*Zea mays*), had been introduced into the lower alluvial valley; by A.D. 1000 the bean (*Phaseolus vulgaris*) had also been introduced. The squash (*Cucurbita pepo* var. *ovifera*) and the bottle gourd (*Lageneria siceraria*), also of tropical origin, had been in Louisiana at least since 325 B.C. Many archaeologists believe that these plant species, added to certain native plants, such as the sunflower (*Helianthus annua*), which was also domesticated; seeds of the marsh elder (*Iva* sp.), lamb's quarter (*Chenopodium* sp.), and knotweed (*Polygonum* sp.); and nuts, fruits, tubers, and roots, provided the necessary food surplus to sustain the large work forces needed to build the earthen constructions. Other archaeologists are of the opinion that our regional native plants, domesticated with or without influence from Meso-America, would have been sufficient to support these groups. And still other archaeologists reason that the then-existing subsistence system, with its reliance on efficiently exploiting wild resources, would have been

49. Harold Edson Driver and William C. Massey, "Comparative Study of North American Indians," *Transactions of the American Philosophical Society*, Vol. 47 (Philadelphia, 1957), 165–456; Neuman, "Atlatl Weights from Certain Sites on the Northern and Central Great Plains."
50. Willey, *An Introduction to American Archaeology*, Vol. I.

adequate to maintain the populations. Depending upon the time and the place of the site, each of these alternatives played its part.

The case for the existence of an efficient agricultural base for the Troyville–Coles Creek Culture in Louisiana is thought-provoking but unresolved. If we consider the squash and bottle gourd remains from the Tchefuncte occupation at the Morton Shell Mound, and the corn and squash reported from the Marksville Site, it would appear that these tropical cultigens had been in Louisiana long enough to have become of significant economic value. Conversely, the fact that not a single specimen of corn, beans, or squash has been reported from all of the thousands of cubic feet of dirt excavated at Troyville–Coles Creek sites would seem to indicate that these foodstuffs were as yet relatively minor and unimportant items in the people's diet. This lack of physical evidence, however, may be the result of excavating in the socioreligious centers rather than in the middens and habitation areas of the supporting farmsteads or settlements. Careful excavation in the latter areas may lead to the recovery of primary evidence in the form of charred remains and/or opal phytoliths of cultigens. Isotopic studies on the human skeletal material from Troyville–Coles Creek sites may also provide dietary evidence. Belmont has suggested that the dearth of such primary evidence as is usually found—charred cobs, kernels, and beans—was possibly due to certain regional culinary practices. Utilizing ethnohistoric data gathered from the Natchez Indians as an analogy, he states that although they "did parch kernels over the fire, there is no evidence that they roasted ears, or in fact used any cooking method wherein the cob would come near fire."[51]

The fact that most of the known Troyville–Coles Creek sites are located along stream systems where soil composition and fertility would have been ideal for plant cultivation is sometimes cited as indirect evidence of agriculture. It is a plausible argument, but it is well to re-

51. Byrd and Neuman, *Archaeological Data Relative to Prehistoric Subsistence in the Lower Mississippi Alluvial Valley*; Irwin Rovner, "Potential of Opal Phytoliths for Use in Paleoecological Reconstruction," *Quaternary Research*, Vol. 1 (1971), 343–59; J. C. Vogel and Nikolas J. van der Merwe, "Isotopic Evidence for Early Maize Cultivation in New York State," *American Antiquity*, Vol. 42 (1977), No. 2, pp. 238–42; John S. Belmont, "The Development of Agriculture in the Lower Valley," *Proceedings of the 22nd Southeastern Archaeological Conference*, Bulletin No. 5 (1967), 16–18.

member that there are numerous nonagricultural riverine cultures worldwide. It has also been hypothesized that, preceding and during the period under discussion in the Southeast, the introduction and adoption of tropical cultigens was largely responsible for an unprecedented population growth that, in turn, provided the needed labor for earthen constructions of Troyville–Coles Creek and subsequent times. This, too, is plausible indirect evidence, particularly when we consider the many examples of comparable population expansion that were due to the adoption of introduced food cultigens, in the post-Columbian New World as well as the Old World.[52] Unfortunately, there are no valid regional data that demonstrate anything but the vaguest demographic counts for the periods prior to the Troyville–Coles Creek Culture, nor are there any applicable to the period of that culture's existence. Archaeologists have been properly cautioned that "agriculture correlates roughly with sedentism in most regions of the world and it is obvious that sedentism, whether or not it results in actual population increases, will result in marked increases in the number of sites recorded simply because permanent sites are more likely to be preserved, and to be found by archaeologists, than are temporary campsites. . . . We are thus left with the impression of a population explosion accompanying the origins of agriculture which may be nothing more than the increase in recognized sites due to the differential preservation of permanent settlements."[53]

The questions and answers regarding the subsistence base for the Troyville–Coles Creek Culture are still largely theoretical. Furthermore, they encompass a number of alternatives. Only after further skillful excavations at productive sites, followed by competent analytical studies, can we hope to derive data to answer some of these queries. For the present it is reasonable to hypothesize that the early Troyville–Coles Creek Culture was a regional population with an incipient agricultural base. Hand in hand with this technology came an ideology that was accepted and that led to the development of socioreligious centers, which, although smaller than those in Meso-America, emulated them in form and function.

52. Crosby, The Columbian Exchange.
53. Mark N. Cohen, "Archaeological Evidence for Population Pressure in Pre-Agricultural Societies," American Antiquity, Vol. 40 (1975), No. 4, pp. 471–75.

IX Caddo Culture

Caddo was the name of the principal tribe of the Kadohadacho Confederation. The Indians belonging to this tribe lived along the Big Bend region of the Red River in Arkansas and Texas. As it is used here, the term *Caddo Culture* refers to a group that exhibited common diagnostic traits through a period of time in a region encompassing large, adjoining parts of Oklahoma, Arkansas, Texas, and Louisiana. The mixed oak-pine-hickory woodlands and prairie transition territory aptly referred to as the Trans–Mississippi South was occupied during historic times by certain Indian tribes who spoke what came to be called the Caddo language.[1] Archaeologists believe the prehistoric manifestations of the Caddo Culture represent the antecedents of these historic Caddo tribes. Admittedly, some of the traits of this construct are not unique to Caddo Culture, but they are more popular, more emphasized, and more cumulative in the region of the Caddo culture.

Clarence Moore's site excavations in the stream drainages of the Mississippi, Ouachita, and Red rivers of Arkansas and Louisiana and

---

1. John R. Swanton, *Source Material on the History and Ethnology of the Caddo Indians*, Bureau of American Ethnology Bulletin 132 (Washington, D.C., 1942); Robert W. Neuman, "Historic Locations of Certain Caddoan Tribes," in Neuman, *Caddoan Indians II* (New York and London, 1974), 9–147; Albert Gallatin, "A Synopsis of the Indian Tribes Within the United States East of the Rocky Mountains and the British and Russian Possessions in North America," *Transactions and Collections of the American Antiquarian Society*, Vol. 2 (1836), 422; Frank F. Schambach, "The Trans-Mississippi South: The Case for a New Natural Area West of the Lower Mississippi Valley and East of the Plains," paper presented at the Caddo Conference, Austin, 1971.

his subsequent publications provided the first substantive data on the archaeological remains of the Caddo Culture.[2]

Following Moore's explorations, no systematic archaeological research was done on Caddo Culture until the advent of federally assisted projects in the 1930s.[3] Although none of the WPA archaeological projects in Louisiana was involved with Caddoan sites *per se*, Winslow Walker's Caddoan investigations, described in the first chapter, were federally funded. It was Clarence H. Webb, however, who developed a systematized construct for the archaeological complexes of the Caddoan area. He organized and hosted the first informal conference dealing with those complexes in 1942, and through his efforts, the first formal Caddo conference convened at the University of Oklahoma in 1946. His keen leadership has been an integral part of all subsequent Caddo conferences to date.

Before describing the traits of the Caddo Culture and their manifestations at sites in Louisiana, it may be well to review briefly the culture sequence of northwest Louisiana and the areas immediately surrounding it. The area was first inhabited during the Paleo-Indian and Meso-Indian periods, with the expected regional variations, particularly in the late stages of the Meso-Indian period. Between that period and about A.D. 500 pre-Caddo cultures inhabited the region. Their artifactual remains consist almost solely of chipped-stone and ground-stone tool assemblages. Partly coeval with these sites, though fewer, are others with comparable stone tool assemblages found in association with clay-or sand- or bone-tempered pottery, occasional copper

2. Robert W. Neuman, "Archaeological and Historical Assessment of the Red River Basin in Louisiana," in Hester A. Davis (ed.), *Archaeological and Historical Resources of the Red River Basin*, Arkansas Archaeological Survey, Research Series, No. 1 (Fayetteville, 1970). Those who are interested in the superlative artistry of certain types of prehistoric North American ceramics can do no better than to study the splendid color plates of selected Caddo vessels in the following reports: Clarence Bloomfield Moore, "Certain Mounds in Arkansas and Mississippi," *Journal of the Academy of Natural Sciences of Philadelphia*, 2nd Series, Vol 13 (1908), Pt. 4, pp. 481–600; Moore, "Antiquities from the Ouachita"; Moore, "Some Aboriginal Sites on Red River"; Moore, "Some Aboriginal Sites in Louisiana and Arkansas." Of course, a more comprehensive illustrative volume was published by the Texas Archaeological Society and the Texas Memorial Museum: Dee Ann Suhm and Edward B. Jelks (eds.), *Handbook of Texas Archaeology: Type Descriptions* (Austin, 1962).

3. Kenneth C. Orr, "Survey of Caddoan Area Archaeology," in James B. Griffin (ed.), *Archaeology of Eastern United States* (Chicago, 1952), 239–55.

and bone artifacts, and low earthen burial mounds. The Resch Site, with its Tchefuncte and Marksville components, and the Coral Snake Mound are notable sites within the Caddo area.[4]

Another pertinent site is the Bellevue Mound overlooking Bodcau Bayou in Bossier Parish. This flat-topped mound, 80 feet in diameter and 10 feet high, was an accretional structure composed of superimposed midden strata and red clay. It was built over a shallow pit about 6 feet in diameter containing the cremated remains of two humans, an adult female and a young child. Encircling the pit was an oval postmold pattern, measuring about 10 feet in diameter, which Fulton and Webb suggest is the remains of a ceremonial structure, perhaps an arbor.[5] Within the mound fill were several strata of midden beneath a red clay stratum on top of which was a flexed interment of an adult female. These remains were mantled with additional midden strata. Most of the 752 sherds from the Bellevue excavations are closely relatable to Marksville ceramics. However, the 14 bone-tempered sherds herald a diagnostic trait of the Caddo area. The stone points, knives, scrapers, spokeshaves, quartz crystals, and grinding stones generally continue to reflect the conservative traits of traditional lithic technologies.

After about A.D. 700 the Troyville–Coles Creek Culture began to manifest itself in northeast Texas, southwest Arkansas, and northwest Louisiana. These remains either underlie or, often, are intermixed with early Caddo deposits. In fact, the cultures are so closely related that archaeologists find it quite difficult—in some cases impossible—to differentiate sherds of Caddoan nonceremonial, utilitarian vessels from those of pottery types thought diagnostic of the Troyville–Coles Creek Culture. And the same situation applies to much of the nonceramic artifactual inventory.

Undoubtedly, the Troyville–Coles Creek Culture and subsequent

4. Harry J. Shafer, "Comments on Woodland Cultures of East Texas," *Bulletin of the Texas Archaeological Society*, Vol. 46 (1975), 249–54; Clarence H. Webb, "A Review of Northeast Texas Archaeology," *Bulletin of the Texas Archaeological Society*, Vol. 29 (1960), 35–62; Don G. Wyckoff, *Caddoan Cultural Area: An Archaeological Perspective* (Norman, 1971).
5. Robert L. Fulton and Clarence H. Webb, "The Bellevue Mound: A Pre-Caddoan Site in Bossier Parish, Louisiana," *Bulletin of the Texas Archaeological Society*, Vol. 24 (1953), 18–42.

Mississippi Valley cultures strongly influenced the developmental stages of Caddo Culture. This is not to say that Caddo Culture necessarily derived from these cultures, but certainly there was significant interaction between them. Meso-American peoples also exerted considerable influence in the formation of the Caddo Culture. The ceremonial centers; temple mounds; corn, bean and squash agriculture; ear ornaments; ceramic vessel forms and their decorative motifs so characteristic of the Caddo Culture, are inescapably Meso-American in origin.[6]

The culture antecedents of the Caddo Culture are complex, but the analyzed archaeological remains provide a substantial framework for tracing the cultural components. To begin with, more than 260 radiocarbon determinations relative to Caddo manifestations in Oklahoma, Arkansas, Texas, and Louisiana have been published.[7] Obviously some of these determinations refer to the late stages of the Caddo Culture, but the earlier ones place the beginnings of the Caddo Culture at a time no later than A.D. 800.

Early Caddo sites range from mound sites associated with village occupations, to mound sites with no apparent village associations nearby, and village sites or small hamlets without mounds. The mounds, either flat-topped pyramids or dome-shaped structures, often of multistage construction, functioned as platforms for buildings and/ or for the interment of specially selected individuals. The remains of structures built atop various mound stages reveal circular and square floor plans, and the human interments are accompanied by a wide array of ceremonial and utilitarian objects (Pls. 54, 55, 56). These mound centers are typically located in the valleys of the major stream systems. Nonmound village sites are usually located on sandy ridges or terraces above small stream systems. These sites are characterized by strewn village detritus, midden concentrations, trash pits, fire pits, cache pits, and postmolds, wall trenches, burnt clay, and daub indic-

6. H. Perry Newell and Alex D. Krieger, *The George C. Davis Site, Cherokee County, Texas*, Memoirs of the Society for American Archaeology No. 5 (Menasha, Wis., 1949).
7. Wyckoff, *Caddoan Cultural Area;* Dee Ann Story and S. Valastro, Jr., "Radiocarbon Dating and the George C. Davis Site, Texas," *Journal of Field Archaeology*, Vol. 4 (1977), No. 1, pp. 63–89.

ative of habitations with circular or square floor patterns. There are also graves at these sites, but the funerary accompaniments are generally not as elaborate as those associated with the mound burials. At some of the village graves, in fact, there is no evidence of funerary objects.

Pottery is found at all Caddo sites (Pls. 57, 58, 59). The details of most of the types have been amply illustrated and presented.[8] There are two main categories of pottery. The first, the type most diagnostic of the Caddo Culture, comprises those vessels usually associated with human burials and/or ceremonial structures. These were manufactured using the coiling technique, and the clay was tempered with grit, sand, clay, and less often, with bone or shell. Vessel shapes include carinated, simple, and compound bowls, and variously shaped jars and bottles with tapered spouts. The vessels may be plain, but more often they are very ornately decorated and highly polished. The Caddo potters used such decorative techniques as incising, excising, engraving, punctating, brushing, stamping, ridging, appliqué, adornos and handles. In addition, some vessel surfaces are covered with a red slip and/or the engraved motifs are colored or filled in with white, red, or green pigments. The second category of vessels, utilitarian or culinary wares, occurs most typically with village detritus. Most of these are represented by sherds (rarely are intact vessels found), difficult to differentiate from contemporary and later Mississippi Valley types. However, the stamped motifs so characteristic of later Mississippi Valley types are infrequent in Caddoan assemblages.[9]

Along the Red River at the community of Gahagan, in Red River Parish, is a Caddo site that was first described and explored by C. B. Moore.[10] There were an unspecified number of mound remnants in the plowed fields. One mound, about 80 feet in diameter and 11 feet tall,

8. Clarence H. Webb and Monroe Dodd, "Pottery Types from the Belcher Mound Site," *Bulletin of the Texas Archaeological and Paleontological Society*, Vol. 13 (1941), 88–116; Dee Ann Suhm, Alex D. Krieger, and Edward B. Jelks, "An Introductory Handbook of Texas Archaeology," *Bulletin of the Texas Archaeological Society*, Vol. 25 (1954); Suhm and Jelks (eds.), *Handbook of Texas Archaeology*.
9. Newell and Krieger, in *The George C. Davis Site*, presented the nuances of these ceramic relationships quite clearly in their superb report on the extensive excavation at that site, an early Caddo mound and village occupation in east Texas.
10. Moore, "Some Aboriginal Sites on Red River."

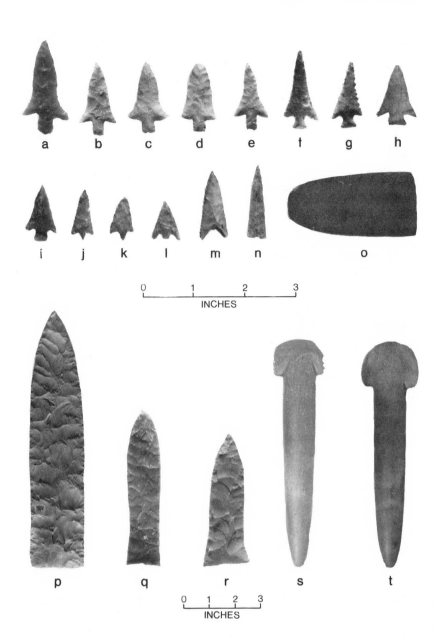

0   1   2   3
INCHES

0   1   2   3
INCHES

PLATE 54

Chipped- and ground-stone artifacts of the Caddo Culture: *a–m*, stone projectile points; *n*, bone projectile point; *o*, stone celt; *p–r*, Gahagan knives; *s–t*, ceremonial celts.

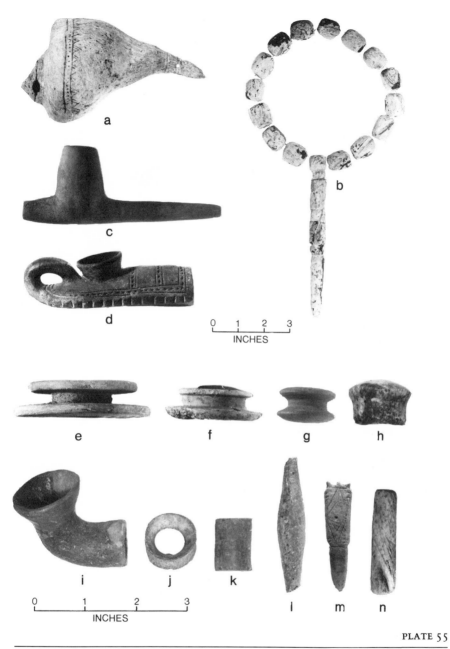

PLATE 55

Artifacts of the Caddo Culture: *a–b*, shell ornaments; *c–d*, clay pipes; *e–g*, clay ear spools; *h*, antler ear spool; *i*, clay pipe; *j*, bone ear spool; *k*, ceramic labret; *l*, copper bead; *m*, shell pendant; *n*, tubular shell bead.

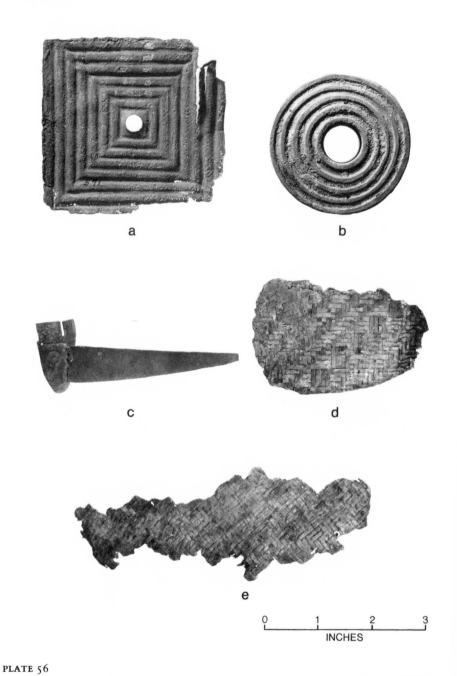

a

b

c

d

e

0 1 2 3
INCHES

Artifacts of the Caddo Culture: *a–b*, copper ear ornament; *c*, Long Nosed God Mask; *d–e*, split cane matting fragments.

0 1 2 3
INCHES

PLATE 57

Ceramic vessels of the Caddo Culture.

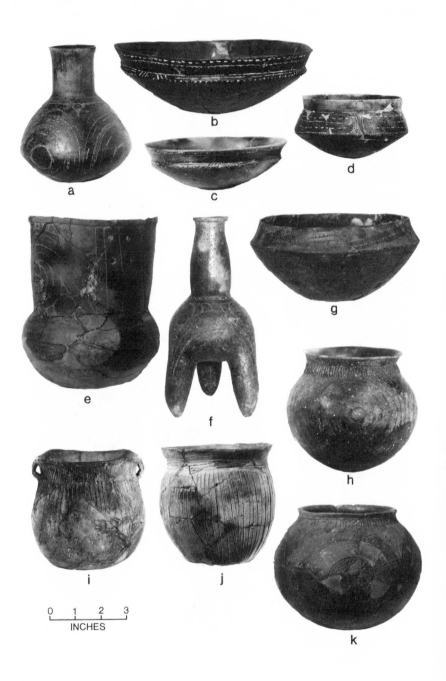

0   1   2   3
INCHES

PLATE 58

Ceramic vessels of the Caddo Culture.

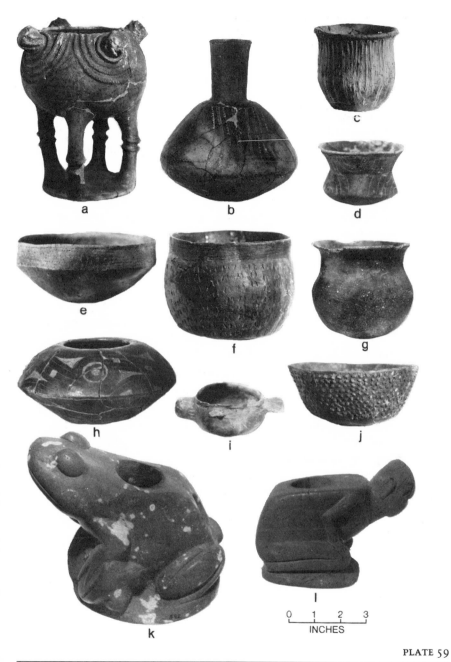

PLATE 59

Ceramic vessels and stone pipes of the Caddo Culture: *a–j*, vessels; *k–l*, effigy pipes.

was excavated and found to contain a central burial pit measuring about 12 feet by 9 feet. The pit bottom was 11 feet below the mound summit. At Gahagan and at a number of other Caddoan sites, excavations have revealed a burial pattern in which mounds were constructed first and then burial pits were dug into them, generally to the depth of the ground surface on which the mound was built but sometimes as much as 7 feet beneath the original ground surface. The human burials at Gahagan, three adults and two adolescents, were in extended supine positions on the pit floor. Three of the skeletons were placed in the middle of the pit, parallel to its long axis, the other two were toward the ends of the pit and oriented perpendicularly to its long axis. Funerary offerings lay near or were associated with particular skeletal elements of three of the burials and were arranged in groups along one of the ends of the pit. The objects included poorly preserved wooden objects that had been copper covered; bone pins; chipped-stone points, knives, and celts; an atlatl weight; lumps of galena; and the remains of rattles. The artifact concentrations at the northern end of the pit included a human effigy pipe; three clay vessels, one vase-shaped and the others bottle forms; fifty-six finely chipped, obviously ceremonial stone points or blades ranging from about 4 to 9 inches in length, most of them arranged in two piles; numerous stone chips; a grooved sandstone hone; a shale chisel; bone pins; and red pigment.

Twenty-six years later, Clarence H. Webb and Monroe Dodd, Jr., conducted further excavations into the same mound at the Gahagan Site. Slightly to the east of the pit Moore had dug, they found and excavated two other burial pits. The first, measuring 19.5 feet by 15 feet, extended to a depth of 8 feet below the east slope of the mound. A row of five human skeletons was found lying along the central part of the pit. A sixth skeleton, oriented perpendicularly to the others, was placed next to one of the side walls, midway between the ends of the pit. The burials—three adult females, two adult males, and one adolescent—were all in an extended supine position. The females were 60 to 68 inches tall, the males measured 67 inches and 72 inches, and the adolescent was also 72 inches tall. In direct association with two of the females and one of the males were copper-covered wood and stone ear ornaments, stone points, and a stone blade. Concentrations of funerary objects had been specially placed along one side wall and at two of the pit's corners. They "were found on the floor and to a height of two feet in the fill along the northwest pit margin. . . . these facts suggest their placement as part of a ceremony while the pit was being filled."[11] In the first concentrations, there were five ground-stone celts, two chipped blades, sixteen bone pins, four bone ear disks, sixteen socketed antler tines, seven shell ear disks, copper beads, unworked copper strips, two copper effigies of human hands, and two of human faces.

These last two objects were "made from two sheets, one cut to form the oval face, the other to form a long grotesque nose which was inserted through a slit in the face and bradded with narrow copper strips. A groove across the forehead with lateral holes allowed for attachment of the mask."[12] Although named "Long Nosed God Masks," these objects (Pl. 56, c), only about 3 inches tall and 2 inches wide with a nose 7 inches long, were not made to cover the face. Instead, they served as ear ornaments. Three pairs of copper masks incredibly similar to these have been reported from other sites in Wisconsin, Missouri, and Florida. One stone mask and three shell versions were recovered from sites in Wisconsin, Oklahoma, Tennessee, and Alabama. It is possible but not very likely that the Gahagan masks were manufactured in Louisiana. Since all of the copper specimens are so very identical, it would appear that they were made in one place and then traded. They cut across cultural traditions in the Southeast, Midwest, and the Caddo area and are excellent time markers.[13]

Between the first and second artifact concentrations was a small, ornately incised, glossy black bowl that had been broken when it was placed in the burial pit. The second concentration contained two groups of small, finely chipped points, thirteen blade fragments, eight ground-stone celts, two stone disks, and a small quantity of unworked quartz fragments. There were also three ear ornaments, a shell spoon, a leather-covered copper object, a red clay stone human effigy pipe (Pl. 59, l), three fragments of cane basketry, and soil discolorations indic-

11. Clarence H. Webb and Monroe Dodd, "Further Excavations of the Gahagan Mound: Connections with the Florida Culture," *Bulletin of the Texas Archaeological and Paleontological Society*, Vol. 11 (1939), 96.
12. *Ibid.*, 107.
13. For a comprehensive study of all the known Long Nosed God Masks, see Stephen Williams and John M. Goggin, "The Long Nosed God in Eastern United States," *Missouri Archaeologist*, Vol. 18 (1956), No. 3, pp. 1–72.

ative of decayed objects. The third concentration consisted of eleven long, chipped-stone triangular blades, called "Gahagan knives," (Pl. 54, *p–r*) and a ground-stone celt. Nearby was a flat-bottomed, long-necked ceramic bottle. Just beyond the bottle was the fourth concentration containing a square, centrally perforated, embossed copper plaque (Pl. 56, *a*), five copper-covered wooden animal-claw representations, several copper objects of unknown purpose, ten barrel-shaped marine shell beads, and two masses of galena. At each end of this northwest side wall were deposits of chipped-stone points. All of the other areas within the burial pit were devoid of artifacts.

Subsequently, but probably not much later, to judge from the continuity of the burial positions and associated artifacts, another human interment intruded into the pit to a depth of 6 feet. It represented a male adult 71 inches in stature, lying in an extended supine position. Copper-covered stone ear ornaments lay on each side of the skull and near the left knee were sixty-one small, finely chipped stone points.

The second burial pit excavated by Webb and Dodd was also on the mound slope, about 6 feet from their first pit. It measured 12 feet by 11 feet and extended to a depth of 8 feet. On the floor at the west end were three human skeletons, two adults and one adolescent, lying side by side in an extended supine position. One adult was a male 71 inches tall; the second adult (sex indeterminate) was 69 inches tall; and the adolescent, lying between the two adults, measured 54 inches. Directly associated with the male adult were four chipped stone points and a Gahagan knife. With the other adult were six stone points, a blade, and a small long-stemmed clay pipe.

Just as in the previous pit, most of the artifacts here were aligned along one side wall. They included sandstone hones, thirteen chipped points, ten Gahagan knives, blade fragments, stone flakes, five ground-stone celts, one mealing stone, eight rubbing stones, a stone disk, one double-stemmed stone pipe, a stone plummet, five ear ornaments of stone and bone, one sandstone frog effigy pipe, seventeen bone pins, four beaver incisors, a copper plaque perforated and embossed in a fashion similar to the one in the previous pit, copper-covered wooden ear ornaments, and a pile of three hundred marginella shell beads. At the opposite side of the pit and at the same end as the burials were another frog effigy pipe (Pl. 59, *k*) and a Gahagan knife almost 10 inches long. The pipe, made of a mottled red clay stone, had been shaped and polished. This large, unusual specimen, which weighs over 7.5 pounds, depicts "a male bullfrog seated on a pedestal, holding a smaller female frog under his chest with the left forepaw. With the right forepaw he presses deeply into the female's lower abdomen, expressing the eggs from the sac."[14]

The people of the Troyville–Coles Creek Culture were the original inhabitants of the large, multiple-mound site at Mounds Plantation in Caddo Parish. In time, there was a gradual shift to the Caddo Culture, which is perhaps best illustrated by the fact that Caddo burials there did not intrude into the earlier Troyville–Coles Creek burials in Mound 5. "This implies knowledge of previous burial locations and respect for them. Such awareness and consideration mitigates against a long time interval and favors a change in culture but not in people."[15]

Most of the information relative to the Caddoan occupation at Mounds Plantation came from Mound 5. We know that Mound 3 had been built over midden accumulations and some sort of poled, ceremonial structure and that the upper levels of the mound contained two separate human burials. One burial was associated with five Caddoan-type vessels and a deer mandible polished from wear, perhaps from use as a corn sheller. Unfortunately, the other human burial and the mound were destroyed before much data could be salvaged. At Mound 5, the reader will recall, Webb and McKinney found a primary mound or stage of construction containing human burials of the Troyville–Coles Creek Culture. A red clay layer, about one foot thick, mantled the primary mound and then the mound was enlarged by subsequent additions of sandy clay lenses. By the time Webb and McKinney dug into Mound 5, its crest was about 10 feet above the surrounding surface.[16] In the mound center were seven rectangular burial pits, five of which can be definitely attributed to the Caddo occupation of the Mounds Plantation Site.

Pit 1, measuring 10 feet by 11 feet, had a depth of 2 feet. On its floor were the fragile remains of five human skeletons. Four of the skeletons, centrally located in the pit, were placed side by side in an ex-

14. Webb and Dodd, "Further Excavations of the Gahagan Mound," 103.
15. Webb and McKinney, "Mounds Plantation," 121.
16. *Ibid.*

tended supine position. The fifth skeleton, in a much better state of preservation, was placed on a dirt ledge about 8 inches high that extended along one of the pit walls. This burial, an adult male 70 inches in stature, was also in an extended supine position, but it was oriented perpendicularly to the others, and there were no direct artifactual associations with it. The other four skeletons, as well as could be determined, consisted of an adult, an adolescent, a child, and the remains of another individual unidentifiable as to age or sex. Associated with various elements of the skeletons were forty finely chipped stone points, Gahagan knives, a ground-stone celt, rattle remains consisting of a turtle carapace and groups of small pebbles, copper-plated ear ornaments, and one unusual leather-covered wooden ear ornament about 4 inches in diameter with a central copper boss and eight radial copper studs. To judge from the artifactual associations, the adolescent was the most revered individual in Pit 1. Just as at the Gahagan Site, however, most of the funerary accompaniments were not directly associated with a particular burial; rather they were placed in the pit corners. Among the objects were chipped-stone points, flakes, cores, ground-stone celts, polished pebbles, hammerstones, sandstone hones, a slab of ironstone, a mass of galena, a small engraved bowl, sherds, and a concentration of charred and fragmented animal bones.

Pit 2, located adjacent to Pit 1, measured about 12 feet by 7 feet and had a depth of 6 feet. On the floor in the center of the pit was a human skeleton representing the remains of an adult about 67 inches in stature, possibly a middle-aged male. Directly associated with him were copper-plated wooden ear ornaments with finger-like projections, five chipped, stone points, eight blades, a ground-stone celt, and a bear canine tooth.[17]

Next to Pit 2 was Pit 3, somewhat trapezoidal in plan, measuring 17 feet by 14 feet, and having the same depth as Pit 2. The human skeletal material here was barely discernible. Nevertheless, it was possible to detect a row of seven individuals—one infant, two children, and several adults—in the pit center. Near one of the skulls were copper fragments and a stone point and in the fill above the remains of three of the skulls was a lens of yellow sand and a green pigment, possibly glauconite.

17. *Ibid.*, 53.

Pit 4, located toward the mound center, was 6 feet by 2 feet and contained only traces of a human skeleton. There were no artifactual associations, and so the cultural assignation of this burial is indeterminate.

Pit 5 at the mound center was the largest deep-shaft burial found at Mounds Plantation. This rectangular pit had been dug through the mound fill and then even further through the premound midden. While digging this pit the Indians, for some reason had carefully thrown the dirt fill up and out along just three sides of the pit. When they finished digging, the pit measured 19 feet by 17 feet and reached a depth of 17 feet. To adorn the pit they colored three of its sides with a red pigment.

A sequence of individuals was interred in Pit 5 over a limited period of time. Most of the skeletons were found in the extended supine position, but several were lying extended on their sides, another was in an extended prone position, and still another individual was sitting slouched against the pit wall. The skeletons included three adult males, eight adult females (three of which contained a flexed fetus), an adult of undeterminable sex, one adolescent, and five infants. Statures of the adult males ranged from 67 to 72 inches; those of the adult females ranged from 63 to 67 inches.

Although the burial pattern manifested at Pit 5 follows the general Caddo tradition at other contemporary culturally related mounds, there are notable embellishments that distinguish Pit 5 from the others because, through a combination of factors, wood and cane were better preserved here than elsewhere. For example, four individuals— two adult females, one of whom had died during pregnancy, her fetus, and an adolescent—were partially covered by a timber framework of cedar. The timbers were about 5 inches wide and 55 inches long. Two of the timbers, lying adjacent to each other, had been drilled and, apparently, were mortised together. Overlying the pregnant female was another wooden framework or structure, which the excavators thought might be the remains of a cradle board. Immediately overlying the skeletons were layers of split-cane (*Arundinaria gigantica*) matting. The mats, sometimes four to eight layers of them, covered the bodies from the knees to the shoulders and were wrapped around some of the individuals. The matting fragments display a variety of weaves and design patterns. The mats were further embellished by dyeing the splints on one or both faces. The splints ranged from natural buff to glossy black, and some were intricately woven to form herringbone, diamond, and bird head motifs. Also associated with the same burials were wooden objects, including three flat lanceolate objects, the side edges of which are smooth and glossy from wear. These range from about 5 inches to 9 inches in length, and Webb and McKinney suspected that they were knife simulations purposely made for burial rites. Other associated wooden artifacts included a comb fragment with three teeth or prongs, two poorly preserved objects that may have been arrow shafts, and a baton-shaped object about 22 inches long.[18]

Slightly isolated from all of the other burials and oriented perpendicularly to them, was the skeleton of an adult male, which the excavators believed to be the paramount burial in Pit 5. He was in an extended supine position with one arm akimbo and both legs slightly bowed. His bones were massive, and he measured 72 inches in stature. Next to his left side was a wooden bow, the first actual physical evidence for the existence of that weapon in prehistoric Louisiana. The bow length was about 66 inches. "The mid-section and lower half were well preserved, including the recurve at the tip, but the upper half was distorted or decayed. There were traces of leather around the middle, with an indicated midbow diameter of only 1.7 cm. We assume that there was a leather handgrip. The wood was identified as bois d'arc or Osage orange (*Toxylon parniferum*), the famous Caddo bow wood."[19] Three other bows, or their remains, had also been excavated from Pit 5. They were curved, between 31 inches and 36 inches in length, and the wood of the shortest specimen was identified as bois d'arc.

Among the other funerary objects deposited with the paramount burial, there were poorly preserved wooden and copper ear ornaments on each side of his skull, five stone points, and a Gahagan knife, which was placed near the left forearm. To the left of the burial was a mass of seeds identified as *Portulaca oleracea* L., of the purslane family, in addition to fragments of wood, leather, and cane matting. Next to the right arm were two red tubular stone beads, a slate pendant, a polished and perforated hematite plummet, three puma canine teeth, "another

18. *Ibid.*
19. *Ibid.*, 104–105.

mass of seeds, and a small mass of calcifying pigment in which were impressions of a bead and the plummet."[20] Interestingly, the excavators recognized that the ground-stone beads, plummet, and pendant are diagnostic artifacts of the Poverty Point Culture, and they interpreted their placement with the paramount burial in this Caddo Culture manifestation as an example of fetishism. It is likely that these objects were found at some long-abandoned Poverty Point occupation, regarded with subjective awe, retained, and then purposely selected as funerary accompaniments for the paramount burial. Other artifactual associations in Pit 5 include a shallow black bowl about 12 inches in diameter and 3 inches deep lying shattered above the skulls of two female adults.[21] It is intricately decorated on the interior and exterior surfaces with incised and excised lines and punctations. These decorative motifs were filled with a green pigment, probably glauconite, and a yellow pigment was used to stain a portion of the base interior. One of the female adult skeletons was holding a cane staff about 44 inches long and an adult male nearby was associated with a comparable staff, one of the previously mentioned wooden bows, five stone points, and a red-filmed clay pipe. The pipe stem is about 8 inches long and less than one-half inch in diameter. The small, plain bowl rests on the stem about an inch from the distal end of the pipe. This long-stemmed variety of clay pipe is particularly diagnostic of the Caddo Culture.[22] The final unusual find in Pit 5 was the skeleton of an adult female that was found seated, leaning against the pit wall, holding a child's skull in the curve of her left arm. Much could be said in detailing the chipped—and ground—stone artifacts found in Pit 5, but it will suffice here to remark that many were made from exotic stone and to note that most of the stone celts, small notched points, and Gahagan knives are diagnostic of the Caddo Culture.

Two other burial pits were exposed in Mound 5 and found to contain Caddo artifacts. Burial Pit 7, measuring about 75 inches by 30

20. *Ibid.*, 56.
21. Clarence H. Webb and Ralph R. McKinney, "An Unusual Pottery Vessel from Mounds Plantation Site, Caddo Parish, Louisiana," *Arkansas Archaeologist*, Vol. 4 (1963), No. 5, pp. 1–9.
22. Michael P. Hoffman, "Ceramic Pipe Style Chronology Along the Red River Drainage in Southwestern Arkansas," *Arkansas Archaeologist*, Vol. 8 (1967), No. 1, pp. 4–14.

inches with a depth of 35 inches contained the remains of an adult female about 62 inches in stature. With her there were three small stone points placed near the chest area. The skeletal remains in Pit 8 were too poorly preserved for sexual identification, but they seemed to be those of an adult 66 inches in stature. The burial pit measured about 10 feet by 5 feet and had the same depth as Pit 7. In this pit, at the end containing the skull, were placed two vessels, one a shallow platter and the other a more ornately decorated bowl with a convex base and barrel-shaped walls. Five small stone points and a Gahagan knife also accompanied this interment.

With Pit 8 we conclude the discussion of the Caddo occupation at the Mounds Plantation. This site and the Gahagan Site are examples of large multimound, ceremonial centers. It is probably no accident that Mounds Plantation is located halfway between Gahagan and the Crenshaw Site, a similar mound center upstream in Miller County, Arkansas. Along the Red River, between Gahagan and Crenshaw, are a number of smaller Caddoan occupations characterized by only one or two tumuli each.[23]

One such occupation is the Belcher Site, located along the bank and natural levee of an abandoned channel of the Red River in Caddo Parish. It was excavated over a period of five years (1936–1941) by Clarence H. Webb and his collaborators and subsequently reported upon in the *Memoirs of the Society for American Archaeology*.[24] Prior to excavation, the primary feature at the site appeared to be a single mound measuring about 100 feet by 80 feet and 8 feet high. A low platform about 50 feet square projected out from the mound in a northwest direction. Excavations soon revealed, however, that the projection and the mound were once two separate tumuli that had since, through erosion, amalgamated. The larger tumulus was designated Mound A, the smaller, Mound B. Further testing demonstrated that site refuse lay at a depth of about 4 feet below the surrounding ground surface and that the occupation area extended from about 100 feet upstream to a half mile downstream from the mound. Webb and his colleagues used

23. W. Raymond Wood, *The Crenshaw Site: A Coles Creek and Caddoan Mound Group in Miller County, Arkansas* (Fayetteville, n.d.).
24. Clarence H. Webb, *The Belcher Mound*, Memoirs of the Society for American Archaeology No. 16 (Salt Lake City, 1959).

techniques that were exemplary for their cautiousness to investigate this complex stratified site. As he wrote in his site report:

> We adopted the combined slicing-stripping technique for the eastern halves of the upper habitation levels and the entirety of the lower two levels. Each successive habitation level was completely cleared by troweling, thus exposing entire floors and all features connected with the respective structure for measurements, photographs and drawings. After removing the house floor by troweling, the subjacent fill was re-moved down to the next habitation level by vertical slicing or shaving, leaving small blocks of soil around each survey stake until the entire habitation level had been cleared, in order to maintain a continuing check on depths of fill, measurements, placements of artifacts, and so forth. After exposing the habitation level, these pillars were removed and the survey stakes replaced before proceeding downward to the next habitation.[25]

Their postexcavation curatorship of the field notes, maps, drawings, and artifacts was just as scientifically precise. The report is a vivid, comprehensive statement on archaeological methodology.

The deep shaft burial pits containing multiple interments in extended supine positions and much of the associated funerary offerings at Belcher mirror the manifestations at Gahagan and Mounds Plantation. The Belcher tumuli served an additional purpose as platforms for two general types of ceremonial or communal buildings. Webb concluded from analysis of the stratigraphy and artifactual remains at Belcher that there was a succession of at least four occupations or stages at the site.[26] They are manifested by premound structures and burial pits and subsequent multistage mound construction associated with additional structures and human interments.

The first occupation, Belcher I, was manifested by a premound structure underlying Mound B. The building (House 4) had burned and collapsed, and the Indians had covered it with sand and a clay cap in order to form a low primary mound. Some parts of the building were outlined by wall trenches containing postmolds, and other wall segments were outlined by postmolds without wall trenches. The floor pattern indicated a rectangular structure 24 feet by 20 feet with a cov-

25. *Ibid.*, 17.
26. *Ibid.*

ered entranceway 3 feet wide and 7 feet long, extending straight out from the middle of the northeast wall. The entranceway floor, a kind of ramp built up about a foot higher than the floor of the structure, slanted down toward the floor of the building interior. The wall trenches, about 10 inches wide and 18 inches deep, contained closely spaced posts with diameters of about 6 inches. These wall trenches did not meet at the corner; instead, the latter were demarcated by three postmolds each. The posts in the wall trenches were embedded as much as 3 feet beneath the floor of the building. Although there were postmolds in several areas of the building interior, their spacing and patterns suggest that they functioned as platform frames or cooking racks rather than roof supports. In fact, there was no evidence of roof supports, and it seems likely that the roof was formed by bending the wall posts inward and interweaving their ends. This supporting frame was then intertwined with split cane and grass-covered with wattle and daub. Edwin N. Wilmsen, in his study of Caddoan house forms, suggests that House 4 may have had vertical walls 5 to 10 feet in height, topped and secured with horizontal poles, which acted as supports for roof poles that leaned inward and intertwined to form a pitched roof. The walls would then have been covered with wattle and daub and the roofs thatched.[27] The floor of this Belcher structure was packed hard and stained with humus and charcoal. There was a shallow central fire pit, about 30 inches in diameter, containing ashes. In the northwest corner was a large ash bed, or bonfire type of hearth, about 4 feet in diameter, which contained animal bones and sherds. Another ash concentration, this one about 10 inches in diameter, was exposed halfway through the entranceway. Elsewhere on the floor detritus was most scanty, but of particular note was a large, brown clay platform pipe about 5 inches long and 3 inches wide, decorated with incised lines, punctations, and notches. The relative lack of detritus on the floor of this structure, in contrast to village dwellings at other sites, may indicate that the building had a religious function.

Two large rectangular burial pits were found within House 4 along

27. Edwin N. Wilmsen, "A Suggested Developmental Sequence for House Forms in the Caddoan Area," *Bulletin of the Texas Archaeological Society*, Vol. 30 (1961), 35–50.

opposite side walls. The northwesterly pit contained five human skeletons, including children and adults of both sexes, lying in the usual extended supine position. Diagnostic artifacts of pottery, bone, and stone were placed on the pit floor near the skulls. One interesting object, a thin lanceolate fragment of bone, possibly a deer scapula, was exposed partially covering "the back of the pronated left forearm and hand" of an adult male.[28] The specimen is 6.5 inches long, 2 inches wide at one end, tapering to less than an inch wide at the opposite end. It is concavo-convex in cross section, with the concave surface facing the arm and hand bones. Three rather evenly spaced perforations had been contradrilled along the midline of the specimen, and the convex surface was decorated with two parallel lines that undulate down the long axis. Webb and Dodd described this specimen in detail, and after considering its place of deposition and wear attributes, they suggested that it protected the forearm against a bowstring.[29] It is just one more bit of secondary evidence for the presence of the bow and arrow in prehistoric Louisiana.

The southwesterly pit contained the remains of three adults and one child in the characteristic burial position. Several pottery vessels and one stone point were near the skulls at one end of the pit. Most of the hand and foot bones of one adult female skeleton were missing, and the lower right femur and the entire left tibia exhibited marked thickness. Webb suggested that these anomalies are symptomatic of syphilitic osteoperiostitis.[30]

In the premound stratum underlying Mound A the excavators found segments of straight wall trenches that probably represented the burned remains of buildings resembling House 4. On top of these remains and only about 60 feet from House 4, the Indians erected another structure, House 8. It was quite different in form from House 4, although the stratigraphic and artifactual data indicate that the two buildings were built and destroyed at about the same time. House 8 had a circular floor pattern, and its outer wall was outlined by fifty-five small postmolds. The building was 22 feet in diameter and had a covered en-

28. Webb, *The Belcher Mound*, 72.
29. Webb and Dodd, "Bone 'Gorget' from a Caddoan Mound Burial."
30. Webb, *The Belcher Mound*.

tranceway 10 feet long and 4 feet wide oriented toward the northeast. The posts on each side of the entranceway were in wall trenches, and another trench of unknown function extended down the center of the long axis of the entranceway. Interior postmolds marked roof supports and platform placements. As had been noted in House 4, there were a central fire pit and ancillary ash beds, but the floor was relatively free of refuse and artifacts. The investigators found only charcoal, animal bones, several bone tools, sherds, burnt clay, and thatch.

During the second stage of construction at the site, Belcher II, the Caddoans built a steep-sided, flat-topped platform 3 feet in height, 66 feet in diameter at the base, and 22 feet in diameter at the summit. This was the primary mound in Mound B. On top of it there were postmolds arranged in two concentric ovals and representing two buildings. The larger oval represented the earlier structure, House 3b, which was 22 feet in diameter. The subsequent structure, House 3a, was only about 15 feet in diameter. Neither building contained central fire basins or ancillary ash beds. Apparently, the buildings had no extended entranceways, although evidence of these may have been destroyed by several burial pits that intruded into this stratum. The smaller structure had burned, and "the red soil surface was charred with small circles or irregular smudges as though small canes or twigs had been stuck into the clay."[31] The floors of both structures were stained with charcoal and contained the usual scattered refuse. In addition, the skeleton of a large unidentified bird was found on the floor of the larger structure.

After House 8 was destroyed by fire, the Caddoans mantled it with dirt, forming the first stage of construction for Mound A. This phase of construction was called Belcher III. House 7, a structure with a circular floor pattern and an extended entranceway facing the northeast, was built atop this primary mound. It measured 40 feet in diameter; the entranceway was about 9 feet long and 4 feet wide. There was also an inner circle of large posts, undoubtedly roof supports, about 8 feet in from the outer wall. There were the usual central fire basin, ancillary ash beds, and interior postmolds suggestive of platforms, partitions, and bunks. More artifacts were found on the floor of this

31. *Ibid.*, 36.

structure than in any other building at the site. Most of them were found in the space between the roof supports and the exterior wall, and they were notably numerous in the ash beds. The list includes eight pottery vessels, perforated pottery disks, an elbow-shaped clay pipe (Pl. 55, *i*), stone points, scrapers, a drill, a celt, sandstone hones, and a long knife; a mammal tooth pendant; nine bone awls; a chisel; worked deer mandibles, a scapula, and antler tines; shell pendants, hoes, saws, scrapers, and an *Olivella* bead. In addition, the refuse contained an assortment of mussel shells, mammal and bird bones, fish bones, gar scales, and turtle carapace fragments. It is notable that House 7 contained an unusually large amount of animal bone and that squirrel skulls, *Sciurus carolinensis* and *Sciurus niger*, were particularly abundant.

During Belcher III times another structure (House 6) was also built, this one on the original ground surface about 10 feet north of Mound B. It, too, had a circular floor plan and an extended entranceway and was about the same size as House 7. There were, however, several notable differences. A pathway extended down the entire length of the very unusual entranceway almost to the central fire basin. This pathway had been dug to a depth of 1 foot below the floor and then filled with superimposed lenses of sand and ash. Between the pathway and the fire basin were two rectangular burial pits dug from the structure floor downward. The smallest pit contained only the remains of a newborn infant. The larger pit contained an adult female with a decorated, bottle-shaped vessel placed next to her right thigh. In House 6 the interior roof supports, in clusters of three to six posts, were set about 7 feet in from the outer wall. Between them were large ash beds 3 to 7 feet long, 2 to 4 feet wide, and as much as 1 foot deep. Between the roof supports and the outer wall were pairs of posts that may have supported a bench or benches that faced the ash beds. The ash beds contained refuse, including sherds and stone, bone, and shell artifacts. Houses 6 and 7 contained most of the freshwater mussel shell found at the site.

Houses 6 and 7 were burned, apparently simultaneously, perhaps as part of a ritual related to the deaths of important personages. Very soon afterward Mounds A and B were expanded until they began to merge and Mound A became the paramount structure. Early in this period of mound expansion a circular structure (House 2), comparable in floor plan to Houses 6 and 7, was built on the summit of Mound B. It, too, was destroyed by fire. The artifactual remains were distributed in an unusual pattern. For example, there were six piles of sherds located around the house in the area between the inner roof supports and the outer wall. Twelve vessels were later reconstructed from these sherds, and in some cases, the sherds for a particular vessel came from more than one pile, "suggesting that the vessels were broken and thrown into the piles shortly before or at the time of the destruction of the building. Ceremonial destruction is entirely possible under these circumstances."[32]

Important evidence of prehistoric subsistence patterns—the preserved remains of persimmons, persimmon seeds, pecans, charred corn cobs, and three charred beans (*Phaseolus vulgaris*)—was recovered. The beans are of particular interest since this is the earliest documentation of the bean from a prehistoric site in Louisiana. This very important tropical cultigen has not been reported in contexts very much predating A.D. 1000 in the lower Mississippi Valley. Its introduction was significant for two reasons. First, primitive corn, although it contains some protein, lacks the amino acids lysine and trytophan, which are needed for protein synthesis. Beans are high in these essential amino acids and the combination of beans and corn results in an increase in readily available protein. Second, leguminous plants, such as beans, return nitrogen to the soil during their life cycle. If beans are grown with corn, the nitrogen content of the soil is replenished, crop yields remain adequate, and the field units may be cultivated for longer periods of time.

After House 2 burned, a burial pit that intruded into the house fill was dug, and one human interment was placed in it. A short time later, about 1.5 feet of sand was added to Mound B, completely covering House 2 and bringing the mound to a height of 6.5 feet above the surrounding ground surface. Seven rectangular burial pits, containing one to three human interments each, were dug into the mound from this new mound surface. Both sexes and all age groups were represented. Funerary offerings, though not evenly distributed, were ornate and

32. *Ibid.*, 34.

plentiful. They included decorated pottery bowls, jars, urns, bottles, a tripod bottle, and cups; incised, ground, and perforated marine and freshwater shell pendants, necklaces, disks, hoes, and cups; animal bone pins, awls, disks, ear ornaments, and labrets; canine-teeth pendants; stone scrapers and a stone point; and piles of animal bones, which are possibly the remains of food offerings. The build-up and burials at Mound B were accomplished at about the same time as two burial pits were dug through the fill over House 6 in the village area to the north. During this late period of Belcher III, Mound A was also expanded, although it was impossible to determine how much was added since the landowner had removed part of the mound.

In the final stages of the site's occupation, Belcher IV, Mound B, was expanded until it reached about 9 feet in height, and Mound A was expanded laterally. On the summit of Mound B the Caddoans erected a building (House 1) with a circular floor plan, clusters of inner roof supports, and ash beds, but without a central fire basin or definite evidence of an entrance. On its floor were several intact vessels and others that had been shattered in place. In addition, there was a portion of a clay human figurine, a conical-stemmed clay pipe with a wide bowl, stone artifacts, and charred persimmons and hickory nuts. As was the custom, the building was burned and then covered with soil and midden during the final period of occupancy at the site. Associated with House 1 were the disturbed remains of a human burial consisting only of a skull and several vertebrae of an adult male lying between two pottery bowls.

In the village area just to the north of Mound B a circular building (House 5) was erected on top of the small mound formed by the collapse of House 6 and the overlying humus. The structure was 38 feet in diameter and at its entrance to the northeast was a steep ramp that projected several feet *inward* from the outer wall. In addition to the usual sort of debris found on the floors of other buildings at this site, there was a concentration of stone points and chips, indicative of an area set aside for stone knapping. There were also two cache pits, each about 2 feet in diameter and 1 foot deep, containing additional debris. And finally, as elsewhere at the site, there were burial pits. Two pits had been dug down from the floor of the building. The smaller pit contained only an infant, perhaps newborn, and several pottery vessels, but the larger pit contained the most unusual human interments and lavish burial offerings of any at the site. There were seven skeletons representing both sexes and all age groups. Unlike other burials at the site, these interments were oriented in different directions, at different angles and overlying or partially overlying each other in a helter-skelter fashion. They gave the impression of being carelessly and/or hurriedly placed. Associated with particular individuals and placed along the side of the pit were thirty-three pottery bowls, jars, urns, effigy pots, and a pedestal bowl; stone points, a celt, and a hone; shell cups, beads, and a pendant; pearls; and a mass of garfish scales. Like the others, House 5 was destroyed by fire and almost one foot of soil and midden accumulated over the top of it.

Subsequent physical anthropological analyses of the human skeletal remains afford us further insights into the people who inhabited the Belcher Site. There were identifiable remains of about fifty people. Adults and adolescents were about evenly represented, but there were only about five infants. Of the adults, females outnumbered males more than two to one. Half of the adult males died between the ages of twenty and thirty years, but adult female mortality ranged from twenty years to advanced ages. Although he was only able to approximate heights, Webb estimated that adult males ranged from 66 to 68 inches and adult females from 60 to 68 inches. Skeletal pathologies were not common, but there were several arm and leg fractures among the adolescents, and one adult female had a fractured mandible. The same adult female and two others also exhibited osseous anomalies suggestive of syphilis. The dentition of the Belcher Site skeletons was particularly poor. In many instances tooth loss was due to disease, sometimes congenital, rather than to violence. There were at least two cases of advanced pyorrhea, caries were rampant, and sinus pockets, abscesses, and instances of osteomyelitis were also present. Webb is possibly the first regional archaeologist to note that the dentition of the early prehistoric corn agriculturalists was inordinately worse than that found among groups who were nonagriculturalists. More recent studies have shown that the switch from a hunting-and-gathering economy and/or the domestication of native cultigens to maize and bean agriculture was not necessarily a nutritional or a cultural boon, particularly during its developmental stages.[33]

The Caddo Culture introduced artificial cranial deformation to Louisiana. The deformation was produced by binding the head of the infant to the cradle board until the head became permanently flattened frontally and/or occipitally. One historical account states that the binding continued until the child was ten years of age.[34] The practice probably diffused into the Caddo area from Mexico. At the Belcher Site it was evident on the skulls of five females and two males. The other adult skulls were too distorted or fragmented for the trait to be discerned. Cranial deformation was a common practice of the prehistoric Caddo Culture, at least among those of higher status.[35] However, it does not seem to have flourished among the historic Caddo groups. Ethnohistories describe the trait among the Houma and Natchez Indians, rather than the Caddoans.

Burials at the Belcher Site were ceremonial. They were associated with a rich assortment of funerary offerings and the ritual destruction of special buildings, most of which were associated with mound construction. Furthermore, the evidence indicates that Belcher was a small ceremonial site supported by communities or hamlets in the area.

The Smithport Landing Site was a nonmound Caddo burial manifestation in DeSoto Parish.[36] Occupational debris of both the Troyville–Coles Creek and Caddo cultures was found scattered along the tops of four cultivated finger ridges that extend out of the dissected uplands and overlook the old bed of Bayou Pierre Lake. The ridges rise abruptly to an elevation of about 20 feet above the lake bed, and the site encompasses a total area of approximately 50 acres. As often happens in this region, rooting hogs had exposed a small Caddoan pot near

33. Webb, "Dental Abnormalities as Found in the American Indian"; Webb, *The Belcher Site*; Clifford J. Jolly and Fred Plog, *Physical Anthropology and Archaeology* (New York, 1976); Robert L. Blakely (ed.), *Biocultural Adaptation in Prehistoric America* (Athens, 1977).
34. Swanton, *The Indians of the Southeastern United States.*
35. Kenneth A. Bennett, "Artificial Cranial Deformation Among the Caddo Indians," *Texas Journal of Science*, Vol. 13 (1961), No. 4, pp. 377–90.
36. Clarence H. Webb, "The Smithport Landing Site: An Alto Focus Component in DeSoto Parish, Louisiana," *Bulletin of the Texas Archaeological Society*, Vol. 34 (1963), 143–87.

the front edge of the crest on one of the ridges. Excavations at that spot exposed nine additional Caddoan vessels, clustered within a radius of about 3 feet and all about 2 feet below the surrounding ground surface. In the same area, also at depths of 2 to 3 feet, excavations by Webb and Monroe Dodd, Jr., exposed fourteen human burials. The vessels and the burials were concentrated in an area no larger than 30 feet by 12 feet. Burial pit outlines, possibly obliterated by cultivation and/or erosion, were not discernible, but Webb surmised, because of their close placement and common orientation, that certain skeletons had been buried together. There were three groups of two individuals each and two groups of three. All of them were in an extended supine position, but in one instance a skeleton overlay two other skeletons crossways. All of the groups, except one of those with three individuals, were associated with Caddoan vessels. There were three adult males, six adult females, and three subadults. In addition, there was a bundle burial and a primary flexed burial of an adult male. Neither of these was in direct association with artifacts, and their burial patterns suggest a closer relationship to the Troyville–Coles Creek Culture than to the Caddo Culture.

From two test pits toward the back of one of the ridges, the burial excavations, and surface collections at Smithport Landing came 19 whole Caddoan vessels, 1,533 sherds, baked-clay fragments with grass impressions, 61 large stone points, 55 small stone points, and a miscellaneous assortment of chipped-stone scrapers, flakes, cores, choppers, and knives, ground-stone celts, a mealing stone, a hammerstone, a stone bead, and a bone bead.

We can only speculate about the factors that led to the selection of this site for a village occupation. Unlike the previously described Caddo Culture sites in Louisiana, the Smithport Landing Site had no burial mounds. Individuals were interred less ceremoniously and with fewer offerings here than at other sites. The location of the site on a ridgetop away from a major stream also differentiates it from the other sites. Actually ridgetop sites are far more common than Caddo Culture mound sites. It is likely that similarly functioning villages occupied other ridgetop sites and that comparable burials would be found there. However, until other ridgetop sites of the Caddo Culture have

been more extensively excavated, this hypothesis must be considered
little more than an unverified assumption.

There is another slightly different nonmound Caddoan burial manifestation at the Bison Site on a low bluff above Brown's Bend along
the Sabine River in Sabine Parish.[37] It was one of a number of sites in
Texas and Louisiana destined to be inundated by the waters of the Toledo Bend Reservoir.[38] Personnel from Northwestern State University
of Louisiana, the University of Texas, and Southern Methodist University conducted excavations here between 1964 and 1966. Preliminary examinations indicated that midden debris in the cultivated fields
extended to a depth of about 10 inches throughout an area of approximately 200 feet by 250 feet. Test pits and extensive trenching revealed
sixteen human interments near the center of highest part of the site.

The burial pits, large enough to accommodate a corpse and funerary
offerings, were oblong, rounded at the corners, and an average of 42
inches in depth. The pits were not aligned with each other, but the long
axis of each was oriented northeast-southwest. In the characteristic
burial pattern, the individual lay in the extended supine position with
the head to the southeast. Each pit at the Bison Site contained the remains of only one individual, sometimes accompanied by artifacts, and
all age groups and both sexes were represented. The skeletons, particularly the postcranial elements, were too poorly preserved to derive
much physical anthropological data. Nevertheless, Barbara H. Butler was able to glean enough information to indicate that the morphology, stature, and pathologies of the Bison Site population do not
deviate significantly from what we know about other Caddoan burial
manifestations.[39] The burial accompaniments included deep and shallow bowls, carinated bowls, straight-walled and globular jars and bot-

37. J. Ned Woodall, *Archaeological Excavations in the Toledo Bend Reservoir, 1966*,
    Southern Methodist University Contributions in Anthropology, No. 3 (Dallas,
    1969).
38. Dan J. Scurlock, *Archaeological Reconnaissance at Toledo Bend Reservoir,
    1962–1963 Season* (Austin, 1964).
39. Barbara H. Butler, "The Skeletal Material from the Bison Site, Area B," in Ned
    J. Woodall (ed.), *Archaeological Excavations in the Toledo Bend Reservoir, 1966*,
    Southern Methodist University Contributions in Anthropology No. 3, pp. 84–
    93.

tles, and a decorated, L-shaped clay pipe.[40] Two of the vessels were filled with the bones of small animals. There were also small chipped-stone projectile points, two ground-stone ear ornaments, a mussel shell, and stains of red, yellow, black, white, and green pigments.

Excavations also exposed a shallow oval pit containing the poorly preserved remains of a secondary human burial. Since no artifacts were found in association with the burial, its cultural assignment is questionable. Several burned areas on the general occupation level were discovered, as well as postmold alignments that may be the remains of an arbor. The occupation level also yielded 2,136 sherds, 50 stone projectile points, knives, scrapers, utilized flakes, cores, and a few specimens of animal bone and mussel shell.

Obviously, the information from the Gahagan, Mounds Plantation, Belcher, Smithport Landing, and Bison sites contributes to our knowledge of prehistoric Caddoan attitudes toward the hereafter, but this is not the whole story. Other sites have revealed more about the everyday essentials in a prehistoric Caddoan settlement. One such site is situated on a relict natural levee, presently being eroded, along the right bank of the Red River near the community of Hanna in Red River Parish. At the time of its occupation, the natural levee probably adjoined an abandoned channel of the Red River. The site excavations, analyses, and report were made possible by federal legislation enacted to preserve cultural resources threatened by federally sponsored construction projects.[41] The Hanna Site was endangered by the proposed construction of a riverbank revetment, and in this instance, the Department of the Army, New Orleans District, Corps of Engineers, cooperated fully to mitigate the impact of the revetment construction.

The principal investigator, Prentice Marquet Thomas, Jr., of the New World Research Institute, gridded the site and then divided it into four cardinal sectors. Initial surface collections, test pits, and trenching in

40. Hiram F. Gregory, Jr., "Vessels from the Bison Site," *Louisiana Studies*, Vol. 5 (1966), No. 2, pp. 159–61; Woodall, *Archaeological Excavations in the Toledo Bend Reservoir, 1966.*

41. Prentice Marquet Thomas, Jr., L. Janice Campbell, and Steven R. Ahler (eds.), *The Hanna Site: An Alto Village in Red River Parish*, New World Research, Report of Investigations No. 3 (New Orleans, 1977). In this report see especially John Lenzer, "Geology and Geomorphology," 32–50. See also Charles R. McGimsey III, *Public Archaeology* (New York, 1972).

the cultivated fields that encompass the Hanna Site, demonstrated that the occupation area covered about 4 acres and only rarely extended to more than 18 inches in depth. These initial explorations also delineated loci that subsequent excavations revealed to be habitations, subsidiary structures, and middens.

In the southwest sector a postmold pattern, somewhat obscured by modern plowing, indicated a rectangular habitation with an entranceway extended to the northeast. The wall and entranceway posts were of various diameters, spaced irregularly, and set into the ground at different depths. The structure measured about 20 feet by 20 feet, and the entranceway was about 7 feet long. Inside it, there were two arcs of postmolds, possibly representing partitions, and scattered repair or replacement postmolds, but no evidence of large support posts. There were also five shallow, basin-shaped pits containing sherds, chipped stone flakes and finished lithic tools, hickory and acorn nut fragments, squash remains, and shells of freshwater mollusks within the structure. Outside it primarily along the sides and to the rear were eleven other pits containing refuse. Two notably large pits, more than 20 inches deep, had burned walls and ash fill containing sherds, stone artifacts, a large quantity of faunal remains, and fragments of bottle gourds and corncobs.

There were two human burials outside the building along opposite side walls. In Burial 1 an adult female, 60 inches tall, along with a child, had been placed in an oblong pit measuring about 75 inches in length. The adult was in an extended supine position and next to her, to the right, lay the child, also extended, but on its left side. In addition to fronto-occipital deformation, the adult exhibited caries, periodontal osteoporosis, trochanter tertius on each femur, perforated olecranon processes on the humeri, and osteoarthritis. Furthermore, Marco J. Giardino, who conducted the physical anthropological study of the human skeletal remains from the Hanna Site, remarked that this adult also "suffered from a cleft palate, a congenital fissure in the roof of the mouth forming a communicating passageway between the mouth and the nasal cavities."[42] The child's skull exhibited frontal deformation

---

42. Marco Joseph Giardino, "Skeletal Remains," in Thomas, Campbell, and Ahler (eds.), *The Hanna Site*, 233.

and indications of a cleft palate. No artifacts were found with either of these individuals. Burial 2 was an adult female lying in a pit comparable to Burial 1 in an extended supine position with her hands covering the pelvic area. She was 64 inches tall, and with the exception of the cleft palate, she exhibited about the same sorts of anomalies as the adult female in Burial 1. Her skull, too, showed fronto-occipital deformation. As in Burial 1, no funerary accompaniments were found.

It is often the case in excavations of village sites that areas of unknown function are manifested by unpatterned concentrations of postmolds, charcoal-stained soil, pits, and detritus. At the Hanna Site one such postmold concentration was exposed adjacent to the rectangular habitation just described. Some of the postmolds, though irregularly set, formed a right angle. Associated with the concentration were several shallow pits containing village detritus. It is not known what activities took place here, but it is reasonable to assume that the postmolds are the remains of the sort of scaffolds, racks, and/or arbors so commonly seen in historic Indian settlements.

In the northeast sector of the Hanna Site Thomas excavated two habitational structures and another unpatterned concentration of postmolds. The first structure was circular and measured about 30 feet in diameter. There was no evidence of an extended entranceway, but a gap of about 6 feet in the row of wall posts along the northeast section of the structure was probably the entrance. Inside the building, there were molds marking the locations of roof-support posts and smaller subsidiary posts. There was also a central hearth and ancillary pits containing a variety of detritus. Of particular note were ten small pits that contained only charred sweet gum fruits, or balls. Similar pits, containing charred remains other than sweet gum fruits, have been the subject of considerable research and discussion. It seems likely that they were smudge pits used to smoke hides or to blacken pottery. The fact that these pits were *within* the house at Hanna suggests to Thomas that, in this case, they might rather have been a means of mosquito control.[43]

43. Lewis R. Binford, "Smudge Pits and Hide Smoking: The Use of Analogy in Archaeological Reasoning," *American Antiquity*, Vol. 32 (1967), No. 1, pp. 1–12; Patrick J. Munson, "Comments on Binford's 'Smudge Pits and Hide Smoking: The Use of Analogy in Archaeological Reasoning,'" *American Antiquity*, Vol. 34 (1969), No. 1, pp. 83–85; Thomas, Campbell, and Ahler (eds.), *The Hanna Site.*

Two human burials were exposed on opposite sides of the house interior. The first was that of a young child lying in a supine position within a shallow oval pit. The legs were akimbo and came together at the feet. One arm was extended, but the other was bent with the hand covering the pelvic area. The second burial was that of a subadult female placed in an oblong pit. She was lying in an extended, supine position. Her skull exhibited fronto-occipital deformation, and the digital bones were missing from all extremities.[44] There were no grave goods associated with these two individuals.

Another circular habitation, about 65 feet northeast of the first structure was only partially excavated, but the exposed wall post-molds indicated an outside diameter of about 30 feet. There were interior support posts and three small trash pits, but no entranceway was found. Inside of the structure toward the wall, an adult female had been buried in a shallow circular pit. She lay in a flexed position, and "the general architecture of the skull differed from that of the other Hanna site females."[45] Like the other burials at Hanna, however, this one had no associated grave goods.

In the southeast sector of the site a third circular structure, about 25 feet in diameter, was outlined by numerous postmolds. The apparent pairing of some of the outer wall posts was its only distinguishing trait. No entranceway was found, and there was no pattern to the arrangement of the interior postmolds. Several small pits, containing little besides hickory nut shells and acorns, were associated with the structure, but the floor area was notably clean. Thomas had the impression that the construction of this habitation was haphazard or undirected.[46] Unlike the other buildings at the Hanna Site, this one was not associated with human burials.

Among the artifactual remains, as the reader might expect, potsherds were the most numerous objects, totaling 25,368 specimens. Pottery was probably manufactured at the site, as evidenced by the numerous pottery coil segments found there, but no whole vessels were found. During the historic period Caddoan potters were women, and we can assume that the same custom existed at Hanna. The vast majority of sherds were from established types of Caddoan ceramics. Some

44. Giardino, "Skeletal Remains."
45. *Ibid.*, 236.
46. Thomas, Campbell, and Ahler (eds.), *The Hanna Site.*

bottle forms and intricately decorated vessels were represented, but most of the sherds come from less ornate, utilitarian jars and deep bowls. As we have seen, however, even the finer vessels at this site were not used as funerary offerings, nor is there any evidence that they were used in connection with any ceremony.

Lithics were the second most abundant class of artifacts, with 15,365 specimens recovered in various stages of manufacture and wear. Small, locally available chert nodules were heat-treated and then chipped to form the desired implement. The tool categories included small projectile points, drills, knives, scrapers, sandstone abraders, a hammerstone, and utilized flakes. Only the drills showed a definite cluster in their distribution. Out of a total of eight drills found at the site, six of them were associated with one of the circular habitations in the northeast sector. Quite surprisingly, no ground-stone artifacts were recovered at the Hanna Site.[47]

Kathleen M. Byrd identified and analyzed the *in situ* faunal material, which amounted to 11,900 specimens of fish, reptiles, birds, and mammals.[48] The species identified indicate that the Hanna Site inhabitants exploited the local mud-bottomed streams and lakes and the dry and wet woodlands. From the list of species it appears that the Hanna Site was occupied year round. The distribution of some of the bones is worthy of note. For example, fish bones predominated in the pits of the northeast sector and they were particularly abundant around one of the circular houses of that sector. The only bird bones at the site were also found in pits of the northeast, while reptile and mammal bones predominated in northeastern middens. In the southwest sector, the only other area yielding an appreciable amount of bone, more fish bone was found in the middens and pits than anywhere else at the site. Deer bones were also distributed peculiarly. In the northeast sector the pits yielded an inordinate number of "meat bones," *i.e.,* upper limb bones, while the middens contained more "non-meat" bones, *i.e.,* tarsals, carpals, metapodials, and phalanges. In the southwest sector the distribution of the same deer bone elements was ex-

47. Newell O. Wright, Jr., "Lithics," in *Ibid.,* 157–83.
48. Kathleen Mary Byrd, "Zooarchaeological Analysis of the Hanna Site: An Alto Focus Occupation in Louisiana," in Thomas, Campbell, and Ahler (eds.), *The Hanna Site,* 189–213.

actly the opposite. Since no comparative data are available from other Caddoan sites, we can only speculate on the socioeconomic implications of these distributions. It does seem certain that the management of deer carcasses was culturally ordained.

Andrea Shea provided more data pertinent to subsistence at the Hanna Site. She analyzed carbonized botanical remains that had been recovered from pits, postmolds, and the general excavation area.[49] These floral remains included hickory nut shells, acorns, squash, gourd, sweet gum, corn, honey locust, pokeweed, grape, persimmon, dewberry, sumac, and wild cherry. Specimens of wood charcoal included hickory, maple, pine, sycamore, cottonwood, oak, willow, and elm. The corn, squash, and gourd remains were found in the northeast, southeast, and southwest sectors, and the cooking pits contained the widest variety of botanical remains, *i.e.*, corn, squash, grape, persimmon, honey locust, and wild cherry. In agreement with the faunal data, the botanical analysis suggests that the site could have been occupied continuously throughout the year.

It is not clear for how long the site was occupied, sometime between A.D. 900 and A.D. 1200, nor do we know why it was abandoned. The houses of this small village were not arranged in any particular order, and there was no plaza or central ceremonial area. Unlike the previously described Caddoan sites, Hanna revealed no evidence of exotic trade items or even status burials. The artifacts, structures, burials, middens, and pits point only to a most languid change through time. The Hanna Site has the look of a backwater settlement whose inhabitants were almost inimical to all but the very basic traits of the Caddo Culture. It is quite likely that Thomas' excellent report on Hanna has provided us with our first real insight into the typical prehistoric Caddoan settlement.[50]

The archaeological remains from early historic Caddoan sites are fundamental to the understanding of the regional culture history (Pls. 60 and 61), for if we are ever to tie in the prehistoric record of an area with a particular historic tribe or tribes, we must apply the direct his-

49. Andrea Shea, "Analysis of Plant Remains from the Hanna Site," in Thomas, Campbell, and Ahler (eds.), *The Hanna Site*, 218–27.
50. Thomas, Campbell, and Ahler (eds.), *The Hanna Site*.

torical approach.[51] If the archaeologist can begin with a site known to have been occupied by a specific tribe in historic times, he can investigate the record of that tribe back into prehistoric times. We can see from the archaeological record of Louisiana that the study of the aboriginal peoples from the earliest historic chronicles into the present time would cover only a very brief portion of their culture history. Hence, by extending our study to include their prehistoric remains, we are able better to understand their origins and the development of their cultures.

In 1931 Winslow M. Walker was searching for definite evidence of the remains of certain historic Indian burials being destroyed by the construction of a federal fish hatchery along Cane River, about one mile south of the city of Natchitoches. Ground scraping and trenching along the right bank and about 450 feet back from the bank, along an elevated, level plain, had exposed a purported 100 burials. Evidence indicated that "this burial ground occupies the site or very nearly the site of the ancient Natchitoches village visited by Henri de Tonti in 1690." After arriving at the site Walker was told by the construction superintendent that the skeletons were buried in an extended supine position, associated with pottery vessels and sometimes with shell and glass beads and metal objects, and most of them no more than 3 feet deep. The informant also remarked that certain of the skeletons had noticeably flattened skulls. Moreover, there were two separate horse burials, and each horse skeleton had "a large earthen bowl placed near the head. The bowls were of plain ware about a foot and a half in diameter and half an inch thick." Other artifacts collected from the burial area included plain and decorated pottery bowls, jars, and bottles, and a small, conical clay pipebowl with an opening for the stem along the side wall near the narrow base. Stone artifacts, though sparse, included chipped projectile points and ground-stone chopping implements. Beads were more abundant; some were made of columella shell and others were of blue glass and white porcelain. Metal artifacts con-

51. Waldo R. Wedel, "The Direct-Historical Approach in Pawnee Archaeology," *Smithsonian Miscellaneous Collections*, Vol. 97, No. 7 (Washington, D.C., 1938).

sisted of scissors, brass hawkbells, bracelets, and "a double-pointed iron spike 6½ inches long." There is no mention of bone artifacts.[52]

While at the site Walker was able to excavate one undamaged burial located near the river bank. The skeleton, that of an adult female, was in an extended supine position just 2 feet below the surface. She was about 67 inches in stature and exhibited extreme fronto-occipital deformation. Placed to the right of her skull were two undecorated shell-tempered vessels: a bowl and inside of that, a small, globular pot.

After comparing the mortuary practices and ceramics from the Fish Hatchery Site with those from other regional sites, some later and some earlier in time, Walker concluded that the Cane River burials dated from a time very early in the eighteenth century. He reasoned that during this period most of the native technologies would persist, although there were undoubtedly significant modifications and innovations resulting from the introduction of European trade items. The native ceramics, at least, remained superlative. Walker's reasoning for the chronological placement of the Fish Hatchery Site remains appears to be sound.[53]

Another early historic cemetery presumed to contain the remains of Caddo Indians—specifically the Natchitoches or their close kindred, the Doustioni—is the Lawton Site located in Natchitoches Parish along the right bank of the Cane River just 8 miles south of the Fish Hatchery Site. Human burials were being exposed there in 1944 by the construction of a cotton gin. Fortunately, A. G. Lawton, the landowner, allowed Clarence H. Webb to salvage some of the archaeological remains as construction of the gin proceeded. Webb was told that early during the grading operations a line of six or seven burials had been exposed.[54] Most of the skulls were to the southeast and the skeletons were generally associated with native pottery and European trade beads. Sometimes the beads were in the neck region, but in one case

52. Walker, "Reconnaissance of Northern Louisiana Mounds"; Walker, "A Caddo Burial Site at Natchitoches, Louisiana," 5, 3, 12.
53. Walker, "A Caddo Burial Site at Natchitoches, Louisiana."
54. Clarence H. Webb, "A Second Historic Caddo Site at Natchitoches, Louisiana," *Bulletin of the Texas Archaeological and Paleontological Society*, Vol. 16 (1945), 52–83.

they were at the wrist. After his arrival at the site Webb had the opportunity to salvage the remains of four burials. There were two adults, one child, and an infant in shallow graves only 2 to 3 feet below the surface. The burial position of the infant was not determinable, but all of the others were in the extended supine position. The skull of the child was to the northwest, but all others were placed to the southeast. There were several glass beads at the neck of one adult, and the other adult was associated with two native vessels. With the child were twelve glass beads and one native vessel, and the infant burial was accompanied by two native vessels and twenty glass beads. No metal, stone, or shell artifacts were recovered from the Lawton Site for comparison, but the native pottery is of the same types as were found at the Fish Hatchery Site. The beads at Lawton are small and of two general shapes, globular and elongated. Of the thirty-six glass and porcelain beads Webb examined, twenty-seven were blue, sometimes with white stripes, and seven were white, sometimes with multicolored stripes, and two were red.

Webb also salvaged two human burials at the Southern Cotton Oil Compress Site located just north of the Fish Hatchery Site near the junction of Cane and Old rivers. Although not reported in detail, they were associated with native Caddo ceramics and "two iron bracelets, fabric, a brass or copper band, and our present sample of 320 European trade beads."[55] The investigators believe these burials also to be the remains of Natchitoches Indians.

James A. Ford briefly noted two other sites in Natchitoches Parish that yielded human burials associated with Caddoan pottery and European trade items. In a discussion of his theories of diagnostic Caddoan ceramics (which have since been accepted by the archaeological community), he alluded to his excavation at the Allen Site. Ford remarked that "this village was accompanied by a cemetery in which the burials were accompanied by European material, principally glass beads."[56] He provided no further details of this excavation, nor of buri-

55. Hiram F. Gregory, Jr., and Clarence H. Webb, "European Trade Beads from Six Sites in Natchitoches Parish, Louisiana," *Florida Anthropologist,* Vol. 18 (1965), No. 3, Pt. 2, p. 16.
56. Ford, *Analysis of Indian Village Site Collections from Louisiana and Mississippi,* 77.

als excavated at the Wilkinson Site where, he mentions, there were an inordinate number of gun flints and glass beads.

Whatever its exact moment of origin, the Caddo Culture coalescence was influence by traits from Meso-America and by the precedent and partially coexistent Troyville–Coles Creek Culture. Without doubt, Caddoan funerary ceremonialism at mound sites and non-mound cemeteries produced the most elaborate prehistoric archaeological manifestations in Louisiana. Several other cardinal developments, whose physical remains first appear together in Louisiana at Caddoan sites, are the bow and arrow and all three of the tropical cultigens, beans, squash, and corn. This culture also introduced the practice of cranial deformation. Caddo Culture is the only prehistoric, cultural development for which we have been able to provide continuous documentation from prehistoric times, as early as A.D. 800, through occupations by historically documented tribal groups in Louisiana. The Plaquemine Culture, to be discussed next, coexisted in part with the Caddo Culture and shared some of its artifactual traits. Nevertheless, the developmental sequence from prehistoric Plaquemine Culture to historically documented Indian tribes is not yet as well documented in the literature.

a   b

c   d

e   0   1   2   3   f
     INCHES

Ceramic vessels from historic Caddo Indian sites.

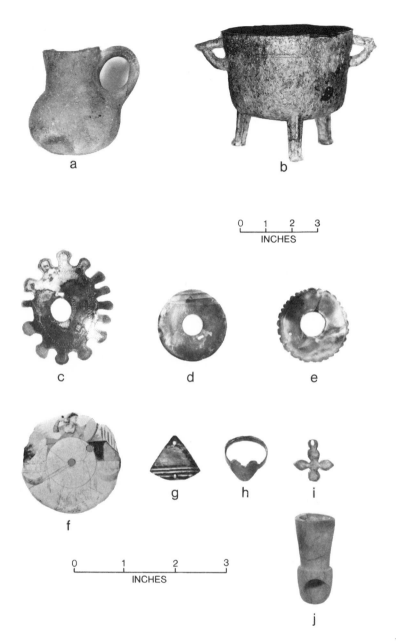

0   1   2   3
INCHES

0   1   2   3
INCHES

PLATE 61

Artifacts from historic Caddo Indian sites: *a*, ceramic pitcher; *b*, three-legged metal kettle; *c–e*, German silver ornaments; *f*, porcelain clock dial face; *g–i*, metal ornaments; *j*, clay pipe bowl.

X Plaquemine Culture

Some archaeologists consider the Plaquemine Culture to be the classic development of temple mound construction in the lower Mississippi Valley. The archaeological manifestations of the culture, as revealed from stratigraphic cuts and more extensive excavations into mounds and village middens, demonstrate conclusively that it was a late or protohistoric development of the Troyville–Coles Creek Culture. The Plaquemine Culture's Troyville–Coles Creek origins are most evident in some of the pottery designs, but they are also apparent in other artifact categories, *i.e.*, elbow-shaped clay pipes, clay ear ornaments, small stone projectile points, and ground-stone celts (Pls. 62 and 63). Multistage mound construction, circular or rectangular structures outlined by postmolds inside of or lacking of wall trenches, and mortuary practices that include mass burials also demonstrate the connection between the two cultures. Caddo-Plaquemine interrelationships, though less evident, are also demonstrable, particularly at sites in the drainage systems of the Ouachita and Red rivers.

It would appear that very little about the Plaquemine Culture is distinctive. In fact, however, certain pottery designs and decorative techniques became predominant and can be easily segregated from Troyville–Coles Creek types (Pls. 63 and 64). The brushing technique is a particularly distinctive Plaquemine design element. Clumps of vegetal matter, such as grass, were apparently rubbed across the clay before it was fired, producing striations of various lengths, widths, and thicknesses on the vessel exterior. Other characteristics of Plaquemine ceramics are the occasional use of shell to temper the clays; small, projecting lug handles on the vessel rims; engraving; and the general absence of stamped designs.

Plaquemine ceramic types overlie Troyville–Coles Creek types in stratigraphic situations, an indication that the former are more recent in time. Since the remains of the Plaquemine Culture during its zenith have not been found in direct assocation with European articles, they must predate the historic era. The published record implies that the Plaquemine Culture is the most likely forerunner of the historic Natchezan and Taensa Indian tribes in the region.[1] In addition to the stratigraphic evidence, there are five radiocarbon dates, ranging from A.D. 975 to A.D. 1640, specifically attributed to Plaquemine Culture occupations. They are from the Avery Island, Thibodaux, Hilly Grove, and Transylvania sites in Iberia, Assumption, Tensas, and East Carroll parishes, respectively, and the Lake George Site in Yazoo County, Mississippi.[2]

Plaquemine occupations are found in a triangular region of which Greenville, Mississippi, forms the apex and the entire Louisiana coastal zone forms the base. At most of the known sites there are two or more rectangular mounds surrounding an open area or plaza. At sites in the northern zone there may be seven to twenty-four mounds surrounding two plazas. Also in the northern zone are the most spectacular mounds of the Plaquemine Culture. In his study, David J. Hally noted that Plaquemine Culture sites are characteristically situated on natural levees where the well-drained and coarse-textured soil would be most suitable for habitation and cultivation. Furthermore, he remarks, the "Plaquemine settlement pattern in the northern half of the

---

1. George I. Quimby, Jr., "The Medora Site, West Baton Rouge Parish, Louisiana," *Field Museum of Natural History, Anthropological Series*, Vol. 24 (1951), No. 2, pp. 81–135; John L. Cotter, "Stratigraphic and Area Tests at the Emerald and Anna Mound Sites," *American Antiquity*, Vol. 17 (1951), No. 1, Pt. 1, pp. 18–32; David J. Halley, "Post–Coles Creek Development in the Upper Tensas Basin of Louisiana," *Proceedings of the 23rd Southeastern Archaeological Conference*, Bulletin No. 6 (1967), 36–40.
2. Gagliano, *Occupation Sequence at Avery Island*; Phillips, *Archaeological Survey in the Lower Yazoo Basin*; Richard Weinstein et al., *Cultural Resource Survey of the Proposed Relocation Route of U.S. 90 (La. 3052), Assumption, St. Mary, and Terrebonne Parishes, Louisiana* (Baton Rouge, 1978).

Lower Valley was a vacant ceremonial center–dispersed settlement type."[3] He infers from ethnohistoric data that the mound sites were utilized by the sociopolitical elite while the populace lived nearby in dispersed hamlets. Known sites in the southern zone have fewer and smaller mounds, and as we shall see, midden deposits in these minor centers are also sparse. Hally noted, however, that early European accounts of the Indians in this southern zone describe tribes living in nucleated settlements.

The first site of the Plaquemine Culture specifically selected for extensive excavation was the Medora Site, a ceremonial mound center on the Medora plantation in West Baton Rouge Parish. The site consisted of two mounds about 400 feet apart and situated adjacent to a small stream called Bayou Bourbeau. The mounds are in a cultivated field at Manchac Point, the narrow neck of a Mississippi River meander. Edwin Doran, Jr., directed the LSU–WPA project that investigated the site during the winter of 1939–1940.

He began with the larger tumulus, Mound A, which was a flat-topped pyramid with basal dimensions of 125 feet on a side and a maximum height of about 13 feet. In the premound stratum beneath Mound A was a thin occupation zone manifested by burned earth, charcoal, midden, and a profusion of postmolds. In one area postmolds and wall trenches outlined the floor patterns of two concentric, circular structures. The inner structure, 25 feet in diameter, had a central fire pit and near it was a flat-topped, circular "clay altar" measuring about 3.5 feet in diameter, and 6 inches high. The floor of the outer structure, 45 feet in diameter, was about 6 inches higher than that of the inner structure. Quimby suggested that these postmolds and wall trenches might represent a single rotundalike building. Just to the southeast of the circular outlines another postmold pattern, this one without wall trenches, outlined a square building measuring 20 feet on a side. The report mentions no entryways for any of these structures.[4]

A flat-topped, slightly ovoid mound about 100 feet in diameter and

3. David J. Hally, "The Lower Mississippi Valley: A.D. 1000–1700," manuscript, Department of Anthropology, University of Georgia, 8.
4. Quimby, "The Medora Site."

2 feet high was built on top of the premound stratum. On its summit were scattered postmolds, midden, and several segments of a square postmold pattern. The Indians later built two small, flat-topped pyramidal mounds on top of and at opposite ends of this primary stage of Mound A. This marked a new innovation in mound construction for Louisiana, although similar mound construction is manifested at the partially coeval Emerald Mound, one of the largest earthworks in the southeastern United States, which is located along the Natchez Trace Parkway in Adams County, Mississippi.[5] At the Medora Site the secondary mound at the northeastern end of the summit was 40 feet square and 5 feet tall. Along its south side was a projecting, stepped earthen ramp, and on top of the mound were postmolds outlining a structure with a square floor pattern. Inside, near the center of the outline, there were three pits measuring up to 6 feet in length and 2 feet deep. They were filled with dirt and contained only a small quantity of cultural debris. The secondary mound at the southwestern end of the summit was quite similar to its mate at the northeastern end, except that it lacked an earthen ramp. It is interesting, once again, that neither of the structures on the secondary mounds revealed an entryway.

The final construction stage at Mound A consisted of a mantle of earth, which covered the two secondary mounds and formed a flat-topped pyramid with a small, domed rise, 25 feet in diameter and 3 feet high, at the northeast end. No pits or postmolds were found on this final construction stage, probably because they had been obliterated by erosion.

At Mound B, about 400 feet south of Mound A, the excavators exposed a premound stratum, which contained midden, a wall trench outlining a floor pattern 20 feet square, "and a similar square of postmolds in a double row. It is possible that the wall trench and post molds do not represent the same building."[6] Mound B was constructed over these remains. It was a flat-topped mound, 100 feet in diameter and about 2 feet high. No structural remains were found on its summit.

5. Cotter, "Stratigraphic and Area Tests at the Emerald and Anna Mound Sites."
6. Quimby, "The Medora Site," 101.

Exploratory trenches were dug in the area designated the plaza, between Mounds A and B, but only thin midden lenses were exposed. No human burials were found at the Medora Site.

As usual, sherds predominated in the artifact inventory. A total of eighteen thousand were found. The only other ceramic object was an engraved ear ornament, and the only finished stone artifacts were three projectile points; two ground-stone celts; a small, smoothed diorite object, concavo-convex in cross section; and a ground-sandstone disk. No bone was reported from the excavation.

Approximately eighteen miles downstream from the Medora Site is another Plaquemine Culture occupation that was also extensively excavated under the auspices of the LSU-WPA program. The investigations were conducted under the direction of Edwin B. Doran, Jr., and Carlyle S. Smith between April, 1940, and July, 1941. The site consisted of two mounds about 600 feet apart, situated along the back slope of the Mississippi River natural levee at the community of Bayou Goula in Iberville Parish. Mound 1 at the Bayou Goula Site was extensively excavated, Mound 2 was only trenched to expose the nature of its construction, and the intervening area between the two mounds was investigated with extensive exploratory trenches.

The excavations of Mound 1 at Bayou Goula, like those at Mound A of the Medora Site, revealed a premound stratum composed of Plaquemine occupation debris. In this stratum was a small pit, 3 feet in diameter and 6 inches deep, lined with cane, leaves, and grasses. Elsewhere, simple plaited, woven impressions were exposed in the soil and, most importantly, one of the few reported instances of fragments of charred corncobs. "These cobs were of small diameter, with eight rows of kernels."[7]

The first stage of Mound 1, built on top of village debris, consisted of a flat-topped pyramid, measuring 70 feet on each side and 3 feet in height. In addition to the usual detritus within the mound fill, there was a cypress log, 6 inches by 46 inches, into which a zigzag design was carved. On the mound summit were charcoal stains, burned spots, and scattered postmolds. The second construction stage enlarged the mound so that it measured 100 feet on a side, but increased its height

7. *Ibid.*, 105.

barely 6 inches. Activity on its summit was indicated by burned areas, charcoal, ash, scattered postmolds, and five stone atlatl weights. The third and final stage of construction at Mound 1 enlarged the mound to measure 140 feet by 110 feet by 6 feet. On the summit at the south end, a small pyramid that measured 40 feet by 110 feet by 3 feet was added. Subsequent plowing and erosion over the top of Mound 1 had obliterated any specific evidence of prehistoric activities on that surface.

Mound 2 resembled Mound 1 in size, and test trenches revealed that its construction was also similar, although Mound 2 lacked the small, pyramidal mound that topped one end of Mound 1.

The diagnostic ceramics, the atlatl weights, the incised cypress log, and the corncobs, were the only artifactual remains attributed to the Plaquemine Culture occupation at the Bayou Goula site.

The Gordon Site, although it is not located in Louisiana, deserves some attention since it, too, was extensively excavated. This site, which consists of two dome-shaped mounds about 225 feet apart and a village area, encompasses about 5 acres. It is situated along the South Fork of Coles Creek, near its confluence with the Mississippi River in Jefferson County, Mississippi. The site was excavated by John L. Cotter of the National Park Service as part of the development program for the Natchez Trace Parkway.[8] Because of erosion, Cotter was unable to discern whether or not the mounds were originally rectangular and flat-topped, but at least one of them, Mound B, was built in two stages and the primary stage had a flat summit. The premound stratum and the mound fill at Mound B also revealed postmold outlines of circular and rectangular structures built in a sequence comparable to that demonstrated at the Medora Site; that is, structures with a circular floor pattern were succeeded by those with a rectangular floor pattern. The circular patterns at the Gordon Site, however, were not associated with wall trenches as they had been at Medora. The opposite situation prevails for the rectangular, postmold patterns; those at Medora were not associated with wall trenches, whereas those at the Gordon Site were. One other notable difference is that rectangular

8. John L. Cotter, "The Gordon Site in Southern Mississippi," *American Antiquity*, Vol. 18 (1952), No. 2, pp. 110–26.

patterns at the Gordon Site had open corners, but those at the Medora Site were closed.

Of particular interest are the human skeletal remains assigned to the Plaquemine occupation at the Gordon Site. In the village stratum near Mound A, a primary flexed burial of an adult male was placed in an ovoid pit with a fish-effigy bowl, two small incised vessels, a small plain bowl, and a polished bowl. Under Mound A, a cluster of human phalanges, cranial fragments, and teeth representing at least two adults, was found. One skull fragment exhibited cranial deformation. Also beneath Mound A was a primary burial in an extended supine position. It, too, exhibited cranial deformation. There were no direct artifactual associations, but near the pelvis were skull fragments of an infant and near the feet was an adult mandible. Within the fill of Mound A, two secondary burials were found. One of these was represented by "massive cranial and thoracic fragments" of an adult male in association with two stone points. The other was the secondary burial of an isolated adult male cranium. In Mound A there was also a primary burial of a dog, "a mature specimen of small to medium size," in association with a stone point.[9]

At Mound B a group of fragmented infant skulls representing four to six individuals was found lying within the circular postmold pattern. One of the skulls exhibited cranial deformation, but there were no direct artifactual associations and no evidence of a pit. In different areas within the fill of Mound B, there were several primary and secondary human burials. The first primary burial was an adult placed in an extended supine position. There was no pit, and the only artifactual associations were a few small stone flakes. The other primary burial was that of a young adult in a pit of indefinite outlines. Cotter did not report the burial position, but he did state that the skeleton was somewhat disarticulated. Associated with the skeleton, near the thoracic region, was a small, polished greenstone celt, and there was a small plain jar 5 feet from the skull. Elsewhere in the mound fill were the associated remains of two children represented by skull fragments that show cranial deformation. There was no pit outline, but deer bone fragments accompanied the remains. Within the outlines of the rectangular structures at Mound B, several burials were found. They were

9. *Ibid.*, 116.

poorly preserved remains of a possible primary burial associated with several stone flakes; an infant burial "in a compact mass, poorly preserved,"[10] associated with a stone point and several flakes; another burial represented by a fragmented adult cranium accompanied by deer bones, stone flakes, and seven sherds; and the bundle burial of an adolescent with no artifactual associations.

The unusually wide array of human burial practices attributable to the Plaquemine Culture is expanded even further if we look at other sites in Louisiana and Arkansas; for example, the Lake Saint Agnes Site. Alan Toth excavated the site using funds provided by the Dupuy brothers, Marc, Jr., Richard, Charles, and Robert, of Marksville, and with their excellent field assistance. The site is a multicomponent mound and occupation area that encompasses about 2 acres of land near Little River in Avoyelles Parish. On the summit of the mound, which measured 45 feet by 55 feet by 11 feet, there was a Plaquemine Culture ovoid burial pit about 7 feet by 4 feet by 2 feet deep. It contained secondary burials representing at least ten individuals. These were manifested by clusters of skulls at each end of the pit and partially articulated skeletal midsections and long bones intermixed elsewhere in the pit. Adults and subadults were represented. The funerary accompaniments within the pit included a bowl, 2 jars, and a bottle, as well as 460 sherds, 2 stone point fragments, a quartz crystal, a hammerstone, and a polishing stone.[11]

At the Sanson Site in Rapides Parish, excavations into a mound about 65 feet in diameter and 4 feet high yielded human burials and funerary objects attributed to the Plaquemine Culture. The details of the excavation data were not reported, but "a wide variety of grave goods, notably sherds and vessels, was recovered. The mound also had contained definite evidence of bundle burials, a mass disarticulated burial, scattered single burials presumed to have been made in the flesh, and three puddled clay repositories with offerings of pottery vessels and two pipes in association."[12] The vessels from the Sanson Site exhibited a particularly distinctive trait. A hole had been made in the base

---

10. *Ibid.*, 117.
11. Toth, *The Lake St. Agnes Site.*
12. Hiram F. Gregory, Jr., "Plaquemine Period Sites in the Catahoula Basin: A Microcosm of East Central Louisiana," *Louisiana Studies*, Vol. 8 (1969), No. 2, p. 112.

of each vessel during its manufacture, usually before, but sometimes after it was fired. The exact significance of this trait is not known, but inasmuch as it is customarily associated with human burials at sites in Florida and Georgia, one would suspect that it is interwoven with beliefs about death and the hereafter. Archaeologists refer to this practice as "killing" the vessel.

The only other place in Louisiana from which "killed" vessels are reported is a mound that contained a Plaquemine Culture component at the Mayes Mound Site on Larto Lake, Catahoula Parish.[13] There Moore's bore holes revealed twenty-three groups of secondary human interments consisting primarily of skulls but including other skeletal elements. The burial pits were generally rectangular, up to 10.5 feet long and 7.5 feet wide, and about 2 feet deep on the average. The pits contained two to sixty-six skulls each, and surprisingly, more than half of the pits yielded more than twelve skulls each. Noting that the clay in the skulls differed from that of the mound, Moore surmised that the individuals had been buried elsewhere, then dug up and reinterred in the Mayes mound. Most of the burial pits contained a few artifacts, including entire vessels, sherds, a clay frog-effigy pipe, an ear ornament, an elbow-shaped pipe, clusters of pebbles probably from rattles, ground-stone celts, a sandstone pipe, chipped-stone points, a knife, and red, white, yellow, and purple pigments. The mound also contained four separate primary burials of adults laid in an extended supine position. None of these burials was associated with artifacts. No children were buried at the Mayes mound.

The Plaquemine occupation at the nonmound MacArthur Site revealed yet another burial practice. The site is in the Bayou Bartholomew drainage of Arkansas, just north of the Louisiana state line. Occupational debris at this site was limited to an area about 26 feet in diameter. Within the postmold outline of a structure having a circular floor pattern about 16 feet in diameter "were extended, supine burials of two adult males and one adult female and four flexed burials of infants, all in separate graves."[14] No artifactual associations were reported.

13. Moore, "Some Aboriginal Sites in Louisiana and Arkansas"; Gregory, "Plaquemine Period Sites in the Catahoula Basin."
14. Martha Ann Rolingson, "The Bartholomew Phase: A Plaquemine Adaptation

Data on Plaquemine subsistence patterns is not very substantial. It is generally assumed that the people of this culture were basically agriculturalists, but this assumption is not well documented in the archaeological record. Since the esteemed crop trinity of corn, beans, and squash had been reported from numerous sites in the eastern United States by this time in prehistory, it is likely that comparable sites of the Plaquemine Culture had an agricultural base as well. The almost total lack of physical evidence for these crops may be a case of poor preservation, or it may be due to the fact that more mound centers than hamlets have been investigated. Both Gregory and Rolingson note that settlement patterns in east-central Louisiana and the Bayou Bartholomew drainage of Arkansas show a preference for bottomland surfaces, *i.e.*, levee ridges and back slopes, rather than higher bluff or terrace edges. They also believe that these people preferred bottomland because the soil was more arable and fertile. "It would appear that the bottom-land resources were more important than locations never threatened by inundations."[15]

From two Plaquemine campsites in southern Arkansas, Rolingson reported an abundance of deer bone and freshwater mussel shells, in addition to fish bones. And in east-central Louisiana Gregory remarked that test pit excavations in east-central Louisiana show heavy exploitation of bear, deer, raccoon, rabbit, squirrel, and particularly, waterfowl. Fish remains, predominantly gar and drumfish, characterize the middens, along with mussel shells of the *Unio*. At the Gordon Site, Cotter found the bones of deer and bear and scales of the garfish. This site also yielded unspecified numbers of rabbit, squirrel, turkey, and wood duck bones, and a limited amount of freshwater mussel shells. Quimby found animal bone in the Bayou Goula site excavations, but he does not specify whether the specimens are from the Plaquemine or post-Plaquemine occupations. We are told, however, that the charred corncobs found at the site are from the Plaquemine component. Farther to the south, in the coastal marshes of Louisiana, McIntire, during his survey in the region, observed that Plaquemine occupations on the cheniers yielded fish and mammal bones, but only

---

in the Mississippi Valley," in Charles E. Cleland (ed.), *Cultural Change and Continuity: Essays in Honor of James Bennett Griffin* (New York, 1976), 114.
15. *Ibid.*, 112; Gregory, "Plaquemine Period Sites in the Catahoula Basin."

sparse quantities of mollusk shells. He found slightly larger concentrations of shell in Plaquemine Culture middens toward the Pearl River.[16] If McIntire's observations stand the test of systematic excavation and quantified analysis, the subsistence patterns of the Plaquemine Culture will be proven to be an outstanding example of a shift in the preferential food selection of prehistoric peoples in the Louisiana coastal region. Most of the other Neo-Indian cultures in this region extensively exploited the molluskan resources.

In summary, the archaeological evidence demonstrates that the Plaquemine Culture was a late prehistoric manifestation that may still have existed at the time of the European entrada into the lower Mississippi Valley. Certain elements of Plaquemine Culture—e.g., stepped mounds with temples on their summits, plazas, secondary burials and funerary offerings indicative of class-structured societies, round and square houses or cabins, and cranial deformation—seem to mesh well with the ethnohistoric record of the region. Of course, the same general traits also have a long and complex prehistoric tradition, and it is true that no European trade items have been repoted from Plaquemine occupations *per se*. Nevertheless, Plaquemine ceramics have been found intermixed as minority wares with other ceramic types excavated in indisputable association with European goods.[17] The distribution and characteristics of the Plaquemine Culture in Louisiana, Mississippi, and Arkansas do not uniformly correspond to the picture we have been given of all of that region's cultures at the time of their discovery by Europeans, but at least in the instance of the historic Natchezan tribes, there does appear to be a developmental sequence from the prehistoric Plaquemine to the historic period.

16. Rolingson, "The Bartholomew Phase"; Gregory, "Plaquemine Period Sites in Louisiana and Arkansas"; Cotter, "The Gordon Site in Southern Mississippi"; George I. Quimby, Jr., "The Bayou Goula Site, Iberville Parish, Louisiana," *Fieldiana: Anthropology*, Vol. 47 (1957), No. 2, pp. 89–170; McIntire, *Prehistoric Indian Settlements of the Changing Mississippi River Delta*.
17. Robert S. Neitzel, *Archaeology of the Fatherland Site: The Grand Village of the Natchez*, Anthropological Papers of the American Museum of Natural History, Vol. 51, Pt. 1 (New York, 1965).

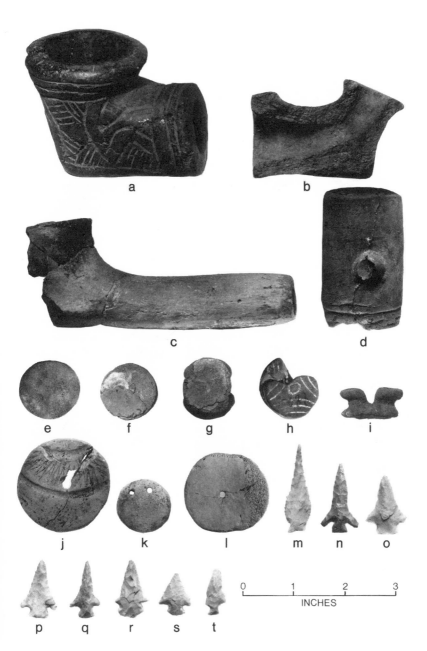

PLATE 62

Ceramic, stone, bone, and copper-coated artifacts of the Plaquemine
Culture: *a–d*, clay pipes; *e–i*, clay ear spools (*f, g,* and *i* are copper-
coated); *j–k*, clay ornaments; *l*, bone ornament; *m–t*, projectile points.

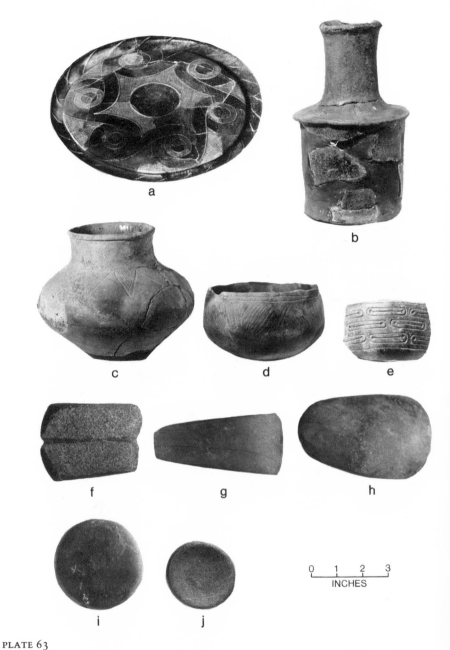

a

b

c

d

e

f

g

h

i

j

0   1   2   3
INCHES

PLATE 63

Ceramic vessels and stone artifacts of the Plaquemine Culture: *a–d*, restored vessels; *e*, vessel fragment; *f–h*, stone celts; *i–j*, stone gaming pieces.

a

b

c

d

e

f

0 1 2 3
INCHES

PLATE 64

Ceramic vessels of the Plaquemine Culture.

XI Mississippian Culture

By A.D. 800 in the vicinity of Saint Louis in the central Mississippi Valley, societies based on agriculture had developed. The cultivation of corn, beans, squash, and a wide array of native cultigens supplemented selective hunting, fishing, and gathering technologies. James B. Griffin quite aptly applies the term *Mississippian* "to refer to the wide variety of adaptations made by societies which developed a dependence upon agriculture for their basic, storable food supply." Of course, this definition also applied to the archaeological manifestations of the contemporaneous Caddo and Plaquemine cultures. Cultural designations are partly arbitrary, but even so, between A.D. 800 and A.D. 1200 those societies in the Saint Louis environs coalesced into one of the largest ceremonial-residential centers ever to have existed in the prehistoric United States, the Cahokia Site near East Saint Louis, Illinois.[1] Like Poverty Point, this center developed near the confluence of the major river systems in the eastern United States. The Cahokia Site encompasses a rectangular area of 6.5 square miles, and within this area of quite diverse environments are approximately 120 tumuli of various sizes and shapes. Near the center of the site is Monks Mound, a massive, rectangular earthen construction that measures 1,000 feet by 800 feet by 100 feet high and contains 21,690,000 cubic

---

1. Bruce D. Smith, *Middle Mississippian Exploitation of Animal Populations*, Anthropological Papers, Museum of Anthropology, University of Michigan, No. 57; Griffin, "Eastern North American Archaeology," 189; Melvin L. Fowler, *Cahokia, Ancient Capital of the Midwest*, Addison-Wesley Module in Anthropology No. 48 (Reading, Mass., 1974).

feet of dirt. Monks Mound is the largest prehistoric earthen tumulus in North America north of Mexico.

Many of the tumuli at Cahokia and other Mississippian centers in the major river drainages of the eastern United States are multistage constructions. The mounds served as platforms for socioreligious buildings, and they were also used for the interment of people of high status. Often human retainers were sacrificed to accompany these burials, and elaborate funerary offerings were made. Grave goods included large quantities of exotic ceramic, bone, stone, shell, and copper items that attest to the exceptionally extensive trade network so characteristic of the Mississippian Culture. Mounds, borrow pits, and wetlands occupied about one half of the Cahokia Site proper; residential space and special use areas that changed through time occupied the remainder of the site. At certain periods, portions of the site were enclosed by bastioned wooden stockades, one of which appears to have bounded an area of 250 acres. Cahokia was a complex urban capital with a population of about 38,000 surrounded by many miles of interconnected subsidiary farming communities.[2]

Cultural influences from Cahokia radiated outward, and smaller but no less prominent Mississippian regional centers developed and flourished in the eastern United States, for example, the Aztalan Site in Wisconsin, the Etowah Site in Georgia, and closest to Louisiana, the Moundville Site in west-central Alabama. Second in size only to Cahokia, Moundville encompasses about 300 acres and contains twenty flat-topped, pyramidal earthen mounds surrounding a central plaza. The site, presently a most attractive state park called Mound State Monument, is situated on a level terrace overlooking the Black Warrior River near Tuscaloosa. The site was protected on one side by a steep river bank and on the other three sides by a wooden stockade. About three thousand people resided at Moundville, and an additional six thousand lived at some seventeen related sites extending for fifty miles along the Black Warrior River.[3] Excavations have revealed differential use of the space within the site. For example, there was a residential

2. Fowler, Cahokia.
3. John A. Walthall, Moundville: An Introduction to the Archaeology of a Mississippian Chiefdom (Tuscaloosa, 1977).

area away from the plaza and close to the river. Civic structures and charnel houses bordered the plaza, and there was a sweathouse within the plaza. There were also special areas for craft technologies, such as ceramics, shell-ornament manufacture, and weaving.

About three thousand human burials were excavated from non-mound cemeteries at Moundville. The physical anthropological data from these skeletal remains indicate that the average stature of the adult males was 65 inches and that of the adult females, 61 inches. The data show a high degree of infant mortality; but if an infant survived to the age of six, he generally lived on into adulthood. The average life-span for the Moundville inhabitants was thirty-five to forty years. High-ranking people, those buried in the mounds, practiced cranial deformation. In addition, funerary accompaniments and depictions on shell and copper items indicate that they dressed lavishly, had more elaborate hair styles, and decorated their faces and bodies by painting and tattooing.[4]

The residential structures at Moundville had rectangular floor patterns, 10 to 30 feet down their long axes. Wall posts were set individually or in wall trenches, entwined with cane, and plastered inside and out with mud. Steep hip roofs were constructed with rafters, wattle, and daub, and then covered with thatch. Characteristically, these were single-room residences with sleeping platforms next to the walls and a central fire pit.[5] Public structures near the plaza and on the mound summits closely resembled the residential buildings, but they were larger than the residences and associated with features and other archaeological remains attributable to rituals. The sweathouse in the plaza was a square building measuring about 25 feet on a side. It was a "double walled structure containing a central room with a hard packed, light colored clay floor. Two fire basins, 1 round and 1 square, were sunk into the clay floor. The square fireplace had vertical walls and indented corners. These corners form . . . a good approximation of the cardinal points."[6]

4. Christopher S. Peebles, "Moundville and Surrounding Sites: Some Structural Considerations of Mortuary Practices II," in J. A. Brown (ed.), Approaches to the Social Dimensions of Mortuary Practices, Memoirs of the Society for American Archaeology No. 25 (Washington, D.C., 1971).
5. Walthall, Moundville.
6. Peebles, "Moundville and Surrounding Sites," 83.

The artifact inventories from Mississippian sites show the expectable regional variations with one notable exception. Wherever the Mississippian Culture existed ceramics were manufactured by an innovative shell-tempering technique. The Indians developed a process whereby shell—generally freshwater mussel shell—was first burned and then pulverized into minute particles. These particles and the accompanying shell "dust" were then incorporated into unfired clay. The process has been verified by x-ray diffraction tests on archaeological samples of Mississippian sherds. "Shell is composed of calcium carbonate which acts to reduce a clay's plasticity in a manner other than the usual introduction of relatively large, nonplastic particles. The minute plate-like clay particles are small enough that the identical ionic charges on their surfaces have sufficient repelling force to keep them slightly separated. Calcium carbonate has the capacity to neutralize this force so that when the clay particles collide during their random movement they tend to stay together. This flocculation process is facilitated by the presence of water and creates 'large' clay particles which consequently enhances the working quality of fine textured clays."[7] Although the Indians knew nothing of atomic structure and the chemical properties of the clay and the shell temper, they discovered the combination of these natural resources that allowed them to manufacture some of the largest and most exquisite ceramic vessels in prehistoric North America. The indications are that shell-tempered pottery originated at Cahokia and rapidly diffused from there throughout the eastern United States.

Mississippian vessels are short and tall globular jars with straight, everted, or recurved rims; deep and shallow bowls; plain and compound long-necked bottles; stirrup handle bottles; straight-rimmed plates; footed vessels; teapot-shaped vessels; gourd forms; and effigy vessels depicting humans, mammals, amphibians, reptiles, birds, and fish. Often the globular vessels and bowls have multiple-lug, strap, or loop handles. Most of the unbroken Mississippian vessels reported from the lower Mississippi Valley were recovered from burials, and they are small. The jars and bowls have orifices about 12 inches in di-

7. Michael G. Million, "Research Design for the Aboriginal Ceramic Industries of the Cache River Basin," in Michael B. Schiffer and John H. House (eds.), *The Cache River Archaeological Project*, Arkansas Archaeological Survey, Research Series, No. 8 (Fayetteville, 1975), 218.

ameter with only a slightly greater vertical dimension. Characteristically, the unpainted vessels range from a dull gray to a shiny black and quite often the exteriors are smudged and fire clouded. Decorative motifs are applied with incising, engraving, brushing, punctating, pinching, nicking, notching, polishing, appliqué, and nodes. There is also positive and negative painting with red slip, red on buff, red on white, and red, white, and black.[8] In addition to pottery, the Mississippians made elegant clay pipes, ear and lip ornaments, disks, and ladles.

The repertoire of stone, bone, shell, and copper artifacts from Mississippian components is no less impressive. Among the stone artifacts are small finely chipped triangular points with or without side or corner notches, drills, chisels, scrapers, axes, knives, ground-stone and polished-stone effigy vessels, human effigies, engraved disks, spatulate and monolithic axes, batons, mealing stones, mortars, hoes, celts, and hammerstones. Items made of bone include handles, pins, needles, awls, flakers, combs, beads, carapace rattles, canine-teeth pendants, deer astraguli game pieces, worked beaver incisors, and points made from deer antlers. From marine and freshwater shell there are numerous beads, disks, pins, dippers, cups, ear and lip ornaments, and elaborately engraved gorgets. Native copper, generally attributed to the Lake Superior region, was used to manufacture masks, beads, pendants, headbands, breastplates, and repoussé plates, and for the plating of stone and wooden ornaments.

One quite notable characteristic of the Mississippian Culture was the "Ceremonial Complex," which began at about A.D. 1000 and reached its pinnacle by A.D. 1500. Although prominent in the Mississippian Culture, this complex cut across cultural boundaries in the eastern United States. It has been called the Southern Cult, the Death Cult, Buzzard Cult, and the Eagle Warrior Complex, because of subjective interpretations of the art motifs and forms. Most of the diagnostic artifacts of this ceremonial complex are from three of the large centers: Spiro, Etowah, and Moundville. The specimens are almost

8. Phillips, Ford, and Griffin, *Archaeological Survey in the Lower Mississippi Alluvial Valley*; Phillips, *Archaeological Survey in the Lower Yazoo Basin*; Roy Hathcock, *Ancient Pottery of the Mississippi River Valley* (Camden, Ark., 1976).

exclusively associated with high status individuals buried in the mounds. The specific motifs, which are strikingly similar, depict in various styles the cross, the sun, the circle, a bilobed arrow, the forked eye, the open eye, the barred oval, the hand and eye and death motifs. All are found separately and/or combined variously on god-animal representations of spiders, serpents, raptorial birds, felines, Long Nosed God masks, and anthropomorphized animal beings. The motifs and god-animal representations appear on shell and copper gorgets, columella pendants, embossed copper plates, badges, emblems, wooden and stone ear spools, some of which are copper plated. Also diagnostic of the ceremonial complex are superbly crafted copper celts, stone celts, monolithic axes, batons, effigy pipes, stone disks, conch-shell bowls, ceremonial flints, and elaborately decorated vessel forms.[9]

Counterparts of these very intricate ritual furnishings, dated to Mississippian times, have been found in Mexico. This evidence, along with the temple mounds themselves and corn and bean agriculture, which also originated in Meso-America, is a further indication of Meso-American influence in the southeastern United States. It is uncertain, however, exactly how Meso-American influences diffused into the Southeast. There is no evidence of mass migrations or invasions from Mexico, by sea or overland, into this region. One quite plausible theory holds that Meso-American traits were introduced northward by Aztec traders called "pochtecas." It is interesting to note the "the God of the Aztec pochteca was Yacatecuhtli, who is sometimes portrayed with a prominent nose (reminiscent of Long-Nosed God Masks). He is sometimes shown with a group of arrows and a disk, which suggest the bilobed arrow, and with a barred staff, suggestive of a serpent staff, held by priests, on shell engravings from the Spiro site in Oklahoma."[10]

By the late stage of the Mississippian Culture, just prior to the historic period, the ceremonial complex had declined greatly, at least in terms of reported archaeological occurrences. In fact, the largest ceremonial centers, such as Cahokia, Aztalan, Spiro, Etowah, and

9. Antonio J. Waring, Jr., and Preston Holder, "A Prehistoric Ceremonial Complex in the Southeastern United States," *American Anthropologist*, Vol. 47 (1945), No. 1, pp. 1–34.
10. Griffin, *Eastern North American Archaeology*, 190.

Moundville, were, for all essential purposes, abandoned by the time of the DeSoto expedition in the mid-sixteenth century. This is not to say that the Mississippian Culture ceased to exist. Quite to the contrary, new large urban centers, towns, and villages proliferated. They, along with older settlements, were formed into provinces governed by chiefs. Furthermore, many of the earlier Mississippian traits—including fortification; temple mounds; rectangular buildings; burial patterns; plazas; corn, bean and squash agriculture; shell-tempered pottery; as well as most of the utilitarian and some of the exotic artifact inventory—persisted on into the historic period. In fact, it was Indians of the late Mississippian Culture who encountered DeSoto and his party during their brief but devastative entrada into the southeastern United States.[11] In Louisiana, certainly the Tunicas and probably some Muskhogean and Chitimachan groups were the historic heirs of the Mississippian Culture.

Little is known about manifestations of Mississippian Culture in Louisiana (Pl. 65). In his synopsis of Louisiana's prehistory, written in 1971, William Haag was unable to present any substantive data on Mississippian Culture. A decade later, very little had been done to remedy this lack of knowledge. Surface collection of shell-tempered sherds at many multicomponent sites provide evidence of Mississippian occupations. Fred Kniffen and William G. McIntire have documented such occupations in the coastal region, particularly in the eastern zone, in the form of *rangia* and/or oyster shell middens and mounds. In addition, Philip Phillips has noted "the possibility of a superficial Mississippian overlay" at certain sites with large pyramidal mounds in the northeastern corner of Louisiana.[12] Although these in-

11. U.S. DeSoto Expedition Commission, *Final Report of the United States DeSoto Expedition Commission*, House Document No. 71, 76th Cong., 1st Sess. (Washington, D.C., 1939); Jeffrey P. Brain, Alan Toth, and Antonio Rodriguez-Buckingham, "Ethnohistoric Archaeology and the DeSoto Entrada into the Lower Mississippi Valley," *Conference on Historic Site Archaeology Papers*, Vol. 7 (1974), 232–89.

12. Haag, *Louisiana in North American Prehistory*; Fred B. Kniffen, "Preliminary Report of the Indian Mounds and Middens of Plaquemines and St. Bernard Parishes," in *Reports on the Geology of Plaquemines and St. Bernard Parishes*, Department of Conservation, Louisiana Geological Survey, Geological Bulletin No. 8 (New Orleans, 1936), 407–22; McIntire, *Prehistoric Indian Settlements of the Changing Mississippi River Delta*; Phillips, *Archaeological Survey in the Lower Yazoo Basin*, 954.

vestigators have given us an idea of the distribution of Mississippian Culture in Louisiana, we still know almost nothing of the lifeways of Mississippians in this state. With but two exceptions there have been no concerted efforts to systematically investigate Mississippian sites in Louisiana.

The first of these exceptions is the work that Ian W. Brown and Nancy Lambert-Brown have done at Avery Island. They conducted an intensive survey of sites, both prehistoric and historic, on the salt dome for the Lower Mississippi Survey, Petite Anse Project. Quite unexpectedly, in light of what is known about the archaeology of the area, the Browns found and excavated two late Mississippian middens. The middens yielded about forty thousand shell-tempered sherds, despite the fact that shell-tempered pottery is rare this far west along the Louisiana coast and this far south, for that matter. Astonishingly, "the closest cultural parallels with the Mississippian component occur in the southernmost portion of the Yazoo Basin of the Lower Mississippi Valley, approximately 185 linear miles distant from Avery Island and at least double this distance by water travel."[13] The Browns surmise that the salt, which we know from ethnohistoric data was highly prized and extensively traded, drew the Mississippians to the area. It is not known whether they mined rock salt or evaporated it from saturated solutions. The many large sherds from thin, shallow bowls, sometimes called salt pans, that have been found may indicate that the Indians employed the evaporation process, but they may also have mined the salt. It is curious that the Indians chose Avery Island over known salines closer to their occupation area. The Browns suspect that the closer salines were, at that period, controlled by other strong Indian tribes and that the Mississippian groups therefore found it less troublesome to obtain their salt from Avery Island, which was situated in a region of small, dispersed native populations.[14] All of these hypotheses are as yet unsubstantiated, but the information forthcoming

13. Ian W. Brown and Nancy Lambert-Brown, "Lower Mississippi Survey, Petite-Anse Project," Research Notes, No. 6.
14. Driver and Massey, "Comparative Study of North American Indians"; C. H. Fairbanks, " 'Salt Pans' from the Southeast," American Antiquity, Vol. 6 (1940), 65–67; Brown and Lambert-Brown, "Lower Mississippi Survey, Petite-Anse Project," Research Notes, No. 6.

from this rather isolated Mississippian component will doubtless provide important information about Mississippian manifestations.

The second exception to our rather meager record of Mississippian Culture is the on-going investigation at the multicomponent Sims Site, located along Bayou Saut D'ours in Saint Charles Parish. David D. Davis of Tulane University's Department of Anthropology is directing the explorations. Surface debris from the Mississippian occupation is scattered over an area of about 15 acres on both sides of Bayou Saut D'ours. On one side of the bayou there are three earthen mounds and the remnants of a fourth destroyed during the first quarter of this century. Remnants of a fifth mound, destroyed about the same time, lie across the bayou from the other mounds. Presently, only one of the extant mounds can be definitely assigned to the Mississippian Culture. Diagnostic shell-tempered sherds have been found along with an abundance of freshwater *Unio* shells in the upper levels of the village area and eroding from the mound. The utilization of this mollusk contrasts quite sharply with subsistence patterns at other sites in the region where brackish-water *rangia* and saltwater oyster shells predominate. The mound has not been excavated, but explorations in the village area have yielded animal bones that indicate that deer, raccoon, and muskrat were heavily exploited. Apparently, the inhabitants were less interested in the swamp rabbit and such fish as the drum, bowfin, bass, gar, and catfish. Davis noted that animal bone was used to manufacture awls and points. As might be expected in this deltaic environment, stone artifacts are extremely rare.[15]

Closely spaced in one area of the village midden were five poorly preserved human burials about one foot below the surface. Three of these were adults represented by an extended burial, a flexed burial, and an isolated skull. The fourth individual was an adolescent in a flexed position, and the fifth was an infant, also flexed and lying next to the flexed adult. There were no purposeful grave goods found in association with these skeletons.

This mound and village site is currently being used as an archaeological field school. The meticulous work being conducted there will

15. David D. Davis, personal communication to the author, March 1, 1979.

no doubt provide much needed data on the Mississippian Culture in Louisiana.

Four artifacts connected with Mississippian Culture, though not invariably associated with it, are of some interest. These objects are representative of the previously discussed ceremonial complex, or death cult. Unfortunately, none of them was systematically excavated, and therefore, their exact archaeological associations are obscure. The first is a small, brownish human-head effigy vessel with intricate bands of incised, zoned cross-hatching that encircles the eyes to form a stylized weeping-eye motif and then scrolls around through the hair region on top of and in back of the head to form a bun. The eyes and pupils are naturalistic, and the mouth is straight with slightly protruding lips. The lobes of the naturalistic ears have been perforated. The nose of the effigy is broken and the very top of the vessel, which may have been a spout, is missing as shown by the coil break. The vessel rests on a flat-bottomed neck in the front of which are two linear crosshatched motifs. In the center of each motif is a plain circle. This unique specimen was collected from a shell midden on the Martin plantation in Lafourche Parish. W. S. Martin gave the vessel to William G. McIntire, who in turn donated it to Louisiana State University (Pl. 65, c). The second artifact, a clay- and grit-tempered rim sherd from a bowl, was an isolated surface find from a bank along Grand Bayou in Plaquemines Parish. On the sherd exterior is a classic representation of the hand-and-eye motif (Pl. 65, d). Only a plaster cast of the third specimen remains. The object is a clay eagle- or buzzard-effigy pipe that depicts the bird holding a human individual down with its talons while with its beak it appears to be plucking the entrails from its human prey (Pl. 65, f). The provenience data respecting this pipe indicates only that it is from southern Louisiana. The fourth object is an example of the batons associated with the ceremonial complex, "in polished stone from Louisiana." This specimen is from Ascension Parish.[16]

It is evident, despite the limited data available, that sites of the Mis-

16. Catalog No. 7098, in Museum of the American Indian, New York, N.Y.; Waring and Holder, "A Prehistoric Ceremonial Complex in the Southeastern United States," 11.

a   b

c

d

e

0   1   2   3
INCHES

f

0   1   2   3
INCHES

PLATE 65

Ceramic objects of the Mississippian Culture: *a–c,* vessels; *d,* hand-and-eye motif on a vessel fragment; *e,* salt pan; *f,* plaster cast of a raptorial bird clay pipe.

sissippian Culture do exist in Louisiana. They seem to predominate in the eastern coastal region and in northeastern Louisiana. The wealth of information about this culture as it existed elsewhere in the south-eastern United States will be an invaluable source for comparison as the Mississippian Culture in Louisiana comes under more serious scrutiny.

XII Historic Indian Archaeology

Archaeology relative to the Indians of Louisiana does not end with the prehistoric period. At several sites archaeological deposits demonstrate an uninterrupted sequence of occupations extending from the prehistoric into the early historic period. Other sites, containing intermixed aboriginal and European artifacts, are single, short-interval occupations (Pls. 66, 67, 68, 69, 70, 71). With thorough archaeological field work and cautious ethnographic and cartographic research, some of these sites may be identified with specific historical Indian tribes.[1]

Two such sites have been explored on the grounds of the Louisiana State Penitentiary at Angola in West Feliciana Parish. The first, called the Angola Farm Site, was discovered in 1934 when deep plowing operations along a broad, flat terrace bench overlooking the Mississippi River bottomland exposed artifacts and human bones. The prison superintendent, R. L. Himes, reported the finds to Louisiana State University, and during that spring of 1934, James A. Ford, assisted by prison labor, spent eight days excavating ten human burials at the site. Two of the burials had been disturbed by plowing, but the eight *in situ* burials lay in extended supine positions about 3 feet below the ground surface. They were oriented in various directions. Accompanying four of the adult males were the remains of flintlock muskets, lead shot, black powder, and gunflints. "Beads were found with almost every burial and were clustered about the neck, chest and ankles. A number of small

1. Stephen Williams, "On the Location of Historic Taensa Villages," in *Conference on Historic Site Archaeology Papers* (Raleigh, 1967), Vol. 1, pp. 2–13.

cones, crudely bent from sheet copper, lay at the ankles of one male. Small turkey bells lay near the feet of two others. In the abdominal region of one male was a small metal pipe and the iron blade of a halberd. Another had an iron axe blade. Three of the males had flat-bottomed, straight-sided, copper kettles about fifteen inches in diameter placed above their shoulders. Two pottery vessels of native manufacture were near the skulls of two different burials."[2] Three adult females were accompanied by three native vessels placed near their heads, and one of these females had a few glass beads near her ankles.

Unlike the adults, the single infant burial was found within the remains of a wooden coffin measuring 19 inches by 43 inches. In association with the infant were nails, hinges, a hasp, a crockery bottle, and near the skull, several pieces of red ochre. From the archaeological findings and archival research Ford determined that these were burials of Tunica Indians who resided in this area during the eighteenth century.[3]

Forty-two years later, in the summer of 1976, Ross Maggio, Jr., then warden of the penitentiary at Angola, notified the curator of anthropology at Louisiana State University that glass beads and other early historic items were being unearthed on the penitentiary grounds along a newly constructed road right-of-way and from nearby graves. Early in August, 1976, I alerted William G. Haag, then Louisiana state archaeologist, and invited him to accompany me to the penitentiary to meet with Warden Maggio, who presented the unearthed artifacts to the state archaeologist and arranged for us to visit the area where they had been found. The site, called Bloodhound Hill, is situated on a small bench of land that extends out about halfway up a high steep slope overlooking the flat terrace that contained the Tunica burials excavated in 1934. Haag and I examined the road right-of-way and the remains of several graves, which had been plundered in the not-too-distant past.

Subsequently, Haag contacted Jeffrey P. Brain of Harvard University, who was able to commence explorations at Bloodhound Hill in

2. Ford, *Analysis of Indian Village Site Collections from Louisiana and Mississippi*, 136–37.
3. Ford, *Analysis of Indian Village Site Collections from Louisiana and Mississippi*.

the spring of 1977 with the assistance of the Louisiana Division of Archaeology and Historic Preservation, prison labor, and a grant from the National Geographic Society. Brain was well qualified to conduct the excavations. For the past seven years he had been researching the archaeology of the Tunica Indians to document their four-hundred-year migration from northwestern Mississippi to central Louisiana.[4]

Brain began his explorations by having the rubbish and vegetation cleared from the general area around the plundered burials and along the terrace bench. Next, electronic metal detectors were used to scan the cleared area, and in this manner, four undisturbed Tunica graves were located.[5] The graves were close together, but they were not all oriented in the same direction. All of the burials were placed in the extended supine position. Despite poor bone preservation, sex and age were determinable. The first grave contained an adult male whose head was oriented toward the east. He was accompanied by a musket, shot, gunpowder, additional gun parts, and several stone tools. The second burial, also oriented toward the east, was that of an adult female who had been dressed in a European cuffed dress coat. A brass kettle, inside of which was a native Natchezan bowl, had been buried with her. Elsewhere in the grave were white glass beads and columella shell ear pins. The third burial was an adolescent with the head oriented toward the east. A quantity of blue glass beads had apparently been woven into the hair; the grave also contained two iron axes. The last burial, oriented toward the west, was that of a child. More funerary items were lavished upon this individual than any of the other three. There were copper bells, hundreds of glass and marine-shell beads, two steel clasp knives, a metal crucifix, and native Caddoan pottery. There can be little doubt that this was the child of some important person in the Tunica tribe.

In addition to these human burials, Brain excavated a midden de-

4. Jeffrey P. Brain, *The Tunica Treasure*, Lower Mississippi Survey Bulletin No. 2 (Cambridge, Mass., 1970); Jeffrey P. Brain, *On the Tunica Trail*, Louisiana Archaeological Survey and Antiquities Commission, Anthropological Study No. 1 (Baton Rouge, 1977).

5. The complete, detailed report on these excavations is not yet available. Brain was kind enough to provide me a copy of his report to the National Geographic Society, however. See Brain, *Tunica Treasure II Project: Final Report to the National Geographic Society, Lower Mississippi Valley* (Cambridge, Mass., 1978).

posit located near the cemetery, and "more than 200 m² of surface area was opened up to an average depth of 50 cm."[6] The midden yielded, in addition to European trade items, a considerable quantity of valuable native artifacts. The Tunica had begun to assimilate European culture, but it is evident that they still attached value to their own artifacts during the period between 1706 and 1731, when the site was occupied.

Another find important to Tunica archaeology in Louisiana is the Trudeau Landing Site in West Feliciana Parish, which was originally reported by Clarence B. Moore.[7] The site is situated on a cleared flat terrace between high, steep, forested hills at the spot where Tunica Bayou enters the Mississippi River only about four miles south of the Angola Farm Site. Moore learned of a metal kettle and other metal objects found at the site, in addition to an ornate catlinite pipe, which he was able to obtain. His own excavations there, however, exposed only midden debris, and he found no graves, so he turned his attention to other sites. Trudeau Landing received no more consideration from archaeologists until it was learned that in the late 1960s an extraordinary number of rare, beautifully preserved artifacts of European and native origin had been looted from approximately one hundred Tunica burials at the site. The human skeletal remains were discarded and the cardinal data that they could have provided were tragically and irreparably lost. Nevertheless, through an unprecedented series of events, much of the collection found its way to the Peabody Museum, Harvard University, where it has been cataloged.[8] The collection has since been returned to Louisiana. The published artifact inventory lists only general categories and gives only approximate quantities. There are about 200 metal kettles, pots, tubs, and skillets; 3 pewter bowls; 100 European ceramic items; 75 Tunican, Natchezan, and Caddoan vessels; 20 wine and gin bottles; 20 muskets or parts thereof; 1 pistol; 500 lead balls; 50 gun flints; 1 grenade; 35 hoes; 25 axes; 15 knives or sword blades; 2 drawknives; 2 adzes; 2 sickles; 1 spade; 10 scissors; 4 spoons; 10 mirrors; 2 chests; 1 kaolin pipe of British manufacture; 3

6. *Ibid.,* 12.
7. Moore, "Some Aboriginal Sites on the Mississippi River."
8. Brain, *On the Tunica Trail;* Jeffrey P. Brain, *Tunica Treasure* (Cambridge, Mass., n.d.).

catlinite pipes of native manufacture; 200 native-made shell ear pins and beads; 200 metal C-shaped bracelets; 60 metal bells; 25 miscellaneous rings, buttons, ear ornaments, and crucifixes; 200,000 glass beads; and 25 pounds of vermilion.[9] This quantity and variety of European objects dating between 1720 and 1740 is indeed unique in the archaeological record of the southeastern United States.

In August, 1972, Brain conducted test explorations at Trudeau Landing, and he was able to expose a number of features that yielded artifacts comparable to those in the Tunica collection.[10] In addition to cleaning several looted grave pits, where he found scattered human bone and artifacts, Brain also excavated three refuse pits and a midden that contained intermixed European and native artifacts. He was also fortunate enough to find an undisturbed Tunica grave about 3 feet deep containing an adult male. Associated with this individual were a musket, a small quantity of gunpowder, a gun flint, a pike head, a clasp knife, and several unidentified pieces of iron.

The 1972 excavations, the Tunica collections, and archival research that includes cartographic data—all corroborate, with reasonable certainty the view that Trudeau Landing is the site of a Tunica settlement occupied sometime between 1731 and 1764. It is unfortunate that so important a site was damaged. Now, though, the land encompassing the Trudeau Landing Site and the picturesque terrain surrounding it has been purchased by the state.

Protected from further vandalism, the site will be developed as a state preservation area for the education and enjoyment of everyone concerned with Louisiana's cultural heritage.

A historical component was exposed at the Bayou Goula Site in Iberville Parish. From ethnohistoric documents and archaeological finds of European ceramics, George Quimby was able to date the component to 1699–1739. He noted that a number of Indian tribes, including the Bayogoula, may have been responsible for this historical occupation.[11] In the upper levels and on the plowed surface of the site, aboriginal sherds, including Plaquemine and Natchezan wares, were

9. Brain, *The Tunica Treasure.*
10. Jeffrey P. Brain, *Trudeau: An 18th Century Tunica Village,* Lower Mississippi Survey Bulletin No. 3 (Cambridge, Mass., 1973).
11. Quimby, "The Bayou Goula Site."

found intermixed with European ceramic, glass, and metal items. Elsewhere in the village area were the remains of houses and segments of a palisade.

The houses were represented by eight rectangular floor patterns outlined by wall trenches containing few postmolds. The houses measured about 25 feet by 17 feet. Four of them were equally divided by interior partitions also manifested by wall trenches, and one of these dwellings also had a 6-foot by 8-foot room attached to one end of the main structure. Six of the houses are aligned as if along a street or lane, with three on each side facing each other. The remaining two structures are around the corner from the end house on one side of the street. No entranceways or interior features were found in the houses because of subsequent plowing at the site. However, fill from the wall trenches yielded late Plaquemine and Natchezan sherds along with a single fragment of European earthenware.

The presence of a palisade at Bayou Goula is indicated only by several long segments of wall trenches. "In one instance several post molds were found in a palisade trench. It is possible, but not likely, that post molds were missed by the excavators in most of the palisade trenches."[12] Ethnohistoric accounts describe a Bayogoula palisade composed of cane rather than wooden posts. This may explain the rarity of postmolds.

Ian W. Brown has offered an alternative view respecting the eight rectangular structures and the palisade at Bayou Goula.[13] Supplemented by more current information gathered from his own excavations and archival research, Brown has reasonably demonstrated that these constructions are most likely the remains of an early eighteenth-century French concession. He notes that the ground plan and the floor patterns contrast quite sharply with any known aboriginal constructions in this region for the period under consideration. Bayogoula residential dwellings were circular, not rectangular. Furthermore, Bayogoula dwellings were not arranged in parallel rows. The archaeological data from the eight structures led Brown to surmise that

---

12. *Ibid.*, 110.
13. Ian W. Brown, "A Reexamination of the Houses at the Bayou Goula Site, Iberville Parish, Louisiana," *Louisiana Archaeology*, Bulletin No. 3, pp. 195–205.

they represent the remains of *de pièce sur pièce* architecture found in French constructions of the time. This architectural form consisted of spaced vertical posts between which were set horizontal planks. The vertical posts were fluted or channeled so as to hold the notched ends of the planks in place. This form of construction could explain the wall trenches and the scarcity of postmolds. Brown remarked that the palisade, too, may well be a French construction inasmuch as they customarily enclosed their concessions.

Eleven historical human burials intruded into Mound 1 at Bayou Goula. The skeletal material was poorly preserved, and age and sex determinations were not possible, but the available evidence indicates that at least nineteen individuals are represented. There was an extended burial, apparently inside a wooden coffin, and a primary flexed burial. All of the others were secondary bundle burials. One of the burial pits yielded only European artifacts, and four of the pits contained European and native objects. Four pits yielded only native objects, but they were sherds of types that elsewhere are found in direct association with European items. The two remaining burial pits contained no artifacts at all, but their stratigraphic provenience indicates that they were contemporaneous with the other historic deposits. In addition to about 235 native sherds, 34 small, finely chipped stone projectile points, 2 quartz crystals, and a bear jaw fragment, there were a variety of European items. These included 10 metal tinklers, 2 tubular metal beads, 3 brass buttons, an object that may have been a fabric seal, a brass dinner bell, and about 190 blue, white and blue, and white glass beads.

Elsewhere at the Bayou Goula Site, generally scattered about near the historic structural remains, were ten refuse pits attributed to the early historic occupancy at the site. They were generally circular, ranging from 20 to 3 feet in diameter and from 6 feet to 1 foot in depth. In addition to artifacts, charcoal, and animal bones in the pit fill, the bottom of the largest pit displayed a scattered distribution of postmolds. Quimby speculated that "this pit may have been part of a semisubterranean house." Objects of native manufacture excavated from the refuse pits included approximately 1,425 sherds and a "Garfish scale projectile point."[14] Among the historical items were 12 iron

14. Quimby, "The Bayou Goula Site," 112, 113.

spikes, found in one of the pits; 7 clay pipe fragments; 4 glass beads; a tubular metal bead; a brass sword guard; 3 gun flints; fragments of rum bottles; chinaware, and crockery; and a bronze French coin dated 1722. The evidence indicates that the Bayou Goula Site was occupied repeatedly by several historical Indian tribes early in the eighteenth century.

Quite unlike all of the other archaeological investigations of historic Indian manifestations in Louisiana are those that were conducted at what is the site of the Presidio de Nuestra Señora del Pilar de Los Adaes (often spelled Adais), the provincial capital of Spanish Texas from 1723 to 1773. The presidio with its associated mission, San Miguel de Los Adaes, was but one of a number of Spanish settlements stretching across Texas from Mexico. They represented a rather abortive attempt to ally the East Texas Indians and to act as a buffer against French encroachments from the east. This particular mission and presidio were erected in the territory of the Adaes, a tribe of the Caddo Confederacy, to lure them away from the French along the Red River at Natchitoches. The presidio was isolated, perilously far from its supply sources and administrative centers in Mexico, on the contested boundary between Spanish Texas and French Louisiana. It stood on a gently rounded finger of upland that extends westward and overlooked a small stream valley about 40 feet below. The site is now part of the Los Adaes State Commemorative Area in Natchitoches Parish. Contemporary Spanish maps of the site show a hexagonal fort with an adobe and wood stockade.

Between 1967 and 1969 Hiram F. Gregory, of Northwestern State University of Louisiana, conducted tests in search of architectural remains and midden concentrations at Los Adaes. He excavated in thirty-two areas to depths ranging from 6 inches to 6 feet. Much of the work was in areas of deposits exposed by modern drainage ditches and access roads. Along a southern slope, in an area of about 10 feet by 3 feet, he excavated a midden containing, in decreasing order of frequency, animal bone, glass bottle fragments, and Indian ceramics. French and Spanish ceramics, metal nails, metal saddlery, brass buttons, rings and jew's harps were also intermixed. On the highest part of the site, Gregory found and excavated what he describes as the remains of a trash receptacle. It was a circular feature, 7 feet in diameter and 2.5 feet deep, that had been capped with clay. The pit fill yielded ash, clinkers, glass fragments, French and Indian sherds, brass pins, segments of copper tubing, and glass "seed beads." Nearby was another pit, 10 feet by 3 feet by 4 feet, which contained five almost whole Indian vessels along with ash, animal bones, brass and pewter buckles, glass fragments, European sherds, and the major portion of a Chinese porcelain bowl. On the surface of the site was a shallow depression 15 feet in diameter. Excavations into this depression indicated that it had once served as a well at least 7 feet deep. Subsequently, during the occupation of the presidio, it was used as a trash pit. Its fill yielded European and Indian sherds, glass fragments, nails, and blanket bale seals. Exposed in a road cut crossing the site was a concentration of limestone slabs, possibly the remains of a chimney and hearth, and three large charred wooden beams. These were associated with metal nails, clinches, hangers, European and Indian sherds, and glass fragments. To Gregory, the items and their provenience suggested the remains of some type of structure, perhaps a dwelling. Evidence of the fortification was found in the remains of a long trench, which was originally 4.5 feet wide and 3.5 feet deep. Gregory excavated sixteen feet of it. Posts, 4 to 6 inches in diameter, had been set into the trench at about 6-inch intervals.[15]

Gregory has offered some interesting remarks respecting the analysis of artifacts from the presidio and contemporary regional sites. From the faunal remains he found that bones of domesticated animals outnumbered native species 10:1. Cow bones predominated, followed, in descending frequency, by horse, chicken, sheep, and swine. The most abundant native resource exploited was shellfish, followed by deer. Fish remains were rare. Indian ceramics, which numbered 6,548 excavated sherds and an additional 1,000 collected from the surface of the site, outnumbered European sherds by a ratio of 6:1. The native sherds were tempered with bone, shell, bone-shell or grit-sherd particles. Bone was the most popular tempering agent, followed by shell and grit-sherd. Gregory noted that bone temper became more popular at the presidio after 1740. He viewed this as an indication of influence from the more westerly Caddoan tribes since at contemporary Caddoan sites to the east bone-tempered pottery is not plentiful. The ves-

15. Gregory, "Eighteenth Century Caddoan Archaeology."

sel types included bowls, beakers, jars, plates, and a few cups with handles. The absence of bottle forms may be due to the fact that they are generally associated with Caddoan burials, none of which were found at the presidio.[16]

In terms of European ceramics the Spanish majolica and French faience sherds, along with fewer English wares and olive jar fragments, date the site between 1720 and 1780, a time period "almost exactly congruent with the opening and closure of the Spanish post."[17] Glass trade beads also were of the types that bracketed the occupation of the presidio. Most of the specimens were of the popular seed bead types, but multicolored beads and faceted types were also present. Only 136 beads were recovered from the excavations, but 72 others were collected from the surface. From his studies of other contemporary Caddoan sites in the area, Gregory surmised that the beads were sewn into clothing for funerary accompaniments, and it is therefore not surprising that few show up in middens or on the site surface. Glass fragments and metal and stone objects were present, in that order of abundance. There were 1,026 glass fragments, mostly from bottles but some from glasses, goblets, and mirrors. No window glass was found, however. Iron, brass-copper, lead, silver, and pewter artifacts included the following: iron nails, a cooking pan, jew's harps, buckles, tableware, segments of wire, kettle fragments, scissors, saddlery accoutrements, and one each of a needle, key, fishhook, hoe fragment, vise jaw, scabbard tip, burro shoe, and stirrup. Brass objects included a kettle and a cup, fragments of kettles that had been mended, tinklers, a buckle, adornos, a candlestick finial, rings, buttons, thimbles, pins, a gun rampipe fragment, a religious medallion, a "fica," and a French *sou* dated 1722. Lead artifacts consisted of two blanket bale seals, an amulet and shot of various sizes. Silver specimens included a bird effigy "identical to the Yalalag cast birds seen in Oaxaca,"[18] ornamental buttons, and fragments of wooden chest covers or overlays. Pewter artifacts consisted of four spoon fragments and a buckle. Stone specimens included four manos, four metate fragments, and twenty-seven gunflints.

16. *Ibid.*
17. *Ibid.*, 136.
18. *Ibid.*, 178.

As Gregory has lamented, the archaeological investigations at the Presidio de Nuestra Señora del Pilar de Los Adaes were of necessity limited.[19] Yet the data recovered are the only substantive data thus far accrued relative to the little-known Adaes Indians during their short period of European acculturation. By 1778 the Adaes were almost extinct. The site has additional importance for the information it may provide about European and Indian relations, and just as significant, for what further archaeological exploration can teach us about Louisiana's colonial affairs.

19. Gregory, "Eighteenth Century Caddoan Archaeology."

0   1   2   3
INCHES

PLATE 66

Ceramic vessels from historic Tunica sites.

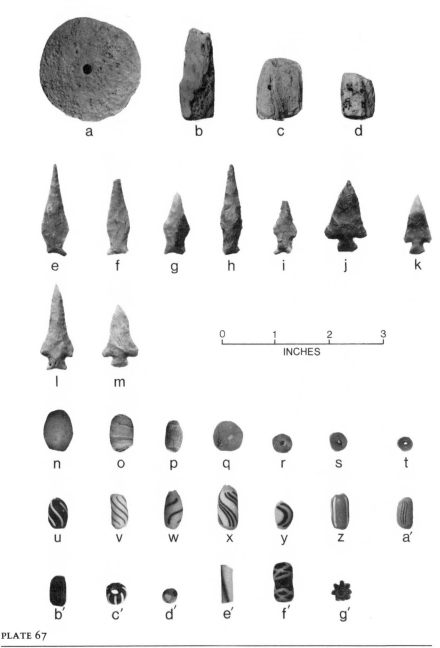

PLATE 67

Shell, stone, and glass artifacts from the Bloodhound Hill and Bayou Goula sites: *a–d*, shell ornaments; *e–m*, projectile points; *n–g′*, glass beads.

a

b

c

d

e

f

0 1 2 3
INCHES

PLATE 68

European objects from the Angola and Bayou Goula sites: *a*, copper kettle; *b*, iron hoe blade; *c*, iron axe; *d*, earthenware jug; *e*, olive green wine bottle; *f*, iron halberd blade.

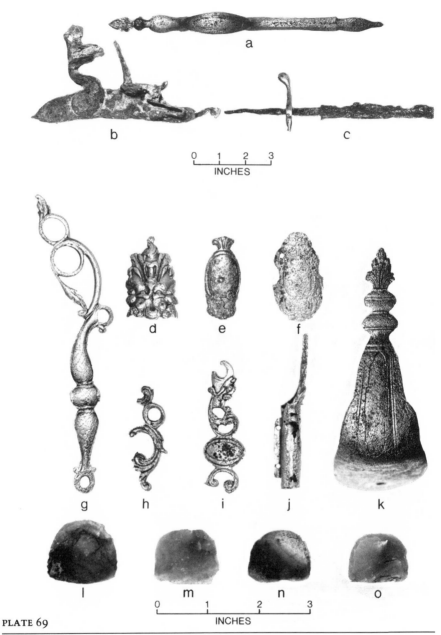

PLATE 69

European weapon objects from the Bloodhound Hill and Angola sites: *a*,
trigger guard; *b*, flintlock; *c*, sword fragment; *d–f*, butt plate fragments;
g–i, side plate and side plate fragments; *j*, rampipe fragment; *k*, butt
plate; *l–o*, gunflints.

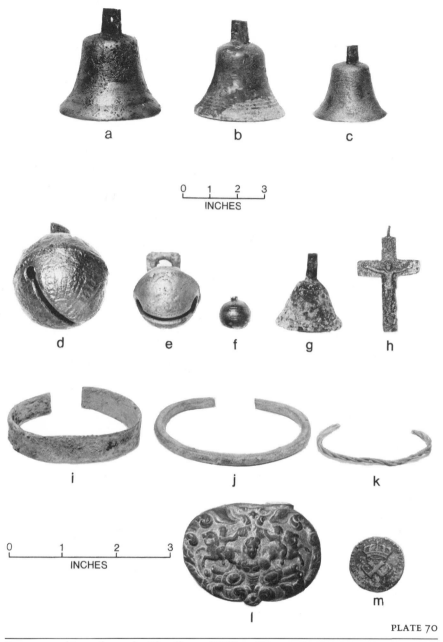

INCHES

0 1 2 3

INCHES

0 1 2 3

PLATE 70

European objects from the Bloodhound Hill and Bayou Goula sites: *a–g*, brass bells; *h*, brass crucifix; *i–k*, metal bracelets; *l*, metal sword guard; *m*, French coin dated 1722.

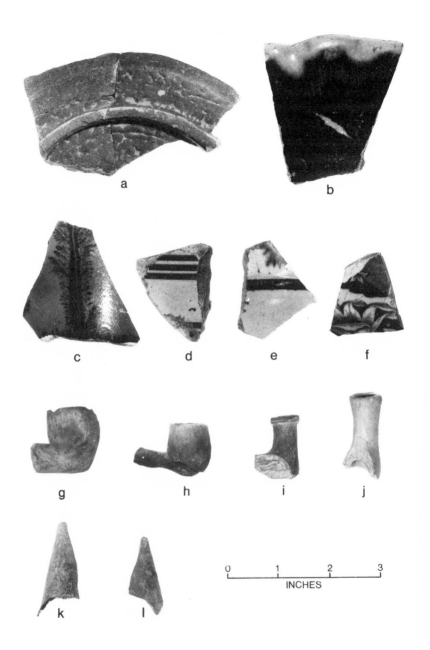

PLATE 71

European objects from the Bayou Goula Site: *a–f*, fragments of European ceramics; *g–j*, clay pipe fragments; *k–l*, copper tinklers.

XIII Summary

Louisiana antiquities have been a matter of record at least since the purchase of the Louisiana Territory in 1804, almost eight years before the state of Louisiana was admitted to the union. By the end of the nineteenth century an impressive roster of military men, jurists, physicians, historians, engineers, naturalists, and antiquarians had reported on prehistoric and historic Indian campsites, villages, shell and earthen mounds, human burials, and an assortment of stone, bone, shell, ceramic, metal, and basketry artifacts. These observers were, by and large, learned men, but they were not, of course, professional archaeologists. They rarely noted site or artifactual relationships, and chronological assignments were limited to distinguishing prehistoric from historic. Nevertheless, the early chroniclers provided invaluable data, from which modern Louisiana archaeology has greatly benefited.

One of the most intriguing and problematic questions of nineteenth-century archaeology in the United States concerned the date of man's arrival in North America. If human remains and artifacts could be found in conjunction with Pleistocene animal remains, it would be an indication of contemporaneity. Such evidence would bolster the theory that human beings had lived in North America far earlier than was generally accepted. It was not a popular theory among the scientific community of the day, and it had even fewer proponents among leading theologians. Every find that was in any way connected with Pleistocene remains generated strong controversy. This was certainly the case when basketry fragments were found with the bones of extinct mammals in Salt Mine Valley at Avery Island, for the circumstances made it possible that the basketry fragments were *older* than the bone deposit. The find was much debated in the literature by prominent scientists of the day, but fate would have it that poor timing and the lack of an adequate effort to clarify the stratigraphy and archaeological association at the site made it impossible to determine conclusively whether human beings lived at Avery Island during Pleistocene times.

Although they were anticipated somewhat by the endeavors of George E. Beyer, who was sponsored by the Louisiana Historical Society in the late 1880s, the only sustained efforts of any magnitude to explore and excavate sites in Louisiana before the 1930s were those of Clarence B. Moore. After many years of experience in other states of the Southeast, Moore came to Louisiana in 1908. With his crew and his paddle-wheel steamboat, the *Gopher*, he spent much of the next nine years here searching out and excavating sites along the major drainages of the state. His excavation techniques and his interdisciplinary approach to the identification and analysis of specimens were equal to, if not better than, those of any of his contemporaries. Nonetheless, Moore is noted most for the volumes of his quickly written but excellent reports describing his fieldwork. The beautifully colored illustrations of artifacts that enhance each volume have not yet been surpassed in the archaeological literature of the region.

Following Moore, from about 1918 until the 1930s, there was a period of general inactivity in the archeology of the United States, and Louisiana was no exception. There were but a few projects in the state sponsored by the Smithsonian Institution, including the Red River survey and excavations of the Marksville Site by Gerard Fowke, and the coastal survey and excavations at the Copell, Morgan, and Veazey sites by Henry B. Collins, Jr.

Fortunately, the cards were reshuffled, and the 1930s ushered in an age of professionalism for American archaeology. State archaeological societies were formed or expanded, the national Society for American Archaeology was organized, and archaeological curricula became increasingly popular at more and more colleges and universities. Louisiana is a case in point. During the early 1930s, the Department of Geography and Anthropology was established at Louisiana State Uni-

versity and soon the faculty were undertaking interdisciplinary studies involving geomorphology and archaeology and were publishing
their findings in the bulletins of the Louisiana Geological Survey. In
fact, the Survey initiated a special publication series, entitled *Anthropological Study*, to publish the results of archaeological investigations. These publications were supplemented by other archaeological
reports that appeared in the *Louisiana Conservation Review*, a journal of what was then the state Department of Conservation.

The federal government also became involved in archaeology during the 1930s, through its sponsorship of relief projects aimed at al-
leviating the unemployment associated with the Great Depression.
Many of these projects were directed toward large-scale excavations at
Indian sites in the southeast region of the United States. Never before
in the history of this country had such an enormous work force been
employed to conduct archaeological investigations, and the results
were generally quite successful and rewarding.

In the late 1930s, somewhat belatedly, large federal relief projects
were funded to excavate sites in Louisiana. Under the coordinated efforts of Louisiana State University and the Works Progress Administration, Indian sites in seven southern Louisiana parishes were
excavated. The projects were planned and directed by James A. Ford,
whose tenacious and tireless efforts for almost the whole of the previous decade had established the chronology and basic diagnostic traits
of ceramics produced by prehistoric cultures in the state. The relief
program enabled Ford to conduct extensive excavations of the type sites
for the Tchefuncte, Troyville–Coles Creek, and Plaquemine cultures,
in addition to the Crooks Site, a component of the Marksville Culture. Ford supervised or coauthored the reports of all of these investigations.

During the 1930s, archaeologists from the Smithsonian Institution
also conducted excavations in Louisiana at the Troyville, Fish Hatchery, and Marksville sites. Winslow M. Walker excavated the last major remnants of Troyville, an enormous, most distinctive site, which
was being needlessly destroyed for the dirt that it could provide for
highway construction. Walker also excavated early historic Caddo remains at the Fish Hatchery Site. His report of those investigations,
which appeared in 1935, was the first scientific, archaeological site re-

port in Louisiana. Frank M. Setzler directed excavations at the Marksville Site under Smithsonian auspices in 1933. The articles that he subsequently published were informative, but despite considerable interest in this important site, no complete report on the investigations there has yet been published.

While most of the archaeological projects were being conducted in southern Louisiana, some very significant work was begun in the Red River Valley of northwestern Louisiana. It was there that the physician Clarence H. Webb began his renowned avocational career in archaeology. In 1934, with the assistance of his brother-in-law, Monroe Dodd, Jr., Webb began excavating Caddo Culture remains at the Smithport Landing Site. Later in the same decade he explored Caddoan deposits at the Belcher Mound and Gahagan sites. Webb's scholarly reports on these investigations, and others to come, soon gained him recognition as an authority on Caddo archaeology.

As elsewhere in the United States, by the end of the 1930s professionalism had left its imprint on Louisiana archaeology. It cannot be denied that there were still many more questions than there were answers. Nevertheless, by that time archaeologists had constructed an outline of the progression of Louisiana's ceramics and the cultures that created them. This outline has stood the test of time. On the other hand, developmental data for the differentiation of preceramic cultures were most vague. Their presence was acknowledged, but their constituents had not yet been assembled.

From the onset of World War II until the 1960s, little archaeology was done in Louisiana. Clarence Webb continued his investigations into sites of the Caddo Culture, and he began to formulate a basic framework for sites of the late Paleo-Indian and Meso-Indian eras. During this interim Webb and James A. Ford, who was then with the American Museum of Natural History, directed their attention to the Poverty Point Culture at the type site in West Carroll Parish. Ford also collaborated with Philip Phillips, of Harvard University, and James B. Griffin, of the University of Michigan, in what was to be called the Lower Mississippi Valley Survey. Between 1940 and 1947, they surveyed and tested selected sites in the Mississippi alluvial valley from the mouth of the Ohio River downstream into Louisiana. The results of the survey, which were published in 1951, have since served as a basic source of data for any scholar involved with the regional cultures of the Neo-Indian Era.

None of these endeavors was sponsored by a Louisiana state agency. In fact, not until 1952 did a state university offer full-time employment to a professionally trained archaeologist. The first such position, in the Department of Geography and Anthropology at Louisiana State University was filled by William G. Haag (Pl. 3), who had conducted archaeological investigations elsewhere in the Southeast.

Happily, from 1960 on through the 1970s, there was an immense acceleration in archaeological activities throughout the United States. The pace of investigation surpassed even that of the public relief programs in the 1930s. Basically, this acceleration was brought about by the alarm of interested citizens who became aware of the devastating amount of archaeological destruction that was occurring throughout our country. The public outcry over this tragic loss and the demand to preserve what remained of the cultural heritage of our country, were heard in state capitols and in Washington. Indeed, anyone who has even the faintest interest in the appreciation of the thousands of years of cultural heritage that preceded the European colonization of North America owes a debt of gratitude to those citizens who made their feelings known to their elected representatives. Thanks to their efforts, Congress enacted several key pieces of legislation, including the National Historical Preservation Act of 1966, the National Environmental Policy Act of 1969, and the Archaeological and Historic Preservation Act of 1974. This federal legislation, together with Executive Order 11593 of 1971, provided the means to locate, excavate, research, preserve, restore, and conserve the prehistoric and historic cultural resources of the United States. Since the 1960s the legislation, through such agencies as the U.S. Army Corps of Engineers, has funded surveys and excavations in areas of federal waterway projects. Numerous archaeological investigations have been conducted on properties administered by the U.S. Forest Service, on federal wildlife refuges, and in conjunction with projects of the U.S. Soil Conservation Service.

The state of Louisiana has also actively supported archaeological projects, particularly through the Louisiana Department of Transportation and Development, along highway right-of-way systems. In my own archaeological endeavors, I have often been assisted by the staff of the Louisiana Department of Wildlife and Fisheries. The Louisiana Department of Culture, Recreation, and Tourism presently administers four state commemorative areas focused on the regional prehistoric and historic Indian cultures. Moreover, in 1974 the state established the Office of the State Archaeologist, under the direction of the Louisiana Archaeological Survey and Antiquities Commission. This office is charged with the responsibilities of maintaining a management program for all sites located on state properties, perpetuating the central state archaeological files, and administering a grant program to survey and/or excavate significant cultural resources. The state archaeologist's office also serves as curator for all artifacts recovered from state properties or donated to the state, and it conducts programs to inform the public about the antiquities of Louisiana. Additionally, this office reviews all federally assisted projects in Louisiana to determine their effect upon cultural resources. The work of the agency is augmented by the Louisiana Archaeological Treasure Act, which was passed in 1974 to protect state antiquities. Along with all of this official recognition, popular interest in archaeology in Louisiana grew to such an extent during the 1970s that before the end of the decade most of the state institutions of higher learning had added professionally trained personnel to their staffs to teach classroom and field courses in archaeology.

In all probability the most rewarding expression of public interest in the antiquities of Louisiana was the formation of the Louisiana Archaeological Society in 1974. The membership presently comprises about 250 professional and amateur archaeologists, organized into regional chapters that schedule meetings, conduct field trips and workshops, and host visiting lecturers. The membership has also instituted an accreditation program whereby individuals, after passing a series of required tests, may receive professional recognition. Each year the society sponsors a two-week summer field school to train members in archaeological techniques. The annual meeting in January is enthusiastically supported and attended by the membership. Furthermore, the society underwrites an interesting and substantive annual bulletin and a quarterly newsletter, both of which contain articles submitted by the society members about Louisiana antiquities and related subjects. As a body and through the endeavors of individual members, the Louisiana Archaeological Society is a cardinal component for the promotion of preservation and conservation of the state's antiquities.

Indeed, during the last two decades a great deal of time and money has been expended on a broad spectrum of archaeological projects. Far fewer sites are destroyed without being surveyed and perhaps excavated, and voluminous stores of reports amassed from the archaeological investigations have been enlightening. It is to be hoped that Louisianians will see the value of these interesting, meritorious, and beneficial contributions and will themselves become the stewards of Louisiana's antiquities.

The archaeological evidence relating to the earliest occupants of Louisiana is as yet quite limited and superficial. This situation is not in the least peculiar to Louisiana. Only in very few of the states have well preserved Paleo-Indian sites been found and excavated. By the very nature of things, the oldest archaeological remains have had the time to dissolve, disintegrate, or become dislodged from their original proveniences. In Louisiana, those problems are compounded by the post-Pleistocene or Holocene climate with its high humidity, abundant rainfall, rising sea level, and the attendant geomorphological changes along the lower Mississippi River Valley and the adjacent continental shelf.

Our earliest finds consist of large numbers of diagnostic stone projectile points that have been collected from the ground surface on such older geological formations as hills, ridges, terraces, and salt domes. Almost without exception these points were manufactured of exotic stone, probably from regions west of Louisiana. Among the point types are Clovis, Folsom, Scottsbluff, and Plainview points, whose counterparts have been documented elsewhere in association with Pleistocene megafauna. In Louisiana, only at the John Pearce Site in Caddo Parish has a Clovis point, along with another similar specimen, been reported from an archaeological excavation. Unfortunately, no other cultural remains were found in association with the points. The published data from the Salt Mine Valley Site, Avery Island, leaves a good deal of doubt about the exact nature of the association between the artifacts and the extinct mammal bone. The radiocarbon determinations, attributable to the Paleo-Indian Era, are also conjectural. Nor do the archaeological data from the Trappey Mastodon Site in Lafayette do much to clarify the relationships between Paleo-Indian and Pleistocene mammals in Louisiana. At the Salt Mine Valley Site, on the other hand, the unusually remarkable state of organic preservation, the abundance and variety of extinct mammal bone, the early radiocarbon determinations, and the indications of undisturbed deposits are major factors for arguing that a systematic archaeological program, unencumbered by industrial salt mining activities, could be most rewarding.

Partially contemporary with some of the above-mentioned point types, but extending into later Paleo-Indian times, are the Dalton and San Patrice points. In Louisiana most of these also occur as surface finds, but unlike the earlier specimens they were made from local lithic resources. Nowhere have they been reported in direct association with Pleistocene fauna. Finds of these artifacts, particularly the San Patrice points, are markedly more numerous than the earlier specimens, which, on its face, would seem to suggest an expanded population. The San Patrice component at the John Pearce Site is the earliest deposit affording us the opportunity to examine a lithic tool inventory composed of other than projectile points. The data clearly demonstrate that the late Paleo-Indians in Louisiana were adept at percussion and pressure flaking, grinding, and secondary retouch techniques in the manufacture of a variety of uniface and biface stone tools for cutting, piercing, scraping, and drilling. However, aside from these lithic artifacts, no other cultural remains were exposed, and so we still know very little about the specifics of the late Paleo-Indians' lifeways. To the extent that any particular lifeway can be discerned, it would seem that by the end of the Paleo-Indian Era, 6000 B.C., Louisiana was inhabited by small bands of hunter-gatherers, who formed larger temporary or seasonal groups and had adapted themselves to the exploitation of a wide range of regional resources.

The end of the Pleistocene period, or Ice Age, was marked by a general climate modification, which raised the sea level and changed weather conditions to those of the present time. Of course, there have been minor climatic fluctuations since the last Ice Age, but we do not yet have very substantive archaeological data respecting their effects upon human adaptations to the environment in most of the southeastern United States.

In the framework used herein, the Meso-Indian Era (6000 B.C.–2000 B.C.) falls within this period of climatic change. During this time a broad spectrum of stone projectile point styles quite unlike those utilized during the Paleo-Indian Era, was introduced. Typically, both points and other stone artifacts were made from local resources, following the pattern that began late in the Paleo-Indian Era, but there was significant expansion in type varieties over the earlier assemblages. Additionally, new stone resources, such as slate, steatite, and scoria, appeared, and new technologies were introduced. Among the new tools were stone adzes and choppers, presumably used to exploit timber resouces, and stone tools and ornaments that were formed by pecking, grinding, boring, and polishing. Also during the Meso-Indian Era the atlatl, a composite weapon that no doubt enhanced the prowess of the hunters, made its first appearance in the region. Although zooarchaeological data from this era are scant for this region, published rosters of identified animal remains demonstrate that the Indians used a variety of hunting, fishing, trapping, and gathering techniques to obtain mammals, birds, reptiles, fish, and mollusks. From the available data it would appear that deer contributed a major portion of the meat supply. Animals not only contributed to the sustenance of the native populations, they also provided the raw material for artifactual items, and it was during the Meso-Indian Era that a diverse variety and large quantity of bone, antler, and shell artifacts made their appearances. The fabricated items included points, hooks, musical instruments, needles, awls, and ornaments. Copper ornaments from this era, although rare, have also been found.

It was during Meso-Indian times that human interments became prominent in the archaeological record of the southeast region. They were manifested as primary and secondary interments of several varieties. All age groups and both sexes are represented in the grave sites, and ordinarily the human remains are associated with funerary offerings, which may include stone, bone, shell, and copper objects, as well as red ochre. Moreover, from the human skeletal elements, physical anthropologists have been able to glean some most interesting data respecting the stature and general health of the Meso-Indian populations.

Following the same pattern as that set by the Paleo-Indian manifestations in Louisiana, a large measure of the evidence for Meso-Indians in the state consists of diagnostic stone projectile points gathered from the surface of older geological formations. It is true that there are published accounts of excavations into Meso-Indian deposits, but the chipped-stone and ground-stone artifact inventories reported do little more than corroborate that data drawn from other sites of this time period in the southeastern region. On the other hand, information obtained from excavations into the two-stage earthen mound at Banana Bayou, on Avery Island, is unmatched in the lower alluvial valley. Although the artifactual remains obtained are sparse and undiagnostic, the radiocarbon date of 2490 ± 260 B.C. obtained from the mound places it in the Meso-Indian Era. Furthermore, the data would indicate that the custom of mound construction in Louisiana began about a thousand years earlier than anywhere else in the Southeast. Although final reports are still forthcoming, preliminary statements informing us of radiocarbon dates from low earthen mounds at the Monte Sano and Hornsby sites in East Baton Rouge and Saint Helena parishes respectively and recent excavations in the Banana Bayou mound yielding diagnostic stone points tend to strengthen the suggestion that mound construction in the Lower Mississippi Valley did indeed commence during the Meso-Indian Era. Obviously, the data on hand is insufficient to give a detailed picture of Meso-Indian lifeways in Louisiana. Certainly recent cultural surveys in the hill and terrace regions of southwest and north-central Louisiana have documented a surprisingly high density of Meso-Indian sites. Moreover, in one location, the Conly Site in Bienville Parish, the Meso-Indian occupation is manifested by an abundant and wide array of chipped-stone and ground-stone tools, along with bone implements, animal bone detritus, and human skeletons. Ongoing investigations into sites of this type will provide some sorely needed data for the Meso-Indian Era in Louisiana.

Following the Meso-Indian Era, the present lines of evidence indicate that the basic stone tool industry remained much the same until possibly as late as A.D. 900. The Indian hunters and gatherers appear to have adapted themselves to a variety of local ecological environments. Some archaeologists believe that this regionalization and its measure of sedentism may have been the outcome of population expansion. In other words, as time passed and population expanded, the

Indian social groups became restricted to smaller territories. Thus they were forced to alter their subsistence and economic strategies and to exploit resources that they had previously ignored or resisted. This seems to have been the situation at the onset of the Neo-Indian Era (2000 B.C.–A.D. 1600) in Louisiana and over much of the southeastern United States, but this is not to say that the local populations were complete isolates. If that were so, we would be hard put to explain the broad southeastern diffusion of such traits as the manufacture of steatite and sandstone vessels, fiber-tempered pottery, and baked clay objects, just to mention a few.

In any event and although the specific determinants are still speculative, the fact remains that around 1500 B.C. there evolved a social organization, perhaps a chiefdom, that was capable of fostering the planning and construction of the immense earthen mound and radiating concentric ridges at the Poverty Point Site in northeastern Louisiana. Although the Poverty Point Site is the most extensive occupation of the Poverty Point Culture, there are other regional centers and satellite sites manifested as middens and purposely formed oval-shaped or horseshoe-shaped earthen mounds or shell middens. One very large horseshoe-shaped shell midden, located on the Gulf Coast in southwest Mississippi, has been radiocarbon-dated earlier than the Poverty Point Site. It is thought to have been a predecessor of the vast regional trade network that reached its zenith later at the Poverty Point Site. More than a hundred sites of the Poverty Point Culture have been recorded in Louisiana, Arkansas, and Mississippi, but its trade network and closely related manifestations extend to Virginia, North Carolina, Georgia, Florida, Alabama, Tennessee, Ohio, Indiana, Illinois, Missouri, Oklahoma, and perhaps the Lake Superior region. To date, archaeologists have examined more than 150,000 artifacts of the culture. The inventory includes the famous Poverty Point baked-clay objects, fired clay ornaments and pipes, chipped-stone and ground-stone tools of exotic or local materials, and ornate artifacts manufactured by a magnificent lapidary technology unsurpassed for its time in all of North America. Bone artifacts are rare at Poverty Point sites and, oddly enough, shell artifacts are not reported. Evidences of habitations and human interments are as yet inconclusive.

There is considerable debate among archaeologists about what sparked the development of the Poverty Point Culture at a time when most of the other regional cultures were characteristically "archaic" in their life-styles. Some authorities are of the opinion that the impetus was a matter of cultural diffusion from the advanced cultures then existing in Meso-America. Among the traits then present in Meso-American cultures were platform mounds, clay figurines, advanced lapidary technology, and manolike and metatelike mealing stones in conjunction with squash and maize agriculture, supplemented by hunting and gathering. Others argue that the Poverty Point Site began and flourished out of a "forest-edge efficiency" subsistence system, whose richness allowed the accumulation of surplus foods and spare time for earthen constructions and the development of nonutilitarian crafts. This group of archaeologists argues, further, that all of this was accomplished without any fundamental stimulus from Meso-America. An alternative view holds that the development of the Poverty Point Culture was indeed influenced by the Meso-American civilizations; its complex of traits seems undeniably Meso-American, although the exact route of diffusion is open to question. Maize and/or squash agriculture was probably not an essential ingredient for the florescence of the Poverty Point Culture. In fact, there is no substantive evidence for an economy based on maize agriculture in the lower alluvial valley until after A.D. 800.

Whatever it was that sustained the Poverty Point Culture, it lasted and flourished for almost a millenium. By 500 B.C. however, it had all but disappeared. The reasons for the decline of this magnificent culture are no more certain than the causes of its inception. Part of the answer may be found among the archaeological remains of the small settlements like the Terral Lewis Site, which supported the socioreligious institutions that we believe were focused at the Poverty Point Site. Following the decline of the Poverty Point Culture, the archaeological data indicate a return to less centralized Indian populations. Never again in Louisiana prehistory were there earthen constructions comparable to those at the Poverty Point Site.

Essentially, what we know about the period between about 500 B.C. and A.D. 100 is subsumed under the rubric of the Tchefuncte Culture. Most of the archaeological manifestations of this culture that have been excavated to any extent are located in the Louisiana coastal zone, although test excavations and surface collections of potsherds reveal that Tchefuncte cultural relationships extend into Missouri, Alabama, Florida, Mississippi, and Texas. The Tchefuncte Culture is the earliest archaeological unit in Louisiana to be characterized by an abundance of pottery. The pottery vessels, of various shapes and podal bases, may be plain or decorated on their exterior surfaces. There are also decorated clay tubular pipes and several styles of baked-clay objects, which carry over from the earlier period, as does most of the lithic tool inventory. The Poverty Point lapidary technology, however, is not represented, nor is there an abundance of stone artifacts manufactured from exotic materials. Unlike the earlier Louisiana cultures thus far investigated, Tchefuncte deposits have yielded large quantities of bone tools and faunal and botanical food remains. As already indicated, much of the Tchefuncte Culture data were obtained from the Louisiana coastal zone shell middens, and these are the earliest data presently available from which coastal settlement patterns and resource exploitation systems may be gleaned. The Indians of the Tchefuncte Culture and all subsequent cultures, for that matter, roamed the marsh and swamp regions and lowlands and selectively exploited the natural resources in these distinctive environments. But for their campsites and more permanent living areas they required dry land. Consequently, we find their habitation sites located along natural levees, cheniers, terrace remnants, salt domes, and lake shores. Farther inland the sites are to be found along secondary stream systems and in slack-water environments. Some very interesting data, relative to the Tchefuncte subsistence economy, are available from several coastal shell middens. These data, and they must be considerably supplemented before any definite cultural patterns can be established, show that the Indians selectively exploited the regional mammals, birds, fish, reptiles, and mollusks, in addition to a variety of wild plant foods, the latter evidenced by their pits, seeds, rinds, and shells. The presence of squash remains at one shell midden may be indicative of horticultural activities. Surprisingly enough, crustacean remains are completely absent from Tchefuncte sites. Indeed, they seem to have been a neglected item of the diet of Louisiana Indians throughout prehistory.

In terms of habitations or structures, very limited archaeological data indicate that the Tchefuncte Indians constructed temporary light-poled shelters having a circular floor pattern. Using ethnohistorical analogies, it is generally surmised that these shelters had thatch or wattle and daub walls and roofs of overlapping palmetto fronds. From one Tchefuncte coastal midden there is postmold evidence of an elongated, shedlike structure.

Physical anthropological data garnered from excavated human interments show the Tchefuncte Indians to have been of medium stature with high cranial vaults. Most of the human bones exhibited pathologies, and dental abscesses were common. The preferred burial pattern seems to have been primary flexed interments, but bundle burials are also present. Funerary accompaniments were not usual. Furthermore, in terms of burial practices, the literature on the Tchefuncte Culture has suggested that the Indians built small, low, domed earthen burial mounds, but a close examination of the published literature shows that this surmise is conjectural or, at the very least, premature. The excavated mounds may instead be harbingers of the mound-building Marksville Culture, which directly succeeded the Tchefuncte Culture and was partially coeval with it. This hypothesis, however, awaits archaeological confirmation.

The Marksville Culture was but a regional example of the Hopewell Culture, so renowned for its elaborate burial ceremonialism. Hopewell ceremonialism developed in Ohio and Illinois, and sometime between 200 B.C. and A.D. 600 it diffused throughout eastern North America. In the Louisiana coastal zone, Marksville ceramics occur in multicomponent shell middens, but very few of the deposits have been extensively excavated and reported upon. From what is presently known, little in the way of funerary ceremonialism has been identified with Marksville components in the coastal shell middens. Inland Marksville sites, manifested as village detritus and multistage earthen burial mounds, appear most common in the central region of Louisiana, with fewer recorded in the eastern region and in the Red River and Sabine River drainages of western Louisiana. Inasmuch as few village areas have been investigated, most of the Marksville Culture data are drawn from excavations into the burial mounds.

Because most of the Marksville human skeletal elements were found in a poor state of preservation, physical anthropological data are lacking. Nevertheless, it has been determinable that the human burials represent both sexes and all age groups. There are primary and secondary interments that vary widely in the number and positions of the individuals interred. Human cremations are reported, as are dog burials. The latter were apparently funerary offerings. Mound A at the Crooks Site was said to contain 1,159 human interments. Marksville Culture burials have been found in various mound stages, on clay platforms or altars, and in deep or shallow pits, sometimes lined with botanical remains. Sometimes they were simply placed on the top of a mound construction and subsequently mantled over as the mound was enlarged. In one instance, at least, the burials were temporarily sheltered by a roofed structure. Most of the Marksville Culture burials were associated with artifacts that included pottery vessels, clay effigies, platform pipes, ornaments, ground-stone and chipped-stone tools and effigies, and objects of exotic stone, copper, shell, and pearls. Bone tools are sparse, but a limited number of awls and fishhooks are reported. Matting fragments, as well as basketry, have been excavated also.

The Hopewellian influence in the Marksville Culture is undeniable in respect to the traits of mound burial and funerary offerings. It is also particularly notable in the very distinctive decorative motifs of the pottery and in the clay platform pipes. Furthermore, from the data presently available, the impetus for the extensive Marksville trade network in exotic stones, minerals, and copper is also attributable to the Hopewell Culture. On the other hand, it must be noted that Marksville burial patterns and mounds do not mirror those reported at Hopewell sites. Despite Hopewell resemblances, the Marksville Culture is a very local expression. Indeed, there was cultural diffusion, but there were no Hopewellian migrations into Louisiana. It would appear that the Louisiana Indians selected particular traits of the Hopewell Culture and altered others to suit their needs and desires. After all, even today in our own cultural milieu, most Louisiana communities have a place of worship, but few of them feel the obligation or even the wish to build a basilica.

Unfortunately, in terms of subsistence economies for the Marksville Culture, we have little data on the purported cultigens and only a very limited number of animal bone items from excavated sites. And the data respecting Marksville Culture habitations are, unhappily, no more conclusive. It would seem that such information must be sought by directing archaeological strategies away from the burial mounds and toward Marksville Culture village sites and coastal shell middens.

From almost A.D. 400 until around A.D. 1200, the Troyville–Coles Creek Culture flourished in Louisiana. From all that we presently know, it was the most expansive culture of the Neo-Indian Era in the state. There are markedly more Troyville–Coles Creek sites in more regions of the state, both inland and coastal, than any of the other Neo-Indian Era cultures discussed in this study. Many Troyville–Coles Creek sites are characterized by several multistage, pyramidal, flat-topped mounds oriented around an open area or central plaza. In plan, the mounds are rectangular and some are known to have stepped ramps extending out from one face. At several sites, two mounds are connected by a low earthen ridge or causeway. The mound area at the famous Troyville Site is partially enclosed by an earthen embankment, whose exact relationship to the mounds is as yet unclear. On the summits of Troyville–Coles Creek mounds, rectangular or circular buildings were constructed of upright posts interspaced with wattle and daub. Little is understood about the roof architecture of these buildings, but it does seem clear that the rectangular structures were gradually replaced by the circular ones. There is widespread agreement among archaeologists that these mounds and the buildings that surmounted them were socioreligious in nature. In fact, multistage pyramidal mounds of this time period and later in the eastern United States are commonly called "temple mounds." This designation is based largely upon evidence drawn from the chronicles of early travelers who visited the Indian settlements and witnessed the socioreligious services conducted there. On the other hand there is a dearth of archaeological information pertaining to the more secular buildings and habitations that must have existed at mound and nonmound sites of the Troyville–Coles Creek Culture.

Although not customarily referred to as burial mounds, Troyville–Coles Creek tumuli generally have been found to contain human interments. Furthermore, nonmound village and campsites of this culture also contain burials. Unlike those of the Marksville Culture, these burials are not characterized by funerary accompaniments, although this certainly was not the situation at the Mounds Plantation Site.

Burial patterns are quite diverse, just as one might expect for a culture that lasted about 800 years, but a study of the chronological sequence of the burial patterns is sorely needed. There are primary burials in extended supine or prone positions and there are flexed burials. One or more individuals may be found in a single burial pit, and in other instances the skeletons are found scattered about on a mound surface and simply covered by dirt of a subsequent stage of mound construction. Secondary burials include single and multiple bundle burials, isolated crania, and partially articulated portions of the skeleton. Cremations are also represented. A major factor of the Troyville–Coles Creek Culture is the physical anthropological research that has been conducted on the human skeletal material. More human skeletal remains from this culture have been studied and analyzed than from any of the other Louisiana cultures discussed in this book. The osseous remains of more than 360 individuals have been examined and there are now data relative to stature, sexual dimorphism, right-handedness or left-handedness, genetic traits, anomalies, diseases, and funerary rite modifications, such as postmortem defleshing.

Of the artifactual diagnostics from Troyville–Coles Creek sites, of course, pottery is paramount. Characteristically, it is clay-tempered, coiled, and paddle-stamped to form variously shaped jars and bowls of different sizes. The vessels are generally shades of buff to black and their upper portions are decorated outside with straight or curvilinear designs executed by incising, hachuring, stippling, and punctating. Other vessels are decorated over their entire exterior with stamped designs. There are also clay pipes, disks, crude human figurines, and stylized zoomorphic effigies. Finished stone artifacts are not particularly plentiful from excavated sites. They include chipped-stone and ground-stone implements, including points, knives, scrapers, drills, hammerstone, mealing stones, plummets, and atlatl weights. The fact that many of the points are smaller than those of the preceding cultures is taken as an indication of the introduction of the bow and arrow into Louisiana. Bone artifacts are not numerous; their inventory includes pins, awls, points, harpoons, and fishhooks. The use of red ochre and copper objects was observed with several of the human burials.

Subsistence data, as well as information on the utilization of non-nutritional resources, have been proffered from several Troyville–Coles

Creek occupations in the coastal region and from inland sites. Zooarchaeological studies revealed a wide array but no particular abundance of animal bone. Freshwater and brackish-water mollusks also contributed to the native diet. Among the botanical remains, leaves, stems, seeds, wood, bark, and cane have been identified. Specimens of the latter three categories relate to features of mound construction. Finally, in terms of subsistence, it is a widely held view that the Indians of this culture were agriculturalists with an economic base of corn, beans, and squash. However, there is nothing in the archaeological record to support that assumption. It is likely that the Indians grew squash, and it is possible that they had begun to experiment with some strain or strains of corn, but there is no substantiating evidence for their dependence upon corn or beans as an economic staple. Rather, the view suggested here is that the Troyville–Coles Creek Indians were agriculturalists who cultivated native species of plants and squash and augmented their larders by hunting, gathering, and fishing in the bountiful environs of the lower alluvial valley.

By at least A.D. 800 there emerged in northwest Louisiana and the contiguous parts of Texas, Oklahoma, and Arkansas an archaeological complex called the Caddo Culture. As the name implies, the prehistoric manifestations of this complex are considered to represent the antecedents of certain Caddo Indian tribes who occupied the region historically. In Caddo Culture we have, for the first time, uncontroversial evidence of prehistoric developments that culminated in establishment of historically documented Indian tribes in Louisiana.

Most of what is currently known about the prehistoric developments of the Caddo Culture at sites in Louisiana pertains to funerary rites involving the construction of earthen mounds. Many of the mounds are of multistage construction, and they functioned as platforms for ceremonial or communal buildings having rectangular or circular floor patterns, walls of wattle and daub, and thatched roofs. Quite often these buildings had extended entryways. Within the buildings burial pits were dug in which one or more human bodies were laid, generally in an extended supine position. The bodies were accompanied by elaborate funerary offerings. All age groups and both sexes are represented, but it would appear that only the elite members of the society were buried in the mounds, and judging from the placement and quantities of artifacts associated with a particular individual in a burial pit, certain adults and adolescents of each sex were highly revered at their times of death. The buildings also contained central fire pits and quite often, smaller ancillary ones. Pottery and bone, stone, and shell artifacts were strewn and/or differentially placed on the building floor. As time passed and for some as yet unknown reason, after they had been used for a time, these prehistoric buildings would be burned and mantled over with dirt. Then another building would be erected. There are other Caddo Culture mounds in Louisiana that were not surmounted by buildings; instead deep shaftlike pits were dug into them. Corpses were placed at the bottom of these pits in burial patterns much like those previously described. In addition, other prehistoric Caddo Culture burials are represented at nonmound cemeteries. At such sites one or more individuals are buried in single, relatively shallow graves. Again, both sexes and all age groups are represented, and the extended supine position remains the most common burial pattern. The funerary accompaniments associated with these nonmound burials are usually less plentiful and they seem considerably less ceremonial than those associated with the burials at the Caddo Culture mound sites in Louisiana.

Without fear of contradiction, it can be said that pottery excavated from Caddo Culture graves ranks with the finest and most ornately decorated pottery known from an aboriginal culture anywhere in the United States. Louisiana sites have yielded many exquisite examples of simple and compound bowls, jars, bottles, platters, and cups. There are remarkably artistic specimens of clay effigy pipes, long-stemmed pipes, and figurines. The nonceramic funerary offerings, which include stone pipes, beads, celts, and ceremonial blades, in addition to a rich array of chipped-stone and ground-stone implements, are also quite beautiful. Mammal bone ornaments include pins, ear disks, labrets, beads, rattles, canine teeth ornaments, and what is possibly an arm guard manufactured from a deer scapula. There are also pearls and marine and freshwater shell containers, beads, pendants, and spoons. Objects made of native copper, the precise source of which has yet to be scientifically determined, include embossed fragments, imitation animal claws, "Long Nosed God Masks," plaques, and copper-plated wooden, clay, stone, and bone ornaments.

Given the limited survival of botanical specimens, we are indeed fortunate to have wooden artifacts and fragments of split-cane matting from Caddo Culture sites. Of cardinal significance are the remains of wooden bows, which represent the first primay evidence for this weapon in Louisiana. Not too surprisingly, two of the specimens were identified as Osage orange, a wood traditionally renowned for bow manufacture. Other wooden artifacts include a comb, a bowl, and copper-plated wooden ornaments. Not only are there fragments of split-cane matting, but some of the fragments exhibit the remains of dye on one or both faces. In addition, the artifact inventory includes two cane "staffs" and some basketry. And finally, variously associated with the Caddo Culture burials were red, yellow, green, black, and white pigments.

Physical anthropological data gleaned from the remains of at least 150 individuals excavated at Caddo Culture sites in Louisiana have provided some most interesting and useful demographic information concerning the sex and stature of individuals and their ages at time of death. Moreover, detailed examination of the skeletal elements and dentition have revealed pathologies such as cleft palates, osteoarthritis, osteomyelitis, syphilis, pyorrhea, tooth abscesses, and caries. It is significant also to note that in these Caddo Culture skeletal remains we have the introduction of the trait of cranial deformation. The origin of this trait in North America can be traced to the Mexican high cultures.

As indicated previously, much of the Caddo Culture data relate to socioreligious aspects and the same may be said for the archaeological information retrieved from sites of the preceding Troyville–Coles Creek and Marksville cultures. On the other hand, explorations at the Hanna Site, a small Caddo Culture community, have furnished valuable insights into the more mundane aspects of prehistoric lifeways by about A.D. 1200. In an area of about 4 acres of strewn and clustered detritus, fire pits, middens, and postmolds indicative of racks, arbors, or scaffolds, were one rectangular and three circular habitations. No whole pottery vessels were found and the sherds, stone, bone, and shell artifacts all reflect utilitarian functions. Lack of ceremonialism is manifested further in four human burials at the site, none of which were accorded funerary offerings. Analyses of the mammal bone and molluscan remains show that the site inhabitants selectively hunted, fished, and gathered the regional fauna, and the data further indicate that the site was occupied year-round. Particularly significant are the botanical remains from the Hanna Site. In addition to a variety of native plant food remains, there are corn and squash specimens. The latter two, taken in conjunction with the corn and beans reported from the Belcher Site, document this Meso-American triumvirate in the Caddo Culture in Louisiana. From the current archaeological data base, however, it is difficult to determine exactly how important corn, bean, and squash agriculture was to the Hanna Site inhabitants and their contemporary neighbors. Fruitful answers to the question of corn, bean, and squash agriculture among the prehistoric Indians of Louisiana will emerge only after other habitation sites like Hanna receive attention.

The archaeological record from early historical Caddo Indian sites indicates that the picture is not too dissimilar from that presented at some of the prehistoric sites, particularly since most of what is reported involves Caddo burials of the early eighteenth century. Generally, it has been found that at the historical burials there is one person to a grave, and the traditional burial position, extended supine, persists. Both sexes and all age groups are represented, and the practice of cranial deformation continues. Funerary accompaniments are not as abundant as those in the prehistoric graves, but now there is a mixture of native and European items. Included in the inventory of European items are scissors, bells, metal bracelets, gunflints, and variously shaped, multicolored glass and porcelain beads. Also, there are two very rare occurrences of horse burials, purportedly associated with Caddo pottery vessels.

The point is worth noting here that these data, pertaining to the prehistoric and historical developments of the regional Caddoan Indians, are not at all common in North American archaeology. In fact, for a multitide of reasons involving the availability and creditability of ethnohistoric and cartographic sources, as well as the integrity of site preservation, only a relatively few of the historic North American Indian groups have been so documented. The archaeological data have markedly enhanced our knowledge and appreciation of no less than twelve hundred years of Caddoan Culture development.

Partially contemporary with and sharing traits with the Caddo Culture is another distinctive archaeological construct called the Plaquemine Culture, whose origins are most apparent in the preceding Troyville–Coles Creek Culture. Plaquemine site deposits have been radiocarbon-dated from about A.D. 1000 into the early historical period, and it is widely argued that they represent the ancestral remains of the historic Natchezan and Taensa Indians. Known sites extend from an apex near Greenville, Mississippi, expanding southward until they are distributed along the entire Louisiana coastal zone.

Most of what is known about the Plaquemine Culture originates from excavations into large, flat-topped, pyramidal, multistage earthen mounds. An interesting innovation in mound construction at several sites is the placement of two small mounds on top of and at opposite ends of a large flat-topped mound. Associated with some of the mounds are circular and rectangular postmold patterns of socioreligious buildings. From the data on hand, it appears that the rectangular buildings continued to be built after the circular form had been abandoned.

Human burials reported from Plaquemine Culture sites are quite diverse. In mounds there are primary and secondary burials, all age groups seem to be represented, and the trait of cranial deformation is reported. The sex of these skeletons has not always been determined, nor have there been physical anthropological analyses of them. Primary burials are in flexed or extended positions, and they may be associated with pottery and stone funerary offerings. Secondary burials are represented by the bones of one or more individuals, isolated skeletal elements, partially articulated skeletal segments, and pits containing as many as sixty-six skulls. They too may be associated with funerary objects of pottery and stone. The primary burials at the nonmound MacArthur Site, in Arkansas, were in separate graves within a structure having a circular postmold pattern. No funerary offerings were reported with these graves.

Artifacts from excavated Plaquemine Culture sites include pottery bowls, jars, bottles, killed vessels, a clay zoomorphic effigy pipe, elbow pipes, and ear ornaments. Chipped-stone and ground-stone artifacts include points, knives, quartz crystals, celts, disks, atlatl weights, and hammerstones. There are also deposits of red, yellow, white, and purple pigments.

It is generally postulated that the Plaquemine Culture Indians were agriculturalists with a subsistence base of corn, beans, and squash, but as elsewhere in the archaeological record of Louisiana, the remains of these plant foods are scant, although fifteen charred fragments of corncobs were reported from the Bayou Goula Site. The agricultural base was supplemented by hunting, fishing, and gathering as attested to by the animal remains found at the sites. Unfortunately these remains are of limited value, because they are not quantified and their proveniences at multicomponent sites are vague.

The archaeological data indicate that the Plaquemine Culture originated in the lower Mississippi Valley during the late prehistoric period, and it would appear that it culminated in the formation of certain regional historical Indian groups, such as the Natchez and the Taensa. Socioreligious mound centers were established, and certain individuals of the elite class or classes were buried in the mounds, generally accompanied by funerary offerings. Quite likely the secular Indian groups were agriculturalists inhabiting the neighboring areas close to and supportive of the socioreligious centers. It should be noted, however, that our assumptions about these farmsteads and settlements in Louisiana are largely speculation and based on meager data from reported excavations in Arkansas. Without doubt, much of what we should know about the lifeways of the Plaquemine Culture Indian in Louisiana awaits discovery.

The last prehistoric unit for which there are archaeological remains in Louisiana is the Mississippian Culture. The origins of this culture are generally thought to have coalesced near the juncture of the great Mississippi and Missouri river systems in the Saint Louis environs. Between about A.D. 800 and A.D. 1200, the Indians of this culture established some of the largest, most populous, planned residential-ceremonial centers ever to have existed in North America north of Mexico. By the end of the sixteenth century, elements of this culture, with expected variations, had diffused throughout much of the eastern United States. In our area it is generally agreed that the Tunica and possibly the Chitimacha, along with some as yet unidentified Muskogean speakers, were the historical heirs of the Mississippi Culture. Just like many of their regional contemporaries, the Mississippians built large, multistage, pyramidal mounds, upon whose surfaces they erected socioreligious structures and in which they sometimes interred invididuals of the elite accompanied with an array of elaborate funerary offerings. Associated with these mound centers were large, supportive, sometimes fortified, agricultural communities with non-mound cemeteries. By the time of European contact, the inhabitants of these settlements were cultivating extensive fields of corn, beans, and squash, along with regional cultigens, and were supplementing those crops by hunting, fishing, and gathering.

The artifactual items most characteristic of the Mississippian Culture are, of course, distinctive pottery styles with new and innovative decorative techniques. Associated with pottery manufacturing is the new trait of pulverizing shell to use as temper in the pottery clay. Found in ceremonial as well as utilitarian ceramics, shell temper is a hallmark of the Mississippian Culture. It is likewise notable that artifacts of the "Ceremonial Complex" make their appearance with human burials at large Mississippian centers. Although recorded at Caddo Culture sites, the "Ceremonial Complex" reached its zenith with and is characteristically most diagnostic of the Mississippian Culture.

From the data on hand, it does not appear that the Mississippian Culture made any great impact on prehistoric Louisiana. Although elements of this culture, principally ceramic motifs, some shell-tempered pottery, and several cult items, are found at contemporary Caddo and Plaquemine culture sites, there is certainly no substantive documentation that would indicate that the prehistoric Indians of the Mississippian Culture overran or displaced any of the native Louisiana populations. With two interesting exceptions, most of what we presently know about the Mississippian Culture in Louisiana is gleaned from surface collections and limited test excavations at multicomponent sites. Admittedly, the data are slim and tentative, but they show Mississippian components to be distributed mainly in the alluvial environs of northeast Louisiana. Another concentration of sites is found in the eastern quarter of the coastal zone. One exception to this pattern is indicated by the preliminary data from the multicomponent Sims Site, where there are remnants of five mounds and a village midden. Thus far, the midden has yielded five human burials lacking funerary offerings and a quantity of faunal remains that provide very tentative conclusions about subsistence patterns. The second exception concerns the Mississippian exploitation of salt resources at the

Salt Mine Valley Site, on Avery Island. Not only is this extremely rich midden deposit quite remote from other known Mississippian occupations, but the economic aspects of salt extraction and trade, as evidenced by the site remains, represent an innovative facet of prehistoric lifeways in Louisiana. Very little else is known about Mississippian Culture in Louisiana, but no doubt, much remains to be discovered.

The waning years of the Mississippian Culture bring us to the historical period. It is notable that although there are excellent ethnohistoric documents relative to Louisiana Indians provided by the DeSoto chroniclers and subsequent explorers of the late seventeenth century, there is a dearth of comprehensive archaeological data for that period. The earliest sites to be extensively reported upon involve Indian occupations dating into the early decades of the eighteenth century.

Historic Indian archaeology is a crucial segment of research, for it offers the most feasible means to connect eons of unrecorded prehistoric cultural developments with a historically documented tribe or tribes. In Louisiana this documentation has been realized with several Indian tribes, namely the Caddo, already discussed, the Tunica, and the historic Indian occupants of the Bayou Goula Site who are thought to represent an amalgamation of the Bayogoula, Acolapissa, and Houma.

Most of the archaeological data we have on the Tunica tribe in Louisiana relates to their burial practices as they existed during the first quarter of the eighteenth century. At the closely situated Angola Farm and Bloodhound Hill sites, twelve undisturbed Tunica graves have been excavated. All of the burials were in the extended supine position. Adults of both sexes and children are represented, and one individual, an infant, had been buried in a wooden coffin. All of the burials were associated with funerary offerings of European trade items and a smaller number of native artifacts, principally pottery. It is thought that the village site or sites are near the cemeteries, but that supposition remains to be proven. About four miles distant from the cemeteries is the Trudeau Landing Site, where perhaps as many as one hundred Tunica graves were looted before archaeologists became involved. Nevertheless, through a turn of events, the unprecedented quantity of grave goods associated with the Trudeau Landing burials was made available for study by archaeologists. The grave goods include European items of ceramic, glass, iron, pewter, silver, copper, weaponry, ammunition, and fabrics and native objects of pottery, stone, shell, matting, basketry, and seeds. Just as importantly, the location of the looted graves was revealed, and subsequent archaeological research has shown that the Trudeau Landing is the site of a historically documented Tunica village occupied between 1731 and 1764.

Other early eighteenth-century Indian burials were excavated at the Bayou Goula Site. Here, however, most of the nineteen individuals were manifested as bundle burials. Two graves contained primary burials, one extended and the other flexed. Some of the graves contained European and native artifacts, one contained only native artifacts, and still others lacked artifacts altogether. Also associated with the historical component at Bayou Goula were the remains of European constructions that may have been a French trading post or concession. A number of early historic Indian tribes are known to have lived in the general area of the Bayou Goula Site, but it is thought that the Bayogoula, Acolapissa, and the Houma tribes were the most likely occupants of the site.

A sense of something quite different is provided by excavations conducted at the site of the Presidio de Nuestra Señora del Pilar de Los Adaes, which was the provincial capitol of Spanish Texas from 1723 to 1773. The establishment of the presidio had its impact, and the Adaes Indians and other neighboring Caddo groups soon became enmeshed with the economic and political affairs of this disputed Spanish and French border area. The archaeological excavations into trash pits and a well, along the stockade line, and in dwelling areas however offer a view of the more practical, day-to-day activities. The processes of acculturation and trade are evident not only from the admixture of European and Indian artifacts found, but also from the animal bone remains, which include those of European-introduced cows, horses, swine, sheep, and chickens far outnumbering those of the native fauna.

Los Adaes, like Trudeau Landing, is a property now administered by the Louisiana Office of State Parks, and it is gratifying to know that future study and archaeological explorations at these sites are being planned. In most instances historical Indian archaeology in Louisiana has been conducted only after sites were reported in danger of destruc-

tion by construction projects or after news that they were being plundered. It is ironic that almost no substantive formulated research, with
the exception of Winslow Walker's endeavors and the LSU–WPA investigations at Bayou Goula, has been directed toward locating a historically documented Indian site, excavating, and reporting it. The
early historic occupations of the Attacapa, Chitimacha, and the numerous Muskogean-speaking Indian groups who inhabited Louisiana
at the time of the European entrada, await identification.

With this summary of historical Indian archaeology in Louisiana,
we come to the end of the present study. The account I have given is
by no means complete; it is but an introduction to what has been accomplished thus far. New data are constantly being presented, and serious researchers will always examine the original documents. The
overall picture presented by the considerable mass of archaeological
data has shown that Louisiana was occupied during the Paleo-Indian
Era, at least as early as 10,000 B.C., by small groups of nomadic hunters and gatherers. They lived here during the waning years of the last
great Ice Age and hunted the now-extinct megafauna that roamed the
region. From then into the Holocene period, or modern climatic cycle,
we see population expansions and a very gradual, yet spiraling, development toward regionalization and sedentism. Concomitant with
these processes are technological developments, some evolving from
within and others resulting from external diffusion, that led to the formation of the agricultural societies first chronicled by the European
explorers. Conversely, but with as yet slight corroboration, it appears
that in the less arable upland hills, prairies, and coastal marshes, the
Indians chose to continue their less sedentary, more leisurely hunting-and-gathering lifeways up into the historical period. The end result was the same for all, however. By the end of the nineteenth century
the native Indian tribes of Louisiana had become almost nonexistent.
A thorough account of that woeful epic still awaits presentation.

In the last analysis the fate of Louisiana's archaeological resources
lies in the hands of her citizens. This very integral and nonrenewable
facet of our cultural heritage will be needlessly sacrificed unless the
present state and federal laws, and those that may be deemed necessary in the future, are enforced. We know without doubt that population growth and the expansion of urbanization will alter the land and

328

waters everywhere in Louisiana. In the process archaeological remains will be affected, but with careful planning, as has been demonstrated, such remains can become an integral part of a developing Louisiana. Without such cooperation all the investigations that have been presented here will have been for nought. Happily, the citizens of Louisiana have shown that they were anxious and proud to bear this stewardship. Archaeological preservation is not too great a task for the scientific knowledge and educational benefits that we all reap in return.

References

Alexander, Herbert L., Jr.
1963 "The Levi Site: A Paleo-Indian Campsite in Central Texas." *American Antiquity*, Vol. 28, No. 4, pp. 510–28. Salt Lake City.

Alt, Rev. Odilo
1934 "A Prehistoric Find at Bedico, La." *Abbey Chronicle*, Vol. 8, No. 4. St. Benedict, La.

Anonymous
1809 "Abstract of a Communication from Mr. Martin Duralde, Relative to Fossil Bones, and c. of the Country of Apelousas West of the Mississippi to Mr. William Dunbar of the Natchez, and by Him Transmitted to the Society. Dated April 24, 1802." *American Philosophical Society Transactions*, Vol. 6, pp. 55–58. Philadelphia.

1847 "Indian Mounds in Louisiana." *DeBow's Review*, Vol. 3, No. 4, pp. 351–52. New Orleans.

1851 "Historical and Statistical Collections of Louisiana." *DeBow's Review*, New Series, Vol. 1, No. 6, pp. 601–602. New Orleans.

1851 Statistical and Historical Sketches of Louisiana." *DeBow's Review*, New Series, Vol. 1, No. 6, p. 611. New Orleans.

1855 "Indian Mounds in Louisiana." *DeBow's Review*, Vol. 18 (New Series, Vol. 1), No. 4, pp. 568–71. New Orleans.

1883 "Abstracts from Anthropological Correspondences." *Annual Report of the Smithsonian Institution for the Year 1881*, p. 686. Washington, D.C.

1962 "Some Paleo-Indian Points in the Williamson Museum." *Louisiana Studies*, Vol. 1, No. 3, pp. 60–61. Natchitoches.

Antevs, E.
1955 "Geological-Climatic Dating in the West." *American Antiquity*, Vol. 20, No. 4, Pt. 1, pp. 317–35. Menasha, Wis.

Aten, Lawrence E.
1970   "Coastal Southeast Texas Archaeology." Manuscript, University of Texas. Austin.

Aten, Lawrence E., and Charles N. Bollich
1969   "A Preliminary Report on the Development of a Ceramic Chronology for the Sabine Lake Area of Texas and Louisiana." *Bulletin of the Texas Archaeological Society*, Vol. 40, pp. 241–58. Austin.

Bass, William M.
1971   *Human Osteology: A Laboratory and Field Manual of the Human Skeleton*. Special Publications, Missouri Archaeological Society, University of Missouri. Columbia.

Bell, Robert E.
1956   "A Copper Plummet from Poverty Point, Louisiana." *American Antiquity*, Vol. 22, No. 1, p. 80. Salt Lake City.
1958   *Guide to the Identification of Certain American Indian Projectile Points*. Oklahoma Anthropological Society Special Bulletin No. 1. Oklahoma City.
1960   *Guide to the Identification of Certain American Indian Projectile Points*. Oklahoma Anthropological Society Special Bulletin No. 2. Oklahoma City.

Belmont, John S.
1967   "The Development of Agriculture in the Lower Valley." *Proceedings of the 22nd Southeastern Archaeological Conference*, Bulletin No. 5, pp. 16–18. Morgantown, W.Va.

Bennett, Kenneth A.
1961   "Artificial Cranial Deformation Among the Caddo Indians." *Texas Journal of Science*, Vol. 13, No. 4, pp. 377–90. Austin.

Beyer, George Eugene
1896   "The Mounds of Louisiana." *Publications of the Louisiana Historical Society*, Vol. 1, Pt. 4, pp. 12–32. New Orleans.
1898   "The Mounds of Louisiana." *Publications of the Louisiana Historical Society*, Vol. 2, Pt. 1, pp. 7–27. New Orleans.
1899   "Ancient Basket Work from Avery's Island." *Publications of the Louisiana Historical Society*, Vol. 2, Pt. 2 for 1898, pp. 23–26. New Orleans.
1899   "Investigations of Some Shell-Mounds in Calcasieu Parish." *Publications of the Louisiana Historical Society*, Vol. 2, Pt. 2 for 1898, pp. 16–23. New Orleans.
1900   "Mound Investigation at Lemar, Louisiana." *Publications of the Louisiana Historical Society*, Vol. 2, Pt. 3 for 1899–1900, pp. 28–33. New Orleans.

Binford, Lewis R.
1967   "Smudge Pits and Hide Smoking: The Use of Analogy in Archae-

ological Reasoning." *American Antiquity*, Vol. 32, No. 1, pp. 1–12. Salt Lake City.

Blakely, Robert L., ed.

1977 *Biocultural Adaptation in Prehistoric America*. University of Georgia Press. Athens.

Bonnin, Jack Charles

1972 *Pimple Mound Occupation in Southwest Louisiana*. Privately printed. Welsh, La.

Brackenridge, Henry Marie, Esq.

1814 *Views of Louisiana, Together with a Journal of a Voyage Up the Missouri River, in 1811*. Baltimore.

Brain, Jeffrey P.

n.d. *Tunica Treasure*. Peabody Museum Press. Cambridge, Mass.

1970 *The Tunica Treasure*. Lower Mississippi Survey Bulletin No. 2. Peabody Museum, Harvard University. Cambridge, Mass.

1971 "The Lower Mississippi Valley in North American Prehistory." Manuscript, Arkansas Archaeology Survey. Fayetteville.

1973 *Trudeau: An 18th Century Tunica Village*. Lower Mississippi Survey Bulletin No. 3. Peabody Museum, Harvard University. Cambridge, Mass.

1977 *On the Tunica Trail*. Louisiana Archaeological Survey and Antiquities Commission, Anthropological Study No. 1. Baton Rouge.

1978 *Tunica Treasure II Project: Final Report to the National Geographical Society, Lower Mississippi Valley*. Peabody Museum, Harvard University, Cambridge, Mass.

Brain Jeffrey P., and Drexel Peterson

1971 "Palmetto Tempered Pottery." *Proceedings of the 27th Southeastern Archaeological Conference*, Bulletin No. 13, pp. 70–76. Morgantown, W. Va.

Brain, Jeffery P., Alan Toth, and Antonio Rodriguez-Buckingham

1974 "Ethnohistoric Archaeology and the DeSoto Entrade into the Lower Mississippi Valley." *Conference on Historic Site Archaeology Papers*, Vol. 7, pp. 232–89. Columbia.

Broadnax, Benjamin H.

1880 "Mounds in Morehouse Parish, Louisiana." *Annual Report of the Smithsonian Institution for 1879*, pp. 386–88. Washington, D.C.

Brown, Clair A.

1936 "The Vegetation of Indian Mounds and Middens and Marshes in Plaquemines and St. Bernard Parishes." In *Reports on the Geology of Plaquemines and St. Bernard Parishes*, Department of Conservation, Louisiana Geological Survey, Geological Bulletin No. 8, pp. 423–40. New Orleans.

332

Brown, Ian W.
1977   "A Reexamination of the Houses at the Bayou Goula Site, Iberville Parish, Louisiana." *Louisiana Archaeology*, Bulletin No. 3, pp. 195–205. Lafayette.

Brown, Ian W., and Nancy Lambert-Brown
1978   "Lower Mississippi Survey, Petite-Anse Project." *Research Notes*, No. 5. Avery Island, La.
1978   "Lower Mississippi Survey, Petite-Anse Project." *Research Notes*, No. 6. Avery Island, La.

Bry, Henry
1847   "Louisiana Ouachita Region." *DeBow's Review*, Vol. 3, No. 3, p. 228. New Orleans.

Bryan, Alan Lyle
1969   "Early Man in America and the Late Pleistocene Chronology of Westen Canada and Alaska." *Current Anthropology*, Vol. 10, No. 4, pp. 339–65. Glasgow.

Bryson, Reid A., and Wayne M. Wendlund
1967   "Tentative Climatic Patterns for Some Late Glacial and Post-Glacial Episodes in Central North America." William Mayer-Oakes, ed., In *Life, Land and Water*, University of Manitoba Press. Winnipeg.

Bullard, H. A.
1847   "Louisiana Historical Researches." *Commercial Review*, Vol. 3, No. 1, pp. 36–37. New Orleans.

Bullen, Ripley P., and James B. Stoltman
1972   "Fiber-Tempered Pottery in Southeastern United States and Northern Columbia: Its Origins, Context and Significance." *Florida Anthropologist*, Vol. 25, No. 2, Pt. 2. Fort Lauderdale.

Bushnell, David I., Jr.
1919   *Native Villages and Village Sites East of the Mississippi*. Bureau of American Ethnology Bulletin 69. Smithsonian Institution. Washington, D.C.
1935   "The Manahoac Tribes in Virginia, 1608." *Smithsonian Miscellaneous Collections*, Vol. 94, No. 8. Washington, D.C.

Butler, Barbara H.
1969   "The Skeletal Material from the Bison Site, Area B." In J. Ned Woodall, ed., *Archaeological Excavations in the Toledo Bend Reservoir, 1966*, Southern Methodist University Contributions in Anthropology No. 3, pp. 84–93. Dallas.

Butler, William B.
1976   "Archaeology and Prohibition." *Plains Anthropologist*, Vol. 21, No. 71, pp. 67–71. Lincoln.

Byrd, Kathleen Mary

1974 "Tchefuncte Subsistence Patterns, Morton Shell Mound, Iberia Parish, Louisiana." M.A. thesis, Louisiana State University. Baton Rouge.

1976 "Tchefuncte Subsistence: Information Obtained from the Excavation of the Morton Shell Mound, Iberia Parish, Louisiana." *Southeastern Archaeological Conference Bulletin*, No. 19, pp. 70–75. Memphis.

1977 "The Brackish Water Clam (*Rangia cuneata*): A Prehistoric 'Staff of Life' or a Minor Food Resource." *Louisiana Archaeology*, Bulletin No. 3, pp. 23–31. Lafayette.

1977 "Zooarchaeological Analysis of the Hanna Site: An Alto Focus Occupation in Louisiana." In Prentice Marquet Thomas, Jr., L. Janice Campbell, and Steven R. Ahler, eds., *The Hanna Site: An Alto Village in Red River Parish*, New World Research, Report of Investigations No. 3, pp. 189–213. New Orleans.

Byrd, Kathleen M., and Robert W. Neuman

1978 *Archaeological Data Relative to Prehistoric Subsistence in the Lower Mississippi Alluvial Valley*. Geoscience and Man, Vol. 19. Baton Rouge.

Caldwell, Joseph R.

1958 *Trend and Tradition in the Prehistory of Eastern United States*. American Anthropological Association Memoir No. 88. Menasha, Wis.

Caldwell, Joseph R., and Robert L. Hall, eds.

1964 *Hopewellian Studies*. Illinois State Museum Scientific Papers, Vol. 12. Springfield.

Cambron, James W., and David C. Hulse

1964 *Handbook of Alabama Archaeology: Part I, Point Types*. Archaeological Research Association of Alabama. University, Ala.

Carr, Archie

1952 *Handbook of Turtles*. Cornell University Press. Ithaca, N.Y.

Carr, Lucien

1892 "The Mounds of the Mississippi Valley, Historically Considered." *Annual Report of the Smithsonian Institution for 1891–1892*, pp. 503–99. Washington, D.C.

Chapman, Jefferson

1975 *The Rose Island Site*. University of Tennessee, Department of Anthropology, Report of Investigations No. 14. Knoxville.

Chawner, W. D.

1936 *Geology of Catahoula and Concordia Parishes*. Department of Conservation, Louisiana Geological Survey, Geological Bulletin No. 9. New Orleans.

334

Chisum, Emmett
1938   "The Excavation of an Indian Village near Sicily Island, Louisiana." *Proceedings of the Louisiana Academy of Sciences*, Vol. 4, No. 1, pp. 54–57. Baton Rouge.

Clemens, Samuel Langhorne [Mark Twain]
1883   *Life on the Mississippi.* James R. Osgood Co. Boston.

Cohen, Mark N.
1975   "Archaeological Evidence for Population Pressure in Pre-Agricultural Societies." *American Antiquity*, Vol. 40, No. 4, pp. 471–75. Washington, D.C.

Coleman, James M., and William G. Smith
1964   "Late Recent Rise of Sea Level. *Geological Society of America Bulletin*," Vol. 75, pp. 833–40. Boulder.

Coles, John
1973   *Archaeology by Experiment.* Charles Scribner's Sons. New York.

Collins, Henry B., Jr.
1927   "Archaeology Work in Louisiana and Mississippi: Explorations and Field-Work of the Smithsonian Institution in 1926," *Smithsonian Miscellaneous Collections*, Vol. 78, No. 7. Washington, D.C.
1941   "Relationships of an Early Indian Cranial Series from Louisiana." *Journal of the Washington Academy of Sciences*, Vol. 31, No. 4, pp. 145–55. Menasha, Wis.

Collins, H. C.
1874   "Geological Notes of Assistant H. C. Collins." *House Executive Documents*, 43rd Cong., 1st Sess., Vol. 2, Pt. 2, pp. 653–54. Washington, D.C.

Cotter, John L.
1951   "Stratigraphic and Area Tests at the Emerald and Anna Mound Sites." *American Antiquity*, Vol. 17, No. 1, Pt. 1, pp. 18–32. Menasha, Wis.
1952   "The Gordon Site in Southern Mississippi." *American Antiquity*, Vol. 18, No. 2, pp. 110–26. Salt Lake City.

Crosby, Alfred W., Jr.
1972   *The Columbian Exchange.* Greenwood Press. Westport, Conn.

Culin, Stewart
1900   "The Dickeson Collection of American Antiquities." *Bulletin of the Free Museum of Science and Art of the University of Pennsylvania*, Vol. 2, No. 3, pp. 113–68. Philadelphia.

Cumbaa, Stephen L.
1976   "A Reconsideration of Freshwater Shellfish Exploitation in the Florida Archaic." *Florida Anthropologist*, Vol. 29, No. 2, Pt. 1, pp. 49–59. Gainesville.

Czajkowski, J. Richard
1934 "Preliminary Report of Archaeological Excavations in Orleans Parish." *Louisiana Conservation Review*, Vol. 4, No. 3, pp. 12–18. New Orleans.

Darby, William
1816 *A Geographical Description of the State of Louisiana.* John Melish. Philadelphia.

DeJarnett, D. L., E. B. Kurjack, and J. W. Cambron
1962 "Stanfield–Worley Bluff Shelter Excavations." *Journal of Alabama Archaeology*, Vol. 8, Nos. 1–2, pp. 1–124. University, Ala.

Dickeson, Montroville Wilson
1846 "Report at Meeting of October 6, 1846." *Proceedings of the Academy of Natural Sciences of Philadelphia*, Vol. 3, No. 5, pp. 106–107. Philadelphia.

1865 *The American Numismatic Manual of the Currency or Money of the Aborigines and Colonial State, and United States Coins.* J. B. Lippincott & Co. Philadelphia.

Dormon, Caroline
1934 "Caddo Pottery." *Art and Archaeology*, Vol. 35, No. 2, pp. 59–68. Washington, D.C.

Dowler, Bennet, M.D.
1852 *Tableaux of New Orleans Daily Delta.* New Orleans.

Dragoo, Don W.
1976 "Some Aspects of Eastern North American Prehistory: A Review." *American Antiquity*, Vol. 41, No. 1, pp. 3–27. Washington, D.C.

Drake, Daniel
1850 *A Systematic Treatise, Historical, Etiological, and Practical, on the Principal Diseases of the Interior Valley of North America, As They Appear in the Caucasian, African, Indian and Esquimaux Varieties of Its Population.* 2 Vols. Cincinnati.

Driver, Harold Edson, and William C. Massey
1957 "Comparative Study of North American Indians." *Transactions of the American Philosophical Society*, Vol. 47, pp. 165–456. Philadelphia.

Fairbanks, C. H.
1940 " 'Salt Pans' from the Southeast." *American Antiquity*, Vol. 6, pp. 65–67. Menasha, Wis.

Featherman, Americus
1871 "Report of a Botanical Survey of Southern and Central Louisiana." *Annual Report of the Board of Supervisors of the Louisiana State University for 1870*, pp. 3–131. New Orleans.

336

Fiser, Jack
1975   "The Treasure of Bayou Jasmine." *LSU Alumni News*, Vol. 51, No. 5, pp. 2–6. Baton Rouge.

Fitting, James E., ed.
1973   *The Development of American Archaeology.* Anchor Books. Garden City, N.Y.

Fontaine, Edward, Rev.
1884   *How the World Was Peopled: Ethnological Lectures.* D. Appleton and Co. New York.

Ford, James A.
1934   "Mound Builders Were Pit Dwellers." *El Palacio*, Vol. 36, pp. 74–75. Santa Fe.

1935   "Outline of Louisiana and Mississippi Pottery Horizons." *Louisiana Conservation Review*, Vol. 4, No. 6, pp. 33–38. New Orleans.

1935   "An Introduction to Louisiana Archaeology." *Louisiana Conservation Review*, Vol. 4, No. 5, pp. 8–11. New Orleans.

1935   *A Ceramic Decoration Sequence at an Old Indian Village Site near Sicily Island, Louisiana.* Department of Conservation, Louisiana Geological Survey, Anthropological Study No. 1. New Orleans.

1936   *Analysis of Indian Village Site Collections from Louisiana and Mississippi.* Department of Conservation, Louisiana Geological Survey, Anthropological Study No. 2, New Orleans.

1939   "Archaeological Exploration in Louisiana During 1938." *Louisiana Conservation Review*, Vol. 7, No. 4, pp. 15–17. New Orleans.

1951   *Greenhouse: A Troyville–Coles Creek Period Site in Avoyelles Parish, Louisiana.* Anthropological Papers of the American Museum of Natural History, Vol. 44, Pt. 1. New York.

1969   *A Comparison of Formative Cultures in the Americas.* Smithsonian Contributions to Anthropology, Vol. 11. Smithsonian Institution Press. Washington, D.C.

Ford, James A., Philip Phillips, and W. G. Haag
1955   *The Jaketown Site in West-Central Mississippi.* Anthropological Papers of the American Museum of Natural History, Vol. 45, Pt. 1. New York.

Ford, James A., and George I. Quimby, Jr.
1945   *The Tchefuncte Culture: An Early Occupation of the Lower Mississippi Valley.* Society for American Archaeology Memoir No. 2. Menasha, Wis.

Ford, James A., and Clarence H. Webb
1956   *Poverty Point: A Late Archaic Site in Louisiana.* Anthropological Papers of the American Museum of Natural History, Vol. 46, Pt. 1. New York.

Ford, James A., and Gordon Willey
1940   *Crooks Site: A Marksville Period Burial Mound in LaSalle Parish,*

Louisiana. Department of Conservation, Louisiana Geological Survey, Anthropological Study No. 3. New Orleans.

1941 "An Interpretation of the Prehistory of the Eastern United States." *American Anthropologist,* n.s., Vol. 43, No. 3, Pt. 1. pp. 325–63. Menasha, Wis.

Forshey, Caleb Goldsmith

1845 "Description of Some Artificial Mounds on Prairie Jefferson, Louisiana." *American Journal of Science and Arts,* Vol. 49, Art. 4, pp. 38–42. New Haven.

Foster, John Wells

1867 "On the Antiquity of Man in North America." *Transactions of the Chicago Academy of Sciences,* Vol. 1, pp. 227–57. Chicago.

1873 *Prehistoric Races of the United States of America.* 2nd ed. S. C. Griggs and Co. Chicago.

Fowke, Gerard

1927 "Archaeological Work in Louisiana." *Smithsonian Miscellaneous Collections,* Vol. 78, No. 7. Washington, D.C.

1928 "Archaeological Investigations—II." *Forty-fourth Annual Report of the Bureau of American Ethnology,* pp. 399–540. Washington, D.C.

Fowler, Melvin L.

1959 *Summary Report of Modoc Rock Shelter, 1952, 1953, 1955, 1956.* Report of Investigations No. 8, Illinois State Museum. Springfield, Ill.

1974 *Cahokia, Ancient Capital of the Midwest.* Addison-Wesley Module in Anthropology No. 48, Addison-Wesley Publishing Co. Inc. Reading, Mass.

Fulton, Robert L., and Clarence H. Webb

1953 "The Bellevue Mound: A Pre-Caddoan Site in Bossier Parish, Louisiana." *Bulletin of the Texas Archaeological Society,* Vol. 24, pp. 18–42. Austin.

Gage, James R., M.E.

1878 "Results of Investigation of Indian Mounds." *Transactions of the Academy of Science of Saint Louis,* Vol. 3, pp. 226–44. Saint Louis.

Gagliano, Sherwood M.

1963 "A Survey of Preceramic Occupations in Portions of South Louisiana and South Mississippi." *Florida Anthropologist,* Vol. 16, No. 4, pp. 105–32. Gainesville.

1964 *An Archaeological Survey of Avery Island.* Avery Island, Inc. Baton Rouge.

1964 "Post-Pleistocene Occupations of Southeastern Louisiana Terrace Lands." *Proceedings of the 19th Southeastern Archaeological Conference,* Bulletin No. 1, pp. 18–26. Cambridge, Mass.

1967   "Kirk Serrated: An Early Archaic Index Point in Louisiana." *Florida Anthropologist*, Vol. 20, No. 1, pp. 3–9. Tallahassee.

1967   "Late Archaic–Early Formative Relationships in South Louisiana." *Proceedings of the 23rd Southeastern Archaeological Conference*, Bulletin No. 6, pp. 9–22. Morgantown, W. Va.

1967   *Occupation Sequence at Avery Island*. Louisiana State University Press. Baton Rouge.

1970   *Archaeological and Geological Studies at Avery Island, 1968–1970*. Progress Report submitted to the International Salt Company, Project Sponsors. Baton Rouge.

Gagliano, Sherwood M., and Hiram F. Gregory, Jr.

1965   "A Preliminary Survey of Paleo-Indian Points from Louisiana." *Louisiana Studies*, Vol. 4, No. 1, pp. 62–77. Natchitoches.

Gagliano, Sherwood M., and Clarence H. Webb

1970   "Archaic–Poverty Point Transition at the Pearl River Mouth." *Southeastern Archaeological Conference Bulletin*, No. 12, pp. 47–72. Morgantown.

Gallatin, Albert

1836   "A Synopsis of the Indian Tribes Within the United States East of the Rocky Mountains and the British and Russian Possessions in North America." *Transactions and Collections of the American Antiquarian Society*, Vol. 2, p. 422. Cambridge, Mass.

Gardner, Joan, and Mary Elizabeth King

1977   "Textiles from Spiro Mound, Oklahoma." Abstract in *Program and Abstracts: Forty-Second Annual Meeting, Society for American Archaeology*. New Orleans.

Genovés, T. S.

1967   "Some Problems in the Physical Anthropological Study of the Peopling of America." *Current Anthropology*, Vol. 8, No. 4, pp. 297–312. Utrecht.

Giardino, Marco Joseph

1977   "An Osteological Analysis of the Human Population from the Mount Nebo Site, Madison Parish, Louisiana." M.A. thesis, Tulane University. New Orleans.

1977   "Skeletal Remains." In Prentice Marquet Thomas, L. Janice Campbell, and Steven R. Ahler, eds., *The Hanna Site: An Alto Village in Red River Parish*, New World Research, Report of Investigations No. 3, pp. 228–38. New Orleans.

Gibson, Jon L.

1966   "Burins from Louisiana." *American Antiquity*, Vol. 31, No. 5, pp. 746–47. Salt Lake City.

1966   "A Preliminary Survey of Indian Occupations in LaSalle Parish,

Louisiana." *Louisiana Studies*, Vol. 5, No. 3, pp. 193–237. Natchitoches.

1968   "Russell Landing: A North Louisiana Phase of the Tchefuncte Period." M.A. thesis, Louisiana State University. Baton Rouge.

1970   "Intersite Variability at Poverty Point: Some Preliminary Considerations on Lapidary." *Southeastern Archaeological Conference Bulletin*, No. 12, pp. 13–20. Morgantown.

1974   "Poverty Point, the First North American Chiefdom." *Archaeology*, Vol. 27, No. 2, pp. 97–105. New York.

1974   "The Tchefuncte Culture in the Bayou Vermilion Basin, South Central Louisiana: A Developmental Case Study." *Bulletin of the Texas Archaeological Society*, Vol. 45, pp. 67–95. Austin.

Gibson, Jon L., and Layton J. Miller

1973   *The Trappey Mastodon.* Research Series No. 27, Anthropology, University of Southwestern Louisiana. Lafayette.

Gill, Edmund D.

1969   Untitled article. *Current Anthropology*, Vol. 10, No. 5, p. 473. Glasgow.

Goodyear, Albert C.

1974   *The Brand Site: A Techno-Functional Study of a Dalton Site in Northeast Arkansas.* Arkansas Archaeological Survey Publications in Archaeology, Research Series, No. 7. Fayetteville.

Grayson, Donald K.

1977   "Pleistocene Avifaunas and the Overkill Hypothesis." *Science*, Vol. 195, No. 4279, pp. 691–92. Washington, D.C.

Gregory, Hiram F., Jr.

1963   "Scottsbluff Points: Trademarks of Texas Tourists." *Louisiana Studies*, Vol. 2, No. 3, pp. 176–77. Natchitoches.

1966   "Vessels from the Bison Site." *Louisiana Studies*, Vol. 5, No. 2, pp. 159–61. Natchitoches.

1969   "Plaquemine Period Sites in the Catahoula Basin: A Microcosm in East Central Louisiana." *Louisiana Studies*, Vol. 8, No. 2, pp. 111–34. Natchitoches.

1973   "Eighteenth Century Caddoan Archaeology: A Study on Models and Interpretation." Ph.D. dissertation, Southern Methodist University. Dallas.

Gregory, Hiram F., Jr., Lester C. Davis, Jr., and Donald G. Hunter

1970   "The Terral Lewis Site: A Poverty Point Activity Facies in Madison Parish, Louisiana." *Southeastern Archaeological Conference Bulletin*, No. 12, pp. 35–46. Morgantown, W. Va.

Gregory, Hiram F., Jr., and Clarence H. Webb

1965   European Trade Beads from Six Sites in Natchitoches Parish, Louisiana." *Florida Anthropologist*, Vol. 18, No. 3, Pt. 2, pp. 15–44. Gainesville.

Griffin, James B.

1967   "Eastern North American Archaeology: A Summary." *Science*, Vol. 156, No. 3772, pp. 175–91. Washington, D.C.

Griffin, John W.

1974   *Investigations in Russell Cave*. National Park Service Publications in Archaeology No. 13. U. S. Department of the Interior. Washington, D.C.

Guthe, Carl E.

1952   "Twenty-five Years of Archaeology in the Eastern United States." In James B. Griffin, ed., *Archaeology of Eastern United States*, 1–12. University of Chicago Press. Chicago.

Haag, William G.

n.d.   "Southeastern United States: Post-Pleistocene Adaptations, 9000–4000 B.C." Manuscript on file at the Department of Geography and Anthropology, Louisiana State University. Baton Rouge.

1939   Untitled article. *Southeastern Archaeological Conference Newsletter*, Vol. 1, No. 2. Lexington, Ky.

1961   "The Archaic in the Lower Mississippi Valley." *American Antiquity*, Vol. 26, No. 3, Pt. 1, pp. 317–23. Salt Lake City.

1962   "The Bering Strait Land Bridge." *Scientific American*, Vol. 206, No. 1, pp. 112–23. New York.

1971   *Louisiana in North American Prehistory*. Mélanges No. 1. Museum of Geoscience, Louisiana State University. Baton Rouge.

Haag, William G., and Clarence H. Webb

1953   "Microblades at Poverty Point." *American Antiquity*, Vol. 18, No. 3, pp. 245–48. Salt Lake City.

Hally, David J.

n.d.   "The Lower Mississippi Valley: A.D. 1000–1700." Manuscript, Department of Anthropology, University of Georgia. Athens.

1967   "Post–Coles Creek Development in the Upper Tensas Basin of Louisiana." *Proceeding of the 23rd Southeastern Archaeological Conference*, Bulletin No. 6, pp. 36–40. Morgantown, W. Va.

Hathcock, Roy

1976   *Ancient Pottery of the Mississippi River Valley*. Hurely Press, Inc. Camden, Ark.

Hay, Oliver P.

1924   *The Pleistocene of the Middle Region of North America and Its Vertebrated Animals*. Carnegie Institution of Washington Publication No. 322a. Washington, D.C.

Haynes, C. Vance, Jr.

1969   "The Earliest Americans." *Science*, Vol. 166, No. 3906, pp. 709–15. Washington, D.C.

Heizer, Robert F.
1937   "Baked Clay Objects of the Lower Sacramento Valley, California."
        American Antiquity, Vol. 3, No. 1, pp. 34–50. Menasha, Wis.
Hester, Jim J.
1960   "Late Pleistocene Extinction and Radiocarbon Dating." *American
        Antiquity*, Vol. 26, No. 1, pp. 58–77. Salt Lake City.
Higgs, E. S., and C. Vita-Finzi
1972   "Prehistoric Economies: A Territorial Approach." In E. S. Higgs,
        ed., *Papers in Economic Prehistory*, 27–36. University Press. Cam-
        bridge, Mass.
Hilgard, Eugene Woldemar
1872   "On the Geology of Lower Louisiana and the Salt Deposit on Petite
        Anse Island." *Smithsonian Contributions to Knowledge*, Vol. 23,
        No. 248. Washington, D.C.
1873   *Supplementary and Final Report of a Geological Reconnaissance
        of the State of Louisiana.* Picayune Steam Job Press. New Orleans.
Hoffman, Michael P.
1967   "Ceramic Pipe Style Chronology Along the Red River Drainage in
        Southwestern Arkansas." *Arkansas Archaeologist*, Vol. 8, No. 1,
        pp. 4–14. Fayetteville.
Holland, Wilbur C., Lee W. Hough, and Grover E. Murray
1952   *Geology of Beauregard and Allen Parishes.* Department of Con-
        servation, Louisiana Geological Survey, Geological Bulletin No. 27.
        Baton Rouge.
Holmes, William Henry
1896   "Prehistoric Textile Art of Eastern United States." *Thirteenth An-
        nual Report of the Bureau of Ethnology, 1891–92, Smithsonian In-
        stitution*, 7–46. Washington, D.C.
1903   "Aboriginal Pottery from Eastern United States." *Twentieth An-
        nual Report of the Bureau of American Ethnology*, pp. 1–237.
        Washington, D.C.
Hotchkiss, T. P.
1873   "Indian Remains Found 32 Feet Below the Surface, near Wallace
        Lake, in Caddo Parish, Louisiana." *Annual Report of the Board of
        Regents for 1872, Smithsonian Institution*, pp. 428–29. Washing-
        ton, D.C.
House, John H.
1973   *Archaeological Salvage in the Basin of Lake Rodemacher, Rap-
        ides Parish, Louisiana, 1972.* Gulf South Research Institute. Baton
        Rouge.
Howard, Calvin D.
1974   "The Atlatl: Function and Performance." *American Antiquity*, Vol.
        39, No. 1, pp. 102–104. Washington, D.C.

Howe, Henry V., Richard J. Russell, and James H. McGuirt
1935 "Submergence of Indian Mounds." In *Reports on the Geology of Cameron and Vermilion Parishes*, Department of Conservation, Louisiana Geological Survey, Geological Bulletin No. 6, pp. 64–68. New Orleans.

Hrdlička, Aleš
1907 *Skeletal Remains Suggesting or Attributed to Early Man in North America*. Bureau of American Ethnology Bulletin 33. Smithsonian Institution. Washington, D.C.
1909 "Report on an Additional Collection of Skeletal Remains, from Arkansas and Louisiana." *Journal of the Academy of Natural Sciences of Philadelphia*, Vol. 14, pp. 171–249. Philadelphia.
1913 "A Report on a Collection of Crania and Bones from Sorrel Bayou, Iberville Parish, Louisiana." In C. B. Moore, "Some Aboriginal Sites in Louisiana and Arkansas," *Journal of the Academy of Natural Sciences of Philadelphia*, Vol. 16, pp. 95–99. Philadelphia.
1916 *Physical Anthropology of the Lenape or Delawares and of the Eastern Indians in General*. Bureau of American Ethnology Bulletin 62. Smithsonian Institution. Washington, D.C.
1940 "Catalog of Human Crania in the United States National Museum Collections: Indians of the Gulf States." *Proceedings of the United States National Museum*, Vol. 87, pp. 315–464. Washington, D.C.

Humphreys, Andrew Atkinson, and Henry L. Abbot
1861 *Report upon the Physics and Hydraulics of the Mississippi River*. Professional Papers No. 4, U.S. Army Corps of Topographical Engineers, U.S. Bureau of Topographical Engineers. J. B. Lippincott and Co. Philadelphia.

Hunter, Donald G.
1975 "Functional Analyses of Poverty Point Clay Objects." *Florida Anthropologist*, Vol. 28, No. 2, pp. 57–71. Gainesville.

Jensen, Harold P., Jr.
1968 "Coral Snake Mound (X16SA48)." *Bulletin of the Texas Archaeological Society*, Vol. 39, pp. 9–44. Austin.

Johnson, Frederick
1961 "A Quarter Century of Growth in American Archaeology." *American Antiquity*, Vol. 27, No. 1, pp. 1–6. Salt Lake City.

Jolly, Clifford J., and Fred Plog
1976 *Physical Anthropology and Archaeology*. Alfred A. Knopf. New York.

Jones, Charles Colcock, Jr.
1873 *Antiquities of the Southern Indians*. D. Appleton & Co. New York.

Jones, Joseph, M.D.
1877 "Explorations and Researches Concerning the Destruction of the
–78 Aboriginal Inhabitants of America by Various Diseases, as Syph-

ilis, Matlazarica, Pestilence, Malarial Fever and Small Pox." *New Orleans Medical and Surgical Journal*, New Series, Vol. 5, pp. 926–41. T. H. Thomason. New Orleans.

Joor, Joseph F., M.D.

1895 "Notes on a Collection of Archaeological and Geological Specimens Collected in a Trip to Avery's Island (Petit Anse), Feb. 1st, 1890." *American Naturalist*, Vol. 29, pp. 394–98. Philadelphia.

Kellar, James H.

1955 *The Atlatl in North America*. Indiana Historical Society Prehistory Research Series, Vol. 3, No. 3. Indianapolis.

Kilpatrick, Andrew B.

1852 "Historical and Statistical Collections of Louisiana." *DeBow's Review*, Vol. 12, Art. 3, pp. 256–75. New Orleans.

Kniffen, Fred B.

1935 "Historic Indian Tribes of Louisiana." *Louisiana Conservation Review*, Vol. 4, No. 7, pp. 5–12. New Orleans.

1936 "Preliminary Report of the Indian Mounds and Middens of Plaquemines and St. Bernard Parishes." In *Reports on the Geology of Plaquemines and St. Bernard Parishes*, Department of Conservation, Louisiana Geological Survey, Geological Bulletin No. 8, pp. 407–22. New Orleans.

1938 "Indian Mounds of Iberville Parish." In *Reports on the Geology of Iberville and Ascension Parishes*, Department of Conservation, Louisiana Geological Survey, Geological Bulletin No. 13, pp. 189–207. New Orleans.

Krieger, Alex D.

1964 "Early Man in the New World." In Jesse D. Jennings and Edward Norbeck, eds., *Prehistoric Man in the New World*, 23–81. University of Chicago Press. Chicago.

Krogman, W. M.

1962 *The Human Skeleton in Forensic Medicine*. Charles C. Thomas. Springfield.

Kuttruff, Carl

1975 "The Poverty Point Site: North Sector Test Excavations." *Bulletin of the Louisiana Archaeological Society*, No. 2, pp. 129–51. Lafayette.

Leidy, Joseph

1866 "Remarks." *Proceedings of the Academy of Natural Sciences of Philadelphia*, 109. Philadelphia.

1889 "Notice of Some Mammalian Remains from the Salt Mines of Petite Anse, Louisiana." *Transactions of the Wagner Free Institute of Science*, Vol. 2, pp. 33–40. Philadelphia.

Lenzer, John

1977 "Geology and Geomorphology." In Prentice Marquet Thomas, Jr.,

L. Janice Campbell, and Steven R. Ahler, eds., *The Hanna Site: An Alto Village in Red River Parish*, New World Research, Report of Investigations No. 3, pp. 32–50. New Orleans.

Lewis, Thomas M. N., and Madeline Kneberg Lewis
1961 *Eva: An Archaic Site*. University of Tennessee Press. Knoxville.

Libby, Willard F.
1955 *Radiocarbon Dating*. University of Chicago Press. Chicago.

Lockett, Samuel Henry
1870 "Report of the Topographical Survey of Part of Louisiana." *Annual Report of the Board of Supervisors of the Louisiana State Seminary of Learning and Military Academy for the Year Ending December 31, 1869*, pp. 49–76. New Orleans.

1873 "Mounds in Louisiana." *Annual Report of the Board of Regents for 1872, Smithsonian Institution*, 429–30. Washington, D.C.

Long, James H.
1975 "The Springridge Site." *Louisiana Archaeological Society Newsletter*, Vol. 2, No. 1, pp. 9–10. Lafayette.

Lowery, George H., Jr.
1974 *The Mammals of Louisiana and Its Adjacent Waters*. Louisiana State University Press. Baton Rouge.

Lyon, Edwin
1976 "The Louisiana WPA Archaeological Project." *Proceedings of the 32nd Southeastern Archaeological Conference*, Bulletin No. 19, pp. 50–52. Memphis.

McClurkan, Burney B., William T. Field, and J. Ned Woodall
1966 *Excavations in the Toledo Bend Reservoir, 1964–65*. Papers of the Texas Archaeological Salvage Project, No. 8. Austin.

MacDonald, George F.
1971 "A Review of Research on Paleo-Indians in Eastern North America." *Arctic Anthropology*, Vol. 8, No. 2, pp. 32–41. University of Wisconsin Press. Madison.

McGimsey, Charles R., III
1972 *Public Archaeology*. Seminar Press. New York.

McIntire, William G.
1958 *Prehistoric Indian Settlements of the Changing Mississippi River Delta*. Louisiana State University Studies, Coastal Studies Series, No. 1. Baton Rouge.

MacNeish, Richard S.
1976 "Early Man in the New World." *American Scientist*, Vol. 63, No. 3, pp. 316–27. New Haven.

Marrinan, Rochelle A.
1976 "Assessment of Subsistence Strategy Evidenced by Shell Ring Sites." *Proceedings of the 32nd Southeastern Archaeological Conference*, Bulletin No. 19, pp. 61–63. Memphis.

Martin, P. S., and H. E. Wright, Jr., eds.
1967 *Pleistocene Extinctions: The Search for a Cause.* Yale University Press. New Haven.

Mason, Otis T.
1881 "Abstracts of the Smithsonian Correspondence Relative to Aboriginal Remains in the United States." *Annual Report of the Smithsonian Institution for the Year 1880*, pp. 441–448. Washington, D.C.

Meigs, J. Aitken, M.D.
1866 "Observations upon the Cranial Forms of the American Aborigines Based upon Specimens Contained in the Collection of the Academy of Natural Sciences of Philadelphia." *Proceedings of the Academy of Natural Sciences of Philadelphia*, 197–235. Philadelphia.

Mercer, Henry Chapman
1895 "The Antiquity of Man on Petit Anse (Avery's Island) Louisiana." *American Naturalist*, Vol. 29, pp. 393–94. Philadelphia.

Million, Michael G.
1975 "Research Design for the Aboriginal Ceramic Industries of the Cache River Basin." In Michael B. Schiffer and John H. House, eds., *The Cache River Archaeological Project*, Arkansas Archaeological Survey Research Series, No. 8, pp. 217–22. Fayetteville.

Monette, John Wesley
1838 "Indian Mounds; or, American Monuments, in the South-West." *South-Western Journal*, Vol. 1, Nos. 15-16, pp. 228–31. Natchez.
1846 *History of the Discovery and Settlement of the Valley of the Mississippi.* Vol. 1. New York.

Moore, Clarence Bloomfield
1905 "Certain Aboriginal Remains of Mobile Bay and Mississippi Sound." *Journal of the Academy of Natural Sciences of Philadelphia*, 2nd Series, Vol. 13, Pt. 2, pp. 279–97. Philadelphia.
1908 "Certain Mounds of Arkansas and Mississippi." *Journal of the Academy of Natural Sciences of Philadelphia*, 2nd Series, Vol. 13, Pt. 4, pp. 481–600. Philadelphia.
1909 "Antiquities of the Ouachita." *Journal of the Academy of Natural Sciences of Philadelphia*, Vol. 14, pp. 7–170. Philadelphia.
1911 "Some Aboriginal Sites on the Mississippi River." *Journal of the Academy of Natural Sciences of Philadelphia*, Vol. 14, pp. 365–480. Philadelphia.
1912 "Some Aboriginal Sites on Red River." *Journal of the Academy of Natural Sciences of Phildelphia*, Vol. 14, pp. 481–644. Philadelphia.
1913 "Some Aboriginal Sites in Louisiana and Arkansas." *Journal of the

Academy of Natural Sciences of Philadelphia, Vol. 16, pp. 7–99. Philadelphia.

1918 "The Northwestern Florida Coast Revisited." *Journal of the Academy of Natural Sciences of Philadelphia*, 2nd Series, Vol. 16, Pt. 4, pp. 514–77. Philadelphia.

Moorehead, Warren K.

1922 "The Hopewell Mound Group of Ohio." *Field Museum of Natural History, Anthropological Series*, Vol. 6, No. 5, pp. 73–184. Chicago.

Morse, Dan F.

1971 "The Hawkins Cache: A Significant Dalton Find in Northeast Arkansas." *Arkansas Archaeologist*, Vol. 12, No. 1, pp. 9–20. Fayetteville.

Morton, George Samuel, M.D.

1839 *Crania Americana.* J. Dodson. Philadelphia.

Mosely, Michael Edward

1975 *The Maritime Foundations of Andean Civilization.* Cummings Publishing Co. Menlo Park, Calif.

Munson, Patrick J.

1969 "Comments on Binford's 'Smudge Pits and Hide Smoking: The Use of Analogy in Archaeological Reasoning.' " *American Antiquity*, Vol. 34. No. 1, pp. 83–85. Salt Lake City.

Nadaillac, Marquis de

1893 *Pre-historic America.* Translated by N. d'Anvers. G. P. Putnam's Sons. New York.

National Research Council

1975 *Understanding Climatic Change: A Problem for Action.* National Academy of Sciences. Washington, D.C.

Neitzel, Robert S.

1938 Quarterly Progress Report WPA Project, Avoyelles Unit. Manuscript on file at the Museum of Geoscience, Louisiana State University. Baton Rouge.

1965 *Archaeology of the Fatherland Site: The Grand Village of the Natchez.* Anthropological Papers of the American Museum of Natural History; Vol. 51, Pt. 1. New York.

Neuman, Robert W.

1967 "Atlatl Weights from Certain Sites on the Northern and Central Great Plains." *American Antiquity*, Vol. 32, No. 1, pp. 36–53. Salt Lake City.

1970 "Archaeological and Historical Assessment of the Red River Basin in Louisiana." In Hester A. Davis, ed., *Archaeological and Historical Resources of the Red River Basin*, Arkansas Archaeological Survey, Research Series, No. 1. Fayetteville.

1972 Archaeological Investigations at the Morton Shell Mound, Weeks

Island, Iberia Parish, Louisiana. Report submitted to National Science Foundation. Washington, D.C.

1974 "Historic Locations of Certain Caddoan Tribes." In Robert W. Neuman, *Caddoan Indians II*, 9–147. Garland Publishing Inc. New York and London.

1975 *The Sonota Complex and Associated Sites on the Northern Great Plains*. Nebraska State Historical Society Publications in Anthropology, No. 6. Lincoln.

1977 *An Archaeological Assessment of Coastal Louisiana*. Mélanges No. 11. Museum of Geoscience, Louisiana State University. Baton Rouge.

Newell, H. Perry, and Alex D. Krieger

1949 *The George C. Davis Site, Cherokee County, Texas*. Memoirs of the Society for American Archaeology No. 5. Menasha, Wis.

Newman, Walter S., and Bert Salwen, eds.

1977 *Amerinds and Their Paleoenvironments in Northeastern North America*. Annals of the New York Academy of Sciences, Vol. 288. New York.

Nott, Josiah Clark, M.D., and George R. Glidden

1854 *Types of Mankind*. J. B. Lippincott & Co. Philadelphia.

Orr, Kenneth C.

1952 "Survey of Caddoan Area Archaeology." In James B. Griffin, ed., *Archaeology of Eastern United States*, 239–55. University of Chicago Press. Chicago.

Owen, Richard

1868 "On the Deposit of Rock Salt at New Iberia, La." *Transactions of the St. Louis Academy of Science*, Vol. 2, pp. 47, 250–52. St. Louis.

Palter, John L.

1976 "A New Approach to the Significance of the 'Weighted' Spear Thrower." *American Antiquity*, Vol. 41, No. 4, pp. 500–10. Washington, D.C.

Parsons, Mary Hrones

1970 "Preceramic Subsistence on the Peruvian Coast." *American Antiquity*, Vol. 35, No. 3, pp. 292–304. Washington, D.C.

Peebles, Christopher S.

1971 "Moundville and Surrounding Sites: Some Structural Considerations of Mortuary Practices II." In J. A. Brown, ed., *Approaches to the Social Dimensions of Mortuary Practices*, Memoirs of the Society for American Archaeology No. 25. Washington, D.C.

Perino, Gregory

1968 *Guide to the Identification of Certain American Indian Projectile Points*. Oklahoma Anthropological Society Special Bulletin No. 3. Oklahoma City.

1971 *Guide to the Identification of Certain American Indian Projectile*

348

Points. Oklahoma Anthropological Society Special Bulletin 4. Oklahoma City.

Phillips, Philip

1970 *Archaeological Survey in the Lower Yazoo Basin, Mississippi, 1949–1955.* Papers of the Peabody Museum of Archaeology and Ethnology, Harvard University, Vol. 60, Pts. 1 & 2. Cambridge, Mass.

Phillips, Philip, James A. Ford, and James B. Griffin

1951 *Archaeological Survey in the Lower Mississippi Alluvial Valley, 1940–1947.* Papers of the Peabody Museum of American Archaeology and Ethnology, Harvard University, Vol. 25. Cambridge, Mass.

Pilcher, Joe Mitchell

1918 "The Story of Marksville." *Publications of the Louisiana Historical Society,* Vol. 10, pp. 68–82. New Orleans.

Poag, C. Wylie

1973 "Late Quaternary Sea Levels in the Gulf of Mexico." *Transactions of the Gulf Coast Association of Geological Societies,* Vol. 23, pp. 394–400. Houston.

Prichard, Walter, ed.

1938 "A Tourist's Description of Louisiana in 1860." *Louisiana Historical Quarterly,* Vol. 21, pp. 1110–1214. New Orleans.

Prichard, Walter, Fred B. Kniffen, and Clair A. Brown, eds.

1945 "Southern Louisiana and Southern Alabama in 1819." *Louisiana Historical Quarterly,* Vol. 28, pp. 735–921. New Orleans.

Quimby, George I., Jr.

1941 "The Tchefuncte Culture." *Southeastern Archaeological Conference Newsletter.* Vol. 2, No. 4, pp. 29–30. Lexington, Ky.

1951 "The Medora Site, West Baton Rouge Parish, Louisiana." *Field Museum of Natural History, Anthropological Series,* Vol. 24, No. 2, pp. 81–135. Chicago.

1956 "The Locus of the Natchez Pelvis Find." *American Antiquity,* Vol. 22, No. 1, pp. 77–79. Salt Lake City.

1957 "The Bayou Goula Site, Iberville Parish, Louisiana." *Fieldiana: Anthropology,* Vol. 47, No. 2, pp. 89–170. Chicago Natural History Museum. Chicago.

Rafinesque, C. S.

1824 *Ancient History; or, Annals of Kentucky.* Frankfort, Ky.

Rau, Charles

1876 "Archaeological Collection of the United States National Museum, in Charge of the Smithsonian Institution. *Smithsonian Contributions to Knowledge,* Vol. 22, Art. 4. Washington, D.C.

1885 "Prehistoric Fishing in Europe and North America." *Smithsonian Contributions to Knowledge,* Vol. 25, Art. 1. Washington, D.C.

Ripley, H. C.
1876 "Report of the Chief of Engineers." *House Executive Documents,* 44th Cong. 1st Sess., Vol. 2, Pt. 1, pp. 889–93. Washington, D.C.

Rivet, Philip George
1973 "Tchefuncte Ceramic Typology: A Reappraisal." M.A. thesis, Louisiana State University. Baton Rouge.

Robbins, Louise M.
1976 "Analysis of Human Skeletal Material from Morton Shell Mound (16IB3), Iberia Parish, Louisiana." Manuscript on file at Department of Geography and Anthropology, Louisiana State University. Baton Rouge.

Rolingson, Martha Ann
1976 "The Bartholomew Phase: A Plaquemine Adaptation in the Mississippi Valley." In Charles E. Cleland, ed., *Cultural Change and Continuity: Essays in Honor of James Bennett Griffin,* 99–119. Academic Press. New York.

Rostlund, Erhard
1952 *Freshwater Fish and Fishing in Native North America.* University of California Publications in Geography, Vol. 9. University of California Press. Berkeley.

Rouse, Irving
1976 "Peopling of the Americas." *Quaternary Research,* Vol. 6, pp. 597–612. New York.

Rovner, Irwin
1971 "Potential of Opal Phytoliths for Use in Paleoecological Reconstruction." *Quaternary Research,* Vol. 1, pp. 343–59. New York.

Rowland, Mrs. Dunbar
1930 *Life, Letters and Papers of William Dunbar, 1749–1810.* Mississippi Historical Society Press. Jackson.

Russell, Richard Joel
1936 "Physiography of the Lower Mississippi River." In *Reports on the Geology of Plaquemines and St. Bernard Parishes,* Department of Conservation, Louisiana Geological Survey, Geological Bulletin No. 8, pp. 3–199. New Orleans.

Russell, Richard J., and H. V. Howe
1935 "Cheniers of Southwestern Louisiana." *Geographical Review,* Vol. 25, No. 3, pp. 449–61. New York.

Ryan, Thomas M.
1975 "Semisubterranean Structures and Their Spatial Distribution at the Marksville Site (16AV-1)." *Proceedings of the 31st Southeastern Archaeological Conference,* Bulletin No. 18, pp. 215–25. Memphis.

Saucier, Roger T.
1974 *Quaternary Geology of the Lower Mississippi Valley.* Arkansas

Archaeological Survey Publications in Archaeology, Research Series, No. 6. Fayetteville.

Sauer, Carl O.

1962   "Seashore—Primitive House of Man?" *Proceedings of the American Philosophical Society*, Vol. 106, No. 1, pp. 41–47. Philadelphia.

Schambach, Frank F.

1971   "The Trans-Mississippi South: The Case for a New Natural Area West of the Lower Mississippi Valley and East of the Plains." Paper presented at the Caddo Conference. Austin.

Scurlock, Dan J.

1964   *Archaeological Reconnaissance at Toledo Bend Reservoir, 1962–1963 Season*. Texas Archaeological Salvage Report to the National Park Service, University of Texas. Austin.

Sears, William T.

1964   "The Southeastern United States." In Jesse D. Jennings and Edward Norbeck, eds., *Prehistoric Man in the New World*, pp. 259–87. University of Chicago Press. Chicago.

Setzler, Frank M.

1933   "Hopewell Type Pottery from Louisiana." *Journal of the Washington Academy of Sciences*, Vol. 23, No. 3, pp. 149–53. Washington, D.C.

1933   "Pottery of the Hopewell Type from Louisiana." *Proceedings of the United States National Museum*, Vol. 82, Art. 22, pp. 1–21. Washington, D.C.

1934   "A Phase of Hopewell Mound Builders in Louisiana." *Explorations and Field-work of the Smithsonian Institution in 1933*, pp. 38–40. Washington, D.C.

1940   "Archaeological Perspectives in the Northern Mississippi Valley." In *Essays in Historical Anthropology of North America: Publications in Honor of J. R. Swanton, Smithsonian Miscellaneous Collections*, Vol. 100, pp. 253–90. Washington, D.C.

1943   "Archaeological Explorations in the United States, 1930–1942. *Acta Americana*, Vol. 1, No. 2, pp. 206–20. Washington, D.C.

Shafer, Harry J.

1975   "Comments on Woodland Cultures of East Texas." *Bulletin of the Texas Archaeological Society*, Vol. 46, pp. 249–54. Austin.

Shea, Andrea

1977   "Analysis of Plant Remains from the Hanna Site." In Prentice Marquet Thomas, Jr., L. Janice Campbell, and Steven R. Ahler, eds., *The Hanna Site: An Alto Village in Red River Parish*, New World Research, Report of Investigations No. 3, pp. 218–27. New Orleans.

351

Shenkel, J. Richard
1974 "Big Oak and Little Oak Islands: Excavations and Interpretations."
Bulletin of the Louisiana Archaeological Society, No. 1, pp. 37–
65. Lafayette.
Shenkel, J. Richard, and Jon Gibson
1974 "Big Oak Island: An Historical Perspective of Changing Site Function." Louisiana Studies, Vol. 13, No. 2, pp. 173–86. Natchitoches.
Shenkel, J. Richard, and George Holley
1975 "A Tchefuncte House." Proceedings of the 31st Southeastern Archaeological Conference, Bulletin No. 18, pp. 226–42. Memphis.
Shetrone, Henry Clyde
1927 Explorations of the Hopewell Group of Prehistoric Earthworks.
Ohio Archaeological and Historical Publications, Vol. 35. Columbus.
1930 The Mound Builders. D. Appleton Company, New York.
Sibley, J. Ashley, Jr.
1967 Louisiana's Ancients of Man. Claitor's Publishing Division. Baton
Rouge.
Silverberg, Robert
1968 Mound Builders of Ancient America. New York Graphic Society,
Ltd. Greenwich, Conn.
Smith, Brent W.
1975 "Prehistoric Settlement Patterns of the Young's Bayou Drainage,
Natchitoches Parish, Louisiana. Bulletin of the Louisiana Archaeological Society, No. 2, pp. 163–200. Lafayette.
1976 "The Late Archaic–Poverty Point Steatite Trade Network in the
Lower Mississippi Valley: A Preliminary Report." Louisiana Ar-
chaeological Society Newsletter, Vol. 3, No. 4, pp. 6–10. Lafayette.
Smith, Bruce D.
1975 Middle Mississippian Exploitation of Animal Populations. An-
thropological Papers, Museum of Anthropology, University of
Michigan, No. 57. Ann Arbor.
Snow, Charles E.
1945 "Tchefuncte Skeletal Remains." In James A. Ford and George I.
Quimby, Jr., The Tchefuncte Culture: An Early Occupation of the
Lower Mississippi Valley, Society for American Archaeology,
Memoirs No. 2. Menasha, Wis.
1948 "Indian Knoll, Skeletons of Site Oh 2, Ohio County, Kentucky."
Reports in Anthropology, Department of Anthropology, Univer-
sity of Kentucky, Vol. 4, No. 3, Pt. 2. Lexington.
Southall, James Cocke
1875 The Recent Origin of Man: As Illustrated by Geology and the

Modern Science of Prehistoric Archaeology. J. B. Lippincott & Co. Philadelphia.

Springer, James W.

1973 "The Prehistory and Cultural Geography of Coastal Louisiana." Ph.D. dissertation, Yale University. New Haven.

Squier, E. G., and E. H. Davis

1848 "Ancient Monuments of the Mississippi Valley." *Smithsonian Contributions to Knowledge,* Vol. 1. Washington, D.C.

Stevens, Edward Thomas

1870 *Flint Chips: A Guide to Pre-historic Archaeology, as Illustrated by the Collections in the Blackmore Museum, Salisbury.* Bell & Daldy. London.

Stewart, T. Dale

1973 *The People of America.* Charles Scribner's & Sons. New York.

Stoddard, Amos

1812 *Sketches, Historical and Descriptive, of Louisiana.* Mathew Corey. Philadelphia.

Story, Dee Ann, and S. Valastro, Jr.

1977 "Radiocarbon Dating and the George C. Davis Site, Texas." *Journal of Field Archaeology,* Vol. 4, No. 1, pp. 63–89. Boston.

Suhm, Dee Ann, and Edward B. Jelks, eds.

1962 *Handbook of Texas Archaeology: Type Descriptions.* Texas Archaeological Society and Texas Memorial Museum. Austin.

Suhm, Dee Ann, Alex D. Krieger, and Edward B. Jelks

1954 "An Introductory Handbook of Texas Archaeology." *Bulletin of the Texas Archaeological Society,* Vol. 25. Austin.

Swanton, John R.

1928 "The Interpretation of Aboriginal Indian Mounds by Means of Creek Indian Customs." *Annual Report of the Board of Regents of the Smithsonian Institution for 1927,* pp. 495–506. Washington, D.C.

1931 "Indian Language Studies in Louisiana." *Explorations and Field-Work of the Smithsonian Institution in 1930,* pp. 195–200. Washington, D.C.

1938 "Historic Use of the Spear-thrower in Southeastern North America." *American Antiquity,* Vol. 3, pp. 356–58. Menasha, Wis.

1942 *Source Material on the History and Ethnology of the Caddo Indians.* Bureau of American Ethnology Bulletin 132. Smithsonian Institution. Washington, D.C.

1946 *The Indians of the Southeastern United States.* Bureau of American Ethnology Bulletin 137. Smithsonian Institution. Washington, D.C.

Thomas, Cyrus

1891 *Catalogue of Prehistoric Works East of the Rocky Mountains.* Bureau of Ethnology Bulletin 12. Smithsonian Institution. Washington, D.C.

1894 "Report on the Mound Explorations of the Bureau of Ethnology." *Twelfth Annual Report of the Bureau of Ethnology*, 3–742. Washington, D.C.

Thomas, Prentice Marquet, Jr., L. Janice Campbell, and Steven R. Ahler

1977 *The Hanna Site: An Alto Village in Red River Parish.* New World Research, Report of Investigations No. 3. New Orleans.

Thomassy, Raymond

1860 *Géologie Practique de la Louisiane.* New Orleans and Paris.

Toth, Edwin Alan

1974 *Archaeology and Ceramics of the Marksville Site.* Anthropological Papers No. 56, Museum of Anthropology, University of Michigan. Ann Arbor.

1977 "Early Marksville Phases in the Lower Mississippi Valley: A Study of Culture Contact Dynamics." Ph.D. dissertation, Harvard University. Cambridge, Mass.

1979 *The Lake St. Agnes Site.* Mélanges No. 13. Museum of Geoscience, Louisiana State University. Baton Rouge.

U.S. DeSoto Expedition Commission

1939 *Final Report of the United States DeSoto Expedition Commission*, House Document No. 71, 76th Cong., 1st Sess. Washington, D.C.

Veatch, Arthur Clifford

1899 "The Shreveport Area." In Gilbert D. Harris and A. C. Veatch, *A Preliminary Report on the Geology of Louisiana*, Special Report No. 2, pp. 152–208. Baton Rouge.

1899 "The Five Islands." In Gilbert D. Harris and A. C. Veatch, *A Preliminary Report on the Geology of Louisiana*, Special Report No. 3, pp. 213–62. Baton Rouge.

1902 "The Salines of North Louisiana." In Gilbert D. Harris, A. C. Veatch, and Jov. A. A. Pacheco, *A Report on the Geology of Louisiana*, Special Report No. 2. Baton Rouge.

1902 "Notes on the Geology Along the Ouachita." In Gilbert D. Harris, A. C. Veatch, and Jov. A. A. Pacheco, *A Report on the Geology of Louisiana*, Special Report No. 4. Baton Rouge.

Vescelius, G. S.

1957 "Mound 2 at Marksville." *American Antiquity*, Vol. 22, No. 4, pp. 416–20. Salt Lake City.

Vogel, J. C., and Nikolas J. van der Merwe

1977 "Isotopic Evidence for Early Maize Cultivation in New York State." *American Antiquity*, Vol. 42, No. 2, pp. 238–42. Washington, D.C.

354

Walker, Winslow M.

1932 "A Reconnaissance of Northern Louisiana Mounds." *Explorations and Field-Work of the Smithsonian Institution in 1931*, pp. 169–74. Washington, D.C.

1932 "Pre-Historic Cultures of Louisiana." In *Conference on Southern Prehistory, Held Under the Auspices of the Division of Anthropology and Psychology, Committee on State Archaeological Surveys, National Research Council, Birmingham, Alabama, Dec. 18, 19 and 20, 1932*, pp. 42–48. National Research Council. Washington, D.C.

1933 "Trailing the Moundbuilders of the Mississippi Valley." *Explorations and Field-Work of the Smithsonian Institution in 1932*, pp. 77–80. Washington, D.C.

1934 "A Variety of Caddo Pottery from Louisiana." *Journal of the Washington Academy of Sciences*, Vol. 24, No. 2, pp. 99–104. Washington, D.C.

1935 "A Caddo Burial Site at Natchitoches, Louisiana." *Smithsonian Miscellaneous Collections*, Vol. 94, No. 14. Washington, D.C.

1936 *The Troyville Mounds, Catahoula Parish, Louisiana*. Bureau of American Ethnology Bulletin 113. Smithsonian Institution. Washington, D.C.

Walthall, John A.

1977 *Moundville: An Introductin to the Archaeology of a Mississippian Chiefdom*. Alabama Museum of Natural History, University of Alabama. Tuscaloosa.

Waring, Antonio J., Jr.

1968 "The Archaic Hunting and Gathering Cultures: The Archaic and Some Shell Rings." In Stephen Williams, ed. *The Waring Papers*, Papers of the Peabody Museum of Archaeology and Ethnology, Harvard University, Vol. 57, pp. 243–46. Cambridge, Mass.

Waring, Antonio J., Jr., and Preston Holder

1945 "A Prehistoric Ceremonial Complex in the Southeastern United States." *American Anthropologist*, Vol. 47, No. 1, pp. 1–34. Menasha, Wis.

Webb, Clarence H.

1944 "Dental Abnormalities as Found in the American Indian." *American Journal of Orthodontics and Oral Surgery*, Vol. 30, No. 9, pp. 474–86. St. Louis.

1944 "Stone Vessels from a Louisiana Site." *American Antiquity*, Vol. 9, No. 4, pp. 386–94. Menasha, Wis.

1945 "A Second Historic Caddo Site at Natchitoches, Louisiana." *Bulletin of the Texas Archaeological and Paleontological Society*, Vol. 16, pp. 52–83. Abilene.

1946 "Two Unusual Types of Chipped Stone Artifacts from Northwest Louisiana." *Bulletin of the Texas Archaeological and Paleontological Society*, Vol. 17, pp. 9–17. Abilene.

1948 "Evidence of Pre-Pottery Cultures in Louisiana." *American Antiquity*, Vol. 13, No. 3, pp. 227–32. Menasha, Wis.

1948 "Caddoan Prehistory: The Bossier Focus." *Bulletin of the Texas Archaeological and Paleontological Society*, Vol. 19, pp. 100–43. Abilene.

1959 *The Belcher Mound*. Memoirs of the Society for American Archaeology No. 16. Salt Lake City.

1960 "A Review of Northeast Texas Archaeology." *Bulletin of the Texas Archaeological Society*, Vol. 29, pp. 35–62. Austin.

1963 "The Smithport Landing Site: An Alto Focus Component in De-Soto Parish, Louisiana." *Bulletin of the Texas Archaeological Society*, Vol. 34, pp. 143–87. Austin.

1965 "The Paleo-Indian Era: Distribution of Finds, Louisiana." *Proceedings of the 20th Southeastern Archaeological Conference*, Bulletin No. 2, pp. 4–6. Cambridge, Mass.

1968 "The Extent and Content of Poverty Point Culture." *American Antiquity*, Vol. 33, No. 3, pp. 297–321. Salt Lake City.

1970 "Settlement Patterns in the Poverty Point Culture Complex." In Bettye J. Broyles and Clarence H. Webb, eds., *The Poverty Point Culture, Southeastern Archaeological Conference Bulletin*, No. 12, pp. 3–12. Morgantown, W. Va.

1971 "Archaic and Poverty Point Zoomorphic Locust Beads." *American Antiquity*, Vol. 36, No. 1, pp. 105–14.

1977 *The Poverty Point Culture*. Geoscience and Man, Vol. 17. School of Geoscience, Louisiana State University. Baton Rouge.

Webb, Clarence H., and Monroe Dodd

1939 "Bone 'Gorget' from a Caddoan Mound Burial." *American Antiquity*, Vol. 4, No. 3, pp. 265–68. Menasha, Wis.

1939 "Further Excavations of the Gahagan Mound: Connections with the Florida Culture." *Bulletin of the Texas Archaeological and Paleontological Society*, Vol. 11, pop. 92–126. Abilene.

1941 "Pottery Types from the Belcher Mound Site." *Bulletin of the Texas Archaeological and Paleontological Society*, Vol. 13, pp. 88–116. Abilene.

Webb, Clarence H., and Ralph R. McKinney

1963 "An Unusual Pottery Vessel from Mounds Plantation Site, Caddo Parish, Louisiana." *Arkansas Archaeologist*, Vol. 4, No. 5, pp. 1–9. Fayetteville.

1975 "Mounds Plantation (16CD12), Caddo Parish, Louisiana." *Bulletin of the Louisiana Archaeological Society*, No. 2, pp. 39–127. Lafayette.

Webb, Clarence H., *et al.*

1969   "The Resch Site (41HS16), Harrison County, Texas." *Bulletin of the Texas Archaeological Society,* Vol. 40, pp. 3–106. Dallas.

Webb, Clarence H., Joel L. Shiner, and E. Wayne Roberts

1971   "The John Pearce Site (16CD56): A San Patrice Site in Caddo Parish." *Bulletin of the Texas Archaeological Society,* Vol. 42, pp. 1–49. Dallas.

Webb, S. David, ed.

1974   *Pleistocene Mammals of Florida.* University Presses of Florida. Gainesville.

Webb, William S.

1974   *Indian Knoll.* University of Tennessee Press. Knoxville.

Webb, William S., and David L. DeJarnett

1942   *An Archaeological Survey of the Pickwick Basin in the Adjacent Portions of the States of Alabama, Mississippi and Tennessee.* Bureau of American Ethnology Bulletin 129. Smithsonian Institution. Washington, D.C.

Webb, William S., and Charles G. Wilder

1951   *An Archaeological Survey of Guntersville Basin on the Tennessee River in Northern Alabama.* University of Kentucky Press. Lexington.

Weber, J. Cynthia

1970   "Thermoluminescent Dating of Poverty Point Objects." In Bettye J. Broyles and Clarence H. Webb, eds., *The Poverty Point Culture, Southeastern Archaeological Conference Bulletin,* No. 12, pp. 99–107. Morgantown, W. Va.

Wedel, Waldo R.

1938   "The Direct-Historical Approach in Pawnee Archaeology." *Smithsonian Miscellaneous Collections,* Vol. 97, No. 7. Washington, D.C.

Weinstein, Richard Alan

1974   "An Archaeological Survey of the Lower Amite River, Louisiana." M.A. thesis, Louisiana State University. Baton Rouge.

Weinstein, Richard A., and Philip G. Rivet

1978   *Beau Mire: A Late Tchula Period Site of the Tchefuncte Culture, Ascension Parish, Louisiana.* Anthropological Report No. 1, Department of Culture, Recreation and Tourism, Louisiana Archaeological Survey and Antiquities Commission. Baton Rouge.

Weinstein, Richard, *et al.*

1978   *Cultural Resource Survey of the Proposed Relocation Route of U.S. 90 (La. 3052), Assumption, St. Mary, and Terrebonne Parishes, Louisiana.* Coastal Environments, Inc. Baton Rouge.

Wheat, Joe Ben

1953   *An Archaeological Survey of the Addicks Dam Basin, Southeast*

Texas. Bureau of American Ethnology Bulletin 154, pp. 143–252. Smithsonian Institution, Washington, D.C.

1971 "Lifeways of Early Man in North America." *Arctic Anthropology,* Vol. 8, No. 2, pp. 22–31. University of Wisconsin Press. Madison.

Willey, Gordon R.

1966 *An Introduction to American Archaeology:* Volume I, *North and Middle America.* Prentice-Hall, Inc. Englewood Cliffs, N.J.

Williams, Stephen

1967 "On the Location of Historic Taensa Villages." *Conference on Historic Site Archaeology Papers,* Vol. 1, pp. 2–13. Raleigh.

Williams, Stephen, and John M. Goggin

1956 "The Long Nosed God in Eastern United States." *Missouri Archaeologist,* Vol. 18, No. 3, pp. 1–72. Columbia, Mo.

Williams, Stephen, and James B. Stoltman

1965 "An Outline of Southeastern United States Prehistory, with Particular Emphasis on the Paleo-Indian Era." In H. E. Wright, Jr., and David G. Frey, eds., *The Quaternary of the United States.* Princeton University Press. Princeton, N.J.

Wilmsen, Edwin N.

1961 "A Suggested Developmental Sequence for House Forms in the Caddoan Area." *Bulletin of the Texas Archaeological Society,* Vol. 30, pp. 35–50. Austin.

Wilson, Thomas

1890 "Ancient Indian Matting—From Petit Anse Island, Louisiana." *Annual Report of the Board of Regents of the Smithsonian Institution for the Year Ending June 30, 1888,* pp. 673–75. Washington, D.C.

1890 "A Study of Prehistoric Anthropology." *Annual Report of the Board of Regents of the Smithsonian Institution for the Year Ending June 30, 1888,* pp. 597–671. Washington, D.C.

1895 "On the Presence of Fluorine as a Test for the Fossilization of Animal Bones." *American Naturalist,* Vol. 29, pp. 301–17, 439–56, 719–25. Philadelphia.

Wimberly, Steve B.

1953 "Bayou La Batre Tchefuncte Pottery Series." In James B. Griffin, ed., *Prehistoric Pottery of the Eastern United States.* University of Michigan, Museum of Anthropology. Ann Arbor.

Winters, John D.

1963 *The Civil War in Louisiana.* Louisiana State University Press. Baton Rouge.

Wood, W. Raymond

n.d. *The Crenshaw Site: A Coles Creek and Caddoan Mound Group in*

358

    Miller County, Arkansas. University of Arkansas Museum. Fayetteville.

Woodall, J. Ned

1969   *Archaeological Excavations in the Toledo Bend Reservoir, 1966.* Southern Methodist University Contributions in Anthropology No. 3. Dallas.

Wormington, H. M.

1957   *Ancient Man in North America.* Denver Museum of Natural History, Popular Series, No. 4. Denver.

Wright, Newell O., Jr.

1977   "Lithics." In Prentice Marquet Thomas, Jr., L. Janice Campbell, and Steven R. Ahler, eds., *The Hanna Site: An Alto Village in Red River Parish*, New World Research, Report of Investigations No. 3, pp. 157–83. New Orleans.

Wyckoff, Don G.

1971   *Caddoan Cultural Area: An Archaeological Perspective.* Oklahoma Archaeological Survey, University of Oklahoma. Norman.

Index